SŌJIJI

MICHIGAN MONOGRAPH SERIES IN JAPANESE STUDIES

NUMBER 94

CENTER FOR JAPANESE STUDIES
UNIVERSITY OF MICHIGAN

SŌJIJI

Discipline, Compassion, and Enlightenment at a Japanese Zen Temple

Joshua A. Irizarry

University of Michigan Press
Ann Arbor

Copyright © 2022 by Joshua A. Irizarry

For questions or permissions, please contact um.press.perms@umich.edu

Published in the United States of America by the
University of Michigan Press
Printed and bound by CPI Group (UK) Ltd, Croydon, CR0 4YY
Printed on acid-free paper
First published June 2022

A CIP catalog record for this book is available from the British Library.

Library of Congress Cataloging-in-Publication data has been applied for.

ISBN 978-0-472-07536-2 (hardcover : alk. paper)
ISBN 978-0-472-05536-4 (paper : alk paper)
ISBN 978-0-472-22016-8 (e-book)

For Gabriel and Raphael

Contents

Digital materials related to this title can be found on the Fulcrum platform via the following citable URL: https://doi.org/10.3998/mpub.11510618

Acknowledgments

No work of ethnography can be accomplished without the help of a great many people who were generous of their time, patience, and most important, trust. However, the need to protect the confidentiality and privacy of my informants overrides any wish to identify by name all those who made the work possible. As is convention in ethnographic writing, the names I use in this book are pseudonyms, and all personally identifiable information has been altered.

Since I cannot thank most of the people I would like to by name, I can only express a deep and lasting appreciation for the generosity and support shown to me over the years by the community of Daihonzan Sōjiji. In particular, my thanks go to the members of Sōjiji's Baikakō and Sanzenkai, who fully welcomed me into their groups with friendship and a sense of humor about my never-ending questions.

I am further indebted to the priests and *unsui* of Sōjiji for their understanding, patience, and willingness to help me make sense of the inner workings of a large Sōtō Zen monastery, and for those valuable glimpses into the backstage that the public rarely gets to see. I am especially grateful to those clergy who invited me to visit and interview them at their home temples throughout Japan and who candidly shared with me their experiences and memories of Sōjiji.

All of this would have been impossible without the introduction of the late Saitō Shingi, who facilitated my initial entrée into the Sōjiji community. I will be forever thankful for his support and endorsement.

My field research from 2006 through 2008 was conducted with the financial support of a Fulbright Graduate Research Fellowship, endowed by the Mitsubishi Corporation. Thank you to the Japan–U.S. Educational Commission (Fulbright Japan) for its support and assistance throughout my fieldwork.

I wish to thank my colleagues at Bridgewater State University—in particular, Wing-kai To, Diana Fox, and Kevin Kalish—for their friendship, encouragement, and support for my scholarship and teaching.

Thank you to Nicole Radanovics for cheerfully providing both inspiration and invaluable research assistance. Special thanks also to Erik Schicketanz and Tim Graf for their warm friendship and for their willingness to help me locate hard-to-find documents and resources over the years.

Sam Meyrowitz, Joe Joffe, John Thiels, Mazen Alsabe, John Paliotta, and Joe Bernier have stood by me through thick and thin as friends and brothers, always with encouragement and good counsel. I met Kōno Yukari at Sōjiji exactly when we needed each other most. Over the course of many meals, coffees, and conversations, she provided friendship, support, and a treasure trove of memories of Tsurumi and Sōjiji.

My warmest love and gratitude go to Akiyama Taka'aki and Kiyōko for bringing me into their home and family so many years ago, but more especially for making my growing family a part of theirs.

Shimazono Susumu has been a voice of support and guidance since my very first trip to Japan in 2001. I am fortunate to count myself among the family of scholars in whose careers Shimazono-sensei has played a formative role.

My deepest gratitude goes to my mentor of more than two decades, Jennifer Robertson. It is due to her painstaking cultivation and care, tireless advocacy, and unwavering confidence in my abilities as a researcher and as a writer that I was able to grow this book from a seed of an idea to full maturity.

My wife, Ita, is the strength behind my efforts and the inspiration behind my words. It has been a long road, and I hope that this work is deserving of the years of love and support and encouragement she gave to me to bring this project to fruition. I love you, always.

Lastly, I dedicate this book to my sons, Gabriel and Raphael. I am beyond blessed to have such vibrant, curious, and affectionate children. May you accomplish your dreams and leave your mark upon the world. I love you both more than words can say.

To all of the people named above and to all those who cannot be named, my gratitude is boundless and eternal. The responsibility for any mistakes, omissions, or inaccuracies in this work is borne solely on my shoulders.

Introduction

Sōjiji, the Forest for a Thousand Years

"People Tilling upon the Dharma Hall"

Stepping out of the train station, it immediately strikes you that Tsurumi is an unlikely place to find a historic Zen temple. If you go on what you think you know about Zen, particularly its associations with nature, tranquility, and artistic and cultural sophistication, then urban, loud, and working-class Tsurumi is surely the exact opposite of that.

The municipal ward of Tsurumi sits in the northeastern corner of the city of Yokohama, immediately adjacent to the industrial city of Kawasaki to the north and Tokyo Bay to the east. Tsurumi is a testament to the rapid industrialization of Japan throughout the twentieth century, a landscape of concrete and metal dotted with pockets of greenery that are more urban planning than nature. The name Tsurumi means "to see cranes," after the majestic birds that used to frequent the shoreline when the town was just a sleepy village. Today, however, the only cranes visible are the massive metal monoliths that service the factories and warehouses situated along the coastline of Tokyo Bay, a landscape redrawn to fit the needs of modern industry and global capitalism.

Tsurumi's location between Tokyo and central Yokohama places the town along the main rail artery and roadways that link the two metropolises. For twenty hours a day, trains thunder along the railway that runs through Japan Railways' (JR) Tsurumi Station, the commercial center of the ward. One either side of the station, wide avenues allow for high volumes of motor traffic throughout the day. At major intersections, the chirping of pedestrian crossing signals is a constant accent to the hum of motor traffic. At major rail crossings, the sound is greatly amplified by bells warning pedestrians and drivers of oncoming trains. Trains run almost constantly through the Tsurumi artery, and the crossing bells ring for nine minutes out of every ten.

Visitors with experience of other large Japanese Buddhist temples are quick to note that the area surrounding Sōjiji proper differs greatly from other temple approaches (*sandō* or *monzenmachi*). In contrast to major urban temples like Asakusa Kannon-dō (Sensōji) in Tokyo and Kawasaki Daishi (Heikenji), there are no storefronts or booths with merchants hawking food or souvenirs, nor are there crowds of tourists pushing along the sidewalk. In its place is a traffic circle used as a bus terminus and taxi stand, with small restaurants, convenience stores, a pharmacy, and a McDonald's lining the road toward the temple proper. Closer to the temple, the street becomes indistinguishable from any other commercial street in Tsurumi save for the quiet but visible presence of florist shops, stores selling stone monuments, and immediately across from Sōjiji's entrance, the branch office of a funeral company.

Neither the temple precincts nor its architecture is visible from the street. Instead, the entrance to Sōjiji is marked by a covered wooden announcement board, two large stone lanterns, and a rough stone sign into which *Sōtō-shū Daihonzan Sōjiji* is chiseled in Japanese characters. A paved pathway leads through the stone lanterns and up a gentle incline lined by tall, broadleaf evergreen trees. With the buildings of Tsurumi University visible through the trees on either side of the path, one might be forgiven for mistaking the path as part of a college campus—which, technically, it is. Like any college campus, groups of students and instructors regularly cross the path on their way to classes, the library, or the cafeteria.

As the visitor climbs the hill, the paved pathway curves slightly, eventually hiding the busy street below. About a hundred meters up the path stands a weathered wooden gate, known as the Sanshōkan. The Sanshōkan is never closed, nor does it connect to any walls that might serve to keep people out of the temple. Rather, the gate's purpose is to be a symbolic barrier between the temple precincts and the outside world. Soon after crossing the threshold of the Sanshōkan, however, the attentive visitor might notice that the constant sounds of the city—the cars, the trains, the incessant ringing of the railway crossing bell—have almost completely fallen away. The sudden quiet is dramatic.

The pathway continues its steady incline toward the imposing two-story Sanmon gate that sits at the top of the hill. Climbing the stairs and passing through the gate, visitors must pass under the threatening gaze of two menacing, larger-than-life guardian statues, their enclosures covered in chicken wire to protect them from the relentless assault of pigeons. Emerging into Sōjiji's precincts proper, signs guide visitors away from the parking lot and manicured lawn in front of them toward the right, up another incline, and toward the temple's main reception hall.

I am here on a hot, humid day in the first week of July. It is still a week before the traditional start of the three-day celebration of Obon, but already the temple is a flurry of activity. Teams of black-robed monks hurry on their way to the homes of parishioner families throughout Yokohama and Tokyo who have requested their services to chant in front of the household's *butsudan* altar. While these families wait for the monks to arrive at their homes, other parishioners are arriving in a steady stream at the temple, most heading straight for the enormous cemetery that frames the temple precincts on three sides.

The Obon festival is the largest of several occasions throughout the year when the Japanese customarily pay their respects to their ancestors at the family grave. At Sōjiji the *sejiki* ceremony held in the temple's enormous Dharma Hall, the Daisodō, is an essential part of the temple's Obon observances.[1] Doctrinally, this ceremony is an opportunity for parishioner families to assist the souls of their deceased loved ones by making a material or monetary contribution to the monastic community, who in turn will recite Buddhist texts (sutra) on behalf of abandoned and wandering hungry spirits. It is only by a series of ritual transfers that the initial donation can be converted into good karma to benefit the spirits of the dead. From my conversations, I know that very few of the laity care about such ritual minutia—the important thing to them is not *how* it works but *that* it works.

Today, the Honzan Baikakō—the temple's musical group—has been invited to perform several songs after the ceremony. As the parishioners begin to fill the great hall, the Baikakō is preparing in their rehearsal room, casually chatting with one another around cups of hot tea. The women wear long skirts and blouses, over which they have put on blue polyester choir robes. The men are spared the robes but wear long-sleeved shirts, blazers, and ties. Even in the oppressive summer heat, proper decorum necessitates formal attire. As a member of the group, I am similarly dressed, constantly dabbing sweat off my face and neck with a handkerchief.

A black-robed monk comes to collect the group and leads us to the ceremony hall. After proceeding single-file down several drafty corridors, the Baikakō enter the Daisodō one by one and bow with their hands pressed together as they walk up the ramp to the inner hall. The group is led to a red-carpeted seating area on the eastern side of the hall, a position of honor. The members take their seats and open bundles containing hand-bells and songbooks, arranging them on the floor in front of them.

The ladies of the temple women's association (Hōon Fujinkai) next enter the hall, escorted by their own usher. Like the Baikakō, the women of the Fujinkai are similarly wearing their finest: most wear skirts and blouses, though a handful of the women are wearing beautifully brocaded kimonos in purples, greens, and pinks. The greetings that both groups extend to the other—less than a bow but more than a head-nod—are cordial and perfunctory. The Fujinkai take their seats next to the Baikakō, but as far as interaction between the groups is concerned, both groups may as well be sitting in a different room.

I mentally note that there are no representatives from the Nichiyō San-zenkai, the lay meditation group that meets on Sundays. I am not too sur-prised: despite being invited by the temple administration to participate in these ceremonies, some in the group view participation in the ritual life of the temple as an unwelcome interruption to their meditative practice. Their absence today, I will later find out, speaks volumes.

The parishioners begin streaming into the hall in earnest now, taking their seats wherever they can find them on the red-carpeted sections of the inner hall. They are directed by a handful of monks who are doing their best to shout over the din and direct traffic using their hands and arms as sign-posts. These ushers encourage everyone to sit as close together as possible to maximize the available seating room, but most of the parishioners are content to cluster themselves as islands of families or individuals. Greetings between the parishioner families are few and far between, no more than there would be at a movie theater or on a crowded bus. Many are wearing the formal clothes that are associated with mourning in Japan: black suits and matte black ties for men; black dresses, dark stockings, and pearls for the women. But others—especially the younger participants, of which there are a surprising number—are wearing jeans, skirts, and even T-shirts and shorts, as if they are on their way to a day out with their friends.

At the southern end of the hall, curious observers take seats in chairs arranged on the linoleum floor in front of the bay doors facing the garden, which are open to let a cross-breeze enter. Some of the visitors are there to escape the oppressive midday heat in the relative coolness of the hall; others are drawn in by curiosity after hearing the sound of the assembly bell as they walked through the garden. Many have their hands full with bouquets of flowers and small gardening tools and are clearly on their way to the cemetery, having stopped off only to throw money into the hall's donation box and to offer incense. Others are tourists sporting day packs and cameras, nearly all of whom comment on the impressive enormity of the hall. Still others are wearing track suits and sneakers, locals for whom Sōjiji is just one stop on their daily constitutional walk. Most of these visitors will be in the hall for less than five minutes, and the chairs will see a lot of turnover in the span of the ceremony.

The next to appear in the hall are fifty young training monks, immediately identifiable by their shaved heads and black robes. They enter by staircase from the basement level of the hall. Upon entering, they kneel in the southwest corner of the room, carefully arranged in rows according to seniority. After a few minutes, the senior clergy, recognizable by their robes of browns or blues, casually enter one by one from the eastern entrance of the hall. They take their place next to the rows of novice monks.

When all have arrived, the assembly bell is struck. An attentive hush descends over the hall as the parishioners look to the ushers who will walk them through the ritual movements of the ceremony. With the ring of another bell, the monks stand as a group, bow, and move into the inner hall with practiced precision. A monk carrying a shoulder-mounted bell signals the assembly to unfold their bowing mats, which are hidden in the folds of their deep sleeves. A reverberating boom from the large bell in the hall signals the start of the ceremony.

The rolling thunder of giant drums announces the arrival of the abbot, who enters the hall with a ten-person entourage. The ushers, who have spread themselves in front of the carpeted areas, simultaneously begin to give instructions to the assembled laity. It is difficult to hear their voices over the reverberations of the drums and bells that fill the hall.

And then, silence.

A visitor at the back of the hall throws a handful of loose change into the donation box. Someone coughs. Outside, crows loudly call to one another over the rhythmic chirp of cicadas. A breeze rattles the glass windows of the hall's side doors.

A bell rings, and the monks stand in unison. From this standing position, they perform nine full prostrations, their foreheads touching the tatami floor each time. When they are finished, the cantor, in a powerful drone, calls out the text that will be chanted.

All at once, the hall explodes with sound and motion. With graceful, practiced movements, each of the participants performs their role like the parts of a finely tuned watch. The assembly of monks chant in unison, their time and speed maintained by the steady beat of a large wooden

Fig. 1. Visitors line up outside of Sōjiji's Butsuden (Buddha Hall) on New Year's Day.

drum. One bell, and stagehands fly from the wings behind the altar, their sleeves flowing behind them, gracefully moving ritual objects into position. Another bell, perfectly timed to synchronize with the rhythm reverberating through the hall, and the abbot starts to slowly move toward the altar to offer incense. Another bell, and the monks begin to ambulate around the hall, their feet moving in perfect precision with the rhythm of the chant and constant drumbeat. Several visitors enter the hall from the outside and sit down to watch the spectacle.

As the abbot returns to his seat, the monks return to their starting positions and continue chanting. On cue, the ushers come by to escort the hundreds of parishioners to incense burners at the front of the altar. Each person will offer a pinch of incense and bow their head, their hands pressed together. The slow-moving line circles the great hall, and the air soon becomes hazy with thick, fragrant smoke.

As I make my way toward the altar, I look around the Daisodō, the largest of its kind in Japan. The movement and activity taking place in the hall, like that within and around the temple, has imbued Sōjiji with a sense of vital energy and purpose. More than five hundred people from all walks of Japanese society are gathered under the roof of the great hall, with hundreds more circulating throughout the temple hallways, precincts, and cemetery. With the reverberations of the time-keeping drum at the front of the hall passing through my body like a heartbeat, I am struck by the sense that, in this moment, Sōjiji is truly *alive*.

A Temple for the Ages

At the end of his life, Sōjiji's visionary founder, Keizan Jōkin (1268–1325), is imagined to have envisioned such a scene as the future destiny of his temple. As his death approached, he gathered his strength to compose a final verse, a poetic capstone to his life that would be recorded for posterity as his legacy:

> *Mizukara tagayashi, mizukara tsukuru kandenchi.*
> *Ikutabi ka urikori, kaisatsu arata nari.*
> *Kagiri naki reimyō no tane, jukudatsu su.*
> *Hattōjō ni kuwa wo sasu hito wo miru.*[2]

> I cultivate and I shape this tranquil field.
> So many times sold and bought, it is made anew.
> Limitless generations of seeds will flourish and decay.
> I see people tilling upon the Dharma Hall.

In the centuries since Keizan's lifetime, his words have proven prophetic. Sōjiji has stood witness to seven hundred years of dramatic history in Japan. Far from its origins as a humble rural chapel on the remote Noto Peninsula (present-day Ishikawa Prefecture), Sōtō-shū Daihonzan Sōjiji today is an impressive temple complex in urban Yokohama and a vital part of the modern city that surrounds it. Situated just forty-five minutes by train from central Tokyo and covering a third of a square kilometer on a hill above Tokyo Bay, Sōjiji ranks among the largest temples in Japan. According to conservative estimates, more than four hundred thousand people visit Sōjiji over the course of an average year. Fully a quarter of this number— one hundred thousand people—will visit the temple within the first seven days of January alone in observance of Hatsumōde, the traditional Japanese New Year custom of visiting a temple or shrine. The other three hundred thousand visitors will arrive in a continuous stream over the course of the year, with surges in visits during festival and holiday observances.

Keizan may have imagined that Sōjiji would prosper, but it is unlikely that he could fathom the scope of the cultural force it would project in Japan. It was through the innovative brilliance of Sōjiji's custodians—Keizan's disciples and heirs—and the accidents of history that a small rural chapel would evolve into a major religious center and that the fledgling sect of Sōtō Zen would flourish throughout Japan for the next seven centuries.

At its height, Sōjiji sat at the pinnacle of a network of over sixteen thousand loyal temples, its priests renowned for their ability to bring in support from every stratum of Japanese society. Sōjiji's cultural impact was equally immense: rituals and practices established by Sōjiji priests in the medieval period were instrumental in shaping Japanese cultural and religious patterns that persist even today.

Nevertheless, by the start of the modern period, Sōjiji was poised on the brink of ruin. Already weakened by political changes that had taken much of its political and financial support, Sōjiji became embroiled in an acrimonious internecine struggle for control of the future of the Sōtō Zen sect. When a catastrophic fire in 1898 utterly destroyed the temple, many feared that Sōjiji would never recover.

After the difficult choice was made to move the temple far from its ancestral home, Sōjiji was rebuilt in 1911 from donated land, buildings, and money in Tsurumi, at the time an otherwise unremarkable coastal village situated between Tokyo and Yokohama that was a station along the famed Tōkaidō road. Tsurumi was in 1911 in the early stages of its own remarkable transformation from farming village to a center of industrial production for the rapidly modernizing nation.

From its new position overlooking Tokyo Bay, Sōjiji sat witness to a century of dramatic change in Japan: modernization, industrialization, militarization, devastation, occupation, prosperity, recession, precarity, catastrophe, and, today, uncertainty. Through it all, Sōjiji has been simultaneously a stalwart bastion of traditional Japanese values and cultural identity and the vanguard of an ambitious religious institution with global aspirations.

Sōjiji is recognized as one of two *honzan*—literally "main mountain," but more precisely translated as "head temple"—of the Sōtō Zen sect of Japanese Buddhism. Today the Sōtō Zen sect is the largest of all the Japanese Buddhist sects, with official estimates placing the number of adherents at over five million people.[3]

As *honzan*, Sōjiji and its counterpart, Eiheiji, sit at the apex of an administrative pyramid under which a complex network of more than fourteen thousand subordinate temples, known as "branch temples" (*matsuji*), is organized. Each sect of Japanese Buddhism has its own *honzan* that serves as the religious, political, financial, and administrative flagship for the religious institution. The abbot of a *honzan* is the nominal and spiritual leader of the sect, tasked with maintaining the authority, legitimacy, practices, and traditions of the religion. To be properly ordained as a member of the clergy, a sect's priests must undergo a period of training at a *honzan* or at a recognized regional training temple that follows an approved clerical curriculum. That the Sōtō Zen sect has two officially recognized *honzan* makes it unique among all other sects of Japanese Buddhism, bringing with it a fascinating history wrought with periods of both fruitful cooperation and bitter rivalry.

A Landscape of Discipline

A first-time visitor to Sōjiji might be surprised by the architectural look of Sōjiji's campus. For a person who has in their mind an image of a "traditional" Zen temple, Sōjiji can certainly be disappointing—I found this to be as true for clergy as it was for tourists.[4] While the buildings are individually consistent in style, taken as a whole, the campus is a unique bricolage of traditional and modern styles and of old and new construction materials and techniques. Knowing how to read Sōjiji's landscape and architecture is an important step to understanding how the temple, as an institution, functions in the present while juggling the contradictions that necessarily result from its being oriented toward both the past and the future.

Sōjiji is constructed in the style of a *shichidō garan*, or "seven-hall monastery," which was characteristic of the major Buddhist temples of China during the Song Dynasty (960–1276). While something of a misnomer—*shichidō garan* campuses usually had many more than seven buildings—the term refers to the seven essential structures that a Buddhist monastery requires in order to support a community of monks and to perform its ritual and administrative functions. In Zen monasteries the seven essential buildings have traditionally been the Buddha Hall (*butsuden*), the Dharma Hall (*hattō*), the Monk's Hall (*sōdō*), the toilets (*tōsu*), the storehouse and kitchens (*kuin*), the bathhouse (*yokusu*), and the temple gate (*sanmon*).[5]

The importing of Zen doctrines and practices from China to Japan occurred gradually, but continuously, throughout the twelfth and thirteenth centuries. Itinerant Japanese monastics such as Myōan Eisai (1141–1215) and Dōgen Kigen (1200–1253)—recognized today as the founding ancestors of the Japanese Rinzai and Sōtō Zen lineages, respectively—spent years living abroad in Song China, observing Buddhism as practiced

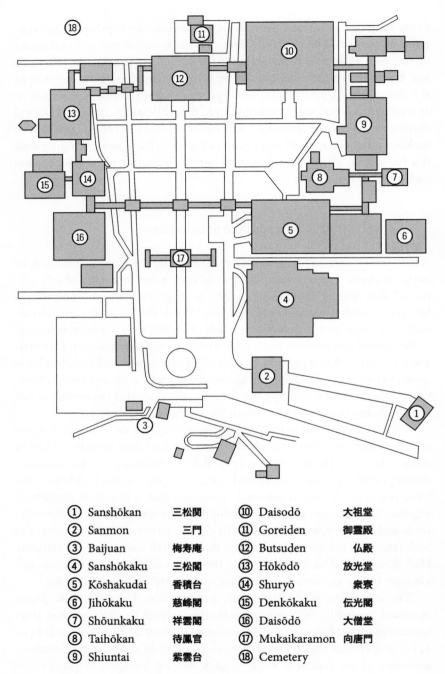

①	Sanshōkan	三松関	⑩ Daisodō	大祖堂
②	Sanmon	三門	⑪ Goreiden	御霊殿
③	Baijuan	梅寿庵	⑫ Butsuden	仏殿
④	Sanshōkaku	三松閣	⑬ Hōkōdō	放光堂
⑤	Kōshakudai	香積台	⑭ Shuryō	衆寮
⑥	Jihōkaku	慈峰閣	⑮ Denkōkaku	伝光閣
⑦	Shōunkaku	祥雲閣	⑯ Daisōdō	大僧堂
⑧	Taihōkan	待鳳官	⑰ Mukaikaramon	向唐門
⑨	Shiuntai	紫雲台	⑱ Cemetery	

Fig. 2. Layout of Sōjiji's buildings and grounds.

in the major public temple complexes and receiving instruction from the famous Zen masters of the time. Deeply inspired by their experiences abroad, these monastics were determined to revitalize Japanese Buddhism by bringing as much of Song Buddhist culture back with them as they could upon their return. When they built their own temples in Japan, it was naturally the Song Chinese monasteries that they sought to emulate in both style and substance. The "exotic" architecture of these temple structures was as much a part of establishing the identity of the Zen lineages in Japan as what took place inside them.[6]

Knowingly or not, these itinerant monastics brought more than just Buddhism back to Japan. In the Chinese public monasteries that Eisai and Dōgen aimed to replicate, the institutional identity of Zen was already deeply interwoven with Neo-Confucianism, a syncretization of Confucian, Daoist, and Buddhist philosophical principles and practices that represented a "systematized cosmology linking individual practice with a metaphysical conception of the cosmos and ethical and political understandings of the importance of social structures like the family, country, and empire."[7] Throughout the Song Dynasty, Zen and Neo-Confucianism developed in dialogue with each other, due in large part to the patronage and influence of the elite literati class and state sponsorship and regulation of Buddhist monasteries.[8] In particular, Neo-Confucianism's strong emphasis on personal cultivation (Ch. *xiushen*, Jp. *shūshin*) as a moral and social obligation was readily incorporated into the framework of Zen monastic practice. The result was that by the late Song period, Neo-Confucianism's focus on individual personal development was inextricable from the philosophical, ritual, and material trappings of the Zen Buddhism that Eisai, Dōgen, and other returning Japanese monastic émigrés had brought home with them.

As a consequence of the close relationship between the two philosophical systems, much of Neo-Confucianism's worldview and cosmology was encoded into the very architecture of Song-style Zen Buddhist monasteries. Buddhist monasteries were spaces of "social and cultural inscription" designed to enculturate individuals into the teachings, ritual practices, and traditions that were believed to promote the cultivation of specific personal, social, and civic virtues.[9] But they were also spaces of collective memory, in which concepts of generational and gender hierarchies, filial piety, and loyalty to civic authority were enshrined and reenacted alongside institutional, genealogical, and cultural narratives and histories. Zen monasteries were complex microcosms of an ideal community, a harmonious earthly kingdom, and a natural world in perfect balance.

One benefit of the intertwining of cosmology with architectural concepts is that a temple like Sōjiji can easily slip between different metaphorical registers for allegorical effect. As a result, Zen temples operate on multiple levels of significance, where rich metaphors and imagery are woven into the architectural narrative of the temple itself. In both China and Japan, by far the most common imagery is to depict Buddhist temples as "mountains" (Ch. *shan*, Jp. *san/zan*), invoking the legends of wise and enlightened sages hermitting themselves on remote mountain peaks to avoid worldly distractions, accessible only to the most determined seekers of wisdom.[10] In reference to this tradition, Sōtō Zen monks are said to be "ascending the mountain" when they arrive at Sōjiji and "descending the mountain" when they depart. This topographical imagery is not restricted to the Zen sects, as virtually all Buddhist temples in Japan have "mountain names" as a prefix to their temple names, despite few temples being located on (or in many cases even near) mountains.

It is also common to depict Zen monasteries as "monastic groves" (*sōrin*) or simply "forests" (*mori*). While quiet and secluded forest temples removed from civilization are, like mountains, idealized places for Buddhist renunciants to devote themselves to their practice, such images are also rich in additional metaphorical significance. As groves and forests are defined by their multiplicity—a solitary tree does not a forest make—the trees of this forest are the individual monastics whose communal life together defines the contours of life and practice in the monastery. For a large temple like Sōjiji, this metaphor is often expanded to include all the participants in the daily life of the temple—the monastics, the parishioners, the practitioners, the employees, and the visitors—whose collective activity brings the temple to life.[11]

Other metaphors imagine Zen monasteries as places of bountiful fertility: "monastic parks" (*garan*),[12] "monks' gardens" (*sōen*), "Zen gardens" (*zen'en*), and, in Keizan's writings in particular, as "fields" (*denchi*).[13] The horticultural imagery is significant since it invokes the idea of cultivation in that growing plants must be regularly cared for, nurtured, and tended to achieve their fullest potential. It also invokes the act of disciplining in that everything in a garden has its proper place and requires strict vigilance to keep the soil free from unwanted weeds and debris.

Slipping again between metaphors, later depictions of the *shichidō garan* introduced by Mujaku Dōchū (1653–1744) present the seven-hall campus as a human body writ large.[14] At a temple's heart is the Buddha Hall, within which the temple's principal image—usually a statue of the Buddha—is enshrined. The other six buildings of the *shichidō garan* have similar anatomical assignations: the Dharma Hall is the head; the Monk's Hall and the kitchens/storehouse are the hands; the toilet and the bathhouse are the feet; and, finally, the temple gate is the genitalia.[15] A landscape thus ordered might be conceivably said to be "alive" in an organic sense: each organ of the body functions in synergy with the others to create a whole that is greater than the sum of its constituent parts.[16]

A *shichidō garan* temple is also a cosmogram, a map of the universe according to Buddhist cosmology. The temple's principal image—in Sōjiji's case a wooden statue of Śākyamuni Buddha, attended by statues of his disciples Mahākāśyapa (Jp. Mahakashō) and Ānanda (Jp. Anan)—sits on an altar known as a *shumidan*, a representation of the axis mundi of the Buddhist universe, Mount Sumeru.[17] Within a temple's walls is a "metaphorical geography" where all points of reference are determined by the orientation of this principal image: regardless of true magnetic direction or geographical orientation, the direction the principal image faces becomes "south." Once this central reference point is established, the rest of the campus buildings can be put in their proper places—the direction to its back is "north," its left hand is "east," and its right hand is "west."[18] In this way, a Zen temple is both a representation of a perfectly ordered universe and a functioning microcosm of that universe itself.

All of these layers of metaphor speak to the fact that Sōjiji, as a *shichidō garan*, is a "lived representation of a social and mental world."[19] It encodes a specific vision of a hierarchical, categorized, and ordered society, world, and universe. It imprints this vision on the movements, the activities, the minds, and the bodies within its walls. It embodies the idea that personal cultivation is key to the development of a perfect society and world and, as such, is the moral and civic responsibility of all humans. Everything must learn its proper place and role within the system, and corrective action must be applied to that which is out of place. Correctly harnessing the direction, flow, and rhythm of what takes place inside the temple walls allows for the whole—the person, the group, the institution, society at large, and the world itself—to thrive and perpetuate.[20]

Shugyō Dōjo

In Japan, Buddhist temples are distinguished according to the specific religious function that they perform. The most common function for a parish temple in Japan is as a memorial temple (*bodaiji*). A memorial temple typically specializes in funerary rites and mortuary rituals, performed on behalf of parishioner families for the benefit of their ancestors. In contrast are prayer temples (*kitōji*), which specialize in securing worldly benefits (*genze riyaku*) for the living, such as health, success, and protection through devotional and ritual performances.[21] As part of its many aspects, Sōjiji fulfills both of these functions. As a *bodaiji*, Sōjiji caters to the ritual needs of over five thousand parishioner families. As a *kitōji*, Sōjiji provides ample opportunities for petitioners to seek benefits directly from a number of powerful beings enshrined within Sōjiji's landscape, to perform activities in pursuit of these benefits, or to generate karmic merit through donations to the monastic community or the sponsoring of a ceremony. But these are secondary functions for Sōjiji.

Sōjiji's primary function is as a *shugyō dōjō*. The word *dōjō* has entered English through martial arts like judo and karate, referring to the room or hall where practitioners train and spar. A common translation of *shugyō dōjō* into English is "training hall," but to rely on this gloss is to miss much of the meaning of the term. Unlike *bodaiji* or *kitōji*, which tend toward traditional Japanese Buddhist architecture,[22] a *shugyō dōjō* does not have to be a temple, though it often is. Technically speaking, any space where an individual improves themselves through the pursuit of an art or activity— including, but not limited to, the martial arts, flower arranging, or tea ceremony—is called a *dōjō*. A *dōjō* is, in Michel de Certeau's terms, a "practiced place," expressed as a function of what is taking place inside it.[23]

One priest described a Zen *shugyō dōjō* to me as "any place where Zen is practiced. That is to say, any place where there is a teacher (*shisō*)." By this definition, as long as there is a legitimate Sōtō Zen teacher present to properly oversee, advance, and correct the practice of the people who assemble there, it is a Sōtō Zen *dōjō*, even though the outward form of the architecture may differ. A *shugyō dōjō* is therefore a space where *shugyō* takes place.

Translating *shugyō* is a trickier task. While *shūgyō* is often translated into English as "spiritual training" or "ascetic discipline," these glosses do not capture the essence of the word as it is used by the Japanese. The first character, *shu*, means "to cultivate or train," with the implication of setting something in order. The second character, *gyō*, implies bodily movement but also performance of an action.

For many Japanese, the term *shugyō* invokes imagery of water ablutions under ice-cold waterfalls, of thousand-day fasts, and of other mortifications of the flesh.[24] It is important to recognize, however, that the concept of *shugyō* is ubiquitous in Japanese society. Contemporary Japanese use the word in a variety of contexts, especially settings where cultivating self-discipline through hardship and self-denial over a long term is seen as the best road to future success.

Dorinne Kondo observes that "in Japanese society generally, hardship is considered one pathway to a mature selfhood."[25] The impetus to self-discipline starts early, with school-age children attending cram schools and working late into the night, as embodied by the maxim "*yontō, goraku*" ("four succeed, five fail"), that a person will achieve success in school, work, and life by limiting themselves to four hours of sleep each night but will become a failure by indulging their body's desire for comfort and rest. In activities like sports and music, the many hours spent perfecting technique through repetition and drills, pushing the body and mind to exhaustion, are done in the name of *shugyō*. For employees, long hours at the office with little sleep or relaxation time, and with little social contact from family and friends is also *shugyō*—a hardship that cultivates a disciplined, reliable, honest, and productive worker and a model Japanese citizen.

While the Neo-Confucian ideals of self-discipline and personal cultivation have been integrated into Japanese society since the medieval period, their study and practice were historically limited to the elite strata of Japanese society, the aristocracy and samurai warrior classes. It was not until the Tokugawa (1600–1868) and early Meiji (1868–1912) periods that the "Neo-Confucian cultivation paradigm" began to permeate and flourish throughout all levels of Japanese society, particularly as a consequence of the spread of popular religious movements.[26] As the Japanese modern state emerged, these values were codified in the Imperial Rescript on Education (1890) in which, in addition to loyalty and filial piety, Japanese schoolchildren were commanded by Imperial mandate to "pursue learning and cultivate arts, and thereby develop intellectual faculties and perfect moral powers."[27] Self-discipline and personal cultivation were presented as means of creating the ideal—that is, loyal, obedient, and disciplined—Japanese citizen. Throughout the early days of the new Japanese polity, and particularly as Japan's modern Imperial Army won increasingly impressive victories against much larger opponents, Zen—the so-called religion of the samurai—was held up by apologists as a means of inculcating these values into the populace at large.[28]

In every activity performed as *shugyō*, an important sleight of hand takes place. The thing that practitioners are working to master—academics, a craft, their job, baseball, piano, flower arrangement, or what have you—is little more than a red herring. What is actually being perfected through *shugyō* is the practitioner themselves. By forcing the physical body to conform to correct movement, correct form, and correct practice, a person's inner self (their *kokoro*, a concept that encapsulates both "mind" and "heart") is transitively acted upon, molding the diligent practitioner into a person of high moral character, worthy of respect, and capable of great feats of concentration, endurance, insight, and wisdom.[29] As Kawano Satsuki writes, in Japan, "properly acting bodies are morally valued bodies."[30]

The purpose of a *shugyō dōjō*, therefore, is to serve as a place of practice where a subject is gradually transformed in both body and mind through the application of intense, coercive pressure.[31] The key here is what Talal Asad calls "conscious intentionality," in which "the inertial resistance of the body, as well as its fragility, need[s] to be addressed deliberately by responsible practice."[32] Through dedicated and repetitive activity, desirable behaviors are reinforced and negative behaviors are hammered away until what remains is a perfected human being as the culture or tradition imagines it.

Using terms like "coercive pressure" certainly makes the *shugyō dōjō* sound like a place of violence. As a place of corrective discipline, it certainly has the potential for abuse and exploitation. Severe as it may be, *shugyō* is nevertheless framed as a compassionate but ultimately impersonal practice. To idly or absentmindedly engage with one's practice is a lost opportunity, worthy of contempt; when the individual stumbles and falters, it is the moral obligation of the community to apply corrective pressure by example, if possible, or by force, if necessary. Embracing *shugyō*, hardships and all, is the only way humans can better themselves, sloughing off the impurities and weaknesses that keep them from realizing their true nature as enlightened beings.

As we will see in the chapters that follow, in Sōtō Zen Buddhism, enlightenment (*satori*) is not a far-off goal that one strives to attain. Rather, enlightenment is a state of perpetual *shugyō*—a constant state of "becoming," in which the process of self-cultivation is truly internalized and fully embodied, resulting in wise and compassionate speech and deeds, graceful movement, and perfect discipline. In Sōtō teachings this is known as *shushō ittō*, "*shugyō* and enlightenment are the same."[33] *Shugyō* is not a means to an end but rather the end itself.

The Rice Paddle and the Pestle

Sōjiji's front office and main reception are in a building called the Kōshakudai. The building's curious name—literally, the "incense stacking platform"—comes from its being Sōjiji's *kuin*, a building that serves as both a storehouse of supplies and a kitchen for the temple community. Because of the bookkeeping necessary to perform both tasks, the *kuin* has also traditionally been the administrative hub of a monastery community,

Fig. 3. The public entrance of the Kōshakudai. The rice paddle (*shamoji*) stands on the right and the pestle (*surikogi*) stands on the left.

tasked with ensuring the smooth day-to-day operation of the temple and keeping close watch on the temple's finances, particularly donations of money, supplies, and foodstuffs from the lay community. Enshrined inside the Kōshakudai is a statue of Daikokuten, the jocular kitchen god who bestows wealth and prosperity. At just over 1.6 meters (about 5.25 feet) tall, this particular statue is the largest of its kind in Japan and often featured on Sōjiji's promotional and tourist material.

The Kōshakudai is usually the first stop that a visitor makes on their way into the interior of the temple itself. With locking cubbies for visitors to remove their street shoes, a gift shop, and a quiet reception area where guests are offered tea, it is a transit hub of sorts, with groups of visitors, dignitaries, cleaning staff, and training monks crossing paths continuously through the corridors on their way to different parts of the temple complex. Underscoring this movement are the sounds of cars picking up and dropping off passengers, footsteps and voices, ringing telephones, the clicking of keyboards, and announcements over the public address system.

On either side of the wooden stairs leading into the Kōshakudai are two curious wooden sculptures—a giant pestle (*surikogi*) on the left and an oversized rice paddle (*shamoji*) on the right. The first (and often only) impression of many visitors is that the larger-than-life kitchen utensils are a fun and curious novelty. But upon closer inspection, their inscriptions reveal an absolute seriousness of purpose, an injunction reminiscent of Dante:

> *Otsu ga mi wo suriherashitezo hito no tame se no tame tsukusu mihotoke no jihi.*
> *Otsu ga mi ha mizu wo mo hi wo mo ito inaku sukuiaguruzo mihotoke no jihi.*

> The Buddha's compassion is your grinding down your body to serve humanity and the world.
> The Buddha's compassion is your body enduring both water and fire to elevate and save others.[34]

"Enter," they command; "surrender yourself to *shugyō*, and through hardship you will be transformed."

Far from the ceremonial grandeur of the Daisodō, the Kōshakudai is clearly a place of human interaction and transaction, a starting point where many different lives and stories intersect. From these steps, Sōjiji's halls reverberate with stories of determination and resilience; of compassion and wisdom; of grief and mourning; of hope and of uncertainty; and of the bonds of family, friendship, history, and tradition. It is therefore the perfect starting point for this book.

Throughout this work, I use real stories from the lives of the people who make up the Sōjiji community. By retelling these stories, my goal is to give shape to a lived and practiced place whose contours are defined by the interactions that take place inside its walls.

Japanese cultural concepts about life and death play a significant role in shaping how the processes of disciplining and cultivation are interpreted by the participants. Some people come out of curiosity after hearing of the benefits of incorporating a "Zen lifestyle" into their daily routine. Others are looking for a way to be more productive at work or simply to become a better person. By far the most common stories are those who come during periods of dramatic personal transition. These transitions, I argue, are moments of "death" of the former social person, marking a shift from one social identity into another.[35] In some cases this is a metaphorical death, such as caused by a divorce, a retirement, or "leaving the world" to enter the ranks of the clergy. In others it is in preparation for one's own physiological death or response to the death of a family member or loved one. Even the spirits of the dead have a reason to be present, as memorial rituals create a space to redefine and reinforce the familial and affective relationships that physiological death threatens to sunder.

The first chapter traces the temple's growth from humble beginnings to its height of power as the seat of the Sōtō Zen sect during the Japanese medieval period, its rapid decline and sudden destruction by fire in 1898, and the controversial decision to move and rebuild across the country in Yokohama. Especially important is Sōjiji's unique vantage point of Japanese history during the twentieth century—Sōjiji was "front and center" during the dramatic development of the Keihin Industrial Corridor; it was a participant in the rise of Japanese imperial militarism; a victim of the devastation of Yokohama at the end of the Second World War; and a beneficiary of the Japanese postwar economic miracle. Woven throughout this history is the fascinating story of Sōjiji's seven-hundred-year relationship with its older sister temple, Eiheiji, a complex and often turbulent rivalry that has helped to shape the practice and identity of Sōtō Zen throughout Japan and, in the last century, the world.

The second chapter begins the framing of Sōjiji's community with the training of the *unsui*, novice monks who live, work, and learn at the temple. The daily life of a Sōtō Zen monk at Sōjiji is highly regimented as well as physically and emotionally taxing. Transitioning into this life of tradition and discipline is often stressful for the young monks, most of whom are recent college graduates who did not choose the clerical lifestyle for themselves but are pressured to carry on the "family business" of their fathers. However, in the strict and disciplined training environment of Sōjiji's Monk's Hall, the *unsui* are slowly remade from hesitant and even resistant young men into living embodiments of Sōtō Zen teachings.

The story of the *unsui* continues in chapter 3 as we follow their transition into fully ordained Sōtō Zen clergy. After so much intense training, the newly minted priests "graduate" from Sōjiji into a world outside of their monastic discipline and are forced to start making a living as clergy in a world of economic precarity, changing cultural values, and modern religious sensibilities. This transition to their new social lives often leads to crises of identity and faith as the priests learn to reconcile their public image as "enlightened beings" with their new worldly responsibilities and human shortcomings. For many, this path leads back to Sōjiji, where they

Fig. 4. A novice monk and a laywoman acknowledge each other on the path to the Butsuden.

serve in teaching or administrative roles and experience a renewed sense of responsibility as caretakers of the temple's legacy and custodians of the future of the Sōtō Zen sect.

Chapter 4 introduces the Sanzenkai, a lay meditation group that sees its weekly meetings at Sōjiji as combining the best of both the lay and monastic lifestyles. While the Sanzenkai represent some of the most devoted Zen practitioners outside of the clergy, they are paradoxically the least likely of all temple groups to participate in the religious aspects of life at Sōjiji. Their belief in a "pure Zen" that eschews ritual and ceremony for a single-minded dedication to meditative practice is a recurring point of tension. Moreover, this "originalist" perspective regularly invokes the lingering specter of the centuries-old institutional rivalry between Sōjiji and its sister temple, Eiheiji, that once threatened to tear the Japanese Sōtō Zen sect apart.

The fifth chapter discusses the Baikakō, a musical group that meets regularly at Sōjiji and other Sōtō Zen temples to sing a type of Buddhist religious music known as *goeika*. Far from the silent meditation of the Sanzenkai, the Baikakō stresses musical performance as a means of cultivating oneself and finding harmony in one's life. At Sōjiji the Baikakō is nearly entirely comprised by elderly women who see *goeika* practice as a means of redefining themselves in their later years, of facing increasing awareness of their own mortality, and of coping with the separation, loss, and loneliness brought on by the death of spouses, loved ones, and friends. Through *goeika* the Baikakō creates a positive communal social space where *shugyō* becomes *dōgyō*— "shared practice." The adoption of *goeika* practice by the Sōtō Zen sect has been one of the most successful lay initiatives of the modern period, with *goeika* groups outnumbering meditation groups in Japan by a substantial margin. Nevertheless, the success of *goeika* has not been without criticism, underscoring the continued marginalization that women have historically faced within Sōtō Zen and Japanese Buddhism in general.

Chapter 6 tackles one of the most important functions of Buddhist temples in Japan, that of providing a space for funerals, burials, and memorial services for the ancestors of temple parishioners. Sōjiji, like the majority of Buddhist temples in Japan, derives a large portion of its income—and consequently expends a large portion of its labor—on the performance of these memorial rituals. The machine-like efficiency by which temple clergy perform these rituals has often brought cynicism and criticism over what many see as the clergy profiteering in the grief of their parishioners or diluting the so-called purity of Zen teachings. Instead of seeing memorial rituals as evidence of "Buddhism in decline," I argue that funerals and memorial rites sponsored by parishioner families on behalf of their ancestors follow the same logic as do other forms of *shugyō* in that they cultivate new life from death, ritually leading both the living and the dead toward compassion and enlightenment.

In the concluding chapter, I discuss developments at Sōjiji since 2011. As has already been well documented, 2011 was a turning point in Japanese history as a consequence of the Great East Japan Disaster, or 3.11, where a major earthquake off of Japan's northeastern coast was followed by a powerful tsunami that killed close to twenty thousand people and triggered a meltdown at the Fukushima nuclear power plant that forced the evacuation of more than four hundred thousand residents and contaminated the air, land, and sea for generations. For Sōjiji, which was celebrating the ascension of a new abbot and its long-planned one hundredth anniversary of its move to Tsurumi, the tragedy did more than force an immediate pivot from celebration to memorialization. The aftermath of the disaster forced a reconsideration of the way that Sōtō Zen clergy engaged with their communities and a reimagination of the role Sōjiji was to play in the face of a transformed Japan.

ONE

The History of Sōjiji

Keizan Jōkin, "Mother" of Sōtō Zen

At the time of Keizan's death in 1325, the small temple known as Shōgakusan Sōjiji was four years old and little more than a handful of wooden structures built upon the remains of an older devotional shrine. It was situated near the sea in the north of the Noto Peninsula (present-day Ishikawa Prefecture), then as today a poor and remote region on the western coast of Japan's main island.

Much of what we know of Keizan's life comes from his own autobiography, as recorded in the *Tōkokki* ("Records of Tōkoku").[1] The *Tōkokki* was Keizan's second major opus after the *Denkōroku* ("Record of the Transmission of the Light"), a series of lectures on the lives of the Sōtō Zen line of patriarchs that he began in 1300.

Keizan compiled the text of the *Tōkokki* in the latter years of his life (ca. 1312–1325), intending for the manuscript to stand as a permanent legacy after he died. Leaving a record of one's life was a common practice of Chinese and Japanese Buddhist masters. In this regard, the *Tōkokki* is not exceptional; indeed, conforming to the genre of which it is a part, much of Keizan's autobiography can be considered apocryphal, with many details of his "extraordinariness" shared in common to the hagiographies of eminent Buddhist masters.[2] From a literary perspective, one of the purposes of Keizan's writing the *Tōkokki* was to write himself into the lineage of Sōtō Zen patriarchs whose lives he had earlier described in the *Denkōroku*.

Still, the episodes from his life he chose to include in his autobiography reveal a man whose activity in this world was deeply intertwined with the visions he saw in dreams. Many of the chapters in the *Tōkokki* begin by describing a dream that Keizan saw, either while sleeping or while sitting *zazen*. The dreams he describes are rich in mythological imagery and personal significance to Keizan, as evidenced by the central role they play in his recollections.

Of note is Keizan's lifelong association with Kannon, the bodhisattva of compassion, through the influence of his mother, a deeply devout woman named Ekan. In the *Tōkokki*, Keizan recounts Kannon's intercession in his own birth: one night, Ekan dreamed that she "was swallowing the warmth of the morning sun."[3] In the morning, Ekan discovered she was pregnant. To his mother, Keizan was a *mōshigo*—a promised child—bestowed upon her by Kannon herself. She redoubled her devotional efforts, prostrating herself before an image of Kannon hundreds of times every day, praying that her unborn child would be born to become a "holy man, an inspirational priest, a heavenly personage."[4]

Keizan was born in 1268 in Echizen Province, in what is now present-day Fukui Prefecture. Keizan's birth name was Gyōshō ("Moving Birth"), a name given to him because his mother gave birth while traveling on pilgrimage. As a child, Keizan was said to be possessed of an unnatural precocity when it came to religious matters and able to recite sutras from memory after hearing them only once.

Ekan took the tonsure and became abbess of a convent, so Keizan spent his early childhood with his grandmother, who had been a lay follower of Dōgen, the founder of the Japanese Sōtō Zen sect.[5] At the age of eight, Keizan received tonsure at Eiheiji by Tettsū Gikai (1219–1309), a priest who would continue to be of significant influence to Keizan throughout the course of his life. Keizan formally entered Eiheiji as a novice at thirteen, where he trained under the abbacy of Koun Ejō (1198–1280), Dōgen's successor. When Ejō died, the abbacy and Dōgen's robe, the symbol of succession, passed to Gikai. Gikai soon left Eiheiji, owing to internal conflict, and established Daijōji in 1292 in what is present-day Kanazawa City.[6] Keizan would soon follow his old teacher to Daijōji.

While in residence at Daijōji, Keizan encountered his two most influential disciples: Meihō Sotetsu (1277–1350) in 1294 and Gasan Jōseki (1277–1366) in 1297.[7] Gikai groomed Keizan for the abbacy of Daijōji and transmitted to Keizan the Sōtō Zen Dharma lineage in 1295. Keizan was thus made fourth in line after Dōgen in the lineage of Japanese Sōtō Zen. Unlike his predecessors, however, Keizan would never hold the abbacy or

any other high office at Eiheiji, a fact that would become politically significant in the centuries following his death.

Keizan succeeded to the abbacy of Daijōji in 1298 and held the office
until 1311. In 1312 Keizan was given land to establish Yōkōji. Yōkōji was to
be Keizan's living legacy, and he and his disciples worked diligently to cultivate relationships with patrons willing to provide financial and material
support to his venture. Both symbolically and architecturally, Yōkōji was
a monument to Keizan's claims to legitimacy as heir to the Japanese Sōtō
Zen lineage. At Yōkōji, Keizan enshrined relics that linked him materially
to the patriarchs who had come before him: to Gikai, to Ejō, to Dōgen,
and, finally, to Tendō Nyōjō (Ch. Tiantong Rujing, 1162–1228), the Chinese priest who transmitted the Sōtō Zen lineage to Dōgen, enabling the
latter to bring Sōtō Zen from China to Japan.[8]

Re-Founding Sōjiji

In 1321 Keizan was offered the stewardship of a small private temple
known as Morooka Kannondō (alternately, Morookadera) situated in a
remote area in the north of the Noto Peninsula. The temple was little
more than a simple wooden enclosure housing an image of the bodhisattva Kannon. While nominally dedicated to the Shingon sect of Japanese
Buddhism, it was common practice at the time for a temple to convert to
whatever sect the resident priest happened to belong—the building itself
was less important than what took place inside. Its most recent occupant
had been a Shūgendō ascetic. Keizan's taking stewardship of the temple
effectively rededicated Morooka Kannondō to Sōtō Zen.[9]

Keizan renamed his "new" temple Shōgakusan Sōjiji. His choice for
the mountain name, Shōgakusan, was simply an alternate reading of
"Morooka." As for the temple name, Sōjiji, there is some mystery. The
word *sōji* can mean "preservation of memory," "preservation of good
works," or "mental concentration"—all auspicious readings for a temple
name.[10] However, the consensus among modern scholars is that *sōji* most
likely refers to a *dharani*, a genre of magico-religious intonations used in
esoteric ceremonies and rituals, often associated with Shingon Buddhist
practice.[11] Since Morooka Kannondō had originally been dedicated to
Shingon Buddhism, Keizan's choice for a new temple name could conceivably be a cleverly elegant way of saying "same temple, new ownership."

Not long after Shōgakusan Sōjiji's rededication to Sōtō Zen, Keizan recorded several wondrous visions about his new temple. In his first vision, he saw Sōjiji not as the lone wooden structure that currently sat on the land, but a large temple complex, bustling with people. When he awoke from the dream, Keizan said prophetically, "This temple is a powerful place from which the destiny of the Buddha's Dharma can be fulfilled. If my own efforts on behalf of the Dharma cry out, my voice will transcend the world."[12]

In a second dream, the bodhisattva Kannon herself appeared to Keizan, commanding him to "build a gate," after which two great birds spread their wings and sailed aloft. After the temple gate was constructed, the bodhisattvas Kannon, Monjo, and Jizō appeared to Keizan above the newly built structure, leading Keizan to enshrine their images in its second story.[13]

Despite Keizan's inspired visions, the newly repurposed Sōjiji got off to a slow start, with Keizan struggling to secure financial support for his new temple. Keizan scored a major political coup by gaining the support of the resurgent imperial faction hoping to win back control of Japan from the military government in Kamakura. In an imperial missive sent to Keizan in 1322, Emperor Go-Daigo proclaimed that Sōjiji was to be the "Foremost center for the spreading of Japanese Sōtō to the world" (*Nihon Sōtō shusse daiichi dōjō*) and authorized Keizan to wear the purple robe, a symbol of imperial favor.[14] This imperial support would reap dividends following the Emperor's "restoration" in 1333, after which prominent families donated financial and material resources to Sōjiji in a show of support for the imperial cause.[15]

Construction of Sōjiji's Monk's Hall, necessary for housing a community of monastics, was completed in 1324. On the twenty-ninth day of the fifth month of that year,[16] the Monk's Hall was dedicated and Sōjiji's monastic order was formally established. In the seventh month of 1324, Keizan stepped down from the abbacy, and Gasan was formally installed as the second abbot of Sōjiji.[17] Sōjiji's inaugural class of monastics was comprised of twenty-eight monks who took the precepts following Gasan's installation.

The nascent monastic community at Sōjiji was given explicit instructions for everyday life in the monastery, daily and monthly rituals, and funeral rites for abbots in a monastic rule known as the *Keizan Shingi*. At a time when monastic practice differed widely, even among temples in the same lineage, Keizan recognized a need to consolidate and standardize the varied monastic customs and traditions, rebranding the whole for use by future generations of descendants.

Keizan died at Yōkōji the following year.

The *Gasan-ha* and the Flourishing of Sōtō Zen

After Keizan's death there were several years of peace between his descendants. The faction who claimed descent from Keizan through Meihō (the *Meihō-ha*) were based at Yōkōji, while the faction who traced their lineage through Gasan (the *Gasan-ha*) were based at Sōjiji. For a time, Gasan even simultaneously held the abbacies of both Sōjiji and Yōkōji.[18]

Despite being the "younger" disciple of Keizan (a critical point in a tradition that emphasizes primogeniture), the prestige and renown of Gasan and his disciples—and, by extension, Sōjiji itself—soon outstripped that of Meihō's line at Yōkōji.[19] Before Gasan's time, the Japanese Buddhist institutions clambered over one another for the patronage of the Japanese aristocratic and warrior classes. Gasan and his disciples, however, understood that much could be gained by ministering to the religious needs of the more populous and less appreciated farming and merchant classes.

Gasan encouraged an entrepreneurial spirit in his disciples. Priests from Gasan's line traveled throughout Japan, bringing with them a new religious innovation: Sōtō Zen–branded funerals and memorial rites that promised immediate salvation to the deceased through posthumous ordination. While innovative in their packaging, these new practices were firmly couched in the language and customs of local funerary practices and were thus easily adopted. The efforts of these charismatic Sōtō Zen teachers drew immense popular support among the poorer agricultural population, which, in turn, influenced the decisions of local landowners and samurai nobility to provide the sect with political, financial, and material patronage.

Another key innovation implemented by Gasan's disciples was to mandate that all priests who traced their line through Gasan share the burden of the abbacy at Sōjiji, as well as to make yearly pilgrimages and donations to Sōjiji to observe memorial rites for Keizan and Gasan. The political and financial effect of these policies was enormous: by pressuring priests in Gasan's line to become abbots of Sōjiji for a set term of service, the faction gained a surplus of "former abbots" when these priests stepped down. The title lent prestige to the priest and increased his standing among the laity, furthering his ability to attract financial support and to establish new temples.[20] As these priests were in Gasan's lineage, the temples they founded would naturally become branch temples of Sōjiji.[21] This surge in temple holdings, combined with yearly donations, allowed Sōjiji's wealth and political influence to expand exponentially.

It was from Sōjiji, therefore, that Sōtō Zen flourished in Japan during the medieval period. Although censuses of sectarian temples were not taken before the eighteenth century, William M. Bodiford conservatively estimates that in the two hundred years between 1450 and 1650, an average of 43 Sōtō Zen temples and monasteries were established each year.[22] By the first official temple census in 1745, there were over 17,500 Sōtō Zen–affiliated temples in Japan.[23] Of these, 16,197 were branch temples affiliated with Sōjiji, with only 1,370 affiliating with Eiheiji.[24]

The Parishioner System

Following the bloody civil wars of the late sixteenth century, the year 1600 saw the dawn of a new political reality in Japan under the banner of the Tokugawa shogunate. From its inception, the Tokugawa regime was on guard against any potential challenges to its rule. While the rival clans who had opposed the Tokugawa forces during the civil wars were relatively easy for the new government to handle—they were banished to the islands of Kyūshū and Shikoku—Christianity, introduced by the Catholic missionaries who accompanied the Portuguese and Spanish trading vessels arriving in Japanese ports, proved a more insidious threat. According to Duncan Ryūken Williams, "The threat of Christianity . . . lay partly in its Biblical teachings that seemed counter to Japan's established religious traditions, but principally in the issue of Christian loyalty owed to God and to the pope over Japan's secular authority."[25] While Stephen G. Covell suggests that the suspicion cast on European missionaries and Japanese Christian converts may have been a deliberate exaggeration that the Tokugawa government "posed to the country as a pretext for implementing measures of social control," Christianity was formally outlawed in Japan in 1614.[26] Over the next several decades, a number of policies designed to root out pockets of Christian holdouts and secure Tokugawa hegemony over the Japanese populace were put into motion.

The Tokugawa shogunate recognized that the existing network of Buddhist temples in Japan was a convenient resource that could be used to mitigate the threat of Christian subversives, as well as to monitor and regulate the activities of the Japanese populace. A policy of mandatory temple affiliation, under which the heads of every household were required to register their families with a Buddhist temple, was enacted in 1635, becoming universal throughout Japan by 1638.[27] In most cases the choice of the temple at which to register—and therefore one's sectarian affiliation—was determined not by belief in or loyalty to any sect's teachings but rather by how close the temple was to one's home. Once a family was registered with a specific temple and sect, it was almost impossible to transfer or otherwise change one's affiliation, save for women who married into a family belonging to a different sect.[28]

These de facto temple "parishioners" became known as *danna* (from the Sanskrit *dāna*, meaning "donating" or "giving"), or more commonly, *danka*, a neologism that combined the characters for "donor" and "family/household." As "donors," the parishioner families were financially responsible for the upkeep of the temple and support of its resident priest. Parishioners were beholden to the temple for the performance of all funerals and memorial rituals, as it was prohibited for the laity to perform funerals themselves or to retain the services of priests outside their registered sect. Moreover, parishioners were obliged to visit their temple on specific festival days and to allow the priest into their homes at least once a year. While clothed in the trappings of piety, this visitation allowed the priest access to inspect the home and ancestral altar for evidence of Christian worship. Failure to fulfill any of these responsibilities gave the temple's resident priest the right to remove the parishioner family from the temple register, exposing the family to social sanction, accusations of heresy, heavy fines, and even the threat of execution.[29]

This compulsory registration was known as the *danka seido* (parishioner system) or *terauke seido* (temple registration system). By making financial support of one's family temple a universal legal obligation across all levels of Japanese society, the temple registration system represented another fundamental shift in the nature of lay-clerical relations in the practice of Buddhism. No longer was patronage of Buddhist clergy and temples the purview of a wealthy few; temple priests were able to draw almost at will upon the financial and material resources of their parishioner base for the needs of the temple and for their own personal livelihoods. No longer were priests required to be charismatic leaders or exemplars of religious practice to draw popular support; temple parishioners were literally captive audiences who added to a temple's coffers whether or not they felt any personal religious conviction or connection to the teachings of the sect. Perhaps most significantly, no longer were performances of funerals and memorial observances the responsibility of members of the local community; with the advent of the parishioner system, these responsibilities shifted to the Buddhist clergy, who now found themselves in a legally defined role as funeral and memorial ritual specialists.

By registering families—rather than individuals—in perpetuity, a temple was guaranteed financial and material support over successive generations, free from the tides of popular or individual religious sentiment. Regardless of whether this support was given willingly or by coercion, parishioner households across all strata of Japanese society now had a vested interest in the daily life and maintenance of what had become, in essence, the "family temple" (*uchi no bodaiji*).

The family temple was the material embodiment of a community's labor and resources expended over time, and as such, it was the temple where a family's (and, in many cases, an entire community's) ancestors were buried and venerated, and where the living and their descendants could expect to be buried and venerated. Caring for the well-being of the family temple ensured that a person could satisfy their filial obligations in life and that they would be given the same respect from their descendants when they died.

Sibling Rivalry

Despite Sōjiji's meteoric rise to prominence and power within the medieval Japanese religious field, Dōgen's Eiheiji was still respected and recognized as the origin point of the Japanese Sōtō Zen sect. However, a variety of factors—including a run of noncharismatic abbots and repeated factioning within its own monastic community—prevented Eiheiji from becoming as politically significant as its position would have otherwise suggested. Eiheiji was recognized as the *honzan* of the Sōtō Zen sect in 1507, but the true political power remained with Sōjiji. In 1589 the Imperial Court reversed its earlier designation, recognizing Sōjiji as the head temple of the Sōtō Zen sect.[30]

For the next three hundred years, Sōjiji and Eiheiji routinely skirmished with one another, with each temple's faction taking sides over a variety of disputes, ranging from the monumental to the trivial.[31] Sōtō Zen practice itself was deeply factionalized, with Eiheiji-line priests and Sōjiji-line priests holding to different ritual standards. Even today, subtle differences in pronunciation, ritual movements, and even the way priests wear their robes communicate to the observant viewer whether a priest was trained at Sōjiji or Eiheiji.

These conflicts might be explained as simple institutional rivalries, but the schism between Sōjiji and Eiheiji hinted at deeper familial issues.[32] For more than three centuries, Eiheiji-line priests resented Sōjiji's widespread influence while Sōjiji-line priests resented having to constantly justify their

status as *honzan* against arguments about Eiheiji's historical primacy. Capitalizing on the major cultural and political shifts that accompanied the
Meiji restoration, the abbot of Eiheiji petitioned the new Meiji government in 1868 to reverse the centuries-old status quo, arguing that Eiheiji
should once again be made the *honzan* of the sect, resparking the intrasectarian rivalry in earnest.[33]

Still, when the political support behind the Japanese Buddhist institutions was withdrawn and the laws mandating parishioner registration were
repealed in 1871, Eiheiji and Sōjiji banded together, issuing a joint statement of solidarity in 1872. For the next two decades, Sōjiji and Eiheiji
would work together to standardize and modernize the sect's practices,
their efforts culminating in the first edition of the Sōtō Zen ritual handbook for use throughout the sect.[34]

This peace was not to last, however. Behind the scenes, both temples
still jockeyed for political position. The institutions themselves were at
war, but the battles were fought in the guise of their historical founders: it was not "Sōjiji versus Eiheiji" but rather "Keizan versus Dōgen."
Dōgen's *Shōbōgenzō* was proffered first as a "bible" (*kyōten*) for the Sōtō
Zen sect; Sōjiji's faction countered by producing Keizan's previously
unknown *Denkōroku* in 1857.[35] Historically, both texts had limited religious significance in a practical sense, but in a new religious field influenced by Christianity—particularly the emphasis on a founder's teachings
as recorded in a written work—the resurfacing of these books reopened
the old wounds regarding legitimacy and authority.[36] The attacks quickly
became personal. From the one side, Keizan was vilified for having cor-
rupted Dōgen's "pure Zen." From the other side, Dōgen's importance was
minimized in light of the contributions made by Keizan and his entrepreneurial descendants. The damage done to both parties' reputations was
such that echoes of this controversy can still be heard today.

By 1892 the Sōjiji faction had had enough. A movement for the "separation and independence" (*bunri dokuritsu*) of Sōjiji led to the cessation of
all formal ties with Eiheiji. On March 19 the abbot of Sōjiji issued a formal
declaration of independence:

> We voluntarily promulgate a statement of separation and indepen-
> dence, notify Eiheiji that all alliances between the two temples have
> been nullified, prohibit the Sōtō sectarian administration, dissolve
> the Sōtō sect assembly, and furthermore petition the Home Minster
> to cancel all sect regulations and recognize our separation.[37]

While Eiheiji still enjoyed its government-mandated status as the *honzan* of the Sōtō Zen sect, it now faced a different problem: Sōjiji's secession had taken with it over fifteen thousand loyal temples, amounting to 90 percent of the sect's total property holdings and income. In the meantime, Sōjiji pushed for official government recognition, either as *honzan* or as head of its own legally recognized branch sect.

After two years of silence between the two factions, it became clear that this was a mutually untenable position. The Japanese government's Ministry of Home Affairs became increasingly involved in the squabble, like a parent struggling to control two fighting children. Eiheiji had more to lose from the secession, but neither was Sōjiji gaining ground on its petitions to the government. Ultimately, the Ministry of Home Affairs forced the two sides to reconcile their differences and in 1894 officially recognized both Sōjiji and Eiheiji as the two *honzan* of the Sōtō Zen sect. The two *honzan* issued a joint statement declaring that "both temples are one body, not two" (*ryōzan ittai funi*).[38]

Correspondingly, Keizan was given equal stature alongside Dōgen, with both holding the title of patriarch (*so*) of the Japanese Sōtō Zen sect. Dōgen is recognized as the apical ancestor (*kōso*) of the sect, but Keizan is honored as *taiso*, the propagator of Sōtō Zen in Japan. Dōgen (and thus Eiheiji) is presented as the stern "father" of Sōtō Zen, the one who planted the seed in fertile soil; in this imagery, Keizan (and thus Sōjiji) became the "mother" under whose care the seeds matured and thrived.[39] Illustrations of the "One Buddha, Two Patriarchs" (*ichibutsu ryōso*), depicting the two patriarchs facing each other mediated by a shining Śākyamuni Buddha seated upon a lotus, became the official image of the Sōtō Zen sect.

The Great Fire and the Relocation

The intrasectarian conflict between Sōjiji and Eiheiji damaged the already tenuous political position of both temples. Less than four years after the two temples made peace, a sudden catastrophe dealt to Sōjiji what should have been a killing blow.

According to the official story, on the evening of April 13, 1898, the monk responsible for the night watch at Sōjiji had gone to bed after neglecting to make his rounds of the temple. Had he done his duty, he would have found candles still burning in the Dharma Hall, which sat at a major juncture of the temple's network of wooden corridors. At approximately nine in the evening, a strong wind knocked over a candle, and the

Dharma Hall was quickly engulfed in flames. A temple monitor raised the alarm bell to wake the sleeping monks, but their access to the hall was blocked by the fire. Gusting winds quickly spread the fire throughout the temple complex in both directions. The monks rescued what treasures they could, but by morning the entire temple complex was gone.[40]

Fire was a common danger to old wooden temples, and the fire of 1898 was not the first time Sōjiji had burned down. In fact, it was not the first time Sōjiji had burned down that century. On the twenty-first day of the first month of 1806, a comparably destructive fire had swept through the temple precincts. Governmental permission to rebuild was granted in 1809, and the temple was gradually rebuilt at the rate of one building per year between 1812 and 1831.

However, there had been major political and economic shifts that made the 1898 fire more threatening for the future of Sōjiji as a viable institution. Under the Tokugawa feudal system, Sōjiji had a powerful friend and benefactor in the Maeda clan that ruled the Kaga Domain (present-day Ishikawa Prefecture). When Sōjiji was destroyed in 1803, the Maeda clan led efforts to rebuild the important temple as quickly as possible, contributing money, resources, and labor. By 1898, however, the old feudal system had been abolished for nearly a quarter of a century, and the Maeda clan—a close ally of the Tokugawa military government—had been stripped of nearly all of its economic and political capital by the new Meiji government. Sōjiji had relied on the support of the Maeda family for nearly three hundred years, but it could not do so any longer.

Moreover, the political and religious landscape of Japan had changed dramatically in the ninety-two years between the fires. In 1898 the Japanese Buddhist institution as a whole was still reeling from the Meiji government's increased regulation of temples and priests. The stakes were high: increased government oversight since 1872 had at times been hostile and even violent in its persecution of the Buddhist establishment.[41] By deregulating the parishioner system, the government drastically limited the ability of temples throughout Japan to compel monetary and material donations from their parishioners. While the overwhelming majority of Sōtō Zen temples were nominally loyal to Sōjiji, the branch temples were themselves in similarly dire financial straits, with some resorting to selling off their holdings to make ends meet. Sōjiji could not rely on its network of branch temples to raise funds for rebuilding either.

Despite its total destruction, all hope was not lost. History credits two visionary men—Ishikawa Sodō (1842–1920) and Asano Sōichirō (1848–1930)—who would spearhead the effort to rebuild Sōjiji. Initially, the hope was to rebuild Sōjiji on the Noto Peninsula, where it had stood for close to six centuries. Within two years, however, a movement was started that would move Sōjiji across the country, closer to the new national capital in Tokyo.

At the time of the fire, Ishikawa Sodō was serving as the rector (*kannin*) of Sōjiji. As the administrative head of the temple, he quickly moved to action, requesting financial assistance from the Sōtō Zen sectarian administration and appealing to Sōjiji's large network of branch temples for aid. In October 1898, only six months after the fire, Ishikawa convened a meeting of Sōjiji's branch temples, where he presented a proposal for reconstruction. Through the auspices of the sectarian administration, the abbots of Sōjiji and Eiheiji issued a joint proclamation calling for the immediate reconstruction of Sōjiji.[42] Ishikawa wrote the preamble to this proclamation.

Across the country in Yokohama, entrepreneur Asano Sōichirō was in the planning stages of a massive project to reshape the landscape of the Tokyo Bay to conform to his vision of Japan's future. Asano would have been familiar with Sōjiji through his first business venture, shipping mercantile goods between Hokkaidō and the Noto Peninsula.[43] After Asano relocated to Yokohama in the 1870s, he began amassing his fortune reselling coal and coal tar to Tokyo factories. As his business empire grew, Asano moved into the cement business, at first leasing a government-owned cement factory and later establishing his own factories. He allied himself with Shibusawa Ei'ichi (1840–1931) and Yasuda Zenjirō (1838–1921), titans of Japan's new financial world. With their financial backing, Asano established more than sixty companies, including TKK Lines in 1898, which would become the leading trans-Pacific service between Yokohama—the "Gateway to Europe and the Americas"—and San Francisco.[44]

Asano had seen for himself the benefits of European and American industrial techniques, most notably the practice of building factories as close to the waterfront as possible to facilitate loading commodities and goods directly onto ships with a minimum of overland transport. While the ports of Tokyo and Yokohama were already being utilized for commerce, Asano recognized that the shallows between the two cities was an ideal landscape for putting his plan into action.

Even fifty years after the start of Japan's modernization, Tsurumi was still an unremarkable village along the Tōkaidō highway, whose major industries were shallow-water fishing and farming.[45] Asano set his sights on a massive land reclamation scheme that would utterly transform the shallows of Tsurumi to allow for rapid industrial and maritime growth.

In May 1900 a coalition of Sōtō abbots and parishioners from Oita and Nagano prefectures sent a letter to Sōjiji's abbot, requesting that temple administration consider moving the temple closer to Tokyo.[46] Their position was strengthened by a growing faction within the sect that saw opportunity in Sōjiji's tragedy: a chance for the temple to relocate itself away from its remote and rural base and closer to the seat of political and economic power.

Although official histories do not detail what, if any, dialogue took place between Asano and his associates and the Sōjiji administration, it is clear that Asano and Yasuda were instrumental in helping to craft the plan to move Sōjiji from its ancestral home on the Noto Peninsula to Tsurumi.[47] Such an arrangement would be mutually beneficial to the two parties. By allying with Asano and his business partners, Sōjiji would gain the patronage of a powerful and wealthy coterie that was destined to become the new political elite of Japan. In addition, Sōjiji would gain first access to international visitors, who were arriving in Japan in ever greater numbers for business and travel. For Asano and his associates, their "new" Tsurumi would benefit from becoming a major religious center virtually overnight. Sōjiji's vast network of temples and priests throughout Japan would ensure investment of capital and resources toward the temple's reconstruction, leading to increased monetary and material investment in the town, as well as bringing visitors who would support the growing local economy.

An inspection committee from Sōjiji visited Tsurumi in 1903 to survey the landscape. The decision to move Sōjiji to Tsurumi was finalized in secret on June 18, 1904, nearly three years before the public would be made aware that such a move was even under consideration. On July 3, 1904, another secret meeting was held with Katō Umio, abbot of Jōganji, the temple that occupied the hill known as Tsuru-ga-oka, the "Hill of Cranes." The meeting was held to hammer out the details of Katō's donation of the considerable land holdings of his temple to the cause of rebuilding Sōjiji in Tsurumi.[48]

With a long history as a devotional site for the medieval cult of Yakushi Nyōrai, Tsuru-ga-oka was an auspicious place to build a temple that would symbolically stand as a guardian of Japan's new national polity. Overlooking Tokyo Bay and oriented with Mount Fuji behind it, Sōjiji was visible from the new harbor being built on Tsurumi's reclaimed shallows and faced eastward toward the Americas and Europe.

In May 1906, Ishikawa ascended to Sōjiji's abbacy. Among his first acts as abbot was to reestablish momentum of the rebuilding office, which had been put on hold as a demonstration of patriotism for the duration of the

Fig. 5. A road leads through rice paddies to the future site of Sōjiji in Tsurumi, ca. 1909.

Russo-Japanese War. At a meeting in Tokyo in July 1907, it was "publicly" decided—the decision having been finalized in secret three years earlier, remember—to move Sōjiji to Tsurumi.[49]

Immediately, an opposition movement formed, comprised largely of citizens of Noto who rightly feared that moving Sōjiji would have a severe impact on the income and development of the region. The Kanazawa prefectural governor was called on to mediate the dispute, and in January 1908 he decided in favor of the pro-relocation group. Plans were quickly put into action to begin the relocation of Sōjiji to its new home.[50]

Starting Over

Following the official decision to relocate, much work needed to be done to enable Sōjiji to open its doors in Tsurumi as quickly as possible. Two buildings were constructed first at the new site in Tsurumi: the Chōryūshitsu, the abbot's residence, and the Hōkōdō, which was to serve as the ceremony hall until a suitable Dharma hall could be built.[51]

The temple was officially opened to great fanfare on November 5, 1911.

The memorial tablets of Keizan and Dōgen arrived by train in the morning; Ishikawa, in his role as abbot, and an entourage of priests and dignitaries were there to receive them at the station. Many thousands of onlookers gathered to witness the tablets' procession to the Hōkōdō, where they would be formally enshrined.[52]

Despite the grand ceremony, Sōjiji began its new life in Tsurumi at a considerable handicap. As part of the decision to move Sōjiji from Noto to Tsurumi, the temple administration was forced to concede that those families who were previously registered as *danka* of Sōjiji would remain parishioners of the old temple, which was reestablished as Sōjiji Betsuin ("satellite temple"; the title was later changed to Soin, "ancestral temple"). It was further agreed that these families would not be tapped for financial resources to build the new Sōjiji in Tsurumi.[53] Despite the donations of considerable financial and material resources from Sōtō clergy and parishioners throughout Japan to establish Sōjiji in Tsurumi, the concessions made to the people of Noto saw to it that Sōjiji arrived in its new home with essentially no parishioners of its own to support the temple in the long term.

For nearly a decade, the new Sōjiji survived mainly on the skill of its administrators in securing donations from Sōtō branch temples, private donors, and through national fund-raising efforts. The land upon which Sōjiji was built was a donation, as were entire buildings like the Hōkōdō and, later, the Taihōkan. Private donations from wealthy and influential patrons helped keep the struggling temple afloat during difficult financial times like the financial depression that gripped Japan after the First World War.

As a consequence, Sōjiji's first two decades in its new home were filled with near-constant construction and expansion of the temple campus. The tragedies of the past informed the decision to build Sōjiji as spread out as possible in order to mitigate the risk of fire ever again being able to destroy the entire temple. Moreover, the new Sōjiji's campus was never a closed circuit: the Buddha Hall (Butsuden) was kept separate from the other temple buildings, creating a firebreak.

The temple buildings were constructed in order of importance to the daily life of both an administrative and ceremonial temple. First up were buildings that were absolutely essential to the ritual life of the temple, followed by a second phase (1912–1915) in which buildings necessary for a community of monks to train and to conduct their daily rituals were built. A third phase (1916–1921) saw the administrative and public buildings come into being, and a fourth phase—which coincided with Japan's surge in imperial nationalism between 1921 and 1937—saw the construction of buildings related to State Shinto and the Imperial Household.[54]

Sōjiji's Taishō era administrators must have realized early on that with the parishioner system having been repealed, the temple could not guarantee a reliable stream of revenue to fill the temple's coffers. Between 1912 and 1921, Sōjiji's policies toward the laity broke from historical precedent, forgoing the establishment of a sizable parishioner base to instead foster a relationship with its new neighbors in Tsurumi through charitable works and establishment of groups and organizations designed to attract "believers" (*shinto*) instead of parishioners.[55] Like many other Buddhist institutions of the time, Sōjiji was clearly borrowing from the playbook of Christian (primarily Protestant) churches and charitable organizations, which provided a model for attracting new adherents while also demonstrating their utility to the state as "useful Buddhism" (*goyō Bukkyō*).[56]

The Great Kantō Earthquake of September 1, 1923, caused a sudden reversal of Sōjiji's priorities back to the idea of a parishioner base. The earthquake caused relatively light structural damage to Sōjiji's buildings, with the most notable casualty being the collapse of the front awning of the Taihōkan. While the earthquake itself was powerful, the real disaster came moments later. Because the quake struck at lunchtime, cooking fires were burning in homes throughout the heavily populated corridor between Tokyo and Yokohama. What began as small, localized fires raged into an inferno that burned for three days, ultimately leaving 71 percent of Tokyo residents and 85 percent of Yokohama residents homeless. All told, the conflagration killed over 140,000 people. Sōjiji's elevated position on a hill above Tsurumi and a protective sheath of trees and vegetation provided a natural firewall that safeguarded the nascent temple from the disaster taking place around it.

In the aftermath of the earthquake and fire, the residents of Tsurumi and the areas adjacent to it sought a place to bury and memorialize their dead. With acres of undeveloped land holdings, Sōjiji was in a unique position to minister to their needs. While the land had originally been set aside for future expansion of the temple precincts, Sōjiji had more than enough holdings to establish a sizable cemetery. Sōjiji was flooded with applications from the laity to establish family graves at the temple, establishing the applicants as parishioners of Sōjiji. Despite having resigned themselves to a future without parishioner support, Sōjiji's administrators found themselves compelled to quickly change course and come to terms with its renewed role as a parishioner temple.

Still, Sōjiji did not abandon its new charitable tack. Under the auspices of its Social Works Department (*Shakai Jigyō-ryō*), 1924 saw the founding of a tide of charitable organizations affiliated with the temple, including a college (now Tsurumi University), a hospital, a home for the blind, a dormitory for single mothers, and a middle school and a high school for girls.[57]

Sōjiji during the Pacific War

Sōjiji's role during the Pacific War is a difficult story to tell. In a temple that prides itself on recounting its long and proud history—in particular, the history of the last hundred years—it was surprising to discover a twenty-five-year narrative gap in Sōjiji's institutional memory dating between 1925 and 1950. Neither the novices nor their supervisors I interviewed could remember ever being told much about what occurred at Sōjiji or its involvement during the war. It was simply not talked about.

Moreover, interviews with elderly priests and lifelong residents of Tsurumi did not reveal many memories of Sōjiji at this time. The oldest person I spoke with who had any firsthand knowledge of Tsurumi during the war was only twelve years old at the end of the war. Other informants were between five and eight at the time. What they remember—vividly, in many cases—was the destruction, the starvation, and the sense of fear, loss, and sadness that permeated their lives. They were too young to remember much else.

What details I was able to discover illuminate Sōjiji's wartime story in relief. Owing to its proximity to the military-industrial port that sat on its very doorstep, Sōjiji did have a working relationship with the Imperial Navy. Although there is very little in the temple that memorializes this relationship, what little evidence there is sits in plain sight as part of the temple landscape. Calligraphy hanging in the main audience hall of the Shiuntai is credited to Admiral Tōgō Heihachirō (1848–1934), a hero of Japan's wars with China and Russia. In addition, Sōjiji is the final resting place of Ōnishi Takijirō (1891–1945), vice admiral of the Imperial Navy, who is credited with establishing the kamikaze pilot corps. A younger priest recalled being told that Sōjiji's precincts were used for a time as a drilling ground for sailors from the Imperial Navy.

Printed records I found came mainly from the temple's self-published bulletin, *Chōryū*, which was initially published in its first series from 1928 until 1943. For the most part, the record from 1936 onward shows a temple whose official message, shared by nearly all Japanese religious institutions at the time, was of nationalistic support for the emperor and for Japan's international expansion. A serial article published throughout 1937 details Keizan's relationship with Emperor Go-Daigo, demonstrating Sōjiji's claim to a long association with and support of the Imperial Household. This series corresponded with the completion of the Go-Daigo-ten Goreiden, a shrine hall dedicated to the emperor, situated directly behind the Butsuden, and Sōjiji's observance of the six hundredth anniversary of Emperor Go-Daigo's death.

Reports of missionary efforts in Japan's colonies were also published in *Chōryū*, including a report of a visit to Manchuria and Korea by Sōjiji's abbot and his retinue (Aug. 1938). These reports regularly accompanied articles such as "The Relationship between Buddhism and the State" (Oct. 1937), "The Task of an Imperial Citizen Is Self-Realization" (Aug. 1939), and "Perfecting Yourself through *Zazen*" (June 1940). As the Pacific War accelerated after December 1941, the language of the temple bulletin becomes increasingly militaristic: "The Great Ideals of Our Nation's Founding" (March 1942), "Faith Is Strength" (Oct. 1942), "Temples and the Greater East Asia War" (Dec. 1942), "Zen and the Warrior Spirit" (Jan. 1943). However, following the sudden deaths of two successive abbots in March and April 1943, and facing wartime paper shortages, *Chōryū* abruptly went silent in July 1943.[58]

Much of the rest of the story can be pieced together by available wartime histories. By 1930 Asano's land reclamation plan for Tsurumi had succeeded beyond anyone's expectations. In Tsurumi alone, over two million square meters of shoreline had been reclaimed for industrial and mercantile use.[59] The shoreline shared by Tsurumi and neighboring Kawasaki created the Keihin Industrial Corridor, as it came to be called, which linked the two metropolises of Tokyo and Yokohama. After Japan's occupation of Manchuria in 1931, the factories of the industrial corridor were increasingly retrofitted for production of materiel to support Japan's military machine.[60]

Following Allied victories in the Pacific Theater, Allied bombers were in range of the Japanese islands by November 1944. Although Tokyo and Yokohama provided important political and economic targets for the air strikes, much of the Japanese war effort was sustained by the factories, metalworks, and shipyards that had been built up along the shallows of Tsurumi and Kawasaki. The factories of the Keihin Industrial Corridor were therefore high-priority targets. From November 1944 to the end of the war in August 1945, Tsurumi and its industries were the target of repeated Allied bombing sorties.[61]

History vividly remembers the atomic devastation of Hiroshima and

Nagasaki, in which tens of thousands of people and the buildings they occupied were blasted out of existence in the blink of an eye. Less remembered is the bombing of Tokyo and Yokohama on the night of March 9–10, 1945, in which Allied forces unleashed a firestorm of incendiary ordinance and napalm along the coastline from central Tokyo to Yokohama, consuming a comparable number of lives.

Standing less than a kilometer from the devastation being wrought on the factories and homes of Tsurumi, an errant bomb or changing winds might have led to the complete destruction of the temple. Yet Sōjiji stood witness while Tsurumi burned, untouched by either the raging flames or the wall of blistering heat carried by the strong winds that night.

For those who could escape the flames, Sōjiji's walls were sanctuary. As the fires slowly died down over many days, the bodies of the dead—when they could be found—were laid out in Sōjiji's hallways and throughout the temple precincts. Residents of Tsurumi came to Sōjiji and walked through its macabre landscape of burned corpses, searching for the remains of family and loved ones. Tsurumi would endure three more devastating strikes, on April 15, May 14, and the worst on May 29.[62] By the end of the war, the Allied destruction of Tsurumi was so complete that most survivors would never find closure.

"After the war, people needed more than a place to bury their dead," one priest told me. "They needed a place where they could come together to celebrate being alive. Sōjiji filled that need." As with the Great Kantō Earthquake, Sōjiji accepted people of all denominations. For many, religious affiliation was less important than practical concerns that the dead be properly memorialized as soon as possible. Once again Sōjiji's parishioner base soared. The space already set aside for Sōjiji's cemetery was insufficient for the demand, and the temple administration was compelled to annex more of the temple's land reserves to accommodate more graves.

Sōjiji in the Postwar Period

The last major push of temple membership came not from tragedy but from prosperity. The postwar reconstruction led to decades of rapid economic growth—Japan's "economic miracle." With its gross domestic product growing at an average rate of over 10 percent every year, Japan became a global industrial and financial superpower. This growth was fueled in large part by a mass exodus of the youngest generation from rural regions to Japan's major cities, like Tokyo and Yokohama. They came to find jobs in the rebuilt factories and offices in the urban areas. By 1964—nineteen years after its almost complete devastation—Tokyo had the largest population of any city in the world, at ten million people.

While it was common to keep close ties with their rural ancestral homes, an increasing number of Japanese flocked to Japan's urban areas with little intention of ever going back. Many of the new urbanites were content with keeping their family's graves at the rural temples where they had stood for generations, but others sought to either relocate or reestablish a family grave at a more accessible temple. From the 1950s through the 1970s, the demand for cemetery space at Japan's urban temples skyrocketed. As real estate prices soared, so too did prices for gravesites. Urban temples like Sōjiji benefited at the expense of their rural brethren. As with the two previous surges in membership, Sōjiji was able to transform its undeveloped land holdings into a more valuable commodity: parishioners. By the late 1970s, Sōjiji's parishioner base had taken on its contemporary character, estimated at over five thousand families. Today Sōjiji's cemetery is almost a hundred thousand square meters in size, fully a third of the temple's total area.[63]

Equally significant, Sōjiji's central location between Tokyo and Yokohama meant the temple sat on a well-traveled route that was to become the major railway and motor artery linking the two cities. Sōjiji became an easily accessible tourist destination for American soldiers during the Occupation and, later, for international travelers arriving by sea at the Port of Yokohama and by air at Haneda Airport. Sōjiji was able to capitalize on this accessibility and emerged from the war having rebranded itself as an "international Zen garden" (*kokusai zen'en*).

Following the war, the temple administrators struggled to come to terms with what suddenly appeared to be the contradictory pull of two forces: one, the outward push toward religious innovation, tourism, and international outreach; the other, the inward pull toward traditional practices, memorial rituals, and dependency on parishioner revenue. In the decades that followed, internal policies and practices at Sōjiji would regularly swing back and forth between these priorities as national prosperity and international interest in Zen led the temple and the Sōtō Zen sect to continuously question its direction.

By the 1960s the United States and Europe were in the midst of a "Zen Boom," in which interest and consumption of all things Zen-related reached new heights. Japan would follow suit with its own Zen Boom during the 1970s, largely in response to this international interest. The surge of attention being paid to Zen was both affirming and profitable to temples in Japan, but it often came at a cost. Influenced by the writing of popularizers such as D. T. Suzuki and Alan Watts, many international visitors were drawn to a Zen that had been sold as a nonreligious "philosophy" or "spirituality," an alternative to Western institutionalized religions that did not require belief or commitment. Those who came to Japan to find Zen—at least as they imagined it—were often turned off by the focus on ritual practices, particularly funerals and memorial rites, that for centuries had defined daily life at Zen temples in Japan. Some enterprising clergy understood this and adapted their temples' daily routine to suit the religious tourists' expectations, adding guided tours, *zazen* sessions, or tea ceremony demonstrations for a fee. Other priests, however, balked at the idea of abdicating their responsibility to their parishioners and their religion by catering to international fads, however potentially profitable, and became critical of those who did so. It soon became clear that two Zens were emerging: religious "Zen" that catered to primarily to Japanese parishioners' ritual needs, and "zen" as an internationally marketable commodity.[64]

Sōjiji's size, status, and location gave it enormous potential to capitalize on both of these trends. While maintaining the daily ritual responsibility to its parishioners, the temple also had the resources to court both national and international interest in Zen. Many of the influential figures involved in spreading Zen to Europe and the Americas during this period—Deshimaru Taisen in France, Suzuki Shinryū in San Francisco, and Maezumi Taizan in Los Angeles, among others—had personal ties to Sōjiji, often providing the impetus for their non-Japanese students to visit. Similarly, the clergy in training at Sōjiji at the time had the opportunity to see firsthand the growth potential in international outreach.

A final push of expansion in the 1960s saw the construction of Sōjiji's largest public buildings. Timed to correspond with the celebrations planned for Gasan's six hundredth memorial anniversary, the Daisodō was completed in 1965 and the Sanmon in 1969. Both structures were specifically designed to be the largest of their kind in Japan: the Daisodō alone can fit more than two thousand people under its roof. They were grand architectural statements of Sōjiji's renewed prosperity and its mission to accommodate all who would come to the temple "to hear the teachings of Keizan." In addition to size, both structures were built for longevity by eschewing traditional cypress wood construction for the more resistant and less flammable reinforced ferroconcrete. Further distinguishing them from other temple buildings whose exteriors were the deep brown of aged wood, both the Daisodō and Sanmon were painted in a bright color scheme of pink and white and capped with vibrant patina-green roofs.

Fig. 6. Sōjiji's Daisodō (Dharma Hall). It is the largest building of its kind in Japan.

While acknowledging their architectural magnificence, more than one priest privately lamented to me that he wished the planners would have had the foresight to choose a more subdued color scheme.[65]

By the mid-1960s, the image of Sōjiji as an "international Zen garden" began to dominate the temple. Articles from *Chōryū* during the 1960s and 1970s show Sōjiji and its priests looking far beyond Japan and actively engaged with the outside world on a truly international scale. Monthly reports from the overseas missions in California and South America are regularly seen alongside travelogues from Sōjiji priests recently returned from trips to Europe, China, and India. Articles about how best to incorporate *zazen* into one's busy modern life are followed by political commentary on international affairs, such as the conflict in Vietnam.

At the height of the bubble economy in the early 1980s, however, Sōjiji's interest in international affairs suddenly diminished, and the temple administration turned its attentions inward. The needs of its Japanese parishioners firmly took center stage, as did issues of sectarian identity and an academic interest in the unique contributions of Sōtō Zen to Japanese history. With the increased income stemming from decades of eco-

Fig. 7. Altar and main ritual space of the Daisodō. Note the brocaded curtains and carefully controlled sight lines.

nomic prosperity, more and more Japanese were in the financial position to indulge in pious conspicuous consumption.[66] In addition to a rise in expensive household religious items like *butsudan* altars, parishioners were increasingly willing to pay for expensive traditional religious services that, owing to a variety of economic and demographic factors, had not been priorities previously. Sōjiji's focus shifted accordingly.

It would be cynical to describe this shift as opportunistic or greedy. Rather, it was a calculated, pragmatic decision. At the time, there was more revenue to be made—and, consequently, a better chance of keeping the temple financially solvent—by cultivating relationships with paying Japanese parishioners who would in theory guarantee a multigenerational affiliation with the temple rather than courting fickle international tourists. At the time, paying parishioners were, as the phrase goes, coming out of the woodwork.

However, when the economic bubble burst in 1992, Sōjiji found itself in a precarious situation. For Buddhist temples throughout Japan, the religious boom ended just as quickly as it began, with parishioner families no longer able to afford the same caliber of funerals and memorial ceremonies that had been primary drivers of temple revenue. The horrific sarin gas attack on the Tokyo subway carried out by Aum Shinrikyō in 1995 and the rise of militant fundamentalist movements around the world further pushed the Japanese away from religion and religious activities.

As the economic recession deepened, many of the temple lay organizations saw dramatic drop-offs in attendance and participation, reflecting the contraction of time, money, and interest among Sōjiji's community. These problems were compounded by the fact that within a single decade Sōjiji had almost completely estranged itself from its previous international reputation. As a consequence, throughout the first decade of the 2000s, Sōjiji's administrators had no choice but to lean hard on the tiller, trying to chart a course for the temple that would see it safely through choppy waters.

The Ethnographic Moment

The research in this book represents two decades of my interest and engagement with Sōjiji and its community. From my first visit to Sōjiji on a hot and humid August day in 2001, I have been a constant correspondent, a privileged participant, and—thanks to the internet, social media, and video technology—a virtual fly on the wall observing and documenting the life of the temple for close to twenty years.

The most active and fruitful period of this research dates from between 2004 and 2011. In August 2006 I arrived in Japan for a twenty-month period of ethnographic fieldwork. For the duration, I lived in an apartment in Tsurumi, fifteen minutes by foot from Sōjiji. By my accounting, I was physically present at Sōjiji for six days out of every seven. In addition, I was in twenty-four-hour "residence" at the temple (which I count as days that I woke up at Sōjiji, spent the day at Sōjiji, and went to sleep at Sōjiji) for over two months of accumulated time through many overnight stays and retreat periods.

By the close of this intensive fieldwork in April 2008, I had logged thousands of hours of on-site participant-observation research and recorded more than two hundred hours of formal interviews and informal conversations with individuals across the spectrum of Sōjiji's diverse community. My experience during this time provides the backbone for the chapters that follow.

TWO

The Training of a Sōtō Zen Novice

In the Kantō region of Japan, late March brings the much-awaited blooming of the cherry blossom trees. Nature is at times difficult to find in the landscape of concrete that dominates Tokyo and Yokohama, but for the two weeks or so that the cherry blossoms are in bloom, city dwellers by the tens of thousands seek out parks and other oases of greenery to take part in *hanami*—flower viewing. The weather is fair and the sun is warm. It is a wonderful time to be outside.

On the lawn outside the Daisodō, Sōjiji's cherry trees are in full bloom. These trees are relatively recent additions to the temple landscape, and there are not many of them—like much of Sōjiji's greenery, they were planted in 1999—but on this particular morning they nevertheless provide a pleasant setting for a group of coeds from Tsurumi University to have a small gathering under a canopy of brilliant white blossoms. Like the thousands of similar gatherings in parks throughout Japan, these students have claimed their *hanami* spot with a waterproof blue tarp, though there is not much competition for space here. They intend to make a day of it, having brought plenty of food to eat and plenty of alcohol to drink. Several in the group will be graduating from college within the month, and today will make for a splendid last hurrah for this circle of friends. The students lounge on the tarp, some sitting, some reclining, their voices and laughter carrying throughout the temple precincts.

Several hours earlier, but seemingly a world apart, five young monks stood in nervous silence outside the entrance of the Taihōkan, the Hall of the Waiting Phoenix. On one of the pillars supporting the ornately carved

47

archway hangs a wooden board, called a *moppan*, with a wooden hammer suspended in a loop of rope at the bottom. A large indentation has been worn into the center of the board, a testament to the thousands of times that the hammer has struck the wood to produce the *moppan*'s characteristic hollow sound. Striking the *moppan* is a signal that a monk has arrived at the temple gates seeking permission to join the temple community. On most days of the year, the *moppan* does not hang here. These past few weeks, however, are different: these five monks are only a handful of the seventy-five novices who will begin their training this spring, and today the wooden board has been hung outside in anticipation of their arrival.

The monks are wearing their long black robes in the traditional manner of a wandering mendicant; the bottom of their robe is bustled into their rope belts to facilitate movement, exposing the hem of their underrobes. On their bare feet they wear rough straw sandals laced at their ankles. Running the length of their forearms is a white sleeve that extends over the back of the hand. Draped over their left shoulders is a bib-like garment called a *rakusu*, identifying them as disciples of the Buddha. Over both shoulders they carry a kind of rucksack fashioned from two boxes secured together with a long cloth strap; one box is carried on their backs, the other on their chests. Carefully packed inside these boxes are a change of robes and undergarments, their over-the-shoulder Dharma robe (*kesa*), a set of lacquered eating bowls, and a small scroll containing an image of the Dragon God, guardian of Buddhist monks. Tucked under their left arms is a black cushion called a *zafu* that they will sit on every day while they meditate; in their right hands, they hold wide-brimmed straw hats like shields. They carry no money save for a five-thousand-yen bill, which will be donated to the temple as "nirvana money" (*nehankin*), used to offset costs for the monk's funeral should he die in training. This is all that a novice monk is allowed to bring with him as he begins his training at Sōjiji. Everything else, all other trappings of his former life, is forbidden.

One of the monks steps forward and removes the hammer hanging from the loop of rope on the bottom of the *moppan*. Taking the rope in his hand, he slowly and deliberately strikes the center of the board three times with the hammer; the sharp crack of wood on wood resonates throughout the temple garden. He replaces the hammer into the loop after the third strike and stands with his palms together with his arms stiffly parallel to the ground. In his loudest voice, he bellows, "*Shintō, yoroshu!*" (New arrivals!)

They wait. Not one of them dares to move or even fidget, nor do they speak to one another. The nervous monks are aware that they are being tested, and they are anxious to not make any mistakes. In their heads, they are likely going over all of the minute details they know they have to remember about living in a training temple, praying they do not make any mistakes that would single themselves out for embarrassment or worse. Perhaps they are grateful for the warm spring sun, knowing that while they stand here, other new arrivals like themselves are being made to stand in freezing rain or even snow outside of monastery gates in regions of Japan where springtime is still weeks away. Perhaps these young monks are feeling the crushing weight of duty and tradition upon their shoulders and wishing they were somewhere—anywhere—else.

The minutes spent waiting seem an eternity. Eventually the gatekeeper emerges at the top of the stairs leading into the hall, wielding a thick wooden stick like a sword. In a stern, quiet tone, he demands to know why the monks have shown up at Sōjiji's gate. "[We have come] to pay respects to the founder of this temple and to enter the temple to train here" (*Gokai-san haitō, narabi ni menkata, yoroshu*), one monk shouts in reply.[1] The gatekeeper warns the new monks that life at Sōjiji is not for those who have any attachment to themselves or those who have any doubts about why they are here. "You can't enter here; go somewhere else," he says dismissively before he turns his back on the waiting monks. "Go home!"

The young monks do not budge. "Didn't you hear me? Leave!" he shouts at them.

This rejection is also part of the test: previous generations of monks were made to stand for hours or even days to prove that they possessed the deep commitment necessary for training at Sōjiji, under the reasoning that those who lacked either self-discipline or a sincere desire to live the austere monastic lifestyle would simply give up and walk away after being rejected. Over the years, the time that new arrivals to Sōjiji are made to stand in front of the gate has gradually been whittled down to about two hours—or half an hour in bad weather.

In the same low, menacing voice as before, the gatekeeper repeats his warning—the path of the Buddha is a difficult road to walk and not to be entered lightly. He asks each new arrival if they are prepared for what awaits them inside the temple gates. Without hesitating, each monk shouts, "Yes!" They are led into the hall, where one by one they step out of their traveler's sandals and into their new lives as Sōjiji monks.

Ascending the Mountain

The act of entering into the community of a Sōtō Zen training monastery is called *jōzan* ("ascending the mountain"). As discussed earlier, mountains, like forests, are important symbols in a Zen temple: calling a temple a "mountain," regardless of its actual topography, invokes the classical Chinese ideal of a hermitage located on a secluded and hard-to-reach mountaintop, far removed from the secular world. While very few temples in Japan are actually on secluded mountains—Sōjiji is located on a hill in the middle of a busy urban city—the custom of giving "mountain names" (*sango*) to Buddhist temples continues today.[2] If a temple is metaphorically a mountain, then those who are entering the temple community for the purpose of *shugyō* are metaphorically climbing it.

Just as the temple is an idealized mountain, the clothing worn and rituals performed by the new monks who are entering the monastery frame them as idealized wandering mendicants, or *unsui* ("clouds and water"). Calling novices *unsui* harkens back to the ideal transient life of the Buddhist monastics of earlier times, who were beholden to "move like clouds and flow like water" (*kōun ryūsui*), never staying in one temple or place for long, always in search of new teachers to deepen their understanding of the Buddha's teachings. The image of the wandering *unsui* in his straw sandals, wide-brimmed hat, and walking staff has been represented for centuries in Japanese literature and art, and even today finds life in Japanese popular imagery in historical dramas, comic books, and animated films.

Like all idealized images, there is a bit of fiction involved in the figure of the *unsui*. As far as anyone at the temple could tell me, it has been years, maybe even decades, since a new monk arrived at the temple after having journeyed for days on foot over mountains and rivers. Nearly all new arrivals have traveled by train or car from their homes to Sōjiji, often accompanied by parents, relatives, and friends. Some even decide to forgo the traditional traveling bags worn over their chest and back for a cloth-tied bundle held in their hands or, in one case I saw, simply a duffle bag.

Likewise, the objects that the *unsui* carry on their person are not actually the only things they will need during their time at Sōjiji. Weeks before their arrival at the temple, prospective monks receive a checklist of all the items they should have: toiletries, school supplies such as notebooks and pens, a seasonal change of robes, bedding and blankets, and plastic shelving units to hold the materials they will acquire over the course of their training. These bulky items have been sent ahead by special delivery service to Sōjiji and are already waiting for the new monk when he arrives at the temple gate.

The *jōzan* ritual itself, with all of the waiting and threatening and shouting, is recognized by everyone involved as little more than a staged performance and a formality. The *unsui* know they will be made to wait for several hours, that the gatekeeper will reject them, and that they will ultimately

Fig. 8. Wearing his traveling gear, an unsui waits at the Sanshōkan gate to be received as a new arrival. He will spend the night in this room before "ascending the mountain" early the next morning.

be admitted into the temple. None of my informants could remember a single instance of an applicant "failing" this test and being sent home. The application for an *unsui* to train at Sōjiji has been submitted and approved months before the new monk arrives at Sōjiji's gate. Indeed, one could make a convincing argument that these new monks who are "ascending the mountain" are less like the traveling monastics of history and legend than they are like freshmen arriving at college for the first time.

By participating in the *jōzan* ritual, a newly arrived monk is playing a role in a narrative that is said to originate in the earliest days of Buddhism in India; monks would congregate in forest retreats to live a communal life during the monsoon season, when traveling was difficult. Throughout their training, the modern-day *unsui* are repeatedly reminded that they are the most recent link in an unbroken chain of tradition that extends back over thousands of miles and two and a half millennia.

This idealized image of the *unsui* is the high standard to which all of the new monks are held. Over the course of his training at Sōjiji, a monk is broken and refashioned from the ground up, transforming his soft and undisciplined body and mind into a living embodiment of Sōtō Zen teachings, practices, and traditions. From the remains of their former selves, *shugyō* is the crucible that transforms them to exemplars of enlightened practice.

A Portrait of the Monk as a Young Man

Wakamatsu-san was twenty-two years old when he arrived at Sōjiji, having just graduated from college only weeks earlier.[3] He is taller than most of the young monks by about a head, but like many of his fellow new arrivals, his frame carried the plumpness of an easy, mostly sedentary, life.

Wakamatsu-san is a "temple son" (*tera no musuko*) and an only child. Unlike the backgrounds of many Japanese men of his age, Buddhism and religion have always played a significant role his life. At his home temple, his grandfather is the nominal abbot, but he has relegated most of his responsibilities to Wakamatsu-san's father, the assistant abbot. Wakamatsu-san grew up watching his father and grandfather perform their ceremonial duties and had many opportunities to observe them interacting with their parishioners. As there were two priests already in the house, it was not necessary for Wakamatsu-san to take the tonsure until recently, which he did as a matter of course before his application to Sōjiji.

Wakamatsu-san's mother and father drove eight hours from their family temple in northwest Japan to bring him to Tsurumi. After checking in, the family paused to take pictures of their son standing in his monastic garb under Sōjiji's large gate. Wakamatsu-san's father had performed his *shugyō* at Sōjiji almost thirty years earlier, and as the family posed for pictures, he gestured around the temple grounds, describing how they had changed since he had been there.

Wakamatsu-san always knew that he would be a Sōtō Zen priest. Like many of the incoming novices, he attended Komazawa University, a Sōtō-affiliated university in Tokyo, where he majored in Buddhist Studies. His choice of study was not due to any particular draw to religion or interest in Buddhism. Rather, he was following a well-paved path that many in the Sōtō clergy had tread before him. According to sectarian regulations, with a background in Buddhist Studies, he could finish his required training at Sōjiji in as little as six months—half the time it would take a university graduate with no background in Buddhism, and a quarter of the time required of monks with only a high school education. Among his peers, Wakamatsu-san was not alone in his assumption that the faster he finished his *shugyō* at Sōjiji, the faster he could get on with the rest of his life as a priest at his family's rural temple.

Nakajima-san arrived at Sōjiji within a few days of Wakamatsu-san. Being of average height and weight, Nakajima-san would have been nearly indistinguishable from the other monks save for his prominent ears, which stuck out proudly from his shaved head. His thick black-rimmed glasses were likewise standard issue for *unsui* who need them, further muting his individuality.

Like Wakamatsu-san, Nakajima-san knew that he had a ready-made career as a priest if he wanted it, but he had dreams of being a computer programmer. Even though he would have received reduced tuition at Komazawa University, his parents had paid for him to attend a private college where he could acquire the skills to design the racing simulator video games that he loved to play. As a second son, his older brother—already a fully ordained priest—was in line to inherit the family temple. Because of this, Nakajima-san's parents were more willing to indulge their younger son's aspirations.

However, the video game industry in Japan is a tough business, and competition for the few jobs there are is cutthroat. After being unsuccessful in securing a postgraduation programming job during his senior year, and faced with looming graduation and unemployment, Nakajima-san became discouraged and concerned for his future. He went to his parents for advice. Although they were supportive, his father suggested that in lieu of a career in game design, he should reconsider the priesthood. If he was diligent and patient, he could work a desk job within the Sōtō Zen administrative offices or even take an overseas appointment in the hope of one day being rewarded for his efforts with a temple of his own. At first Nakajima-san resisted, but he gradually began to warm to the idea. In a blur, Nakajima-san received tonsure from his father, and his paperwork and applications were rushed so that he could enter a Sōtō training temple immediately after graduation. Nakajima-san's father had performed his required *shugyō* at Eiheiji, but he was concerned that a monk's life at a temple famous for its strict discipline would be too severe for his son, who was only beginning to come to grips with his new vocation. In the end, Nakajima-san says, it was a toss-up between Sōjiji and a small regional training temple with only a handful of monks. As he would later admit, Nakajima-san chose Sōjiji hoping there would be safety in numbers that would allow him to get through his *shugyō* without being singled out for the mistakes he was almost certain to make.

Biographies like Wakamatsu-san's and Nakajima-san's are common among each new crop of *unsui* who come to Sōjiji. For the majority of new *unsui*, pressure to inherit the family temple has long made a career in the priesthood a foregone conclusion. While previous generations of *unsui* came from more diverse backgrounds, temple sons today comprise more than 90 percent of new Sōtō clergy, with only 10 percent entering the priesthood based on other personal motivations.[4] Statistically, this would mean that in an entering cohort of seventy-five *unsui*, only eight will come from non-temple family backgrounds.

As temple sons, nearly all of the new *unsui* at Sōjiji are already somewhat familiar with the texts and protocol of daily life at a Sōtō Zen temple. The depth of this background, however, varies from individual to individual. One *unsui* who took tonsure at an early age to assist his father in daily ritual life (like Wakamatsu-san) will have substantially more of a foundation in temple life than another temple son (like Nakajima-san) who received the tonsure just before entering Sōjiji. Similarly, temple sons are almost guaranteed to have more familiarity with temple life than a layperson who takes the tonsure after discovering a personal religious commitment. Early experience translates into definite advantage in a training temple: the more exposure an *unsui* has to the ins and outs of daily life at a Sōtō temple, the smoother their acclimation will be into the disciplined and regimented life of *shugyō* at Sōjiji.

If one were to sketch out an "average" *unsui* at Sōjiji, both Wakamatsu-san and Nakajima-san would come very close to the description. The ages of the incoming *unsui* typically range from eighteen to forty, with the majority being twenty-two or twenty-three years old. With the exception of several *unsui* who hold only a high school diploma, virtually all of the incoming *unsui* are college graduates, most commonly graduating from the two Sōtō-affiliated universities, Komazawa and Aichi Gakuin.[5] Although non-Japanese are permitted to train at Sōjiji (provided they are suitably fluent in the Japanese language), they have typically been few and far between; the last foreign national—a Brazilian—trained at the temple in 2000.

Most significantly, if not readily apparent, all *unsui* at Sōjiji are male. Women play an active role in the daily operations of Sōjiji, and female monastics are not uncommon visitors to the temple.[6] However, only men are allowed to train as *unsui* at Sōjiji, with women relegated largely to support roles, such as working in the gift shop, assisting in the kitchens, or housekeeping for the guest rooms.

Contrary to popular belief, very few of the young *unsui* would describe themselves as having a "religious calling" in the sense that the term has been used in the Christian monastic tradition. It is important to remember that the decision to enter the monastic life was in most cases not theirs to make. As Covell describes, temple families that cannot produce an heir either by birth or adoption, or those who have sons who choose vocations other than the priesthood, are commonly forced out of their temples by their parishioners.[7] Financial realities and the need for a suitable successor mean that temple families often cannot afford to indulge their sons' dreams of a life outside of the priesthood. This is especially true when it comes to the eldest son of the family: Nakajima-san was fortunate to have an older brother who was already being groomed for succession, but his older brother was not given the same freedom as his younger sibling to choose his own future.

The uncommon *unsui* is the one who comes of his own volition to the monastic lifestyle as opposed to the one who merely comes to terms with it. In this regard, for many temple sons, the act of following in their father's footsteps to become a Sōtō priest is treated in the best of circumstances as a convenient eventuality. These *unsui* describe being fortunate that they have a certain measure of job security in rough economic times. For others, the pressure to take over the difficult and often unrewarding "family business" can feel like an inescapable prison. Having absolutely no personal interest in a life of religious obligation, these *unsui* enter into their *shugyō* harboring feelings of resentment and even open animosity toward those who do.

It is not an exaggeration, therefore, to state that the incoming *unsui* who are most drawn to a deeper, personal connection to Zen Buddhism and the lifestyle of a monastic are those who are least likely to come from a temple background. Free from the financial or filial obligations that would have pressured them into the priesthood, these *unsui* usually had the freedom to make life choices and have experiences that are often not available to temple sons. Not surprisingly, these *unsui* are typically older than the average entrant, having spent years working in an office, attaining graduate degrees, raising a family, or traveling. In the majority of these cases, their interest in Zen derives from years of regular *zazen* practice in temple settings, often accompanied by an appetite for books about Zen and an idealized view of monastic life.

Monks with nonclerical family backgrounds often report being led to Zen practice through a sense of dissatisfaction with one or more aspects of their secular lives. One priest I met at Sōjiji described dropping out of a doctoral program at a prestigious university mere months before he was scheduled to graduate. Another monk was previously employed at a law firm where he was growing increasingly unhappy as a result of overwork and a feeling that he was being "bullied" by his overcritical superiors. He began practicing *zazen* as a way of dealing with the pressures of his job, but he found himself fantasizing about abandoning it all for a monastic life. Other monks in this category report that it was being laid off due to company downsizing or coping with the aftermath of a divorce that led them to pursue a life in the clergy.

The *unsui* come from all parts of Japan, with the majority from the main island of Honshū. Of these, most come from the Kantō region, the area that includes the Tokyo Metropolitan Prefecture and Kanagawa Prefecture (which includes Yokohama). All but a handful of the remainder come from the northern half of Honshū, particularly the Tōhoku region, where Sōtō Zen traditionally has had a deep foothold of parishioner support.

A prospective Sōtō Zen priest has several options as to where he can perform his *shugyō*. In addition to Sōjiji or Eiheiji, a monk can choose from a network of smaller, regional training temples where there are fewer *unsui* (some with as few as ten training monks) and where practice is more intimate.

Since over 90 percent of Sōtō Zen branch temples are nominally affiliated with Sōjiji, one might assume that Sōjiji would get the bulk of the new initiates. This, however, is not the case. *Shugyō* at Eiheiji has the reputation for being stricter and more mentally and physically demanding, and training there carries a greater level of social prestige both within the sect and among parishioners. Enrollment at Sōjiji has steadily declined over the past several decades while Eiheiji's numbers have swelled to over two hundred entrants per year.

In my experience, an *unsui* at Sōjiji often has a ready answer to the question of why they chose Sōjiji over Eiheiji. In many cases two or three previous generations of a monk's family have trained at Sōjiji, making *shugyō* at Sōjiji a family tradition. Others choose Sōjiji, as Nakajima-san did, for its reputation for not being as strict or harsh as Eiheiji or a smaller temple. One monk told me that since his temple's rituals historically have more in common with Sōjiji's than Eiheiji's, he thought it would be a smoother transition for him. Some described wanting to be closer to a big city, and one admitted that he chose Sōjiji because the weather was less extreme in Tsurumi than in Fukui Prefecture, where Eiheiji is located.

Debates between which temple's training is stricter, which practices are more authentic, or which monastic lifestyle is more demanding remain a constant source of rivalry between Sōjiji and Eiheiji. However, a quantifiable difference between the two *honzan* is that Sōjiji ministers to the ritual needs of over five thousand parishioner families; Eiheiji, in contrast, has none. The responsibilities and lessons that an *unsui* is exposed to during his time at either temple are thus dramatically different, with training at Sōjiji providing on-the-job training for clergy whose future ability to make ends meet greatly depends on their skill in anticipating and catering to the needs of their parishioner families.

Leaving Home

For many Japanese youths, the college years are remembered as a time of relative freedom and socially acceptable irresponsibility sandwiched between the stresses of high school and the responsibilities of adulthood. For those who enter monastic training, their college years are ended by the very real personal sacrifices and austerities required of *shugyō* in a Sōtō Zen training temple. For many new monks, the sacrifices are involuntary at best, made all the more painful in light of the recent memories of their former identities. Only weeks earlier, many of these young men were seniors in college. They styled their hair, wore jeans, ate meat, drank alcohol, hung out with their friends, listened to music, watched movies, played games, and went on dates. As they stand at the gates of Sōjiji, all of that is now behind them. They are expected to leave behind the lay trappings of their former lives and embrace their new identities as Sōtō Zen clergymen.

The weeks leading up to their arrival at Sōjiji can be among the most jarring and life-changing of a young monk's life. The transition from lay life into his new identity as a Sōtō Zen monk begins several weeks before the actual arrival, when the *unsui* receives tonsure from an ordained Sōtō Zen priest, most often his father or close male relative. The tonsure ceremony, known as *shukke tokudo*, is considered to be the first step along the Buddhist path. As is common in many initiation rites, *shukke tokudo* visibly marks the initiate's body by shaving the hair, thus communicating the end of the initiate's identity as a regular member of society and the start of a life defined by a liminal status as world renouncer and a disciple of the Buddha.

In previous times, the concept of leaving home had a much greater social significance than it has today. A literal translation for the term *shukke* is "home-leaver," meaning one who has given up their families, houses, and property for a life of mendicant transience. In Buddhist practice throughout Asia, this status is contrasted with "house-holder" (*zaike*), a general category for all non-monastic Buddhist laity.[8]

Prior to the modern era in Japan, "leaving home" was literal; an initiate who had been tonsured through *shukke tokudo* was struck from the household register (*koseki*) of his lay family. From a legal and societal perspective, the act of being struck from the household register "unmade" a person. A person who did not appear on a household register was outside the law and outside established social order. All rights to property, title, and caste were taken away. While he lived, there would be no record of his having been born; when he died, there would be no record of his death for future generations to venerate him as an ancestor. For the unfortunate outcaste, it would be as if he had never existed.

For a layperson, being removed from one's family record was a punishment available to secular or religious authorities as a form of "social execution" that rendered the subject an outcast and a nonperson in this life and doomed him to be a wandering, hungry ghost in the next. The monastic, however, was saved from this fate by having his social identity and personhood reconstituted by being added to the temple register of the priest who tonsured him and to the clerical register (*sōseki*) kept at the head temple of his sect. By transmitting the tonsure and administering the Buddhist precepts, the tonsuring priest became an initiate's master (*shisō*) and "Dharma father." The ritual of tonsure therefore became the birth of a new social person into a family understood through participation in a "Dharma lineage" (*hōkei*)—that is, a system of descent predicated upon the transmission of teachings passed down from one generation to the next, and that are believed to originate in the Buddha Śākyamuni, who sits as the apical ancestor.

Prior to the twentieth century, "leaving home" made it possible for Buddhist clergy to free themselves from the obligations and responsibilities of their former lives. Today, however, the particularities of Japanese history and Buddhist doctrine collide in the *shukke tokudo* ceremony, putting the very idea of "home-leaving" to the test for monastics in modern Japan. The majority of these ceremonies are performed in Sōtō Zen temples where the initiate's socially recognized father—biological, adoptive, or in-law—is resident abbot. Unlike former times, an initiate is no longer struck from his household register when he is added to the temple register of the tonsuring priest.[9] In effect, the erstwhile "home-leaver" today actually *gains* a family as well as the social and ritual obligations owed to both the ancestors and living members of each. For a temple son, the family he gains is, for the most part, the family he started with. For Sōtō Zen clergy who come from lay families, however, they immediately gain generations of Dharma parents and grandparents, Dharma siblings, and Dharma cousins.

For all of its implications, the Sōtō Zen *shukke tokudo* ceremony is brief and intimate. The tonsuring priest shaves all but one lock of hair on the initiate's head to symbolize his casting off of worldly obligations. The initiate then receives a set of black robes. After he puts on these robes, the last lock of hair—symbolizing his final attachment to his former self—is shaved. To mark his transformation into his new social identity, the initiate is given a new name known as an *anmyō* (refuge name) or *hōmyō* (Dharma name).[10] The name consists of three parts, with the second part acting as a new personal name for the initiate.[11]

After receiving his Dharma robe (*kesa*), bowing mat, and eating bowls from the tonsuring priest, the initiate formally takes refuge in the Three Jewels and vows to uphold the Three Pure Precepts and the Ten Major Prohibitions. Finally, his master presents him with a *kechimyaku*, a lineage chart that places the initiate—now known by his new refuge name—into a single, unbroken line of descent that begins with the historical Buddha, Śākyamuni, and continues through generations of master-disciple relationships to the current master and the new initiate. The line becomes a closed circle when a line is drawn from the initiate to Śākyamuni, essentially showing the initiate to be the teacher of the Buddha himself.

The ostensible cutting of the worldly ties of one's former life and the receiving of a new name is as much a death as it is a birth into a new world of social relationships and filial responsibilities as Sōtō Zen clergy. Over the course of the ceremony, the master's actions are meant to replicate the raising of a child: the master clothes the initiate (with the Dharma robe), names him (with a Dharma name), and, finally, provides him with the means to feed and sustain himself (with the eating bowls). Despite its brief duration, the *shukke tokudo* rite establishes the foundation for the relationship of filial indebtedness and obligation (*on*) that the initiate is beholden to honor for the rest of his life. By being provided a new Dharma name and a lineage chart, the initiate is given the means to reorient his new identity to the family to which he now belongs and, by extension, the parents and ancestors to which his bonds of obligation must be repaid (*hōon*).[12]

After the ceremony, the initiate's refuge name and the details of the initiation are registered with the administrative offices of the Sōtō Zen sect. The initiate now has two names, a secular name and a Dharma name, both of which have significance for him. Today a member of the clergy keeps their Japanese family name but may legally change their personal name to their new Dharma name. For many temple sons, this is an easy transition on paper; practical-minded parents often give their sons a Japanese personal name written using characters whose pronunciation can be easily changed so that the written name will stay the same even after he is given a "new" name during his initiation.[13]

However, even if an *unsui* has a conveniently transferable written name, he will most likely grow into adolescence using the Japanese pronunciation of his personal name. In my conversations with the *unsui*, several expressed difficulty in relating to their new name and, by extension, to their new Buddhist identity. While it may be that the attachment to their former name is often difficult to break, it may also be the case that the symbolic significance of receiving an *anmyō* no longer carries the force that it once did: "Truth is, I don't have any connection with my new name," one *unsui* confided to me. "For twenty-two years, my name has been Masao. Now I'm Shōyū." He shrugs. "It really doesn't mean anything to me."[14]

After the *tokudo* and registration with the Sōtō Zen sectarian administration, the new initiate has ten years to become a fully ordained priest. The requirement is that the initiate spend between six months and two years in *shugyō* (depending on the highest level of education attained) at a certified training monastery. As this period of *shugyō* is the only thing standing in the way of their full ordination, most new initiates aim to complete this part as soon as possible after their tonsure.

Prior to the modern period, governmental edicts prevented a monk from receiving full clerical ordination until they could prove that they had spent twenty years in *shugyō*.[15] Today *unsui* arriving at Sōjiji's gates have had scant weeks to come to grip with the realities of their new social status and public identities. While several informants reported arriving at Sōjiji with excitement for their training, far more reported feelings of anxiety and nervousness for what was to come.

The First Days

An *unsui* needs to assimilate very quickly to his new life within the temple community, as the rhythm of daily life at Sōjiji cannot be interrupted in order to ease the new arrivals into their new routines. Because of this, each new *unsui* spends their first week at Sōjiji in the Tanga-ryō (Guest Quarters). It is here that the fresh and nervous *unsui* are given a crash course in temple policies, personal comportment, and the schedule that will become their daily routine over the next year of their lives.

The Tanga-ryō is a "temporary place" in several senses. Previously, being led to the Tanga-ryō was a continuation of the probationary tests of the *jōzan* ritual; for seven days, a new monk was made to sit *zazen* from morning to evening, stopping only to eat (when meals were brought to him) or to sleep (when bedtime was announced). Today, however, the week spent in the Tanga-ryō is used as a period of orientation for the new monks: they participate in morning ceremonies, are led around to the various departments of the temple so that they can see firsthand what jobs are expected of them, and, most importantly, receive instruction on daily life at Sōjiji so that when they formally enter the community at the end of their probationary week, their transition is as smooth as possible.

In another sense the Tanga-ryō is temporary because it "exists" only during the limited time frame in which Sōjiji is expecting new arrivals. While every other temple department has a space dedicated to its purposes, the Tanga-ryō comes into being when newly arrived monks are taken to a multipurpose room on the first floor of the Denkōkaku. The room has tall windows that, in addition to making the room bright, allow the new *unsui* to be observed from outside the room. In order to maximize wall space—*zazen* practice in the Sōtō tradition necessitates that a sitter face a wall or opaque surface—temporary wooden dividers with low shelves are set up, giving each new *unsui* a place to set down their traveling gear, take their meals, and sit *zazen*. Paper sheets detailing Sōjiji's daily schedule and protocol are hung high on these walls to allow the *unsui* to reference them. Once the last of the new arrivals has left the Tanga-ryō, the dividers are taken down and the Tanga-ryō disappears until a new batch of *unsui* arrives.

New arrivals of former times were treated politely as guests; the *unsui* in the Tanga-ryō today have much in common with military recruits at boot camp. An *unsui*'s time spent in the Tanga-ryō is essential for jump-starting the transformation of the new arrivals into disciplined—and, specifically, Sōjiji-trained—Sōtō monks. To survive at Sōjiji, an *unsui* must unlearn much of what they have learned growing up in modern Japan: they have to relearn how to walk, how to stand, how to sit, how to eat, how to sleep, and how to speak. If they do not—or if they resist—the consequences can be severe.

The reeducation of the *unsui* begins immediately upon stepping over the threshold of the Taihōkan and into Sōjiji's corridors. While taking instruction from their superiors, the *unsui* are made to stand at attention for long periods with their hands and arms raised in *gasshō*, a position of respect whereby the hands are held palms together with the point of the fingertips at the level of one's nose, and the arms held parallel to the floor. Holding *gasshō* for extended periods of time is not as easy as it looks.

Because of the precise way the arms and hands must be held, the shoulders and dorsal muscles in the upper back used to support the arms become fatigued and quickly begin to ache. The pain soon moves to the lower back, and very quickly the effort of trying to maintain the *gasshō* position becomes a daunting physical challenge in and of itself.

Adding to this is the requirement that the initiates must learn to sit for extended periods of time in *seiza*, a formal kneeling position in which the buttocks rest on the heels of the feet while the upper body is held upright, with the weight of the body resting on the shinbones and tops of the feet. This position quickly cuts off blood to the legs, starting first with numbness in the feet and soon creeping up toward the thighs. For the beginner, the "pins and needles" feeling begins in the feet in a matter of minutes. If the position is maintained for longer, the legs go completely numb. This is the position that the *unsui* must sit in during formal occasions such as morning ceremonies, which can easily take upward of forty-five minutes. The average person can somewhat mitigate the pain in the legs by shifting one's body weight or moving to a cross-legged sitting position, but these are not options allowed to the *unsui*.

When *gasshō* and *seiza* are combined—for example, when reading from a text while chanting—virtually every muscle group in the body is forced to work in ways that they are rarely made to do in everyday life outside of a temple. After as few as three days, the otherwise pliant tatami floor begins to feel as hard as stone, and tension in the upper-body muscles begin to resist all attempts to hold *gasshō* for any length of time.

Pushing the new arrival's body to its physical limits is precisely the point: physical resistance to the pain caused by holding *gasshō* and *seiza* is equated with mental attachment to the comforts of the monk's former life. Yet, as one experienced informant told me, it is not enough for the *unsui* to merely try to endure the pain; rather, the *unsui* must come to accept the pain and understand it as a necessary part of the *shugyō* experience. It is only when this is understood that attachment to comforts of body and self can be cast aside and the training can truly begin. For now, the *unsui*'s "unenlightened" body must quickly reach a point where it can do what is expected of it despite the pain he is experiencing.

Equally important is that the new arrival demonstrates the willingness to unquestioningly obey the commands of his superiors, which, as new arrivals, is everyone.[16] For the most part, communication to a superior is limited to "yes!" (*hai*), "no!" (*iie*), and "thank you!" (*arigatō gozaimashita*) responses, shouted at the top of one's lungs in the style of a military recruit. The *unsui* are also expected to not waste time when required to be somewhere: groups of barefoot *unsui* routinely thunder down the wooden hallways at top speed on their way to their chores. Likewise, the *unsui* are required to stop what they are doing and stand to the side to salute a superior with a deep bow in *gasshō* should they encounter one in the temple corridors.

This first week is a physically and emotionally trying time for all the new *unsui*. Most have no experience with being spoken to with such severity, enduring such physical demands, or living under the strict gaze of superiors who are quick to punish any infractions of the rules. As his body begins to buckle under the mounting physical stressors, doubts begin to race through the *unsui*'s mind. The thought of persevering through a year of such a lifestyle is so daunting that fleeing the temple becomes more and more tempting. It is not unknown for scared *unsui* to try to escape during this period.

On the seventh day after having stood in front of the gate of Sōjiji requesting admittance, an *unsui* leaves the Tanga-ryō. At this point he is formally admitted into the community of monks in a private ceremony in the Monk's Hall known as the "Entering the Hall Ceremony" (*nyūdō shiki*). He is assigned a single tatami mat in the hall, over which his name is hung. This is where he will sleep and sit *zazen*. At the head of his assigned mat he has two wooden drawers—one for his bedding and another for his limited personal belongings.

By the first of April, all of the new *unsui* who will be entering Sōjiji have arrived. Those who arrived last have already left the Tanga-ryō and have been integrated into the monastic community. Each of the seventy-five monks has been assigned a temple department that they will report to on a daily basis for their work detail.

On April 2 all of the new novices participate in an induction ceremony known as the "Entering into Residence Ceremony" (*menkata shiki*). This ceremony marks the official beginning of the summer retreat period, and the assembled monks are now said to be "inside the rules" (*seichū*). For the next one hundred days, all of the newly arrived *unsui* are prohibited from leaving the temple grounds, receiving phone calls or letters from home, or reading a newspaper.

After the ceremony, a commemorative photo is taken for the occasion, featuring the abbot flanked by the senior teachers and their assistants, who are assigned to supervise the new monks. The cohort of *unsui* will be known for posterity as that year's class of "summer retreat new arrivals" (*natsu angō shintō*). More importantly, from this point forward, the *unsui* will refer to themselves collectively as *wareware shugyōsō*—"we priests-in-training."

The Heart of *Shugyō*

From the exterior, there is little to distinguish the Monk's Hall from the other buildings in the temple precincts. The stairs that lead to the main doors—which may be opened slightly to allow air circulation when the weather is particularly nice or hot—are blocked by the same wooden barricade and "no entry" sign that are found near many other temple structures. In fact, two nearby service roads provide enough foot and motor traffic to make this one of the least quiet places in the temple complex, especially when a newspaper delivery motorcycle goes by. The only visible indication that this is the sanctuary of the monks-in-training is a weathered sign hanging above the hall, written in stylized calligraphy, which indicates that this building is the "Place Where Buddhas Are Chosen" (*senbutsujō*).[17]

Of all the buildings that comprise a traditional seven-building monastery, only the Monk's Hall (*sōdō*) can really be called the monk's own. An *unsui* will spend approximately a third of his life at Sōjiji in this hall alone, with most of that time spent sleeping or sitting *zazen*. Formerly, meals were also taken in the Monk's Hall, but on most days of the year the hall is no longer used for this purpose. The monks now gather to take their meals in the communal dining hall above the main reception. For the most part, the monks' lacquered eating bowls remain stowed in little cubbies in the Sōdō.

On all but a few rare occasions, the laity is forbidden from entering the hall. Even in those situations where members of the laity are allowed to enter, they are restricted to the outer hall (*gaitan*), which is little more than a wide perimeter encircling the protective sanctuary of the inner hall (*naitan*). The heavy sliding doors leading to the hall from the interior corridors are nearly always closed; all that most visitors to Sōjiji ever see of the interior of the Monk's Hall are three staged photographs of daily life in the hall that have been posted above the closed entryway.

Over the course of my research, I was allowed to enter the outer hall a handful of times with a small number of other practitioners for the week-long intensive meditation retreats known as *sesshin*. On several occasions, however, I was secreted into the inner hall by my monastic informants for a quick peek for "research purposes." I could write down what I saw, but I was expressly forbidden from taking pictures.[18]

The squat sliding doors that connect the Monk's Hall with the main corridor of the temple do not convey the immensity of the hall beyond it. Stepping over the threshold into the Sōdō, one is struck by the cavernous size of the space, despite only the outer hall being immediately visible. The ceiling of the hall is easily more than twelve meters (forty feet) high, punctuated by wooden buttresses and hanging light fixtures. The walls constructed of cypress wood have, like the temple corridors, darkened with age. The dark walls stand in stark contrast to the paper-covered sliding panels that begin just above eye level and the white plaster walls that stand above them. The hard, cold concrete floor has been sealed with a high gloss and is kept sparkling by repeated daily washing. The outer hall is comfortably drafty in the summer but frigid as an icebox in winter.

The outer hall is little more than the space between the exterior walls of the building itself and the walls that enclose the inner hall. The eastern portion of the hall is the widest, having two tatami platforms with room for ten seats, split by the entryway to the inner hall placed in the center of the wall. In this entryway, an opaque rattan curtain is rolled down from the ceiling to the floor most days of the year, limiting curious eyes (such as those who may have snuck into the Sōdō) from seeing into the inner hall. A two-sided metal sign hangs from the center of the entryway at eye level. On one side is written "*zazen*" for the days in which the *unsui* wake at the usual time to sit for the morning meditation session. On the other is written "*muzen*" ("no meditation"), for those rest days when the *unsui* are given an extra half hour to sleep in. Over the door hangs another name for the Sōdō, "Cloud Hall" (*Undō*).

The inner hall itself is a simple wooden construction. Seventy-four tatami mats encircle the perimeter of the space; at the head of each are the drawers the monks use to place their bedding and their personal belongings. Two islands of ten tatami mats—five on each side, separated by shelving—flank the devotional image in the center, essentially bifurcating the room along the horizontal axis. On each tatami mat sits a single black *zafu* with a vertical white tag upon which the name of the owner is written. These are the cushions that the *unsui* carried with them to Sōjiji, one for each monk in residence.

On an elaborately decorated platform in the very center of the hall sits a finely detailed image of the bodhisattva Monju, embodiment of wisdom and protector of the Buddhist clergy. Monju is pictured as the idealized monk. Seated in perpetual *zazen*, he is eternally vigilant and maintains perfect form, never faltering in his practice. Monju's eyes, half opened in meditation, gaze at the floor of the entryway into the hall. A small altar with flowers, candles, and an incense burner sit on the dais in front of the image. On a lower table in front of this lies the flat-ended stick used to mete out discipline in the hall. A raised bowing platform sits on the floor immediately in front of this image.

Altogether, Sōjiji's Sōdō has room for 86 *unsui* in the inner hall and 20 additional seats in the outer hall. If one adds the raised chairs reserved for the abbot and the principal instructor, known as the Godō (lit. "rear of the hall"), the total number of seats in the hall becomes 108, a number with cosmological significance in Buddhism.[19]

An *unsui*'s space within the Sōdō (and, by extension, his place in the community) is assigned to him by virtue of the order in which he arrived at the temple relative to other monks. An *unsui* entering the Monk's Hall for the first time finds his place by locating his name tag, posted high off the floor in advance of his arrival. This name tag—white characters written on a thin black-lacquered board—lists the *unsui*'s prefecture of origin, followed by his family name and his Dharma name.

In principle the latest arrival to Sōjiji is assigned the seat on the western side of the hall, immediately to the left of the main entryway. The next most recent arrival is given the seat to his left and so forth. As one moves clockwise around the hall, the stature of the monk (as determined by tenure in the temple) can be seen to increase. The tatami mat immediately to the right of the main entryway is reserved for the *shuso*, a monk elected to be the representative of the corps of *unsui*. To his left is the raised cushioned chair where the abbot sits on the occasions when he joins the assembly for *zazen*. A complete circle of hierarchy links the highest-ranking monk with the lowest meets at precisely the point where Monju eternally gazes. It is possible to draw a parallel between the construction of the Monk's Hall and the visual symbolism of the *kechimyaku* certificate a monk receives during his tonsure. Ultimately, the lowest student is the teacher of the highest master.

The inner hall of the Monk's Hall is called the "heart of *shugyō*" (*shugyō no chūshin*) not only for its central place in the monks' lives but also for the fact that there are more prohibitions and rules governing behavior associated with it than with any other hall in the temple complex, save for the toilet and bath.[20] In the inner hall, monastic discipline is expected to be the most strict and severe. While in the hall, the assembled monks are enjoined to follow the impossible example of perfect self-discipline set by the image of Monju in the center of the hall: unfaltering in their practice of proper protocol and regulation, unwavering in their devotion to *shugyō* as a means of transforming themselves, and unmoving in the face of exhaustion or the passions of the world. When a monk cannot be these things, the hall monitors are deputized to beat a monk back to diligent observance of his *shugyō* with wooden rods—an act of violent, but impersonal, compassion.

By design, the Monk's Hall is a perfectly disciplined—and perfectly disciplining—space. Physically present on their assigned tatami mats, each *unsui* in the hall is placed within a visible network of relations that renders hierarchy and rank immediately knowable and incontrovertible.[21] The Monk's Hall is partitioned in such a way that the individual becomes the subject of constant and unrelenting disciplinary forces.

In the context of a temple the size of Sōjiji, this single tatami mat is virtually microscopic. A single tatami mat is the space of one *jō*, a unit of measurement roughly the dimensions of a human body, approximately .8 meters (2.6 feet) in width and 1.82 meters (6 feet) in length. This makes the *unsui*'s personal space in the temple little more than 1.5 square meters (16 square feet). Each tatami mat touches the mat next to it with only a hairbreadth of space between them, and it is expressly forbidden for an *unsui* to "spill over" into adjoining spaces.

Even when an *unsui* is not physically present in the hall, his name tag and *zafu* cushion (also inscribed with his name and positioned such that his name is always visible) remain behind as material stand-ins for the monk within the network of relations encoded in the layout of the hall. Such precise coordinates within the space of the hall allow for the monk—in every other way superficially identical to those around him—to be individuated and monitored. Monks whose behavior causes them to stand out from the assembly can be immediately identified and corrective discipline applied. On the occasions when an *unsui* flees the temple, his absence is immediately revealed to those sitting near him and to those who are observing him.

In this regard, the inner hall of the Sōdō is a perfect panopticon, a disciplinary apparatus in which coercive power is internalized in those who are to be made into obedient subjects of the disciplinary gaze. On the one hand, the image of the bodhisattva Monju in the center of the hall is a gentle reminder of the potential in all of the training monks to achieve enlightenment (*satori*) in the form of a continuous state of perfect discipline that carries over into every aspect of life. On the other hand, Monju is an ever-present taskmaster whose central position in the hall grants him a vantage point from which to monitor the entire monastic community. His high expectations of obedience and discipline are enforced by the hall monitors who patrol the Monk's Hall like guards with drawn swords. While sitting *zazen*, and even while they sleep, the monks are always aware of the disciplining forces being applied to them from every direction.

Embodied Lineage

Every morning at precisely four o'clock (four-thirty in the winter), two *unsui* begin a running course through the long wooden corridors of the temple, each brandishing a large handbell that they ring the entire way. This is known as *shinrei*, a word that refers to both the act of waking and the bell that is used for the task. The ring of the bell and the heavy footsteps of the sprinting *unsui* pierce the darkness of the temple night like a passing train, starting quietly in the distance, rising to a near earsplitting volume as the *unsui* passes by, and then quickly fading away as he moves on to the next building. Dawn is still hours away, but morning has come to Sōjiji.

The monks in the Sōdō, many still exhausted from a late night spent finishing their responsibilities in one of the temple's various departments, quickly rise to put their bedding away. They rush as a group to the bathroom to relieve themselves, wash their face and head, and brush their teeth. It is crucial that they move quickly, as they have only ten minutes before the bell is rung to mark the start of morning *zazen*, the official start of the temple day.

The single tatami mat that the *unsui* have only moments before used for sleeping is the same space upon which they will sit for *zazen*; rows of bedding have been replaced by rows of black *zafu* cushions. The *unsui* return to their tatami mats, raise their hands in *gasshō* and bow once toward the wall, and then turn clockwise and bow again to the center of the room in a show of respect for those who will be sitting next to them and for those who will be sitting across from them. Taking care to avoid touching the wooden board at the front of the platform with either their buttocks or their feet, the *unsui* use their arms to push themselves onto their cushions and pull their feet up into a cross-legged position, carefully arranging their slippers on the lip of the floor beneath the platform.

Every morning, the hall monitor (*jikidō*) makes a brisk review of the assembled *unsui*, ostensibly to see if any of their faces show traces of spiritual awakening, but really to verify that none of the young monks has fled during the night. He carries a thick wooden stick horizontally in his hands, almost as a presentation, and visible to all he passes. The *unsui*, in turn, salute the monitor by raising their hands in *gasshō* as he passes by. When he has completed his rounds of the hall, the metal gong is struck three times; on the third strike, the lights are dimmed, and the monks turn to face the wall for morning *zazen*.

The concentration required to sit *zazen* is difficult to maintain no matter what time of the day it is attempted, but the combination of the silence of the hall, the dimmed lighting, and the very fact of having been asleep only minutes earlier all work against the sitting *unsui*. At this hour, in these conditions, it is easy to surrender to the lure of "just closing my eyes for a bit." Before long, the poor *unsui* is nodding off, his head falling forward toward the wall.

Sometimes the *unsui* can catch himself in this process, restore his posture, and reestablish his concentration with a few deep breaths. Usually, however, the hall monitor—who has been slowly and silently patrolling the hall behind the backs of the *unsui* with his stick (*kyōsaku*) now held vertically front of him—catches the sleeping *unsui* first. The monitor stops behind the sleeping monk and presents the stick to the *unsui*'s back. The monitor then firmly taps the *unsui* on the right shoulder with the stick to announce his presence. The monk, suddenly shocked back into wakefulness, realizes he has been caught. He raises his hands in *gasshō*, bends forward in his seat, and leans his head to the left to expose his right shoulder to receive a blow from the *kyōsaku*.

The stick whistles through the air as the monitor swings it firmly against the *unsui*'s shoulder. The sharp crack of wood connecting with muscle shatters the silence of the hall. Both the *unsui* and the hall monitor then place their hands together in *gasshō* and bow. The *unsui* resumes his *zazen*, and the hall monitor continues his round of the hall.

The characters comprising the word *kyōsaku* can be translated literally as "warning whip." For the *unsui* thus struck, the blow indeed serves as a punishment that may be light or severe, depending on the monitor who delivers the blow. (On at least two occasions, I personally received hits from a monitor that had me seeing stars at the moment of impact and left a visible bruise on my shoulder that lasted for about a week.) The strike of the *kyōsaku* is a well-placed jolt to a sleepy *unsui*'s system intended to wake him up by unlocking the energy and tension that gathers in the shoulders, long recognized in Chinese medicine as a key pressure point of the body. The sound of the *kyōsaku* also serves as a warning to the monks sitting nearby: one punishment has already been meted, and another might follow should you become careless or lazy.

But the *kyōsaku* is not a purely punitive instrument. A restless or sleepy *unsui* can request a blow from the hall monitor at any time by raising his hands in *gasshō* as a signal to the monitor as he passes by. Such self-disciplining is encouraged by the *unsui*'s superiors as an essential part of responsible and diligent practice.

For twenty minutes, the *unsui* sit facing the wall. The silence of the hall is punctuated only by periodic coughing and the crack of the *kyōsaku* as it connects with the back of another drowsy *unsui*.

At the end of the sitting period, the voice of the cantor breaks the stillness: "Let us receive our *kesa*" (*kesa o itadakimasu*).²² Still facing the wall, the *unsui* place their folded *kesa* on the top of their heads.

With their hands in *gasshō* they chant:

Daisai gedatsu puku	How great, the robe of liberation,
Musō fukden e	a formless field of merit.
Hibu nyorai kyō	Wrapping ourselves in Buddha's teaching,
Kōdo shoshujō	we free all living beings.²³

After reciting this chant three times, the monks then unfold and don the *kesa*.

Of all the material trappings of Buddhism, the toga-like *kesa* (commonly translated as "Dharma robe") is the most universal, worn by monastics in Buddhist countries throughout Asia. The *kesa* has its origins in ancient Indian ascetic practices, where it was often the only body covering that a world-renouncing mendicant would allow themselves. The Buddhist *kesa* was originally a patchwork sewn from unclean and discarded cloth, such as soiled rags and funeral shrouds. In the Indian context, this choice of materials communicated to observers that the mendicant had abandoned material attachments and renounced the dualities of purity and defilement and of modesty and impropriety that characterized daily social life.²⁴

As Buddhism traveled across Asia, monastic clothing was adapted to suit the climate and culture, but the monastic *kesa* has remained a constant. The modern Sōtō Zen *kesa* maintains the patchwork pattern of the Indian *kasaya*, but it is now sewn from swatches of clean cotton, silk, or even artificial fabrics.²⁵ A black *kesa* is given to the monk by the tonsuring priest during the *shukke tokudo* ceremony. When the novice becomes a fully ordained Sōtō Zen priest, the color of the *kesa* changes from black to an earthen tone to mark his change in clerical status.

While the *kesa* is nearly universally accepted as the mark of a Buddhist monastic, it has further significance in the Zen context. According to Zen historiography, the Buddha, sensing that his departure from the world was imminent, assembled his followers to choose a successor. When his disciples had assembled, the Buddha held aloft a flower. This gesture confused all but one of his disciples, Mahākāśyapa, who smiled at the sight of the flower. As the story goes, the Buddha chose Mahākāśyapa to be his successor, and the Buddha bestowed his *kesa* upon him to symbolize the transfer of authority.[26]

The daily practice of receiving the *kesa* in Sōtō Zen temples has its origins in an episode appearing in both the "Merit of the Kesa" (*Kesa Kudoku*) and "Transmission of the Robe" (*Den'e*) fascicles of Dōgen's *Shōbōgenzō*. Dōgen describes traveling through China as a young man and visiting a temple where the Chinese monk sitting next to him quietly performed this small ceremony. He writes, "At that time, there arose in me a feeling I had never before experienced. . . . Seeing it done now, before my very eyes, I was overjoyed." Dōgen vowed to transmit this practice to Japan, where he says it was previously unknown.[27]

For the monk to "receive" the *kesa* on a daily basis is therefore an act with multiple levels of symbolic significance. On one level, placing the *kesa* on the head recalls the hair that was shaved to separate the monk from the laity. As the monk is made to recall his responsibility of performing his *shugyō* for the salvation of all beings, the act of removing the *kesa* from the head and wrapping it around his body is a daily reenactment of his tonsure and a renewal of his personal monastic obligations.

On a deeper level, the community of monks is made to personally reenact the foundational myths of the Zen (and particularly Sōtō Zen) sectarian genealogy. Like Mahākāśyapa, the first patriarch, the monks receive the *kesa* to signify their legitimacy as successors to the Buddha's True Dharma. Like Ānanda, the second patriarch, the *kesa* has come to rest on their heads to signify the moment of awakening and receipt of the teachings. Like Eka, the first recipient of the teachings supposedly transmitted from India to China by Bodhidharma, they are enjoined to "pass on the *kesa* by which the authenticity of our line is established."[28] In this way, the *unsui* are reminded daily of their inheritance of a uniquely Sōtō Zen tradition.

These themes are reinforced immediately following the receipt of the *kesa* through the performance of the *Dentō Fūgin*, a recitation of three foundational texts whose reading serves as a daily reinforcement of Sōtō sectarian identity. The first text, the *Sandōkai*, is attributed to Sekitō Kisen (700–790); the second, the *Hōkyō Zanmai*, is attributed to Tōzan Ryōkai (807–869), the first to claim that his teachings were of a distinct Sōtō (Ch. *Caodong*) school. The third text, the *Gōjūshichi Butsu* (The "Fifty-Seven Buddhas") is a recitation of the names of each of the ancestors in the lineage of Sōjiji's founder, Keizan Jōkin. Beginning with six "historical" Buddhas, the lineage traces the unilineal master-student descent from Śākyamuni Buddha through the Twenty-Eight Indian Patriarchs, from Bodhidharma through the Twenty-One Chinese Patriarchs, and finally with Dōgen and Japanese Sōtō patriarchs that succeeded him. The recitation of lineage in the *Gōjūshichi Butsu* ends with the master of the founder of a temple: in Sōjiji's case, the chanting ends with Tettsū Gikai, the third Japanese Sōtō patriarch and Keizan's master.

A single strike of the gong signals the end of both *zazen* and the *Dentō Fūgin*. With this complete, the monks rise from their positions on the tatami platform and process out of the Sōdō in double file toward the Daisodō for the morning service.

The Food Makes the Monk

By the time the morning service has ended, an *unsui* has been awake for nearly two hours, and it has been twelve hours since his last meal. He is famished. The concentration needed for *zazen* and almost an hour and a half of nearly continuous chanting demand a surprising amount of energy from the body. The monks assigned to the kitchens know this and have been following the progress of the morning services on a closed-circuit video feed from the Daisodō. It is their responsibility to have the morning meal ready to be served to 150 hungry monks in the communal dining hall within minutes of the end of morning services.

Breakfast in a Zen temple is quite spartan. The *unsui* are served a simple rice gruel (*kayu*) made from white rice and water, often accompanied by a mixture of powdered seasonings and herbs that give the otherwise bland gruel a measure of flavor. To the gruel is added a side dish of pickled vegetables that serve as both a palette cleanser and a means of mopping up the gelatinous residue left in the eating bowl by the gruel. Toward the end of the meal, any remaining residue is cleaned from the bowl by the addition of hot water poured from brass kettles. The *unsui* are free to drink this water, or they can dispose of it in wooden buckets that are brought around for this purpose.

Time, even this early in the morning, is precious, and the *unsui* have only moments to eat before the hot water is passed around to signal the end of the meal. While food is understood as a basic necessity of life, it is treated as a medicine—a means of alleviating the pain of hunger—rather than a luxury to be enjoyed. Because of this, very little time is allowed for casual eating or for savoring the meal. An *unsui* must learn to eat quickly enough to have finished every grain of rice he has been given by the end of the eating period, but he must also learn to maintain proper eating etiquette and not slurp down his food.

In principle, the *unsui* are permitted to eat their fill, either by signaling to the server to fill their bowls with more than a ladleful or by returning to the servers for seconds. In practice, however, I seldom saw an *unsui* take more than a ladleful, and I almost never saw them request seconds. Why was this? Had the monks internalized repeated instruction from their superiors that a monk should exercise restraint and moderation? Perhaps it stemmed from a desire not to stand out from the rest of the group by asking for more than others took or were given. Maybe it was a result of a "monkish machismo" from which the *unsui* competed with one another to show off how austere or how diligent they were in their performance of *shugyō*. Was their hunger actually sated by the portions given to them?

It is likely that the monks' mealtime restraint may be a combination of all these factors. During a meditation retreat, I witnessed an example of servers having fun at the expense of a hapless monk who had the misfortune of being caught asking for too much. The initial "infraction" might have been an accident: the new monk most likely forgot to give the upward hand motion that signals "enough," leading the server to give him more than he wanted or could finish. The joking started with the next meal, when the servers began filling his bowl to the brim with rice, even after he frantically signaled for them to stop. The following day, they filled his bowl beyond its limits, this time heaping four or five portions into the bowl, which the monk diligently ate. When the servers repeated the trick again with the next meal, the poor monk had come prepared, bringing with him a piece of plastic wrap to save the rice for later. On the last day of the retreat, the servers brought the *unsui* afternoon tea in a finely crafted porcelain teacup on a small red-lacquered pedestal—a piece normally reserved for honored guests and high-ranking clergy. The servers began calling him *rōshi* (a term of respect reserved for fully ordained priests) and responded to his embarrassment with over-the-top displays of bowing and honorific language. When the meal was over, the smiling servers crowded around the defeated *unsui* while the temple photographer took a picture. Although this joke was a harmless lesson in the effectiveness of communal discipline, the message sent to the *unsui* by his peers was clear: training monks don't take seconds.

The new arrivals I spoke with were unanimous in telling me that the dietary restrictions of *shugyō* were the most difficult adjustment they had to make in coming to Sōjiji. Between the primarily vegetarian diet and the pressure to restrict one's portion size, an *unsui* consumes only about a thousand calories per day. For a healthy twenty-two-year-old male, this diet is emaciating. By their own estimate, a new arrival loses between five and twenty kilograms (twelve to forty-four pounds) within the first ninety days of their *shugyō*, with the average weight loss being around nine kilograms (twenty pounds).

While vegetarianism is usually associated with health benefits, the traditional monastic diet is not only insufficient for basic dietary needs, but it is also demonstrably unhealthy. For centuries the menu at a Zen temple was dictated by which foods could be preserved in large quantities for long periods of time. This means that milled white rice has traditionally been the foundation for temple meals owing to its long storage life and ability to make the eater feel full. Yet, in preserving the rice, there is a trade-off: virtually all naturally occurring nutrients, most notably thiamin (Vitamin B_1), are removed from the final product during the husking process. The pickled vegetables and soups that accompany rice-based meals are similarly empty, delivering high amounts of sodium for very little return in essential nutrients.

As late as the 1990s, *unsui* were regularly afflicted with debilitating illnesses caused by the vitamin, calcium, and protein deficiencies in the monastic diet. The most dreaded of these diseases was beriberi, a disease of the nervous system caused by thiamin deficiency that begins with painful swelling in the extremities and, if left untreated, causes nerve damage, paralysis, and eventual death. One monk who trained at Sōjiji in the 1980s told me, "In my time, everyone got beriberi during their training. Oh, it was painful! Of course we were afraid of getting it, but it was something that you waited for, because it was inevitable. When you got sick, you went to the hospital and they gave you medicine. When you got better, you went back to Sōjiji and continued your *shugyō*."[29]

Since the 1950s, subtle changes to the monastic diet at Sōjiji have been implemented by administrators who sought ways of maintaining the health of the temple community while preserving the dietary and religious traditions of Sōtō Zen training temples. One adaptation was to allow the *unsui* to eat a raw egg over a bowl of rice in the morning to add fat and protein into their diet. At the time, this was a controversial decision and compromise was needed. It was decided that before they eat the egg, a monk must temporarily "defrock" himself by removing his *rakusu* (a functional stand-in for the full Dharma robe) and hanging it on a peg. By so doing, the monk would not be held culpable for any violation of the monastic precept against the taking of life. Later innovations, such as drinking a pint of milk once a week on Sunday or taking daily multivitamins, did not include such compromise measures. In the years since these small changes were adopted, the debilitating diseases caused by deficiencies in the monastic diet have fallen off dramatically, though not entirely.

Still, the low-calorie diet and the strict work regimen enact a profound change on the *unsui* from the moment he steps into the temple. By the end of his first hundred days, the novice no longer has the plump softness of a youth spent in a comfortable, mostly sedentary lifestyle. His face is drawn and angular. He has lost most of his body fat, leaving only wiry, lean muscle behind. Kneeling for extended periods in *seiza* actually becomes easier for him, as there is less weight for his folded legs to support. His very body becomes a living testament to the austerities that he has endured.

Twenty-Four-Hour-a-Day *Shugyō*

The day at Sōjiji officially begins at four in the morning and officially ends at nine in the evening. For most of the *unsui*, however, fitting all of their responsibilities into these seventeen hours is a very elusive goal. For the monks who have been assigned to the responsibilities of waking up the temple, preparing the Dharma Hall for the morning ceremonies, or working in the kitchen, the day starts at 2:30 a.m., a full two hours earlier than the rest of the temple. For those who work in the administrative and accounting departments, or who have responsibilities preparing items such as the handwritten tablets used in memorial ceremonies (*tōba*), the day commonly ends well after midnight. On average, an *unsui* at Sōjiji is operating on fewer than four hours of sleep a night for nearly their entire time at the temple.

Over half of the incoming *unsui* are assigned first to the Kandoku-ryō, the "Department of Silent Reading." In previous generations, the monks in this department spent the majority of their day in the large study hall situated across from the Monk's Hall, memorizing the daily liturgy and studying Buddhist scriptures. Twice daily, after breakfast and after lunch, the novices would gather to listen to a sermon. In addition to this, the *unsui* of the Kandoku-ryō were obliged to take part in the midday and evening services in the Daisodō. This full-time study was intended to quickly bring the *unsui* up to speed with the basic liturgical knowledge necessary for daily life in a Zen temple and to provide a seminary education to transform the young *unsui* into future Sōtō clergymen.

Today the *unsui* have regularly scheduled classes and lectures in the

Fig. 9. The unsui listen attentively and take notes during a lecture.

afternoons and evenings. Correspondingly, time that an *unsui* might spend in independent study has largely been done away with. So too has the mid-day service. The study hall is now reserved for lay visitors to sit *zazen*, and the time that was formerly scheduled for study and sermons is now occupied by work detail (*samu*).

Sōjiji is an impressively large temple, and the manpower required to keep it clean must be equally impressive. Twice a day the *unsui* of the Kandoku-ryō are expected to clean every wooden surface in the temple, following a circuit that begins at the doors of the abbot's residence and makes a nearly complete clockwise circle through the temple corridors. When corrected for linear distance, the entire cleaning circuit is more than eight-tenths of a kilometer (about half a mile) long and more than four meters (twelve feet) wide in most places.

Cleaning almost a kilometer of wooden flooring twice a day is a demanding chore in its own right, but the *unsui* are armed for the task only with buckets of water and rags. Further, the *unsui* are made to sprint this entire circuit arched over, barefoot, with their hands sliding on damp rags while their legs propel them forward. This cleaning technique is often used in the martial arts in order to discipline the student to respect their practice space while simultaneously building leg and back muscles.[30] Yet, unlike most martial arts halls—or most Japanese temples, for that matter— the sheer size of Sōjiji transforms this traditional training technique into a punishing trial of endurance.

Before they begin, the *unsui* change out of their monastic robes and into loose-fitting work clothes (*samue*). They wrap a white towel around their heads to prevent sweat—and there will be sweat!—from falling on the floor while they clean. The *unsui* start their on-their-hands sprint through the temple, with each monk covering as much surface area as they can before their wet rags dry up and lose their ability to slide. The *unsui* make it look easy, but it is a grueling workout that affects every muscle group, especially the muscles of the legs and the back.

On several occasions, I volunteered to help out with the cleaning. I was in good shape, and I expected that I would be able to keep up with the *unsui*. My failure to be able to do even a fraction of their work detail was catastrophically comical. Either I couldn't push the rag (it was too dry) or I slipped belly-first onto the wooden flooring (it was too wet). In the instances where I got it just right, I could only push the rag for about ten meters (about thirty feet) before I was breathing heavily and my legs and arms wanted to give out.

This entire circuit is repeated by the *unsui* twice a day, regardless of summer heat or winter chill. The repeated washings have prematurely darkened the once-light Japanese cypress lumber from which the temple floors are constructed, making the temple look centuries older than it really is.

Walking through the temple corridors one rainy day with Aoki-san, a senior priest, I asked him why the *unsui* are made to clean the temple as often as they do. Wouldn't once a day be enough? We briefly stopped our walk in the Daisodō, where four *unsui* were using wicker brooms to systematically sweep the entirety of the enormous hall—mat by mat, row by row, one thousand mats in all.[31]

"The goal of *samu* is not to make things clean," Aoki-san told me, not taking his eyes off the monks making their slow progress through the hall:

> The goal of *samu* is *samu* itself. If we wanted them only to clean, we would give them a vacuum cleaner or a mop, and they could make the floors sparkle. But "cleanliness" and "dirtiness" are in your mind. You make something clean and just like that [he snaps his fingers], it's dirty again.

In a Zen temple, *samu* and *zazen* are the same. During *zazen*, we are "just sitting" (*tada suwaru*). *Zazen* has no goal. We try to keep our minds from wandering off from where we are and focus on "now and here" (*ima, koko*).

Samu is the same thing. There is no use in trying to make things clean. It is "just cleaning" (*tada sōji suru*). With every step you need to think, "I'm sweeping, I'm sweeping."

You know, people think enlightenment is a moment when you say, "I get it!"(*Wakatta*). It's different than that. There's a saying: "*issun suwareba, issun hotoke*"—"sit for a moment, buddha for a moment." When you concentrate on now and here, even for a second—that's enlightenment.

Samu is just another way of walking the path of the Buddha. When you eat, think, "I am eating." When you sit, think, "I am sitting." When you walk, think, "I am walking." It is hard at first, but eventually it becomes easier and you can do it for longer and longer. *Shugyō* trains us to keep this up for twenty-four hours a day.

He walked over to make sure that the incense burner was lit and added a pinch of fragrant incense to the keep the coals burning. When he came back, we stood for several minutes in silence in the darkened hall, watching the *unsui* and listening to the heavy summer rain falling on the roof overhead.

Under Pressure

Two days out of every ten—the days ending in the numbers four and nine—are designated rest days. On these days, morning *zazen* is cancelled, giving the *unsui* an extra half hour to sleep in. On the afternoons before these rest days, *unsui* who are no longer restricted to the temple grounds can leave Sōjiji to go on personal errands in Tsurumi, provided they have finished their responsibilities for the day and have received permission to do so. The monks have at most two hours of free time to spend, so they tend to stay in the immediate vicinity of the temple. Still, on these days it is a common sight to spot *unsui* from Sōjiji, still in their monastic robes, shopping for toiletries or browsing the comic book section of the local used bookstore.

On all other days, the *unsui* are left to steal a few minutes of break and rest where they can get it. Most departments in the temple have a break room where the *unsui* can have a few moments to relax, smoke a cigarette (a surprising number of the monks are habitual smokers), or even to lie down for a quick nap. The break rooms are safe spaces for the *unsui*. They are placed well beyond the sight of temple visitors, and even the *unsui*'s superiors take a more permissive attitude toward monastic proto-col while in these rooms.[32] The result is that the monks of all ranks have a chance to relax, mingle, and enjoy surprisingly casual conversation with one another.

Besides being tucked out of the way, the break rooms are themselves nondescript, often containing a motley assortment of sitting mats and chairs brought in from around the temple. All the break rooms I saw had a communal table, clocks, and at least one (and usually more) ashtrays.

Like the Monk's Hall, the break rooms are treated by the monks as a sacred space but for opposite reasons: whereas the Monk's Hall is special because of the strict discipline it commands, the break room is valued for the *absence* of discipline. Being a part of the conversations in the break rooms revealed a side of the monks I had been unable to capture in any of the public spaces of the temple complex. Formalities and regimentation were, for the most part, set aside. Topics in the break room were never over matters of religious significance but, rather, over the things of importance to young Japanese men in their early to mid-twenties. The *unsui* talked animatedly about their favorite bands or movies or about clubs where they used to hang out. When it came out that two *unsui* who had been working side by side for weeks had a similar taste in hard-core punk music, one ran to grab paper and pens so each could write down the artists they wanted the other to listen to when they left the temple. Another monk revealed an encyclopedic knowledge of American basketball teams and players and told the group how he gotten a passport specifically in the hope of getting to see the Los Angeles Lakers play. On one memorable occasion, a supervising priest came into the room with an old guitar he had found discarded and, after restringing it, launched into a blisteringly fast guitar solo.

The conversations and time spent in the break room reminded the *unsui* that there was a world "out there" outside of Sōjiji and that the extreme limitations of their *shugyō* were only a temporary condition. In this regard, the break room was the single greatest foil to the disciplinary apparatus of the Monk's Hall: the limited minutes spent in the break room reinforced not just the monk's individuality and humanity but also a sense that *shugyō* was something that had to be endured only for the time being. While the atmosphere in the break room did not contribute to the prescribed "twenty-four-hour-a-day *shugyō*," the time spent assuredly helped the *unsui* endure the remaining twenty-three hours of training.

Too Much to Bear

Even with these periods of calm, the pressures of the monastic life at Sōjiji are too much for some. In the relative safety of the break room, my informants told me in hushed tones that within the past year, there had been seven *unsui* who had tried to escape from the temple. Follow-up inquiries indicated that this number is on par with a yearly average of between five and ten escapes a year, down from an average of twenty in the 1980s.

Most escapes take place at night while the temple is asleep. Seldom does escape take place without advance planning. A monk bent on escaping will have made preparations in secret to set his plan into motion. In order to facilitate his escape, the novice has to leave most or all of his personal belongings. The doors to the temple are opened when the early rising monks wake up at 2:30 a.m., so provided a monk is able to leave the Monk's Hall unnoticed, he is able to literally run out the front door of the monastery.

At this point the escapee is likely terrified at what he has done. A successful escape attempt has disastrous ramifications for the professional prospects of the monk in question and any future he might have in the sect. This stigma extends to the priest who sponsored his application to his temple, who in most cases is the monk's father. This priest is obliged to submit a formal apology to the temple and sectarian administrative headquarters on behalf of his disciple, but the damage to the reputation of both has already been done. Should the disciple sincerely want to continue as a monk—or should his obligations to the family temple make his renouncing the clergy an impossibility—and should the Sōtō Zen administration accept his appeal, the *unsui* might try his *shugyō* again from the very beginning, this time at a smaller, regional training center where the daily regimen may not be as strict and where he can be watched much more closely.

What would lead a monk to flee from Sōjiji? A commonly heard response was that an *unsui* who had committed himself to escaping was likely subject to bullying or outright hazing by his fellow monks or his superiors. While an awareness of bullying in schools, sports, and the workplace has received increased attention in Japan over the past generation, the potential for corrective discipline to descend into abuse represents the darker side of *shugyō*. In previous times, one priest reported, a novice at Sōjiji could not go through the day without at least fifty hits from the *kyōsaku* stick, resulting in horrible and painful bruising and other flesh wounds. Another priest, describing similar treatment, repeatedly punched his open palm to capture the sound of the physical abuse that an *unsui* might endure for any infraction of the rules, which were often minor. A third priest whom I interviewed at his home temple began to noticeably rock back and forth while recalling the daily abuse he had endured decades earlier.

All, however, agreed that any abuse in the temple was previously much worse than it is today, following new policies and careful monitoring by the Sōjiji administration. The temple administration reportedly listens carefully to any allegations of abuse, under the premise that "if it leaves the impression of bullying, then it *is* bullying." Still, such abuse can be rectified only if the *unsui* speaks up, which even today many are reluctant to do.[33]

Despite the potential for *shugyō* to slip into hazing and abuse, former novices at Sōjiji often report that their most memorable experiences at the temple involved the sensation of being pushed beyond the boundaries of physical and mental limitations. The often-painful realities of *shugyō*, with all of the demands required of the *unsui*'s body and mind, were commonly remembered with fondness, though several were quick to admit that these memories are pleasant only in hindsight. "The things that are in front of your eyes are quite difficult," one priest told me.

The *Bon* Dance

Throughout Japan, the summer Obon festival is a time of homecomings, celebrated with feasting, drinking, and dancing.[34] During Obon the spirits of one's ancestors and departed family, especially those who have died within the past year, are believed to return to the world to visit the living. For the *unsui*, Obon marks the end of both the summer retreat period and the hundred-day-long probationary period during which they were forbidden from leaving the temple grounds or receiving mail and phone calls from family and friends. This is a major milestone in the life of an *unsui* at Sōjiji and certainly one worth celebrating.

The normally tranquil temple garden is transformed during the three nights of the Spirit Festival (*Mitama Matsuri*), which lasts from July 17 through 19. The main approach to the temple is lined on either side with colorful booths and the smells of fried eggs, fried noodles, and fried octopus, culinary staples of Japanese festivals. From the main street into the temple complex, a long train of thousands of people are crammed into a space that sees only a handful at a time on most days of the year. It is impossible to move by your own will, and a person quickly falls into the rhythm of the crowd.

The crowd pushes toward Sōjiji's main parking lot, which has been con-verted into a space for dancing. In the center of the lot, there is an elevated circular stage with a large *taiko* drum in the center. The stage is adorned with the pattern of alternating red and white stripes that indicate celebra-tions throughout Japan. Large speakers and flashing lights are mounted on the stage, and long strings of multicolored flags extend outward and are attached to poles on the outside of the parking lot.

This year, as every year, the Obon festivities are planned by a joint committee of *unsui* and a group from Tsurumi University High School (formerly the Tsurumi Girls High School). In many ways the Sōjiji Obon dance is truly a festival for the young. Families, especially those with young children, have staked out space on tarps or blankets they have brought for the occasion. The children are usually the most "traditionally" dressed of any group at the festival, with their parents going out of their way to dress their children in kimono-like *yukata* complete with wooden shoes. Young women and men of high school and college age are everywhere.

The *unsui* have given up their monastic robes for the festival. Those who have assigned tasks during the dance, such as wading among the crowd to hand out fans or selling beer and alcohol from under a tent across from the stage, are wearing work pants, headwraps, and souvenir "Zen" T-shirts from Sōjiji's gift shop. Other monks are wearing *yukata* and are tasked with getting the attendees to dance. This often means spending a good deal of time chatting up clusters of girls and occasionally leading them by the hand into the dancing circles.

Despite their best efforts, it is hard to get people to dance. Some well-known songs are played back-to-back in order to get the attendees to stay in the circles. It is clear that there are certain songs that are more popular than others, and after a while the deejay begins to come to terms with the reality that only certain songs will get the people into the dancing rings. After a while, the same three songs are played over and over.

While the parking lot is loud and full of energy, the main temple com-plex is much more serene. The paved path that runs through the center of the complex is lined with small paper cups, each with a single candle burn-ing inside of it. On every one of the hundreds of cups a name is written: the candles are part of the *Mantō-e* ("Ten Thousand Candles Observance") and are tiny memorials purchased in remembrance of a loved one, family member, or friend. In other parts of Japan, Obon is celebrated by floating candles in lakes or rivers to ferry the souls to the "other shore" for another year. Here the candles are kept close, arranged in a pattern that illuminates the path to the Buddha Hall. Very few people walk among the candles, choosing instead to join in the revelry elsewhere in the temple.

Fig. 10. The unsui perform a choreographed dance routine at the Obon Spirit Festival (*Mitama Matsuri*).

As the sun sets, fireworks are set off in the sky over the festival. The end of the fireworks is the limit for many families with tired children. As the families leave, they are replaced by young adults, for whom the party is just beginning.

After eight o'clock, the deejay adds a popular new song to the dance rotation, a song specifically chosen by the *unsui*. They have choreographed a dance number that they perform for the crowd. As the song starts, the *unsui* take the stage and position themselves in the circle closest to the stage for their performance. As they dance, the cheering from the crowd is explosive, and the young monks ride the energy like superstars. As the song ends, one of the monks on the stage jumps up on the railing, balancing himself precariously over the crowd. He shouts into the microphone:

"Say Dai-hon-zan!" The audience shouts back, "Dai-hon-zan!"

"Say Sō-ji-ji!" "Sō-ji-ji!"

"Say Tsu-ru-mi!" "Tsu-ru-mi!" The crowd cheers.

Another monk with a microphone climbs onto the railing, and the two of them begin an energetic freestyle rap. The audience starts clapping to the monks' beat, and cheers erupt when they finish. The deejay immediately plays the song again from the beginning, keeping the energy alive.

When the song ends, the deejay makes the mistake of following up the song with one of the family-friendly dance songs that was popular earlier in the night. The crowd immediately begins drifting away.

After the pop song is repeated for the fourth time, I decide to head for home. As I make my way toward the gate, I notice Kawase-rōshi sitting at a picnic bench away from the crowd, his arms casually folded across his chest as he leans against the table. I walk over and sit down next to him, and I notice that from where he is sitting, he can see both the large crowds dancing in the parking lot and the light trickle of people who are walking up the candle-illuminated pathway to the Buddha Hall. When the pop song comes on for an unbelievable fifth time, I ask him over the noise of the crowd whose idea it was to add such a song to the mix. The *unsui* chose it themselves, he replies. "I don't think it's a good thing," he confesses with a sigh. "I'm happy everyone is having fun, but they've forgotten why this festival was started in the first place." It's not just the *unsui* who have forgotten, he tells me. The people of Tsurumi have forgotten it too:

> Sōjiji started holding the Spirit Festival right after the war. When Tsurumi was bombed, Sōjiji was lucky—it wasn't damaged. The damage to the rest of the city was so bad that some people couldn't even find the bodies of their loved ones. They were buried in their houses or burned up by the flames. People would lay out the dead bodies here [he gestures, indicating the entire temple precincts], so their families could find them and give them a proper funeral.
>
> But there were so many bodies that were never found. Sōjiji started the Spirit Festival to calm their souls. The point of the dancing was to remind the people that in the face of great tragedy, the other side of life is happiness.
>
> In the first years after the war, the festival was a way for the *unsui* and people of Tsurumi to come together to celebrate being alive and rebuilding the town. There was a slogan back then—"The town is all together!" (*ichidō machi yo*). I think that those of us who have never known war need to remember what has happened in the past.

"But," Kawase-rōshi says with a smile and a shrug, "the *unsui* do something like this every year. It's their way of rebelling. In time, they'll come to understand."

Coming Home

Throughout the year, there are multiple occasions for priests trained at Sōjiji to return to Tsurumi and participate once again in the ceremonial life of the temple. How does it feel to come back? "Whenever I come back to Sōjiji, I always have a feeling of 'welcome home'" (*okaeri nasai*), one priest told me during a visit to his home temple in Niigata. It wasn't the exhaustion, or the restrictions, or even the constant threat of looming discipline that were embedded in his mind. Instead he remembers faces and voices and the echoes of conversations and jokes. When he returns to Sōjiji, he can still see his friends running through the halls beside him as they cleaned the long wooden corridors together. He remembered those priests above him who looked after his well-being and who took a personal interest in molding him from a scared *unsui* into the priest he is today. Through the social media and Sanshōkai, Sōjiji's alumni group, he is still in contact with many of the priests he trained with. With pride, he says that the bonds of camaraderie he formed in Sōjiji's halls have lasted decades.

For the Sōtō clergy trained at Sōjiji, the days spent in *shugyō* will always have an important place in their lives: Sōjiji has left its imprint on their bodies, their words, their actions, and their identities. Many express a sense that their time at Sōjiji made them a part of something larger than themselves, of being links in a chain that extends across rivers and mountains, across oceans, and across the centuries. They no longer belong to only one family; their *shugyō* has transformed the priests into custodians of their sect, their temple, their Dharma line, their legal family, and the families of their parishioners. When they leave Sōjiji, they leave with the understanding it will one day be their sons who will one day nervously stand outside in the cold sunlight of a March morning shouting for permission to enter the temple for *shugyō*, scared and unaware of what awaits them inside.

THREE

Bearing the Mantle of Priesthood

The months or years that a Sōtō Zen priest spends cloistered as an *unsui* at a training temple like Sōjiji is by far the most time-consuming and personally trying part of the initiation process. At the end of his period of *shugyō*, a priest is likely anywhere from six months to two years along in his clerical career. From this point, the remaining three ordination rituals are usually scheduled to take place in rapid succession, often with only a few months or even weeks separating them. All that is officially required for a priest to undergo the remaining rituals is the timely submission to the Sōtō Zen sect's administrative offices of the necessary documents applying for each successive stage. When the official approval is received by the applicant, the rituals can move forward at the convenience of the priest and his sponsor.

Yet far from being mere formalities, the participatory reenactment of ritual, I argue, is key to a person's transformation into a priest. Even more so than as novice *unsui*, priests are legitimated in the eyes of the sect and the public only insofar as they can appear as legitimate embodiments of the teachings of Sōtō Zen. The rituals of ordination are therefore not mere performances. Rather, these rituals operate on two levels: first, through the bodily reenactment of important moments of the Sōtō Zen religious history, with the priests in the roles of key historical figures, and, second, through having priests recreate these moments anew, allowing them to both participate in and perpetuate this history.

At the same time, the realities and obligations of contemporary Japanese society have had dramatic consequences for a priest's identity both inside and outside the context of Sōjiji. As we shall see, the past hundred years in particular have had very important ramifications for the day-to-day lives of post-training priests trying to reconcile their traditional roles as renunciant priests with their modern lives, lived very much "in the world." As fully ordained priests negotiate their roles as professional clerics, they find themselves responsible for the well-being of their families and their parishioners, the continued survival of their sect and *honzan*, and the training of future generations of clergy.

Descending the Mountain

Most *unsui* are eager to get their *shugyō* over and done with as soon and as fast as possible, and many are the *unsui* who count down the days to their *sōan* ("leaving the retreat") celebration, the day they finally "descend the mountain" (*asan*) and return to a world outside the strict discipline of the Monk's Hall.[1]

An *unsui* who has fulfilled his required duration of training can schedule his departure at any time, but there is an understanding that he should try to wait until after any major ceremonies or holidays to avoid leaving the temple understaffed. Because of this, larger groups of *unsui*—sometimes upward of ten or fifteen at a time—tend to leave the temple together.

On the afternoon before their departure, the *unsui* go around to each temple department to formally thank the department head for his time and care during their training. As they did when they first arrived, the *unsui* stand as a group with their arms raised in *gasshō* and shout to the closed door that they have come to pay their respects. The department head emerges and offers a few words of congratulations and encouragement. Shouting as one, they thank him for his time, apologize for their intrusion, and move on to the next department.

On the morning of their departure, the *unsui* participate in the morning rituals and breakfast as usual. After breakfast, they once again prepare themselves in the manner of traveling monks—robes tucked for ease of movement, straw sandals on their feet, and their traveling bags suspended on their chests and backs.

At eight o'clock, the entire temple community gathers in the front of the Kōshakudai and takes up positions lining both sides of the driveway. The graduating *unsui* emerge from the hall to cheers and applause from their friends, who rush to place cellophane-wrapped bouquets of brightly colored flowers into the *unsui*'s already full hands. From the wooden stairs

Fig. 11. The unsui assemble on the steps of the Sanmon gate for a commemorative "Graduation Day" photo.

of the interior of the hall, the rector of the temple comes out to address the graduating *unsui* through a handheld public address system: "We are proud of you and what you have accomplished here. We are a family, and you will always be welcome to come home."

After the rector has given his congratulations, the graduating *unsui* begin their walk down the hill toward the temple gate. As they pass through a gauntlet of applauding friends, the two lines fall in behind them, following them down the circular drive. At the Sanmon, the entire community poses for several commemorative pictures, with the graduating *unsui* in the center of the group.

When the pictures are finished, the senior priests remain behind on the steps of the Sanmon while the *unsui* join the graduates in their final walk to the Sanshōkan, the wooden gate that serves as the formal boundary between Sōjiji and the outside world.[2] Taking one of the most meaningful steps of their lives, the graduates step over the wooden threshold of the gate, symbolically stepping out of their lives as training monks. The crowd around them erupts into cheers as the closest well-wishers pat the graduates on their backs and shake their hands. Small groups then grab each graduate *unsui* and throw them three times into the air.

After lingering for a couple of minutes with the graduates, the assembly of *unsui* turns back and runs up the hill in order to be on time for their morning cleaning duties. The graduates remain at the Sanshōkan so that the temple photographer can take several more commemorative photos.

At this point, the graduates, having stepped over the threshold, have symbolically reemerged from their cloister into the mundane world. Their "departure" thus completed, the now-graduated monks anticlimactically walk back up the hill and into the temple complex, retracing their steps without fanfare into the reception hall, where they are greeted by an attendant who collects their borrowed straw hats. The graduates take off their straw sandals, step into their old slippers, and disappear back into the temple halls.

In the corner of the temple gift shop sits a pile of plastic crates and bedding bundles, all tagged and ready for pickup from a special delivery service. The graduates now wait for rides from parents, relatives, or friends who will come to the temple to pick them up and bring them home. The *sōan* ceremony, like the *jōzan* ritual, is a symbolic mixture of traditional appearance and modern convenience. As they arrived, so shall they leave.

Following his *sōan*, I was able to catch up with Nakajima-san before he left with his mother, who had arrived by train the night before. They were on a tight schedule, with bullet train tickets that would have them home by mid-afternoon. He told me how excited he was to see his family and friends for the first time in over a year. He expected that his "welcome home" party that night would be a lot of fun.

As several newly graduated former *unsui* described to me, their return to a non-monastic lifestyle was filled with a sense of liberation and relief. One expressed great satisfaction in the knowledge that he would never be forced to wake up before sunrise to sit *zazen* again. Another proudly recounted that his first act upon leaving the temple was having a hamburger at the McDonald's that sits on the corner of the busy street leading up to Sōjiji: "It made my stomach hurt, but every time I passed that McDonald's, all I could think of was how much I wanted a hamburger!"

Still, for many *unsui*, the transition to life outside of the monastery is a difficult one, similar to the return experienced by others who have been through an intense liminal and communal experience. One priest, now in his forties, told me that when he finally went home after spending almost eighteen months at Sōjiji (a time that, in retrospect, seemed to him "too short"), he was surprised to find himself depressed and lethargic. He began with good intentions to continue the routines of his training at home, but he quickly found that he was unable to maintain the disciplined schedule as he had intended. His commitment to daily *zazen* fell away within a month, and soon after he experienced difficulty waking up in the mornings to over-see his ritual obligations to the ancestors of his temple's parishioners. Over time, he reported, he came to terms with his difficulties but only through compromise: he would forgo daily *zazen* entirely but made it a point to wake up at seven to perform his morning duties.

Whatever disappointment this priest felt at his lapse in personal disci-pline, having to make such compromises after one's return to life outside of Sōjiji is a story that resonates with many Sōtō Zen priests. Other priests I spoke with reported similar dissonance– what Nara Yasuaki describes as a "gap between the monastic life and life in the temple."[3] The most common sentiment voiced was of missing the communal life of the training temple: "Without the feeling of camaraderie (*nakama ishiki*), daily life just isn't the same," one priest told me. Most of all, the sudden absence of the near-constant disciplining gaze within the temple walls also means that daily life can begin to lack structure and, in some cases, even meaning. As soldiers and students can attest, a regimented life is easiest to maintain in a group, all of whom function under continuous disciplinary pressure.

The Sōtō Zen sect recognizes that one is already a priest (*sōryo*) once tonsure has been performed. Nevertheless, becoming a fully ordained Sōtō Zen priest requires a succession of four primary initiatory rituals, of which tonsure is only the first step.[4] From the time the paperwork certifying ton-sure is processed and approved by the sectarian administrative offices, the newly minted priest has ten years to complete the remainder of the initia-tory process. This road can be very long for some, but most priests aim to receive full ordination within two to four years after tonsure.

Following tonsure, the novice priest is given the clerical title of *jōza* ("ascending the seat"), a term that refers to a priest's entrance into the monastic life in a training temple. As we have seen, successful completion of *shugyō* of any duration is a significant accomplishment in a priest's life, as the hardest part of a priest's training is behind him.

Dharma Combat

Completing the monastery training requirement makes the priest eligible to participate in the second initiatory ritual, the Dharma Combat Cer-emony (*Hossenshiki*).

The Dharma Combat Ceremony is intended to be a public demonstra-tion of a fledgling priest's ability to be a powerful proponent and exemplar of the Sōtō Zen teachings and practices. The historical precedents for the

Dharma Combat Ceremony date back to India, when wealthy and power-ful elites would invite rival philosophic schools to engage in public debates. The schools that accepted the patron's invitation would arrive and hoist their school's banner at the gates; two schools simultaneously displaying their banner signified that the debate battle was under way. These debates could rage for many days, but they would ultimately be judged to have a clear winner and loser. The loser was forced to publicly concede the superiority of the winner's argument. The losing side's flag would then be lowered, leaving only the victor's to wave in the wind.

The historical Buddha and his disciples were party to this practice of high-stakes philosophic debating. Over time, the Buddhist canon became filled with examples of the overwhelming power of the sermons of the Buddha and his followers. It was not merely humans that could be swayed by coming into contact with the Dharma; all manner of beings, from gods to animals to demons, were won over simply by hearing the Buddha's Dharma as spoken by an enlightened priest.

The Sōtō Zen canon, likewise, has many historical precedents for Dharma combat. Most significant for the Sōjiji-trained clergy is the con-version story of Gasan Jōseki, who would become the second abbot of Sōjiji. Gasan began his monastic career at Mount Hiei, where, like Dōgen, he trained within the Tendai school. After a chance meeting with Keizan in Kyoto, Gasan challenged Keizan to a "question and answer" (*mondō*) debate to determine the merit of the other's teachings. Gasan was well-educated and already wise beyond his years, but Keizan's Sōtō Zen lineage gave him the weight of the True Dharma behind his words. Gasan was reportedly so moved by the sheer force of Keizan's arguments that he fell into a personal crisis, ultimately questioning his Tendai training.[5] Some-time later, Gasan returned to Keizan to dedicate himself to Sōtō Zen and became one of Keizan's two most eminent disciples.

Today the Dharma Combat Ceremony symbolically reenacts this pros-elytizing tradition within Buddhism by publicly placing the soon-to-be ordained priest in a role through which he must demonstrate his ability to personify the teachings of Sōtō Zen to any and all challengers. Like the daily recitations of lineage and key texts in the Monk's Hall, participa-tion in a Dharma combat ritual is multifunctional in that it affirms and preserves key moments of Buddhist—and specifically Sōtō Zen—history while bodily placing a priest into this tradition through participatory reenactment.

The Dharma Combat Ceremony is in many ways the equivalent of an oral defense of a thesis or dissertation, save that all sides of the exchange are memorized from a standardized text.[6] In this regard, and despite its name, the ceremony is not "won" but rather performed. In today's Dharma combat there are no surprises: the protagonist always wins.

In a training monastery like Sōjiji, the title of "first seat" (*shuso*) is given to the monk who is elected by his peers to serve as the primary representative for the community of training monks.[7] In previous times, the monk who was granted the honor of serving as *shuso* was the one who was recognized as the most likely candidate to inherit the Dharma lineage of the Zen master. While it remains a position of great prestige at a large training monastery, it has largely become a ceremonial role, with few everyday responsibilities.

Only two *unsui* per year have the honor of performing a Dharma Combat Ceremony at Sōjiji. For the remainder, their chance comes upon their return to their home temple after their training, where they are granted the title of *shuso*. Since most priests go on to inherit a small parish temple, it matters little if the "first seat" is technically the *only* seat at a given temple; the term *shuso* indicates that the priest is the heir apparent to his sponsor's Dharma lineage.

The *Hossenshiki* takes place twice a year at Sōjiji, in May and November, in the middle of the summer and winter retreat periods, respectively. It is an important ritual in the yearly cycle of the temple and one of the few rituals in which the entire temple community participates. As the date of the ritual approaches, the novice *unsui* begin practicing in earnest for the ceremony. In the weeks leading up to the ceremony, the usual quiet of the temple landscape is broken by the monks practicing their questions, phrased in classical Japanese shouted at the top of their lungs in a gruff and forceful manner.

On the day of the ceremony, the *shuso* enters the hall alongside the abbot and an entourage of ranking priests, all carrying partly open fans as a mark of their office. The community of *unsui* are seated in their usual positions flanking either side of the inner hall, with the *shuso* taking his place in the position closest to the altar in the first row. The abbot sits in the center, facing the altar. Attendants bring a small table and place it in front of the abbot. First an incense burner is placed on the table, and afterward a three-foot-long staff known as a *shippei* is placed in front of the burner. Of all the material implements used in a Zen temple, the *shippei* is the only one that is literally a weapon; its stylized shape is intended to be that of an unstrung bow.

After an opening recitation of the Heart Sutra and offerings made to the patriarchs, the Dharma combat begins in earnest. The *shuso* makes a round of the hall, prostrating in front of the ranking priests, and finally making four prostrations to the assembly: one to the abbot, one to the left, one to the right, and then a second prostration to the abbot. The *shuso* then approaches the abbot and with his permission takes the *shippei*.

Thus armed, the *shuso* kneels in front of the main altar. Spatially, this position is one of importance and also of mediation. In the hall this position is usually occupied by the statuary of the Sōtō Zen patriarchs who sit above the altar gazing down and out at the assembled community, their faces obscured by curtains and shadow to ensure that their gaze cannot be returned. During Dharma combat, however, the *shuso* occupies this ritual position. Facing out at the assembly from the front of the hall, he is symbolically made to be the focus of the ceremony (a right normally reserved for the patriarchs alone), but his placement on the floor is a humbling reminder that the *shuso* is not yet worthy to be counted among his revered forebears.

The *shuso* opens the combat by raising the *shippei* and fan to the level of his eye, a gesture of offering. Holding the fan in his left hand, he takes the *shippei* in his right hand and slams it with a loud boom into the tatami floor. As he does so, he shouts a strong challenge to the assembly. Dharma combat has begun.

The challenges come from *unsui* seated around the hall, who open their questions by shouting, "Oshō!" the equivalent of "Hey, priest!" The challenges are brash; the *unsui* shout their questions in the deep, threatening voices characteristic of Japanese gangster movies. The back-and-forth exchanges are brief and aggressive on both sides, with each confrontation lasting under a minute. Each exchange ends with a characteristic exchange of "*Chinchō!*" ("Take care of yourself!") and the response "*Banzei!*" ("Stay well!"), which the *shuso* punctuates by slamming his *shippei*. The challenger, humbled, is grateful for what he has just learned. The *shuso*, the winner of the debate, is similarly graceful in his victory.

For over an hour, the *shuso* fends off these philosophical "attacks" by his peers. The challenges come from all directions in seemingly random fashion. It is significant to note that at no time do the ranking priests offer their own challenges or enter into the fray. For the time being, they are silent observers, watching the *shuso* fend for himself by deftly responding to the attacks being thrown at him.

Nearing the end of the ceremony, the back-and-forth shouting abruptly ends. The *shuso* returns the *shippei* staff to the table sitting in front of the abbot. Making another set of four prostrations, the *shuso* returns to each of the ranking priests to pay his respects and a prostration, this time in reverse. Emerging from the left side of the hall, the *shuso* takes his place at the head of the assembly of *unsui*.

Now it is the priests' turn to address the *shuso* and his cohort. Where there was chaos—novice monks shouting at each other from random directions—now there is order. The ranking priests speak in turn, in ascending hierarchical order, moving clockwise around the hall, and culminating in a comment from the abbot himself.

The floating, almost musical voices the ranking priests use to make their comments stand in dramatic contrast to the gruff, aggressive voices the *unsui* used to issue their challenges. By responding to his attackers in an appropriately aggressive voice, the *shuso* met fire with fire, addressing the unenlightened *unsui* on their own terms. However, this audible shift in tone and language is a performative demonstration that while the *shuso* may show promise, he still has a long way to go. The actual words spoken by the ranking, experienced priests are congratulatory, but the underlying message is clear: enlightened words must issue from cultivated, graceful bodies.

That the Dharma Combat Ceremony is the capstone event to a novice's *shugyō* underscores this point. It is very easy to speak the right words, especially if they are memorized from a book. It is a far more difficult thing to *embody* these words. Ultimately, the *Hossenshiki* demonstrates, a priest will be judged not only for the enlightened words he speaks but more so for the way his lessons are manifested in his everyday behavior.

Dharma Transmission

Once the *Hossenshiki* has been completed and certified, the priest gains the clerical title of *zagen*, "principal seat." But he will likely hold this title for only a few weeks, as the ceremonies that finalize his ordination happen in rapid succession.

The priest's success in the *Hossenshiki* publicly demonstrates that he has been properly prepared in body and mind to be a vehicle of the Buddha's teachings. If before his training he was a formless lump of wax, his *shugyō* has painstakingly shaped him into a candle capable of holding a flame.[8] But this candle is as yet unlit. In the Dharma Transmission Ceremony (*Denpō-e*), the flame of the Buddha's teachings—the True Dharma—will be passed to him by his master, one candle lighting another.

The Dharma Transmission Ceremony is conducted behind closed doors, with just two participants: the master (*shisō*) and the disciple (*deshi*).

The transmission itself is said to take place through a powerful "mind-to-mind" (*isshin denshin*) connection between the two participants, empowering the master to share with his worthy disciple the enlightened wisdom passed down from the Buddha himself.[9] When the disciple emerges from the ceremony, he is visibly transformed: the *kesa* he now wears is the subdued earthen color (brown, mustard, or moss green being the most common colors) worn only by a fully ordained Sōtō Zen priest.[10] His transformation marks him as a productive member of the Sōtō sect, a public recognition of his qualifications to perform all of the ritual responsibilities that will be required of him as an officiant in a parish temple. With more experience, he will become eligible to be a *reproductive* member of the sect: a living representation of the continuity between Sōtō Zen's mythological past and its present, capable of transmitting the Dharma to future generations.

The precedent for the ceremony is the archetypal story of the Buddha passing the "light" or "flame" (*denkō*) of his Dharma, including the leadership of the fledgling Buddhist community, to his disciple Mahākāśyapa through a symbolic gesture that only Mahākāśyapa understands. In the *Denkōroku*, Keizan writes that the story of the Buddha's "offering up of a flower" to Mahākāśyapa "has been passed on from ancestor to ancestor; those outside the ancestral line are never allowed to know about it without good cause."[11] This archetypal story establishes the hallmark of the Sōtō Zen Dharma Transmission Ceremony: the carefully controlled generational transfer of privileged knowledge that publicly establishes the legitimacy of the recipient within the genealogy of the transmitter.[12]

What takes place during the Dharma Transmission Ceremony is a trade secret; instructions for conducting the ritual must be specifically requested from and approved by the Sōtō sectarian administration on a per-case basis, and the materials must be returned once the ceremony is completed. One consequence of this is that, to many outside the clergy, the Dharma Transmission Ceremony is shrouded in an aura of mystery and fascination—and with good reason. Like all secret initiatory rituals, only a very privileged few will ever experience it, and by participants refusing to discuss what took place, the allure of the secret itself becomes the fodder for rumor and speculation. Indeed, this "secretism"[13]—the implied access to hidden knowledge and powers, the intentional vagueness that fires outsiders' imaginations about what is being concealed, and the calculated dissemination of stories that bolster the reputation of the secret-bearers—sits at the core of the Sōtō Zen clerical identity and fuels the mystique of the "Zen master" in popular culture as well.[14]

Putting aside the specifics of the ritual, what exactly is being "transmitted" in a Dharma Transmission Ceremony? It is not correct to say that *nothing* is transmitted; rather, no "thing" is transmitted.[15] In this sense, T. Griffith Foulk describes how "the Dharma transmitted from master to disciple is literally inconceivable: it has no specifiable content and no marks by which it can be recognized."[16]

However, the Dharma Transmission Ceremony is far from an empty gesture. Instead, as Bodiford identifies, the significance of the ritual lies in its selective mobilization of seven cultural dimensions—ancestral, biological, linguistic, ritual, legal, financial, and temporal—that work to enmesh the master and disciple into an ideal familial relationship as informed by Confucian family values and obligations. The Dharma Transmission Ceremony "encapsulates these dimensions in a mythological framework, unites them in genealogical terminology, and reveals them through concrete ritual performances."[17] No "thing" changes hands; rather, what is transmitted is a new locus of identity for the recipient within a nesting set of relationships––as a disciple of his master, as a member of a historical Dharma lineage, as a public representative of the Sōtō Zen sect, and as an heir of the Buddha himself—with all of the legal, ritual, financial, and filial values, obligations, and expectations these relationships traditionally entail.

What is *not* transmitted in the Dharma Transmission Ceremony is enlightenment (*satori*) itself. Rather, the performance of the ritual strongly implies that some sort of transformation has already occurred in the recipient to make him a suitable vessel for the Dharma. If one accepts the Sōtō sect's doctrinal position that the provenance of the True Dharma has remained unbroken from the moment of the Buddha's awakening to the present day, and if both the transmitter and recipient are understood to be worthy and legitimate (and, today, sect-approved) inheritors of the Dharma, then by logical implication, the recipient must also be enlightened. When and where did this "awakening" take place? Under the principle that "*shugyō* and enlightenment are the same" (*shushō ittō*), the answer is that the newly certified priest must have achieved *satori* during his training as an *unsui* at Sōjiji. It is not surprising then that the laity—and particularly non-Japanese Zen enthusiasts, in my experience—are inclined to over-idealize the clergy, whose certification documents silently mark them as enlightened beings, even if the priests themselves tacitly refuse to do so.

Still, an interesting problem remains. Jihō Sargent estimates that in order to maintain current levels of clerical operations in the Japanese Sōtō Zen sect, the sect needs to certify Dharma transmission to approximately six hundred new priests every year, the vast majority of them young men between twenty and thirty years old.[18] One has to ask whether it stretches the meaning of the word "enlightenment" if, for the purposes of institutional continuity, six hundred new young men and women each year are assumed to have come into possession of the wisdom of the Buddha himself.

In answering this question, it might surprise the reader as to how rarely enlightenment, often perceived to be the purpose or end goal of Buddhist practice, is actually mentioned in the context of a Sōtō Zen temple. Not a single priest I spoke with—of any age, rank, or office—ever referred to themselves or their brethren as having "attained enlightenment" (*satori o eta*, or *satori o hiraita*), nor was enlightenment the goal of their practice. Indeed, those few times that a priest did make explicit mention of their epistemological state was to lump themselves with everyone else on earth in sharing the same desires, fears, and weaknesses that make us all human.[19]

In this regard, *satori* is conceived and taught in contemporary Sōtō Zen in quite a different manner than the sublime, noetic experience that is commonly portrayed in the popular imagination. A genuine experience of *satori* is still held to be a significant event, to be certain, but Sōtō teachers stress that it is only one's first—and brief—insight into the possibilities of living one's life in a state of perfect and continuous *shugyō*. To confuse it with a phenomenological or existential change of state is akin to confusing one's acceptance letter into college as the entirety of a college education.

Instead, the teachers stress to their subordinates that one is "enlightened" only insofar as their actions and behavior can be said to be enlightened. As Taigen Dan Leighton explains, "The point is to enact the meaning of the teachings in actualized practice, and the whole praxis . . . may be viewed as ritual, ceremonial expressions of the teaching, rather than as means to discover and attain some understanding of it."[20] The *kechimyaku* lineage chart and the certification of transmission (*inshō*) that is bestowed upon Dharma transmission are therefore not a certification of wisdom, but rather an in-house certification that the newly minted priest has attained the necessary proficiency and dramaturgical discipline—the ability to act, move, and talk as an enlightened person should, and to do so convincingly and with discretion—that will allow them to aptly and publicly perform as a member of the Sōtō Zen clergy.[21]

"Abbot for a Day"

At this point there is only one ritual left before the priest is a fully ordained Sōtō Zen clergyman. This last ritual is known as *zuise haitō*, in which a priest is required to serve as "abbot for a day" (*ichinichi jūshoku*) at both Sōjiji and Eiheiji.

For nearly six hundred years, this ritual was the cornerstone of Sōjiji's rotating abbot system (*rinjūsei*). The rotating abbot system began as a clever means of sharing the responsibility—or, more accurately, the burden—of being abbot of a temple that was both remote and rapidly increasing in size and significance. Sōjiji's rotating abbot system was loosely based on a similarly named system traditionally employed at the "Five Mountains" public monasteries in China. In actual practice, however, Sōjiji's rotating abbot system was a unique innovation that inadvertently cemented Sōtō Zen— and Sōjiji—as a major player in the religious landscape of Japan.

Sōjiji's unique rotating abbot system was instituted in 1390 by the five principal Dharma descendants of Gasan Jōseki.[22] Under the agreement, each of the five Dharma branches that inherited Gasan's Dharma line would provide a priest who would serve as abbot of Sōjiji for a period of three years. When the priest's term was completed, the abbacy of Sōjiji would move to another Dharma branch, which would send their own representative, and so on.

In a period when it was customary for clergy to spend twenty years in training before they could even receive Dharma transmission, very few Gasan-line priests were initially eligible to hold the office of abbot. Complicating matters, in addition to his ritual and administrative responsibilities at Sōjiji, each abbot was required to maintain his home temple as well, which was often many days' travel away from Sōjiji's remote location on the Noto Peninsula.[23] Sōjiji's abbacy quickly became a "hot potato" that priests were eager to get off their hands and no one wanted to be stuck holding.

During his lifetime, Gasan entreated his disciples to be energetic and active popularizers of Sōtō Zen. His original five disciples likewise transmitted this proselytic spirit to their own students. Throughout the medieval period, Gasan's Dharma descendants spent much of their time traveling the Japanese countryside, actively courting patronage from both aristocrats and commoners by conferring the Buddhist precepts on the laity and performing funerals and memorial services. What was originally an onerous burden turned into an unforeseen boon; having the title of "former abbot of Sōjiji" only served to help the priests' mission, granting an added dimension of prestige and legitimacy.[24] Where these itinerant monks traveled, a new "temple"—often just a simple wooden construction housing an enshrined image—dedicated to Sōtō Zen would often be founded soon after.[25] Since the founding priests were in Gasan's Dharma line, these new temples became branch temples of Sōjiji, contributing materially and financially to their parent temple's welfare.

Over the next few centuries, the number of priests eligible to ascend to Sōjiji's abbacy increased exponentially. As this pool of abbots deepened, the required residency of the abbacy decreased from three years, to one year, to six months, and, finally, to a single day. Each of these "abbacies" brought with them substantial monetary donations from the now merely visiting priest to fill Sōjiji's coffers.[26]

By the first temple censuses in the eighteenth century, Sōtō Zen proselytization efforts throughout Japan had created an impressive network of temples founded and populated by "former abbots" who were politically loyal to Sōjiji. By the time the rotating abbot system was abolished by governmental edict in 1871, Sōjiji had seen 49,766 abbots in five and a half centuries.[27] Sōjiji's branch temples outnumbered Eiheiji's by nearly a ten-to-one margin.

The modern *zuise haitō* ritual was established as a result of the Meiji era compromises that led to historically significant Eiheiji and the politically powerful Sōjiji coming to their uneasy truce over the leadership of the modern Sōtō Zen sect.[28] Today a priest's officiating of a short ceremony at both head temples serves as a ritual confirmation of the priest's ordination—a sort of victory lap. Often, priests will do this back-to-back, performing the ceremony at Eiheiji one day and then boarding a train bound for Yokohama to perform the ceremony again at Sōjiji the following morning.

The *zuise* ceremony at Sōjiji is actually a very simple process. Anywhere from one to five newly minted priests emerge into the hall after morning services wearing bright red *kesa*, with similarly colored bowing mats and slippers. This bright red color is visually reminiscent of Bodhidharma's red cloak, often featured in representations of the famous patriarch as he ventured over mountain and desert to bring Buddhism from India to China. (This red color is particular to Sōjiji; at the *zuise* at Eiheiji, they wear a more humble brown.) The priests are responsible for officiating—that is, offering incense and prostrations—during a special fifteen-minute *zuise fūgin* ceremony dedicated to the founding generations of each head temple, which takes place after the morning services. After the ceremony, congratulations are offered and, as always, commemorative pictures are taken.

After the date of *zuise* has been registered and confirmed with the Sōtō Zen administrative office, the priest gains the title of *oshō*, the official distinction of a fully ordained priest. At this point they are fully vested clergy, eligible to perform all of the ritual and administrative responsibilities of an assistant abbot of a parish temple.

In practice, the title *oshō* is rarely heard today. In the Sōtō Zen sect, the title *rōshi*—literally translated as "elderly teacher"—is used as a generic title of respect for fully ordained clergy, in the sense that "Reverend" is used in English. At Sōjiji the title is often tacked on to the titles of other currently held offices; for example, the priest who holds the office of Tenzo (temple cook) will be known as "Tenzo-rōshi." Like the honorifics "-*san*" or "-*sensei*," *rōshi* is never used in reference to oneself. Rather, it is a term of respect used by clerical subordinates to their superiors and by lay men and women to the clergy generally.[29] As with other honorific titles in Japanese, superiors almost never refer to their subordinates as *rōshi*, substituting more informal labels where appropriate (-*san*, -*kun*).

While in the Sōtō Zen sect the title *rōshi* has lost much of its age-related connotation, newly minted priests sometimes experience a sense of dissonance when they begin hearing themselves being referred to as *rōshi* for the first time, since it is a term they have previously reserved for their elders and superiors. One priest I spoke with was bothered enough by this to insist that people refer to him with the less-common -*oshō*, which is technically correct, but unfamiliar to most laypeople.[30] When I pressed him for an explanation, he explained that he felt genuine discomfort whenever he was called *rōshi*, because he did not yet have the experience and wisdom that he believed the title conveyed.

Zenji-sama

In Sōtō Zen the abbots of the two *honzan* serve as the spiritual heads of the temples and as living exemplars of the sect's teachings. The position of abbot is largely ceremonial; as with many Japanese institutional hierarchies, the abbacy of the head temples can be said to be a reward for a life lived in service to the Sōtō Zen sect.

In addition to being the formal abbot (*jūshoku*) of Sōjiji, the abbot has two titles that convey the multiple roles he plays. The first is *kanshu*, which is used in reference to his being the head administrative officer of a large training facility. The second is *zenji*, translated directly as "Zen master," which is used to characterize his role as the spiritual leader of the temple. In such a way, the dichotomous nature of a *honzan* like Sōjiji—being both an administrative and a religious center—is mediated in the very person of the abbot.

A future abbot of Sōjiji or Eiheiji is chosen by special election, with all officially registered Sōtō Zen clergy eligible to cast votes. Unlike the

Catholic papacy, for example, the abbacy of the two Sōtō Zen head temples is not directly chosen. Rather, the winner of the election is named to the position of deputy abbot (*fuku-kanshu*) of the temple.

The deputy abbot is nominally subordinate to the abbot, but the two offices are often blurred, placing them on essentially equal footing within the temple hierarchy. Among other functions, the deputy abbot serves as a representative for the temple during important ceremonies and functions where an abbot's presence is required but he cannot be present. Since the abbot is in residence at Sōjiji, the deputy abbot spends the majority of his time away from Tsurumi, regularly traveling back and forth between Sōjiji and his home temple as needed.

The deputy abbot is the heir presumptive to the abbot, assuming the abbacy ceremoniously but without challenge when the current abbot steps down or dies in office. This allows for a smoother transition between abbacies, as the deputy abbot is elected years before he will actually take office. When the new abbot is installed, an election is held soon after to fill the deputy abbot's vacated position. However, since the priests elected to the offices of abbot and deputy abbot are generally elderly, it is not uncommon for a sitting abbot to outlive his deputy.

With the exception of the deputy abbot, all subordinate temple officers serve at the invitation and pleasure of the abbot. The priests he calls to service in his administration greatly determine both the ideological and practical directions the temple will take over the course of an abbot's tenure. While the new abbots are charged with maintaining the traditional practice of the Sōtō Zen patriarchs, in reality each new administration is an opportunity to enact major shifts in temple policy and practice. These shifts have profound effects not only on the quality and content of the training for hundreds of *unsui* who will enter Sōjiji during an abbot's reign, but they can also dramatically affect the way temple parishioners, practitioners, and visitors relate to Sōjiji. In this way, it is possible to speak of different administrative "eras" at a temple just as one would a governmental or presidential administration. A brief look at the policies enacted by four recent abbots demonstrates this fact.

Umeda Shinryū-zenji (1906–2000, r. 1982–1996) is well remembered by the monks who trained under his administration. One longtime officer at Sōjiji fondly recalled being inspired as an *unsui* by Umeda-zenji's (then in his late eighties) unbridled energy: "Umeda-zenji loved calligraphy. When the Daisodō wasn't being used for a ceremony, he would turn on all the lights and roll out long pieces of paper on the floor of the hall. He had a big paintbrush, and he would jump around like he was a child, making strokes here and there. I remember thinking, 'What an energetic and healthy *zenji* he is! I hope I'm that lively when I'm that old!'"

Umeda-zenji similarly instilled in his *unsui* a concern for human rights. Human rights had been a charged topic within the Sōtō Zen sect in the wake of a 1984 controversy in which a Sōtō priest publicly revealed decades of institutionalized discrimination toward the Japanese *burakumin* outcastes.[31] It was under Umeda-zenji's abbacy that Sōjiji established a special classroom for the "Protection and Advancement of Human Rights" (*Jinkin Yōgo Suishin-shitsu*), with lectures and twice-monthly small-group seminars in which all training *unsui* are required to participate.

Still, many of the veteran lay practitioners remembered Umeda-zenji's fourteen-year abbacy as a time when Sōjiji closed off into itself, a conservative reaction to the popular and international focus of Sōjiji during the "Zen boom" of the 1960s and 1970s and a response to the rise in pious conspicuous consumption of Japanese parishioners and practitioners made possible by the bubble economy of the 1980s.

The abbacies of Narita Hozui-zenji (1906–1998, r. 1996–1998) and, in particular, that of Itabashi Kōsō-zenji (1927–2020, r. 1998–2002) went a long way toward reversing Sōjiji's years of introversion by making an active effort to reinvent Sōjiji as both a leader in environmental conservation and a public religious institution that welcomed both Japanese and international visitors. To many in the lay community, Itabashi-zenji's administration is remembered as a "golden age" (*ōgon jidai*) at Sōjiji. In addition to being a prolific author, Itabashi-zenji revitalized Sōjiji's failing Baikakō and regularly sat *zazen* with the Sunday Sanzenkai. The clergy too remembered him fondly, as Itabashi-zenji would take his meals in the common meal hall with the *unsui* and even personally make a nightly review of the temple, turning off lights to conserve energy. Under his administration, he enacted the "Open Sōjiji" (*Hiraita Sōjiji e*) policy, with the goal of making Sōjiji more welcoming to guests and more involved within the greater Tsurumi community. Symbolically, the Mukai Karamon gate, traditionally open only during the New Year holiday and on visits from the Imperial Household, was now opened to the world. In addition, when it wasn't in use, the Shuryō was made available to anyone who wished to sit *zazen* at any time. Perhaps most significantly, Itabashi-zenji greatly transformed the temple's physical landscape by working with local environmentalist Miyawaki Akira to build the Sennen no Mori—the "Forest of a Thousand Years"—a revitalized natural landscape that would serve to attract generations of visitors who would feel at home and at peace at Sōjiji.

However, there were many who felt that Itabashi-zenji's populist approach to reinventing Sōtō Zen was going too far. My informants among both the laity and clergy discussed in hushed tones how intrasectarian politics had pushed Itabashi-zenji out of the abbacy after only four years. His successor, Ōmichi Kōsen (1917–2011, r. 2002–2011), became the twenty-fourth abbot of the new line in 2002.

Ōmichi-zenji held many offices at Sōjiji over his long life, but to many, his abbacy was a sharp about-face from Itabashi-zenji's tenure, focusing more on ensuring Sōjiji's continued survival in the long term through religious conservatism. Those among the laity who had been attracted by Itabashi-zenji's populist style felt alienated by Sōjiji's return to policies that they believed reaffirmed, rather than broke down, the traditional barriers between priest and layperson. Nevertheless, it was my experience that Ōmichi-zenji's presence at official ceremonies guaranteed a large turnout from parishioners and members of the temple community.[32]

In addition to the *zenji*'s abbacal duties at Sōjiji, he also shares the nominal leadership of the Sōtō Zen sect with Eiheiji's abbot. Each *zenji* serves as the titular head of the sect for two years, with the office alternating between the temples. Despite these lofty responsibilities, the *zenji*, according to one priest, is essentially a politician in that aside from ceremonial responsibilities, the abbot's job is to be the public face of Sōjiji and Sōtō Zen by meeting with influential public figures and donors, as well as standing as a model for a life spent in service to the Buddhist path. All of the administrative concerns of the temple are delegated to members of his administration.

Dividing Labor

Following the tradition of the Song-style Chinese monasteries, Sōjiji is split along an invisible east-west axis that serves to divide the labor that takes place within the temple's walls.[33] The Western Division (*seibu*) is the educational half of the temple, overseeing the training of new monks and the coordination of the ritual and ceremonial life of the temple community. In a training temple like Sōjiji, the Western Division can be best described as a seminary; it is in the *seibu* that the novice monks learn the ritual, protocol, and doctrine that they will use in their future lives as professional clergy. The Western Division is nominally under the guidance of a principal known as the Seidō-rōshi. Like many positions in the temple, the Seidō-rōshi is largely a ceremonial role, seldom requiring the priest holding the office to be present. The actual daily life and education of the *unsui* is managed by the Godō-rōshi, the Tantō-rōshi, and the Ino-rōshi, known collectively as the *seibu yakusan* ("officers of the Western Division"). While the positions of Godō and Tantō have long existed in Japanese Zen monasteries, their present portfolios at Sōjiji are a relatively recent innovation, dating from the sectarian reforms of the Meiji period. These two offices were developed to diffuse the heavy burden placed upon the Ino-rōshi, who, as cantor, was not only responsible for the liturgical order and keeping of ritual time during ceremonies, but whose purview also included maintaining the daily schedule of the entire temple, serving as de facto "headmaster" of the training novices, keeping discipline in the Monk's Hall, and ensuring that the temple rules were enforced and proper protocol observed at all times. Below these three teachers are the hall monitors who are tasked with keeping discipline among the *unsui*.

In contrast, the Eastern Division (*tōbu*) houses the administrative and operational offices that govern the daily operations of the temple. If the abbot is the CEO of the temple, then the COO is the rector (*kannin*). The rector is technically third in the hierarchy behind the abbot and deputy abbot, but to his office falls the responsibility of keeping the temple administratively and financially sound both in the present and toward the future. Given the intensity of the work involved, as well as the intimacy with temple operations that comes with the job, the rector is arguably the true head of the temple. As a consequence, rectors are often rewarded for their service by being nominated for the deputy abbacy upon its vacancy.

Below the rector at Sōjiji are seven sections (*ryō*) between which are split the various aspects of temple administration: Planning and General Affairs (*Rokuji*), Comptroller (*Fūsu*), Kitchens (*Tenzo*), Maintenance and Labor (*Shissui*), Propagation and Public Outreach (*Fukyō*), and Ceremony (*Jishin*). The priest in charge of each department takes the title of that department.

While the majority of the *unsui* in the temple are assigned to the "catchall" General Assembly (*Kandoku*), more experienced novices (or younger novices with specialized needs) and recently ordained priests are often assigned to staff a specific administrative department for a period of three months. In each of these departments, responsibilities run from the secretarial (answering phones, receiving guests, serving tea) to the managerial (coordinating work schedules, compiling inventories and budgets, supervising assignees). In some cases, departments that have famous or otherwise absent heads are often run on a daily basis by an assistant department head, who effectively serves as middle management.

The officers who will comprise the temple administration of an abbot's tenure are formally "summoned" to service by the abbot, a tradition that masks the fact that they were selected for the position by the rector and his administrators. If the position is accepted, the priests are expected to serve a term of three years, renewable on a case-by-case basis yearly for up to a total of five years. The priests are monetarily compensated for their work and receive private rooms at Sōjiji during their tenure.

For a younger priest, especially those who are not in line to inherit a temple (for example, second sons and priests who were not born into a clerical family), staying on at Sōjiji after ordination is an important means of establishing a name for oneself within the temple and sect. While a priest with the proper educational pedigree can "graduate" from Sōjiji after six months to a year, many *unsui* are in no rush to start the responsibilities of working at their home temple. Especially for those whose fathers (and even grandfathers) may still be in their working prime, staying on for additional time at Sōjiji is a means of alleviating the financial burden from the clerical family while better preparing himself for his own parish temple.

For an elderly priest, returning for service at Sōjiji can be a comfortable gig—assuming, that is, that the priest wants it in the first place. There is often considerable difficulty in staffing the upper echelons of the temple hierarchy. This is not due to a lack of qualified candidates but rather to a lack of *willing* candidates. As was the case with Sōjiji's rotating abbots during the medieval period, the time and dedication required to adequately do one's job as an officer at a large training temple like Sōjiji conflict and detract from the responsibilities required in caring for one's home temple. Since many of these priests are either close to or at retirement age, it is common for them to turn down positions that would jeopardize their retirement. If they do accept the positions, these older priests often delegate much of their work to their immediate subordinates, younger priests who can be relied on to oversee much of the day-to-day tasks.

The most competitive positions are the "middle management" roles, the immediate assistants to the department heads. As is typical in Japanese corporate structures, these assistants are the ones who are inevitably saddled with the most responsibility. Most often such positions go to mid-career priests—those who often already have significant responsibilities as assistant abbots at their home temples and who are also usually married with children. The additional income from working at a *honzan* is the major reason why the positions are so competitive, often saving priests from having to find second jobs outside of the priesthood to supplement their wages. Still the pressure and need to sacrifice time with one's family and responsibilities is often a difficult price to pay. Although the burden is somewhat lessened the closer one lives to Yokohama, for those whose home temples sit on other coasts or other islands, the result is extended periods away from home (sometimes for weeks or months at a time) or a commute between Sōjiji and their home temples that requires long car, train, or even plane trips.

Priests in these roles arrive and leave at the beginning of their tenure as the novice *unsui* do, in full traveling regalia, as if they were "ascending the mountain" for the first time. However, the older priests have none of the oppressive restrictions on diet or movement that the *unsui* do. For these priests, *shugyō* is in the pressure to perform their responsibilities to the best of their abilities. As they move up the temple hierarchy, they will have more and more people who depend on their decisions and effort. At the same time, they are now expected to keep up appearances. Their subordinates and the visiting public will be watching their every move.

The Idealist Monk

As morning wake-up bells pull the *unsui* out of sleep in the Sōdō, elsewhere in the temple the monks assigned to the kitchens have already been awake for over an hour and a half. The temple kitchen—the Tenzo-ryō—is located in the basement of the Jihōkaku, a modern multistory building behind the Kōshakudai that also houses Sōjiji's administrative offices.[34]

The kitchen prepares food for the monastic community and the temple employees on an industrial scale. Over six hundred servings of food—three meals for more than two hundred people—are prepared each day. Cooking and serving a day's worth of hot meals are important and time-consuming tasks. While the kitchen monks are freed from the obligation of participating in *zazen* and morning ceremonies, theirs is hardly leisure time. From about 2:30 a.m. until about 5:00 p.m., the kitchens are alive with near-constant activity.

Sōjiji's kitchens are thoroughly modern in appearance, resembling the large, bright industrial kitchens of a school or hospital. The walls are a sterile white and dominated by large stainless-steel stoves, shelves, and preparation space. Along two walls are large steel vats where huge batches of white rice are prepared—as gruel in the mornings and as rice to accompany lunch and dinner. Other vats are large enough to contain two hundred servings of soup or whatever else is on the menu for the day. Several pairs of stainless-steel islands are placed throughout the kitchen for chopping vegetables and food preparation. Two walk-in refrigerators dominate another side of the kitchen.

On the wall, a closed-circuit television shows a live video feed from the Daisodō. As soon as morning services are over, the kitchen monks must have breakfast prepared and loaded onto serving trays to be brought to the communal dining hall upstairs. Indeed, the job of the kitchen monks does not end when the food is prepared. In the dining hall, the monks of the kitchens are also the servers who ladle out food to the community. After the meal is finished, they bus the tables and collect the used bowls, chopsticks, and serving utensils. They then clean all of the bowls, cooking instruments, and kitchen area by hand.

It is nearly 7:00 a.m. by the time the kitchen workers are finished with these chores, and they have been awake for almost four and a half hours. Having the discipline to serve others before yourself is a virtue, and it is only when their morning work is finished that those in the kitchen are able to break their own fasts. If everything goes as scheduled, they have enough downtime for a break or even a quick nap before the whole process begins again at 8:00 a.m. for lunch.

Work in the kitchens is physically and mentally demanding, but it was an assignment that a monk named Kodama-san specifically requested. Kodama-san had been at Sōjiji for nearly a decade and was older than the incoming *unsui* by about eight years or so. He had a round face, and his mustard-brown *kesa* hid a healthy fullness that was not shared by the calorie-restricted training *unsui*. He did not wear black thick-rimmed glasses like the younger novices. Rather, he wore clear, round frames that gave him the likeness of a bald John Lennon.

Outside of the kitchens, Kodama-san was a consummate storyteller. He took great pleasure in connecting with the visitors who came to Sōjiji, and he would often stay behind after a ceremony to give a brief sermon to the people sitting in the open area at the rear of the Daisodō. If he felt he had a large enough audience, he would send an *unsui* to fetch an over-the-shoulder PA system, and he would stand in a well-trafficked area to sermonize to anyone who would listen.

In both his sermons and his conversation, Kodama-san masterfully played at double entendre and used Japanese and English homophones to great effect. When he really got going, his speaking was fast, animated, and interlaced with pantomime, funny faces, and sound effects. He often carried a sketch pad with him, on which he would draw cartoon bears and other animals playing the parts of the characters in his stories. At other times, he would pull magic tricks and joke props from the pockets in his robe sleeves to punctuate his stories.

While Kodama-san's role in the kitchens was subordinate to the temple cook, the priest who held the office at the time was in demand throughout

Fig. 12. Kodama-san gives an impromptu sermon on the steps outside the Daisodō.

Japan for his *shōjin ryori* vegetarian cooking and spent very little time at Sōjiji. The day-to-day operations of the kitchens therefore fell to Kodama-san, who bore the responsibility of ensuring that there was always enough food prepared and that the temple community was served exactly on time, three times each day.

Kodama-san took his responsibilities in the kitchen very seriously, knowing that he must serve as a teacher and an exemplar to the younger *unsui* who were assigned to work beneath him. He certainly had his work cut out for him: in addition to having to plan menus for three meals a day, the kitchens are almost always critically understaffed. By Kodama-san's own estimation, it takes about thirty monks to efficiently run the kitchens. However, Sōjiji was understaffed as it was, and the kitchens were requisitioned only twenty bodies. It was Kodama-san's challenge to inspire the *unsui* to push their *shugyō* to the next level.

Kodama-san saw his appointment as a great opportunity to demonstrate to the younger *unsui* lessons like those given by the Chinese temple cook who is said to have deeply influenced Dōgen's understanding of Zen. According to the autobiographical *Tenzo Kyōkun* ("Instructions from the Cook"), Dōgen describes a fortuitous meeting with the cook of a nearby monastery who had come aboard Dōgen's boat while docked in the port of Qinyuan hoping to purchase Japanese mushrooms. Dōgen, sensing ethnographic opportunity, invited the cook to tea and began to ask a series of probing questions about the monk's life and work at the monastery. When Dōgen tried to extend the interview by offering to buy the monk dinner, the monk politely but firmly refused:

> "If I do not oversee the preparations for tomorrow's meal offering, it will not turn out well." [Dōgen] said, "Are there not co-workers in the monastery who understand the meals? What will be deficient if only one officer, the cook, is not present?" The cook said, "I took up this position in my later years, it is this old man's pursuit of the way. How could I hand it over to others? . . ."
>
> [Dōgen] again asked the cook: "You are venerable in years; why don't you sit in meditation to pursue the way or contemplate the words of the ancients? It is troublesome being cook; all you do is labor. What good is that?"[35]

The cook laughed at this brash question: "My good man from a foreign country, you do not yet understand the pursuit of the way and do not yet know about written words!" Dōgen was confused by this statement initially, but he later came to grasp the deeper wisdom behind what the cook had told him: that the work of the temple cook—indeed, the work of any temple officer or administrator—may be time-consuming and mundane, but if one mindfully approaches their responsibilities as *shugyō*, any job or task is a viable path to enlightenment.[36] From this perspective, cooking in the kitchens for twelve hours a day is no different from sitting for twelve hours in the meditation hall.

By his own admission, Kodama-san identified with this temple cook and took seriously his responsibility to provide similar kernels of wisdom and insight to his charges. Every morning, Kodama-san would draw cartoon bears in monastic robes on the whiteboard in the kitchen's small office, conveying through word bubbles lessons of mindfulness or gratitude for the donated food that the monks were preparing and eating. Often, Kodama-san would challenge his subordinates to prepare food in creative ways. On one of the days I volunteered in the kitchen, Kodama-san gave a bored *unsui* a "Zen puzzle" (he used the English loanword). Taking a square block of fried tofu, Kodama-san cut it diagonally into four triangles. He then told the *unsui* to make a shape using three of the four triangles to be served on small dishes and ensuring there was enough tofu for everyone in the temple. The *unsui* played around with the pieces, making various two-dimensional trapezoids and parallelograms that barely fit on the plates. Finally, the *unsui* came up with an answer that fit the serving dishes: a three-dimensional pyramid. Kodama-san praised the *unsui* for his solution and clapped the younger monk on the shoulder.

At other times, Kodama-san would skillfully transform reprimands into teachable moments. One particularly poignant lesson I witnessed occurred when Kodama-san stopped an *unsui* who had been throwing away too much of the head of cabbage that he had been cutting. Kodama-san challenged him to consider the moment that something is transformed from "food" to "garbage." When the *unsui* responded to his question with silence, Kodama-san explained that there is no objective moment in time when "garbage" happens. Rather, the transition happens only in your own mind, at the moment when you mentally determine something is useless and act upon throwing it away. Kodama-san took a strip of stray cabbage from the counter and narrated its slow trajectory into a garbage can: "food, food, food, food, food, garbage." If you are less quick to label something as trash, Kodama-san explained to the *unsui*, you will find that you have a lot less to throw away.

Kodama-san told me that he tried his best to be a good and fair superior (*senpai*) to his subordinates (*kōhai*). The dichotomous *senpai-kōhai* system is a staple of Japanese social organization, found in nearly every aspect of life. When it works best, it establishes a lifelong relationship between superior and subordinate. Ideally, the *senpai-kōhai* relationship forms a chain between past and future: the former were once *kōhai* themselves, while the latter will one day become *senpai* to their own subordinates. At the same time, the system lends itself easily to the possibility of exploitation. Stories of physically and mentally abusive *senpai* are widespread, but so are stories of the dangers of insubordinate and disrespectful *kōhai*.

Kodama-san admitted that he was often frustrated by his charges, who viewed their early morning wake-ups and their tasks in the kitchen as a three-month-long punishment to be endured rather than an opportunity to bring deeper personal meaning to their *shugyō*. He lamented that the *unsui* largely treated the Tenzo-ryō "as a part-time job (*arubaito*), as if they were flipping hamburgers." When he spoke to them, he was fairly certain they were tuning him out completely.

In his own experience, Kodama-san had dealt with several mean and abusive *senpai*, and—like every one of the supervising priests I spoke with—he was determined not to perpetuate a cycle of psychological or physical violence. At the same time, he acknowledged that fear of violent discipline (or lack thereof) did have an effect on the way the *unsui* comported themselves. Without it, the *unsui* were "*otokoppoi*"—"manly"—by which Kodama-san meant arrogant and prideful, swaggering around the temple "like Marlon Brando in *Rebel without a Cause*."[37]

"Pride (*puraido*)," he said with visible frustration, "has no place in a Zen temple."

Not long after this conversation, Kodama-san requested and was granted a transfer to a different temple department when his current term was up. He told me that he felt he had learned all he could in the Tenzo-ryō and was looking forward to a new opportunity to deepen his *shugyō*. While I did not doubt that this was true, I also suspected that—like dedicated teachers everywhere—the daily effort of trying to inspire his team of exhausted and apathetic *unsui* had taken its toll on this humble temple cook.

The Delinquent Monk

Kodama-san's idealized relationship to his priestly role and his work was not shared by all, however. Kodama-san had introduced me to Yanagi-san, a temple priest from a prefecture near Tokyo, one afternoon while the latter was visiting his friend at Sōjiji. The two men's time at Sōjiji had overlapped, and they were twice assigned to the same temple departments. Consequently, they spent a lot of time getting to know each other and had become close friends. Unlike Kodama-san, who stayed behind at Sōjiji to get more experience, Yanagi-san left Sōjiji after a year to return to his home temple. On paper these two men had the same training and qualifications and in fact came from very similar family backgrounds. As I was to discover, however, their personalities and perspectives were polar opposites: Kodama-san's dedication to the ideals and techniques of monastic *shugyō* was met by a spirit of cynicism and rebellion in Yanagi-san that questioned the entire system of which he was a part.

I had arranged to meet up with Yanagi-san on a warm April evening at a small bar near Tsurumi Station. He arrived wearing a worn blue *samue*, the loose-fitting work clothes worn by the monks when they perform manual labor. He was wearing old white sneakers, and a small white towel, tied in the back, covered his shaven head. He carried a shopping bag from a department store and an over-the-shoulder messenger bag. Nothing about the way he carried himself necessarily advertised "Zen monk." The only thing that had the potential to give away his status was the work clothes, which are often worn as street clothes by Buddhist clergy of all sects. Unlike the formal robes and *kesa*, however, a *samue* can be purchased and worn by anyone.

Once we were seated in our booth, I ordered a beer and Yanagi-san ordered a glass of water. I assumed I would be drinking alone, but just as soon as our waiter dropped off our drinks and left, Yanagi-san poked his head around the corner and, seeing that the coast was clear, reached into an inner pocket to pull out a hip flask full of liquor. He poured several quaffs of the alcohol into his water and mixed the drink with his finger. "Alcohol gets expensive, you know?" he shrugged with a smile. "This way is cheaper." He deftly slipped the flask back into his pocket, raised his glass in cheers, and took a deep sip.

Our conversation was casual and quickly turned toward shared interests. Yanagi-san had always loved American movies, and he mentioned recently having seen *The Godfather, Part III*. The movie made an impression on him, he said, particularly "the story about the bad priest," referring to the character of Archbishop Gilday, the sinister Vatican priest who plots to embezzle millions from the Corleone family and is instrumental in the fictional conspiracy that ends in the murder of the pope.

Yanagi-san described feeling struck by the parallels between the movie's portrayal of greed and other ethical compromises within the Vatican hierarchy with his own experiences as a clergyman in an institutionalized religion. In his mind, it was not difficult to trace the moral progression from a priest who started his career with honest and pious intentions to one who later extorts sizable bribes from rich donors wanting to redeem their guilty consciences. Religious institutions like temples and churches are dependent on donations, he told me, but instead of helping all people equally, much time and energy is spent—"wasted" (*sutete shimatta*), in his opinion—courting and catering to the wishes of wealthy benefactors:

If you have money, you can get anything you want from a priest: a prestigious posthumous name (*erai kaimyō*), a big grave for your family, even your own private temple! We're happy to accept donations from anyone: politicians, businessmen, and criminals. It doesn't matter. We don't ask where the money came from. Even if the money came from crime, we tell the person that they're doing a good deed. If they give enough money, we'll inscribe their names on the temple. In a hundred years, people will remember them as a great friend of Buddhism instead of a criminal.

Even in fiction, watching the Vatican bestow a papal honor on gangster Michael Corleone in exchange for $250 million helped Yanagi-san come to the conclusion that, despite superficial differences, Sōtō Zen is no different from any other institutionalized religion.

Yanagi-san explained that the archbishop in the movie probably didn't start off intending to be bad. His descent into malfeasance likely started with an ethical compromise or a bad choice. Like a reverse *shugyō*, the poor moral choices he cultivated became habitual until the priest had strayed absolutely from his path, nothing more than a charlatan in clerical robes. "As I watched the movie, I wondered what he thought about himself. I thought that it must have made him feel very guilty."

For a moment, Yanagi-san looked past me, staring at the wall. "I thought that maybe I was a lot like him, you know?"

As our friendship progressed, he started signing his emails as "delinquent monk" (*furyō bōzu*). The more I got to know him, the more he opened up to me about his "vices." He drinks. He has eaten meat all of his life. He smoked while he was at Sōjiji, but his wife made him quit.

Are drinking alcohol, eating meat, and smoking sins worth the guilt Yanagi-san was feeling? This is a complicated question.

While Buddhist tradition holds that the Buddha himself handed down clear instructions for the daily living and comportment of his followers, compilations of these rules of conduct for Buddhist monastics (known as *vinaya*) are a literary genre unto themselves, with many competing versions and no singular definitive work. In China the most commonly used list of monastic vows based on the *Four Part Vinaya* counted 10 precepts for novices and 250 precepts for fully ordained clergy.[38] The taking of these vows was a matter of official certification and set the state-recognized clergy apart from the laity as well as from charlatans. Later, a separate list of 10 major and 48 minor prohibitions, known as the Bodhisattva precepts, was developed primarily to be administered to lay adherents in large public ceremonies that doubled as fund-raising events. By the late Tang period, it was common for Chinese monastics to receive the exhaustive list of *vinaya* precepts as well as the newer list of Bodhisattva precepts.

When Buddhism arrived in Japan from the mainland in the eighth century CE, the first Japanese monastics continued in this tradition of receiving both the *vinaya* precepts and the Bodhisattva precepts. Not long after, Saichō (767–822), the founder of the Japanese Tendai Buddhist sect, argued that the 250-article *vinaya* precepts were no longer relevant to Japanese monastics.[39] To his disciples, Saichō transmitted only the ten major and forty-eight minor bodhisattva precepts. Dōgen, originally ordained as a Tendai monk at Mount Hiei, would have received them in this manner.

During Dōgen's journey to Song China, he faced difficulty securing permission to train at official state Ch'an monasteries; having not received the *vinaya* precepts, he was not recognized as a legitimate Buddhist monastic.[40] No records indicate that Dōgen ever took the *vinaya* precepts in order to practice in China; instead, it is believed that Dōgen's Chinese teacher, Rujing (Jp. Tendō Nyōjō), likely accepted Dōgen's limited bodhisattva precepts as they were.

Sōtō tradition holds that when Dōgen returned to Japan bearing the Sōtō Zen lineage, he began ordaining both monastics and the laity using a new list of sixteen precepts as opposed to the fifty-eight that he received during his own Tendai ordination.[41] As described in the *Shushōgi*, this abridged list includes the Three Refuges (in the Buddha, the Dharma, and the Sangha), the Three Pure Precepts ("renounce all evil, perform every good, and save all sentient beings"), and the Ten Major Prohibitions:

Do not kill	不殺生戒
Do not steal	不偸盗戒
Do not engage in improper sexual conduct	不邪婬戒
Do not lie	不妄語戒
Do not deal in intoxicating beverages	不酤酒戒
Do not criticize others	不説過戒
Do not praise oneself and slander others	不自讃毀他戒
Do not covet either the Dharma or property	不慳法財戒
Do not give way to anger	不瞋恚戒
Do not disparage the Three Treasures[42]	不謗三宝戒[43]

Of crucial importance to the establishment of a clerical identity in Japan generally was the observance of the first, third, and fifth prohibitions: following a strict interpretation, premodern Buddhist clerics were specifically prohibited from eating meat, from having sex and getting married, and from consuming alcohol. By the Tokugawa period, these religious precepts became codified into the law of the state; a Buddhist cleric found in violation of these three precepts could incur punishments ranging from defrocking to public shaming to execution.[44]

During the period of Imperial restoration after 1868, the new government of the nascent Japanese polity realized that the Buddhist institution, which had willingly collaborated with the Tokugawa government for more than two hundred years, presented a danger to the new political hegemony. In an attempt to limit the numbers and authority of the Buddhist clergy in the new political field, the Meiji government passed a series of ordinances that became known as the *nikujiki saitai* ("Eat Meat and Marry") laws: after 1872 the Japanese Buddhist clergy was permitted—and in some cases mandated—to eat meat, drink alcohol, and have sexual relations.[45] In theory, this amounted to a legal defrocking of the Buddhist community intended to deny the clergy their previous tax-free status, diminish their authority in the eyes of the populace, and limit their ability to organize and mount a resistance against the nascent government on ideological grounds. In practice, however, these laws would fundamentally transform how Buddhist clergy would negotiate and understand their clerical identities in modern Japanese society.

Most crucial was a change in the force of the precepts within the Buddhist sects themselves: what had previously been "grave prohibitions" became personal aspirations, lacking the ethical and punitive force they once carried. Interestingly, this reinterpretation of the precepts coincided with the rise in influence of Japanese Buddhism's traditional religious antagonist: missionary Christianity. Corresponding to the rise of Christian missionary and charitable activities in Japan in the late Meiji and early Taishō periods, the Ten Major Prohibitions were publicly presented in counterpoint to the Judeo-Christian Ten Commandments. Whereas the Ten Commandments proclaimed "thou shalt not" (-*suru na*), the Buddhist clergy claimed that the Buddhist precepts carried the message of "thou shalt try not to" (-*shinakute miyō*), evidence that Buddhism was a more loving and forgiving religion than Christianity claimed to be.[46]

In many ways this reinterpretation of the precepts from religious mandate to a lifestyle suggestion was a double-edged sword. On the one hand, it rendered the new legal "freedoms" of the clergy intelligible to both the clergy and the laity while preserving the clergy's self-image as faithful custodians of Buddhist tradition. On the other, it virtually dissolved the key social barriers distinguishing the clergy from the laity, leaving the Buddhist clergy to come to terms with what "maintaining the precepts" actually means in modern Japan.[47] For some in the clergy, these blurred lines contribute to a personal crisis of identity and responsibility that they are often forced to face alone.

From my interviews and conversations, I found members of Sōjiji's lay community to be quite comfortable with the idea of the Buddhist clergy drinking alcohol and eating meat. They realize that it is the exceptional priest who does *not* partake of these things. In contrast, I found that it is largely American and European Zen enthusiasts who most often express a sense of disenchantment and even anger when they see the Buddhist clergy eating meat or drinking alcohol. At one English-language *zazen* group I attended in Tokyo, I was taken aback when the post-meeting discussion turned vitriolic toward the Japanese Zen clergy, who the non-Japanese members of the group believed were ignoring or even purposefully violating their monastic vows.

Still, many priests that I met during my fieldwork, especially those in leadership and teaching roles at Sōjiji and in the Sōtō Zen sect, were conscious of the potential for such behavior to be seen as contradictory and even hypocritical by the laity.[48] Even when alcohol was served at temple functions, funerals, or end-of-year celebrations, I rarely saw a ranking priest eating meat or imbibing alcohol while publicly performing his role as clergy. It was only afterward, either in private parties or in groups with other clergy, that I saw priests eating and drinking with less inhibition.

The priests I spoke with who kept to vegetarianism or avoided alcohol usually had a ready explanation as to why they did so, often citing the health benefits of a meat-free diet or a dislike for the taste or the effects of alcohol. Not a single priest I spoke with said they refrained because of their clerical vows or because it was something they were supposed to do. If eating meat and drinking alcohol were Yanagi-san's vices, he was certainly not alone among his fellow Sōtō clergy.[49]

It was only toward the end of my first fieldwork trip, after months of hanging out with Yanagi-san, that he finally revealed what had been weighing so heavily on his conscience. In the middle of dinner one evening, he innocuously paused the conversation to call his wife. But then he handed me his cell phone: "Joshua, would you explain to my wife that I'm out with you, and not another woman?" I assumed he was joking, and using my politest Japanese, I introduced myself and apologized to his wife for keeping her husband away from home.

After ending the call, he immediately apologized and explained what had just happened. He was in a miserable marriage, he confessed, and his wife's bursts of anger were regular and fearsome. "She yells at me for coming home late. She yells at me that I don't make enough money. She yells at me that we don't live close enough to a train station. I'm happier when I'm not at home," he said, visibly browbeaten.[50]

He and his wife were an arranged marriage. She was the daughter of a close friend of his father's, and on the three or four dates they had, she "seemed like she would make a good wife." They were married in a Buddhist wedding ceremony soon after, about two years before I met him. Hearing him tell the story, they sounded like the worst two years of his life.

Arranged marriages like Yanagi-san's are relatively commonplace within the Buddhist clergy in Japan. A priest's father is often the one to introduce his son to a potential wife, often the daughter of another clergyman or of a parishioner. Such marriages, once arranged, happen quickly, usually too soon for either party to really get to know their future spouse. Frequently they are marriages of mutual benefit: if a family has two sons, as in Yanagi-san's case, the second son is often married into a clerical family that has a marriageable daughter but no son. In this arrangement, the eldest son will inherit his natal family's temple, and the second son will be adopted into his wife's family and become heir to his father-in-law's temple.

An arrangement such as this is usually a relationship of mutual convenience; since parishioners are generally interested only in the continuity of custodians to care for their ancestors, they retain the right to force out a parish priest who does not have a successor lined up. Particularly if a priest has only daughters, finding a suitable son-in-law can mean the difference between a priest and his wife being allowed to remain in their homes in advanced age or not. While this follows many of the strategies that the Japanese have traditionally employed to guarantee continuity of the family line, it bears mentioning that such strategies are a relatively new innovation for the Sōtō Zen clergy—at most four or five generations, at this point.

I asked Yanagi-san if it would be possible to get a divorce. While it is legally possible, he told me, priests who get divorced run the risk of mortally wounding their reputations and professional prospects. "I'm a priest. How would it look to the parishioners if priests get divorced?" he rhetorically asked. "We're responsible for caring for our parishioner families, but if priests get divorced, all it shows is that we can't even take care of our own families."[51] Making matters difficult in his case was that the temple is not yet "his"—as assistant abbot, it still belongs to his father-in-law. A divorce from his wife would certainly cost Yanagi-san his current position and, quite possibly, his chance at ever having his own temple.

Treading carefully, I asked him why his wife would think that he was out with another woman. "Before I met her, I was with a lot of women. My wife asked me about it once, and I told her. *That* was a mistake!" He took a sip of his drink.

Yanagi-san described, matter-of-factly, that he is a man with a sex drive. He had resigned himself that there is nothing—no ascetic practice, no religious precept—that can stop that. He thinks about sex often and he dreams about it. It only gets worse when he drinks.

But there was something more. He hesitated for a moment. "I'm in love with another woman," he finally told me. A mutual friend introduced them at a gathering, and they hit it off immediately. As Yanagi-san described her, this woman sounded like everything that his wife was not: understanding, nurturing, and even-tempered. He told me that his wife suspects that there was someone else, if she didn't know outright. "Every night, it's 'Where were you? Who were you with?'"

Of all of his clerical vows, the vow to not have "improper" sexual relations was the one that was causing him the most concern. "I'm allowed to have sex with my wife, who I don't love. I'm *not* allowed to have sex with my girlfriend, who I do love. That's backwards, don't you think?"

Complicating matters further is the fact that his wife had just given birth to a child. He didn't want to tell me its name or gender. "I don't want to get attached to the baby. The baby is adorable. But my wife has already threatened to take it away and never let me see it." I asked him if he thought she was serious about this threat. "Probably," he said with sadness.

"Even if my wife leaves *me*, everyone will say it's my fault. They'll say I abandoned my wife and child. She probably won't get remarried, because in Japan women only get 'one strike.'[52] My child will get bullied for not having a father. When I think about these things, all I want to do is run away." The weight on his conscience was palpable.

"Do you know what I don't understand? Why can the Buddha be a bad father and not me?"

This statement requires some explanation. According to some Buddhist textual traditions, the historical Buddha was, to use the modern term, a "deadbeat dad." After his royal wife gave birth to a son, a not-yet-enlightened Śākyamuni woefully proclaimed that "a bondage has been born." When the future Buddha fled his palace and pleasure garden to pursue the transient life of a world-renouncing ascetic, this also meant abandoning his wife and infant son.[53] "Even the Buddha knew that babies and monks are like oil and water," Yanagi-san said. "They can't mix."

Yanagi-san missed the freedom he had before he was married (an ironic statement, given his religious obligations and the public pressures of his profession), and he believed that the custom of arranged marriage really failed in his case. He had no one to talk to about his problem and had been suffering in silence for more than a year. He didn't feel that he could tell his father or older brother, and he was afraid of confiding in his friends for fear that gossip would come back to haunt him and his career.

I slowly came to realize the weight of what Yanagi-san, the self-proclaimed "delinquent monk," was wrestling with. In both their training and in their professional lives, Sōtō Zen clergy are expected to embody in word and deed the enlightenment, grace, and compassion of the Buddha. Indeed, an overwhelming majority of Sōtō clergy report a desire to "live their life as a priest proudly" and to be an "example for their parishioners."[54] To a large extent, however, many in the clergy are ultimately left to their own devices to navigate contradictory personal, social, and familial obligations and pressures—pressures that the Buddha himself famously could not reconcile. The Buddha was able to escape from his worldly responsibilities, but Buddhist clergy in Japan today do not have this option. Instead, they face public and private pressure to resolve an existential contradiction that has vexed Buddhism from its very beginnings: how can a person balance the expectations to live the ascetic, disciplined life of a world-renouncer with the everyday obligations to one's family, community, and the state?[55]

For those like Yanagi-san who struggle with these questions, the answer can be a life spent in perpetual guilt, a never-ending struggle to reconcile the high personal standards and social expectations of their profession with not only the financial, professional, and familial obligations common in contemporary Japan but also with their own human desires, passions, and fears. It's not fair, Yanagi-san conceded, but he feels that all he can do is to "endure" (*ganbare*).

Still, he tries to be optimistic. He told me that he had read an article in a magazine that gave him a measure of comfort. According to the author, the best marriage is the one where the husband and wife have different hobbies and interests and don't talk to each other, even to the point where they are living virtually separate lives. "That's the most comfortable (*raku*) way," he says. "And that's probably the only way for me."

"The Path of the Buddha Is a Difficult Road"

Kodama-san and Yanagi-san are only two of the more than two dozen priests from across the Sōtō sect who shared with me their stories, memories, and reflections of their time at Sōjiji. While these two priests' personal narratives are not necessarily generalizable—it would be incorrect to say that all priests who come out of Sōjiji are as idealistic as Kodama-san or as conflicted as Yanagi-san—their stories are instructive in demonstrating how Sōtō clergy differently internalize the lessons of *shugyō*, and the dif-

ferent ways this mandate to self-cultivation shapes the experience and perspective they bring to their clerical careers.

As of 2019 there are over twenty thousand registered Sōtō Zen clergy
in Japan, but they all have two experiences in common: a period of time
spent in a *shugyō dōjō* and the difficulties inherent in being a Buddhist priest
in modern Japan.[56] Between the conflicting personal, social, familial, and
religious obligations; the income and opportunity costs of living the life of
a clergyman; and the energy and dedication required to keep and attract
parishioners against the powerful tide of demographic change, a priest's
life is neither easy nor comfortable. As the *unsui* are warned as they take
their very first steps into the temple, the path of the Buddha is a hard road
to walk.

There is a general recognition within the sect that, owing to the "stag-
nating of the religious life of the temple" (*jiin no shūkyō katsudō no tait-
eika*), attracting and retaining new clergy is becoming increasingly difficult.[57] Compared to previous generations, there is a particular difficulty
in attracting people from outside the temple family who are interested or
willing to take on the roles of a priest. In 1985 non-temple sons made up
more than a quarter of the Sōtō clergy; now they account for just over a
tenth of the clerical population.[58]

This problem dovetails with the issue that the Sōtō clergy, like the Japanese population in general, is aging quickly. The median age of a parish
priest is now 61.1 years and has been steadily increasing over the past thirty
years.[59] On average, a temple son will not inherit his home temple until he
is close to 50 years old, more than twenty-five years after he finishes his
training.[60] A prospective or newly minted priest is aware that he will not
have a livelihood from the temple for more than half of his life, virtually
necessitating his finding a second career if he wants to support a family of
his own. This hard calculus has led to a crisis of manpower within the sect,
and today almost a quarter of all Sōtō temples—more than two thousand
temples—do not have plans for succession.[61]

For Sōjiji's administrative officers, attending to the future of the sect
is just one of several simultaneously pressing concerns. From the abbot
on down, *shugyō* means dedicating themselves to the daily operation of a
large institution whose mission it is to ensure that the history, traditions,
rituals, teachings, and values of Sōtō Zen are successfully passed on to the
next generation of clergy and, through them, to the sect's parishioners and
adherents. But to impart the past necessitates an engagement with both the
present and the future, and this is something with which the Sōjiji administration has at times been slow to come to terms.

As with many traditionalist institutions, there is an understandable resistance among the administration to making compromises or concessions to the present. Indeed, in these contexts the value of tradition is believed to lie precisely in its applicability *to* the present. From the perspective of the priests responsible for training a generational cohort that is often spoken of as lacking in cultural values, obsessed with themselves, and emotionally soft, monastic *shugyō* is a necessary corrective to the ills of the modern world. In this light, considering changes to the monastic education program to appeal to and address the future needs of younger generations is a slippery and dangerous slope. Herein lies the tension between the idealistic Kodama-san and his exhausted and disinterested subordinates in the kitchens. Here, as well, lies the tension between the traditional Buddhist and Confucian values that were impressed upon Yanagi-san during his time at Sōjiji and his lonely struggle to reconcile them with the complexities of the modern world and human heart.

However, in my observations, interactions, and conversations with the ranking priests within Sōjiji administration, what I witnessed more than anything else was an understanding that the rigid discipline of *shugyō* must be tempered with generous compassion. Veteran priests, particularly those in supervisory roles, were not blind or deaf to the difficulties of the strictly disciplined and regimented life of an *unsui*. Still, they understood at a personal level that the *unsui*'s time at Sōjiji, difficult as it may be, is nothing compared to the actual journey of life as a temple priest that is ahead of them. The *unsui* who have the best chance to succeed in their careers are not necessarily those who have a rote mastery of ritual (though this is, of course, important) but rather those who are most able to cultivate compassion for the suffering of others out of the discipline and rigors of their training. Embodying enlightenment, these priests knew, is a twenty-four-hour-a-day job.

FOUR

Struggling for Enlightenment (While Keeping Your Day Job)

On any given Sunday, Sōjiji and its precincts are alive with the sounds and sights of activity. Spend even an hour doing nothing more than watching and listening, and a person will come to understand that the sound of Zen is far from silent.

From the Daisodō and the Hōkōdō, the deep boom of the large bell and metallic ring of the assembly gong marks the rhythm for the memorial ceremonies that take place all day, with one ceremony blending seamlessly into another. As one approaches the buildings, the rhythmic drone of the monks' chanting fills the air.

A steady stream of visitors climbs the stairs to the Daisodō, likely drawn as much by the impressive size of the hall as they are by the sounds of activity coming from the inside. Upon entering the hall, Japanese visitors generally have a sense of what to do: pinches of incense are offered, hands are pressed together, and heads are briefly bowed. As a capstone to the visit, anywhere between several to a handful of coins are thrown into the massive wooden donation box that stands between the doorway and the inner hall. At Sōjiji the sound of the coins falling through the layers of wooden slats built into the coffer provides a staccato to the continuo of the ritual taking place in the inner hall. Some people even try to time their offering of coins to conspicuously correspond with key moments in the ceremony.

Outside the hall, cars and taxis regularly drive up the paved driveway, bringing parishioners to the cemetery to visit family graves. Tourists walk through the garden, stopping regularly for selfies and posed photographs that try in vain to capture both themselves and the entirety of the buildings behind them. Other visitors are locals from Tsurumi for whom Sōjiji, sitting on its hill above the city, is a regular stop on their daily walks. Picnickers, often several mothers together with their children, camp out on the green spaces underneath the trees. Their children are free to run around the temple buildings, their voices transforming the landscape from a disciplined space into a playground of discovery. From the treetops, the crows that make Sōjiji their home call out to each other. The light wind that blows through the broad leaves of the evergreen trees rattles the wooden windows and doors of the halls in their frames.

Inside, a constant rumble of footsteps echoes through the temple halls. Groups of *unsui* barrel up and down the corridors of the temple on their way to various parts of the temple complex. Visiting tour groups—often between five and thirty people—are led through the halls by monks serving as tour guides, each step creaking the wood beneath their feet. Likewise, black-clad parishioner families are led through the halls in fifteen-minute intervals on their way to their individually sponsored ceremonies in the Hōkōdō or the Daisodō.

Every so often the public address system comes alive to make an announcement, audible from speakers in every part of the temple complex. The announcement always begins and ends with a noticeable pop as the microphone is turned on or off.

The bell in the clock tower is rung every twenty minutes, a constant reminder of the passage of time. If one does manage to lose track of the time, be assured that the daily newspaper is delivered to the doors of several of the temple's residence halls by motorbike courier precisely at three in the afternoon.

But while the rest of the temple precincts are filled with noise and movement, the members of Sōjiji's Nichiyō Sanzenkai—the Sunday *zazen* group—sit cross-legged within a darkened hall in meditative silence. A sign outside the door reads "*Zazen* in progress. Please be quiet."

The participants of the Sanzenkai have come from all over the Tokyo and Yokohama metropolitan area—some traveling for more than two hours each way—to spend their Sunday afternoon at Sōjiji sitting silently on a cushion and gazing with downcast eyes at a wall in a darkened room. For many, this time is the highlight of their week—a refuge from the constant bombardment of information and stressors of the modern world.

Zazen

The practice of *zazen* is in many ways fundamental to the identity of the Sōtō Zen sect. The Japanese word *zen* is an abbreviation and localization of the Chinese *chan'na*, itself a transliteration of the Sanskrit word *dhyana*, and which, as a fourth-order rendering, is glossed into English as "meditation."[1] The character *"za"* lends itself to a simpler reading, meaning "to sit." A common translation of *zazen* from Japanese to English, therefore, has been "seated meditation."

On the one hand, this translation allows for an expedient means of conveying to a nonspecialist reader what the practice of *zazen* might be like. Thanks to popular media, the word "meditation" conjures images of a person sitting cross-legged on a cushion, eyes closed, and drawing deep breaths. This is not far off from the truth.

What makes the brand of *zazen* put forth by the Sōtō Zen sect distinctive is that it lacks a focal point upon which practitioners are supposed to train their attention. While the body is positioned similarly to other forms of meditation, a *zazen* practitioner is specifically instructed *not* to focus on any image or thought. One priest described it to me this way: "If meditation (*mokusō*) means 'focus on an object', then *zazen* is different. *Zazen* is also different from 'empty mind' (*mushin*). If empty mind happens during *zazen*, then it's by accident. It's not something you should focus on doing."

Instead, Sōtō *zazen* practitioners are entreated to "just sit" (*tada suwaru*). This "just sitting" is the core of the Sōtō Zen concept of *shikantaza*: the idea that any mental effort—even focusing on the act of not-focusing—is a tether that ties the mind to the material, and thus ephemeral and illusory, world. In the *Fukan Zazengi*, Dōgen writes that the practitioner must "give up the operations of mind, intellect, and consciousness" and "stop measuring with thoughts, ideas, and views."[2] Similarly, Keizan, writing in the *Zazen Yōjinki*, tells the practitioner to "sit without doing anything."[3] By training the body to "just sit," a *zazen* practitioner ideally trains the mind to do the same. According to Sōtō Zen teachings, it was in this way that the Buddha was able to learn to let go of his mental associations and physical and emotional attachments to the world. This perfect state of living fully in the present moment without the chain reaction of thoughts about the past or the future is the essence of enlightenment (*satori*).

The practice of *zazen* has a foundational place in the historical identity of the Japanese Sōtō Zen school, as it is through their roles as inheritors of this practice that the Zen clergy claim their legitimacy as heirs of the Buddha's enlightenment. However, there is the danger of essentializing meditation as being *the* characteristic of Zen practice. Sōtō Zen priests today spend remarkably little of their lives in *zazen*—at best, an hour a day while undergoing the rigors of monastic training and seldom after that once their training is done. To state categorically that *zazen* defines the Sōtō Zen tradition is to miss or ignore that the reality of Sōtō Zen religious practice is found in the regular performance of rituals, funerals, and memorial services.

Worse, this identification of *zazen* with Zen contributes to a situation in which some in the public perceive that priests who do not focus their efforts on meditation are somehow "doing it wrong." For non-Japanese in particular, this association fuels the Orientalist fantasy in which all Zen temples feature round-the-clock meditation and all Zen priests are fonts of enlightened wisdom willing to drop everything to further the spiritual journey of the religious tourist knocking at their temple door—a not uncommon misconception that can lead to disillusionment and outright resentment when the reality proves differently.

It is another common misperception that all Zen temples have opportunities for laypersons to practice *zazen*; today only about 20 percent of Sōtō temples do, up from roughly 10 percent in the 1980s.[4] Many would-be Zen seekers are surprised to find that in the vast majority of Sōtō Zen temples in Japan, *zazen* is not practiced at all; the model priest is the one who diligently ministers to the ritual needs of his parishioners and their ancestors, not the one who meditates.

Nichiyō Sanzenkai

As a training temple, Sōjiji can perhaps be held to a different standard than a neighborhood parish temple: at Sōjiji daily *zazen* is expected of the training priests. For many of the *unsui*, this is the only time in their lives that they practice *zazen* with any regularity. Moreover, having put forth *zazen* as a lay-accessible form of physical, mental, and spiritual cultivation since the Meiji period, it would be odd for the flagship of the Sōtō Zen sect not to offer the public a setting for the practice of *zazen*. Sōjiji's Sunday Sanzenkai has been in existence since the earliest days after Sōjiji's move to Tsurumi, though its character has changed dramatically over the course of the last century.

The word *sanzen* has traditionally been used in Chinese and in the Japanese Rinzai and Ōbaku Zen contexts to refer to the act of a person who comes to learn at the feet of a wise Zen teacher. Dōgen, however, dramatically reinterpreted this usage in the *Zazengi* fascicle of the *Shōbōgenzō*. The first lines of this fascicle state unequivocally that "*sanzen* is *zazen*" (*sanzen wa zazen nari*). This statement by Dōgen has been used in modern times to show how the Sōtō Zen sect "democratized" (or, alternatively, "laicized") meditation practice by removing the status differential inherent in the traditional usage. Indeed, the remainder of the *Zazengi* fascicle details instructions for the proper practice of *zazen*, none of which require the presence or instruction of anyone but the practitioner.

Historically speaking, it was not the accessibility of *zazen* that gave Sōtō Zen its broad appeal. Despite Dōgen's instructions, *zazen* was considered to be the sole purview of the clergy rather than an activity accessible to the laity. Indeed, the practice of *zazen* by the Sōtō Zen clergy contributed to their public mystique and was perceived to be the source of the priests' power over death itself, allowing them to perform funerals and memorial ceremonies for the laity that could bestow immediate enlightenment on the dead.[5]

After the sudden loss of political and economic influence in the wake of the Meiji Restoration, the Sōtō Zen sect—and indeed the Japanese Buddhist institution as a whole—scrambled to demonstrate their loyalty to the new political hegemony, as personified in the figure of the emperor. Brian Victoria demonstrates that from 1904 to 1945 *zazen* was increasingly and publicly put forth by influential Zen clergy and scholars as a disciplining tool that could forge a powerful and obedient military and citizenry that was unwavering in its loyalty to the Japanese polity.[6] Ironically, this use of *zazen* to create obedient subjects of an authoritarian regime was the strongest argument for the democratization of *zazen* practice: "Everyone in contemporary Japan could utilize the power of Zen, just as everyone could benefit from its 'strikingly clear and thorough teaching on life and death.'"[7]

As with the founding of social charities, Japanese Buddhism in the post-Meiji era borrowed much from the playbook of Christian missionaries and churches. The Buddhist clergy, long accustomed to their status as the legally mandated recipients of material and financial donations from the laity, now turned to missionary, charitable, and catechistic works in an effort to stay competitive in the widening religious field in Japan.[8] Sōjiji, recently moved to Tsurumi, was in a unique position to reinvent itself and its efforts as a religious institution. Almost immediately following Sōjiji's official opening, a Sunday school was established to encourage young people to identify with and benefit from Sōtō Zen teachings. Local women were similarly invited to join the temple's women's group (Fujinkai). The women of the Fujinkai not only provided a ready source of participants for ceremonies but also served an auxiliary purpose by sewing and repairing the robes of the *unsui* as they took tea and listened to sermons. It is in this same vein that the Nichiyō Kōwakai (Sunday lecture group) was established in 1916 as a means for the temple to reach out to its new neighbors. With women and children having their own organizations, the Kōwakai was primarily—though not exclusively—a men's group that would meet on Sundays to listen to the clergy deliver sermons.

This emphasis on sermons declined in the years following the Pacific War, and around 1950 the Kōwakai was reborn as the Nichiyō Sanzenkai, as a group focused on the practice of *zazen*. Throughout the "Zen boom" of the 1960s and 1970s, Sōjiji was poised to attract much of the international interest in Zen, as made popular by the writings of authors such as Eugen Herrigel, D. T. Suzuki, Jack Kerouac, and Alan Watts. Owing to its fortunate placement between the Port of Yokohama and what would become Haneda Airport, Sōjiji was uniquely situated to attract the waves of international visitors who were arriving in Japan. Photographs of the Nichiyō Sanzenkai from the 1970s reveal an ethnically diverse participant base, with international practitioners sitting alongside Japanese members. However, when Sōjiji's introspective turn came during the 1980s, the Sanzenkai followed suit. Participation by non-Japanese dropped off dramatically as the temple increasingly devoted more of its energies toward the ritual needs of its Japanese parishioner base.

Today the Sanzenkai is the largest and most accessible of lay organizations at Sōjiji, with over four hundred newcomers coming to try *zazen* each year. Of all the temple groups, the Sanzenkai remains the best equipped to handle non-Japanese speaking visitors, since a good number of members possess conversational English skills because of educational or professional necessity. The Sanzenkai was established as a not-for-profit group, and the modest participation fees collected each week are put toward a donation to the temple in gratitude for the use of space, in addition to the purchasing and upkeep of cushions and slippers, and other incidental costs. A small group of volunteer officers (*sewanin*) form the administrative core of the group. Though officially under the auspices of Sōjiji's Propagation Department, the group's operations are managed almost exclusively by these lay officers.

Membership and Motivations

The average attendance at a Sanzenkai meeting is sixty people, making Sōjiji's group one of the largest *zazen* gatherings in Japan. Attendance by over eighty participants is considered exceptional but not uncommon. Of these participants, between five and twenty people are first-time visitors, with roughly half of this number formally joining the group as "new members" (*nyūkaisha*).

This last figure should strike the reader as curious. Assuming six new members per week, the Sanzenkai should see an increase of approximately three hundred new members over the course of a year. Indeed, this is precisely what the official numbers show, and the Nichiyō Sanzenkai boasts more than four thousand officially registered members. On paper, all of the other lay groups at Sōjiji put together have only a fraction of the membership of the Sanzenkai.

These numbers require some explanation, however. The figure of four thousand members represents the total number of *registered* members, not active members. If one were to look at *active* membership, just 1–2 percent of the official membership are ever accounted for during a regular Sunday practice. When I mentioned this to one of the officers of the group, I was told that a long-standing joke is that "if all of the members of the Sanzenkai decided to show up on the same day, the line would stretch all the way down to Tsurumi Station."

Why, then, is there such a dramatic difference between the official membership number and the number of actual practitioners? One answer might be the low cost of membership. When a person comes to the Sanzenkai for the first time, they are given the option between a "one-day experience" (*ichinichi taiken*) and full membership in the group. While the one-day experience costs 500 yen (US$4.75), the onetime "membership fee"—which comes with a welcome packet containing instructions for *zazen*, a membership certificate, and a slim sect-published handbook titled "Essentials of Sanzen" (*Sanzen Yōten*[9])—is only slightly more expensive at 1000 yen (US$9.50). Since membership in the Sanzenkai comes with no additional personal or financial obligation, many first-time participants simply find full membership to be the better deal. Statistically speaking, however, the odds of a new member becoming a regular participant are astonishingly small. Most new members come for one session and never come again.[10]

Some conversations and observations over the course of my research were very instructive as to possible reasons for the low retention rate of younger members and women generally. Conversations with "onetimers"— members who officially registered with the group but never came back— show that in many cases they paid for their membership in the Sanzenkai with the best of intentions. Time constraints were one of the main reasons people cited for not continuing with *zazen* practice at Sōjiji. One woman I spoke with really enjoyed her experience of *zazen* at Sōjiji but since that first meeting simply had not found the time to return. She worked full-time as a nurse while attending night classes, and a six-hour commitment on Sunday—four hours of the Sanzenkai itself plus commuting time—was just too much for her to regularly commit to participation. "I always think to myself, 'This week, I'll go,'" she told me. "But when Sunday comes, I always have something to do." Other people acknowledged that their experience of *zazen* was a welcome break from their always-on-the-go daily lives, but, ironically, many of these participants could not find the time to sit *zazen* a second time.

Other reasons for short-term membership hint at a disjunction between expectations generated by representations of *zazen* in the popular media and the realities of *zazen* practice in a temple setting. One man had attended Sōjiji's Sanzenkai three or four times since joining but complained that the group was too big and impersonal. He preferred to find a smaller *zazenkai* closer to his home, where he might have a chance to interact and ask questions of the temple priest. One woman found that *zazen* really wasn't what she thought it would be and instead found a yoga group that gave her the spiritual and meditative outlet she was looking for. Another man thought that *zazen* would be a good way of deepening his martial arts practice but left Sōjiji after complaining that *zazen* practice there was too "easy." Several people reported that their first experience was marred by the discomfort of sitting and feelings of stress and anxiety they felt when left alone with their thoughts.

However, the most troubling answer came from a woman named Ms. Kojima, a three-year member of the Sanzenkai. Ms. Kojima enjoyed *zazen* practice and "loved" the atmosphere at Sōjiji but struggled with her feeling that Sōjiji's Sanzenkai is an unwelcoming environment for younger female practitioners. During an interview at a local coffee shop, Ms. Kojima told me that whatever relief she felt while sitting *zazen* was quickly undone by the overly strict and critical environment perpetuated by the older men of the group. "It is not a place where women can feel at ease" (*kimochi ii tokoro ja'arimasen*), she told me, her voice dropping to a whisper:

> When I first started here, I didn't know what *kinhin* [meditative walking] was. Just after I joined, one man pushed me from behind for walking too slowly. The week after that, someone yelled at me because I didn't know which way to go. As a woman, I don't get to enjoy the feeling of *zazen*, because I always feel as if someone

is watching me. I think it would be different if I were a man. I'm always nervous about making mistakes.

Unlike those who walked away from *zazen* at Sōjiji, Ms. Kojima made a legitimate effort to attend the Sanzenkai at least once a month. Still, her negative experiences were difficult for her to overcome, at one point emotionally preventing her from attending the group for four months. While the question remains how pervasive experiences like Ms. Kojima's are among other women who may have been inclined to be more permanent members, the relatively low retention rate for women led me to believe that hers cannot be an isolated case.

The Propagation Department does what it can to introduce younger people to the benefit of *zazen*—for example, sponsoring overnight *zazen* retreats for the students of Tsurumi High School and Tsurumi University. For its part, the Sanzenkai does its best to accommodate the priorities of the Propagation Department. However, assuming that all of the reasons given above are true, an even simpler scenario might be the culprit for members not returning to the Sanzenkai—namely, that the membership of the group is caught in a circular pattern that keeps membership to a certain demographic makeup.

Women account for more than half of visitors and new members, but among regularly attending members, men outnumber women by approximately a six-to-one margin. Similarly, based on visual estimates, the average age of a visitor or new member (male and female) is mid-thirties to mid-forties. In contrast, the average age of the forty-one regular members who shared with me their age was fifty-seven years.

Since the Sanzenkai is comprised largely of older men, younger visitors and particularly women may simply feel that the group caters primarily to older men and is therefore not for them. Together the Sanzenkai and the Propagation Department do what they can to combat this reputation, and the Sanzenkai's presence in temple literature and on the internet is designed to appeal to the widest possible audience. Still, the message that "everyone is welcome" may not coincide with what a visitor sees.

Not My Temple

Compared to other lay groups at Sōjiji, the members of the Sanzenkai were the least likely to participate in other activities at the temple, such as the monthly sermon (less than a quarter had ever attended), the vegetarian cooking classes (only one respondent out of forty had attended), or the monthly sutra-copying classes (only two out of forty). In contrast, of the members of the Baikakō (discussed in the following chapter), 83 percent had attended a monthly sermon, and over a quarter had attended the cooking classes or sutra-copying class.

Similarly, members of the Sanzenkai were least likely of the lay organizations to participate in religious ceremonies and festivals held at Sōjiji, such as Hatsumōde (New Year), Setsubun (Lunar New Year), or Obon (the summer ancestor commemoration festival). While this does not necessarily demonstrate a lower rate of religiosity, it does demonstrate a lower rate of *personal affiliation* with Sōjiji, despite the fact that the various groups overall contain a comparable number of registered parishioners of Sōjiji. Sanzenkai members may practice *zazen* at Sōjiji, but compared to other temple groups, they do not consider Sōjiji to be "their" temple—that is, a place to go to fulfill their religious needs and obligations. From my informants' responses, this is not surprising. Of the forty-one people I spoke with, only fourteen identified with the Sōtō Zen sect as their primary religious affiliation, and of these, only three were parishioners of Sōjiji. Of the remaining respondents, fifteen identified with a different sect of Japanese Buddhism, and twelve told me they do not identify as being a member of any organized religion at all.

The motivations that brought these members to *zazen* practice are therefore understandably diverse. The most common response to the question "Why did you start practicing *zazen*?" was a description of a period of personal crisis or reevaluation in that person's life, with over a third of interviewees responding in such a manner. While some mentioned a lasting sense of stagnation or disillusionment in their lives, for others the crisis was more acute: a loss of employment, a divorce or heartbreak, or a death of a relative or friend often led people to turn to *zazen* to cope with their feelings. Several people independently spoke of "losing their path" or of "seeking relief from their worries." One member described his motivation to come to grips with the transiency of life after his mother suddenly passed away.

A striking example of finding *zazen* through personal crisis was Mr. Satake, a businessman from Tokyo in his mid-forties. About five years before I met him, Mr. Satake was on a downward spiral of self-destruction. The pressures of his job and his failing marriage had led him to drink too much, but the breaking point happened when his father suddenly passed away. "When my father died, I went crazy," he told me. His wife divorced him, and he came close to hitting bottom through drinking and gambling.

Nearing his lowest point, his mother told him that, as oldest son, he was responsible for the memorial rituals for his father. He knew that his family were parishioners of Sōjiji, but he knew nothing about Sōtō Zen. He also knew that every sect of Japanese Buddhism had some practice that distinguished it from the others, so he searched the internet for answers. Every search he did came up with references to Dōgen and *zazen*, so he started reading books on *zazen*. Soon after, he visited Sōjiji's Nichiyō Sanzenkai.

The disciplined quiet of *zazen* was an immediate fit for him. For months, he never missed a single meeting. Soon he was waking up every morning at four ("even on my days off," he proudly added) to sit *zazen* for an hour before work, a routine that he claims helped him deal with the daily stresses of his job. He credits *zazen* for helping him learn to deal productively with his problems and for turning his life around.

This perception of *zazen* as a kind of therapy for the stressors or troubles in one's life was a common theme during my conversations. Another take on a similar theme was to see *zazen* practice as a prophylactic: roughly a third of my informants sought out *zazen* as a means of *preventing* the stress that came with their responsibilities before it became problematic. A common reply was that *zazen* helped to maintain "spiritual balance" (*seishin antei*). One member, a retired company worker, described how *zazen* helped him to develop this spiritual balance by being able to focus on his work but also allowing him to let go of stress at the office and at home.

Along this vein, several respondents reported first being exposed to *zazen* during training retreats sponsored by their employers "to foster better relationships between people as well as to reduce stress in the office." Although these retreats have fallen out of vogue in recent years, they were popular in the 1970s and 1980s as a means of cultivating a culture of the "corporate warrior." The retreats were often overnight or weekend affairs at Zen temples led by priests who doubled as corporate training consultants. In addition to team-building exercises, the retreats incorporated aspects of Zen philosophy and practices in order to develop a disciplined (and, more importantly, obedient) corps of employees.[11] Today high schools and colleges also sponsor *zazen* retreats, advocating the use of *zazen* as a means to create a diligent and productive student body.

Several longtime practitioners remember finding initial inspiration to practice *zazen* in the work of modern authors such as D. T. Suzuki, Thich Nhat Hanh, and "Homeless" Sawaki Kōdō. Others had first encountered the idea in a magazine or newspaper. One man told me simply, "I had read about *zazen* in a magazine, and I wondered what it was. So I came to Sōjiji."

Lastly, three respondents were inspired by family members who were themselves avid practitioners of *zazen*. In two of the three cases, the relative was a grandfather. One woman told me that memories of her grandfather sitting *zazen* when she was a child was what motivated her to begin practicing *zazen* when he passed away, as a way of remembering and sharing in an activity that he was passionate about. Similarly, another member recalled his sitting *zazen* as a middle-school student with his grandfather, who encouraged the practice by saying it would make him successful in school and in work. The member regretted not finding the time to do *zazen* during his career, but as a retiree and a grandfather himself, he is an assiduous practitioner, encouraging his own grandchildren to sit *zazen* with him.

The Community Hall

The building known as the Shuryō ("Community Hall") sits directly across from the Monk's Hall on the western side of the temple. The Shuryō is one of the oldest buildings at Sōjiji, dating to the initial phase of construction of the monastery. The building was completed in 1915 and dedicated as the Monk's Hall in September of that same year.

As Sōjiji grew in size and reputation, it began to attract more monastic recruits than the hall could hold. When the current Monk's Hall was dedicated in 1933, the older hall was renamed the Shuryō. No longer serving as a place to house and feed the monastic community, the Shuryō was repurposed as a study hall for the monks. In previous generations, the community of *unsui* would gather in the hall to listen to a *teishō*, a lecture given by one of the superior priests expounding on a religious text. At all other times, the hall was available for the monks to quietly read, study, and memorize the many texts they would need to know to function in their priestly duties. The signboard over the entrance to the inner hall is inscribed *kokyō shōshin*—"illuminate your mind through the old teachings."

The Shuryō is architecturally similar to the current Monk's Hall in its construction, albeit on a humbler scale. Like the Monk's Hall, the Shuryō is constructed as an inner hall encircled by an outer hall, with platforms of tatami placed along the walls. Unlike the Monk's Hall, the platforms run lengthwise rather than widthwise along the walls of the inner and outer halls. Architecturally, the limited number of mats restricts the number of people who can sleep comfortably in the hall to about thirty. However, since three people can sit on a single tatami mat, the Shuryō can comfortably seat three times this many, making it ideal for a room dedicated to study and *zazen*. Today the room is arranged to seat ninety-four, and more cushions can be added if needed.

In its center sits a statue of Juntei Kannon attended by two Dragon Kings, a donation to Sōjiji by the Bishō Tokugawa family. The many-armed, three-faced image of Kannon rising from a lotus flower is a representation of compassion, rising out of the "mire" of the world to provide hope for the salvation of all living things. This statue of Kannon serves as a complement to the statue of Manjū enshrined in the Monk's Hall, and together the two represent the dual nature of the ideal Buddhist monastic: an image of enlightened discipline on the one hand and a paragon of selfless compassion for all living beings on the other.

Since the construction of the three-story Denkōkaku, a modern-style building with classrooms and a lecture hall for the *unsui*, the Shuryō has become primarily a hall for lay use. It remains empty for most of the time and sees the most use on weekends when visiting tour groups and corporate and school retreats come to Sōjiji. In 1999 it was announced that as part of the "Open Sōjiji" policy, the Shuryō would be made open for use by anyone who wanted to use it, at any time. While this policy has since been rescinded (reservations are now necessary), most visitors who come to Sōjiji to experience *zazen* leave with lasting memories of the Shuryō.

On Sunday afternoons the room belongs to the Nichiyō Sanzenkai. So strong is the affiliation between the Sanzenkai and the space of the Shuryō, the two are almost synonymous to many in the group, occasionally leading to a feeling that borders on possessiveness concerning the hall.

Unlike the Monk's Hall, seats in the Shuryō are not assigned, and in theory people are free to sit wherever they like. However, in practice, there is a tendency for long-time members to arrive early to claim "their" seats, which can be a particular mat or even a particular cushion where they tend to sit week after week. There is an unspoken, but implicit, logic to this arrangement: more experienced members replicate the hierarchical seating of the Monk's Hall such that the eastern side of the hall is populated by long-term members, in order of seniority. A new member entering the inner hall would likely see this patterning over their first weeks and soon learn not to look for seats on the eastern side, even if they are unoccupied.

Newer members, in contrast, tend to sit in the outer hall that encircles the outside wall of inner hall. Again, nowhere is it stated that this is the "place" for new members, but, by and large, less-experienced practitioners choose to sit there for quite some time after they have joined the Sanzenkai, in addition to several long-time members who have grown comfortable sitting there over a period of months or years.

Their reasons for doing so are varied. One woman commented that she felt that the relatively confined outer hall (with lower ceilings and walking room only two body-widths wide) allowed her to keep her focus better than in the openness of the inner hall. One longtime male practitioner said he preferred the outer hall *because* of the regular distractions taking place outside of the Shūryō's walls. "The point of *zazen* is to teach us not to hold on to distractions," he told me. "Why would I want to sit in a place where there are no distractions to practice letting go of?" Another man said that because he consistently arrives late, he always goes for a seat in the outer hall, since he is more likely to disturb people if he walks around the inner hall to find an empty seat.

Still, hierarchical distinctions do play a part in many practitioners' choice to sit in the outer hall. The inner hall is a high-stakes environment: one's practice—including any missteps or faux pas—is thought to be more visible in the open space of the inner hall than it is on the periphery. Consequently, the inner hall has become, by reputation, the place where the "serious" practitioners sit. One newer member told me that he assumed he would "know" when it was his time to move into the inner hall but had not yet gathered the courage to do so.

Preparation

Both Dōgen and Keizan thought it necessary to briefly address proper attire for *zazen* practice in their writing. In Dōgen's several manuals concerning *zazen*, his only mention of clothing is for the practitioner to "loosen their robe and belt" and to wear the monk's *kesa*.[12] Keizan, in the *Zazen Yōjinki*, advises practitioners only to avoid either dirty or luxurious clothing and to mend and clean their garments before sitting *zazen*.[13]

In this regard it is important to remember that both Dōgen and Keizan's instructions were intended primarily for a world-renouncing monastic audience as opposed to the unordained laity; the monastic practitioners likely did not need additional instructions on clothing, as proper clothing was addressed in the monastic rules (*shingi*) that governed life in a temple. Suggestions that clothing worn for *zazen* practice should be comfortable and in "cool" colors, such as blues, browns, and blacks, were later extrapolations from the Sōtō patriarchs' writings, added to bring a measure of decorum and consistency to lay *zazen* practice.

In actual practice, members of Sōjiji's Sanzenkai are largely free to wear whatever they wish. Only a small minority—no more than fifteen or twenty men and women—change into traditional clothing like a *hakama*, a training outfit usually worn by martial arts practitioners, or a *samue*, such as the monks wear for their daily work detail. An equal number arrive already wearing or change into sweatpants, while the greater majority of the group stay in their street clothes such as jeans or slacks.[14]

The clothes a person wears for *zazen* are a not-so-subtle public declaration of how dedicated that person is to their *zazen* practice: while wearing jeans or tight slacks is seen as a rookie mistake, wearing sweatpants or tracksuits demonstrates familiarity and comfort with *zazen*. Wearing traditional Japanese attire such as a *hakama* or *samue* conspicuously marks the wearer as being a devoted (*nesshin*) practitioner—"the real deal" (*honkakuteki*), so to speak. Functionally, these outfits are no different from wearing sweatpants in that they are loose and comfortable and allow the legs to move freely, but being expensive and individualizing, they grant their wearer the appearance of serious and earnest dedication to *zazen* practice, regardless of actual experience.

Perhaps the most conspicuous status-granting item worn by Sanzenkai members is the *rakusu*, the bib-like garment that serves as a utilitarian stand-in for the monastic *kesa*. Laypersons who wear the *rakusu* have participated in a ceremony known as *zaike tokudo*, a modification of the clerical "home leaving" initiation ritual. In this ritual a layperson accepts the sixteen Sōtō Zen precepts and becomes a disciple of an established priest but does not take the complete plunge into priestly ordination. The *rakusu* is inscribed on its reverse with a calligraphic "certificate" from the teacher, along with the date and details of the ceremony.

What is interesting about the *zaike tokudo* ceremony is that it results in a situation in which the participant straddles the worlds of priest and layperson, blurring the lines between Buddhism's traditional home-leaver/householder distinction. While clearly a symbol of dedication to Buddhist practice—it is a form of the clerical Dharma robe, after all—many *rakusu* wearers report that they are not particularly "religious" but rather formed a relationship with a charismatic teacher with whom they wished to affiliate themselves. The *rakusu* in this regard is a complicated status symbol, paradoxically demonstrating both proximity and distance from both the clergy. Like the Sanzenkai itself, the *rakusu* wearer signifies that they are *almost* clergy and *almost* a layperson but not quite either.

The Complicated Art of "Just Sitting"

After leaving their bags in the changing rooms, a participant is free to seat themselves in the Shuryō. Upon entering the hall, the participant takes a pair of slippers from a rack on the wall and, as quietly as possible, moves through the hall to find an empty seat.

The close attention to detail that is paramount for *zazen* practice begins the moment a person enters the hall.[15] Participants are told to keep their hands held in *shashu*, a position in which the left hand is held in a fist over the heart with the right hand covering. When crossing over the threshold into the hall itself, a person must keep their left shoulder to the left door frame, remembering to enter the hall left foot first.

For those entering the inner hall, the process is repeated, with the practitioner stopping to hold their hands together in *gasshō* and bow their head toward the image of Kannon. The rules for moving through the inner hall are somewhat intricate and, to the beginner, can be quite daunting. One can pass to the left of the image of Kannon, but never to its right.[16] If one wants to sit in the front of the room, they have to walk around the center islands and approach from the back. One can sit anywhere except on the four cushions that flank both entrances. For an *unsui*, proper movement in the hall is a drill that is part of their monastic repertoire. For a layperson unfamiliar with the intricacies of movement through a ritual space, moving about the inner hall is fraught with the danger of committing an embarrassing faux pas.

When an available spot is located, the participant pulls the *zafu* cushion forward, places it on its side, and fluffs it until it is nearly spherical. With their seat properly prepared, the participant then bows in *gasshō* twice in greeting—once to the other practitioners sitting next to them and once again to those sitting across from them.

The next step takes a little practice. Every platform of tatami mats in the Shuryō has an approximately six-inch wooden lip (the *jōen*) that is used for meals. The trick is for a person to seat themselves on their cushion without their buttocks or feet touching the wooden lip. Since the platform is about three feet off the ground, the effort to avoid the *jōen* can be somewhat acrobatic, with people using their arms to carefully guide themselves onto their cushion and then sliding their cushion back so that their feet and buttocks clear the wooden surface in one smooth movement.

Once a participant is safely on the tatami, they take a few moments rocking back and forth to adjust the cushion to the shape and contours of their lower body. When this is done, they fold—and in some cases pull by force—their legs into one of several cross-legged positions. The two most accepted sitting positions for *zazen* are "half lotus" (*hankafuza*) and "full lotus" (*kekkafuza*). Of the two, full lotus is the more difficult, requiring substantial flexibility in the joints of the hips, knees, and ankles in order to get both feet on the opposite thighs. While this puts strain on each of the joints, the benefit of the full lotus position is a firm base with three points of contact with the floor (both knees and the buttocks), which reduces strain on the back.

In contrast, the half lotus position simply requires folding the right leg over the left and does not cause nearly as much strain on the joints. For this reason, it is recommended to newer practitioners. The tradeoff here is that *hankafuza* necessitates that the sitter overuses the muscles of the lower back in order to sit up straight. After sitting in this position for an extended period of time, the back begins to fatigue, first in the lower back and then radiating into the shoulders and neck.[17]

While the ability to sit in half lotus is doctrinally accepted—Dōgen describes it in the *Fukan Zazengi*[18]—there is nevertheless a measure of stigma attached to it. The ideal for experienced *zazen* practitioners is full lotus, the more difficult and ostensibly more "authentic" position, since religious iconography commonly depicts the Buddha sitting in full lotus position. Among themselves, long-time members pay attention to who sits in which position, and the ability to sit in full lotus becomes another measure by which a person's skill and dedication to their practice can be compared.

While half lotus is certainly easier than either full lotus or the kneeling *seiza*, the modern Japanese spend as much time in chairs as any of their postindustrial counterparts. The result is that the Japanese—like anyone else not physically accustomed to sitting in certain positions for extended periods of time—find the seated positions used in *zazen* to be uncomfortable and even painful. Physical sensations in the legs and back can range from a "pins-and-needles" feeling to a dull numbness to throbbing inflammation, often cycling through all of the above. The modern body simply is not used to being coerced into such positions.

In sermons and in conversation, many in the Sōtō Zen clergy lament this transformation of modern Japanese society into a "chair lifestyle" (*isu seikatsu*). From this perspective, the rise of the use of chairs in homes and the workplace over the course of the last century corresponds with the decline of traditional Japanese morals, values, and customs. While not an evil in and of itself, the "chair lifestyle" has become a metonym for all that is wrong with modern society: the chair represents laziness, anxiety, selfishness, violence, a loss of respect for authority, and a weakening of the family. Indeed, in this usage, the "chair lifestyle" (and its implied origins in "Westernization," *seiyōka*) is contrasted with more "traditional" modes of sitting, which, by association, correspond with a nostalgic view of the Japan of the past as ordered, harmonious, holistic, and cooperative.

A corollary of this is the hope that if the "chair lifestyle" can be unlearned—or at least compartmentalized—there is still a chance for modern Japanese society to be redeemed. For many in the clergy, encouraging others to undertake the process of redisciplining the body to be able to sit *zazen* carries the urgency of a public service program. Part of the message is that the Japanese "of former times" understood that enduring discomfort was a virtue in itself, that cultivating the ability to mentally overcome discomfort is an inescapable part of effectively disciplining the body and mind.

Indeed, the connection between traditional styles of sitting and an idealized Japanese society of the past invokes the specters of cultural essentialism: as one priest explained it to me, "Americans think that painful things equal bad things. However, we Japanese see discomfort as part of *shugyō* and something that has to be gotten used to. For us, pain is an opportunity." On the flip side, racialized notions of biology also came into play: on one occasion, I found myself being criticized for not sitting in full lotus. My critic pointed out that my choosing to sit in *hankafuza* was indicative of laziness and a weak spirit on my part. His rationale was that since *"gaijin* [non-Japanese] have longer legs than Japanese do," sitting cross-legged was ostensibly biologically easier for me than for Japanese people. It did not seem to register (or matter) that not only was he taller than I was, but his legs were also longer than mine. This, however, was beside the point: by not sitting in full lotus, I was demonstrating to him that I was unwilling to subject myself to even the mildest of hardships—a critique he would later extend to Americans in general.

Shikantaza

Once the practitioner is properly seated on their cushion, they compose themselves and wait for one of the monks assigned as a hall monitor (*jikidō*) to come by with the *kyōsaku* stick. At each row of tatami, the monitor stops and raises the stick in offering. The practitioners salute him in *gasshō*, bowing as he passes. When the monitor has done a full walk-through of the entire hall, the session begins.

Zazen begins non-ceremoniously. A metal gong is struck three times to announce the beginning of the period. The practitioners turn clockwise to face the wall. The lights in the hall are dimmed to the bare minimum. After that, silence. Suddenly the hall becomes a sensory deprivation chamber. By creating an environment where external distractions are minimized, the *zazen* practitioner is left alone with their body and mind for an uncomfortable period of time.

Newcomers to the Sanzenkai likely have heard of *zazen* through a book, magazine article, or television program extolling the benefits of meditative practice to balance the hectic modern lifestyle. For them, these first hours can pass slowly as their "modern" minds, accustomed to the sensory barrage of an always-connected life, distractedly jump from thought to thought and from worry to worry, often returning to the growing discomfort of forcing their body to sit erect and their legs folded in a manner that cuts off circulation.

Adding to the mental burden, practitioners are instructed to regulate their breathing by inhaling and exhaling slowly through their nose. Their eyes are kept open during *zazen*, keeping their gaze at a forty-five-degree angle in front of them. Their hands are placed in their lap, in a gesture known as the "cosmic *mudra*" (*hokka jōin*). In this position, the right hand cups the left hand while the two thumbs touch, forming an egg shape that is said to "contain the whole universe."

Many new practitioners spend much of their time shifting, adjusting, and correcting their position. The fact that their body is not "relaxed" during *zazen* comes as a surprise to many beginning practitioners. Indeed, there is quite a bit for their body to remember: in addition to enduring the growing discomfort in their legs without changing positions, the sitter must keep their back perfectly straight, breathe slowly, not move their head from side to side, not yawn, not close their eyes, and keep their hands perfectly positioned. Interestingly, it is this last, seemingly minor, point that is of the utmost importance. According to experts, the best way to know the internal state of the practitioner is by watching the bridge formed by the thumbs touching: if the bridge has collapsed, the sitter has become lax or distracted.

It is not surprising that the single most commonly asked question from beginners following a *zazen* gathering is how long the discomfort will last before it begins to get better. As one member explained to me, "I thought it would be exciting when the pain finally went away. I looked forward to that moment. But it was a slow process. Gradually, it just got easier for

me. I was able to sit *zazen* for longer and longer." Through repeated practice and constant policing of the body, unfamiliar positions become muscle
memory, and the effort required to sit in *zazen* becomes more familiar and
easier to maintain.

But the redisciplining of the body is only a first step. Recall that the
logic of *shugyō* is based on the principle that the disciplined body leads to
a disciplined mind. However, one does not lead effortlessly to the other.
Even when the resistant body is seemingly mastered, *zazen* practitioners
face a greater struggle: a wandering mind.

In both the *Fukan Zazengi* and *Zazenshin* fascicles of the Shōbōgenzō,
Dōgen gives the *zazen* practitioner the cryptic instruction to think of "not
thinking" (*fushi*), further clarifying this to mean that the practitioner should
engage in "non-thinking" (*hishi*).[19] While this statement might make sense
to someone couched in the philosophical nuances of medieval Chinese and
Japanese philosophy, the modern-day practitioner is left to their own devices
to make sense of the contradiction of non-thinking. When pressed, the most
common response is to invoke metaphor: one practitioner explained that he
had been taught to think of the mind like an empty sky, with thoughts being
like clouds. When clouds fill the sky, the result is a storm or a gloomy day.
Non-thinking is like the sky letting the wind blow so that clouds cannot
gather. When I asked for clarification, he suggested asking a priest, who
would be able to explain better than he could.

So I did. The priest I spoke with, familiar with the metaphor, explained
that thoughts "are just the changing landscape of your mind, momentarily
passing through. A person is like a container that contains these passing
experiences. 'Non-thinking' means just noticing your thoughts and letting
them happen without involving yourself."

From an intellectual perspective, the *zazen* practitioners might understand what they are being instructed to do mentally. Doing so in practice,
however, is a different animal altogether, and I came to appreciate how
frustrating "non-thinking" could be. Any distraction—footsteps in the
hallway, a person coughing, an itch under your nose, a car driving up the
driveway—can easily become the jumping-off point of a cascade of mental and emotional responses. The mind swims with random thoughts:
bills to be paid, work that needs to be done, emails to be written, food for
dinner, a catchy song, a phone call to make. By the time the practitioner
realizes where their thoughts have taken them and how far from "non-
thinking" they have traveled, minutes or even the entire period have
passed. The very act of cognition becomes the elephant in the room. The

only advice available is frustrating in its simplicity: let the thoughts pass, and start again.

Every person I spoke with identified with this struggle, and only a handful were willing to say that they have experienced even the briefest moment of *shikantaza*. "The moment you recognize that you're doing it," one person explained, "it's over. And then you spend the rest of the period wondering how you did it and thinking how to do it again."

Through all of this is the shadow of the hall monitor brandishing his *kyōsaku*, quietly patrolling the hall behind the backs of the practitioners. While the *unsui* who are assigned to assist the Sanzenkai are more lenient than their counterparts who patrol the Monk's Hall, the constant presence of the hall monitor is a reminder of the bodily and mental discipline necessary for *zazen*.

In the meditation hall, time is kept in an innovative manner: by watching the progression of a burning stick of incense. Similarly, regular *zazen* practice trains the body to mark the passage of time. Like students nearing the end of class, one begins to hear sounds of increased restlessness as the thirty-minute mark approaches. When the incense has burned down to the sand, the monitor rings the bell twice to mark the start of *kinhin*. Slowly and gingerly, the practitioners unfold their legs, stand up, and stand at attention, their right hand covering the tight fist of their left hand over their heart.

Kinhin is a slow meditative walk that allows practitioners to stretch their legs without breaking the atmosphere of concentration in the hall. As would be expected, steps are deliberate, and movements precise: with each step, a person moves exactly half a foot length, as measured by placing the heel along the instep of the opposite foot. While the step is measured, the timing is not: it is common to see a logjam situation when a person decides to be more "meditative" than those behind him.

Kinhin is brief—no more than three minutes, long enough to get the blood flowing back to the legs—and the bell is rung once to signal the practitioners to return to their seats. Hearing the bell, the practitioners bow in place and then quickly follow masking-taped arrows on the floor to cycle back to their cushions. When they get there, they get back on the platform and turn around to continue their *zazen* for another period.

And Now a Sermon

After the second period of *zazen*, the bell is rung once to signal the end of the sitting. After dismounting from the platform, stepping into their slip-

Fig. 13. The members of the Zazenkai gather in the reception room of the Shiuntai for a sermon.

pers, and repositioning their cushions, the group again stands at attention, their hands held close to their hearts. The group then processes single file out of the hall and down Sōjiji's long corridor like a giant snake.

Walking briskly in ill-fitting slippers, the group thunders through the temple corridors to the Shiuntai, a large hall traditionally used for Sōjiji's abbot to formally receive visitors and guests. Though the hall is visibly impressive from the outside, the interior hallway is dimly lit, appearing to be just another dark wooden corridor. Nondescript sliding doors flank the hallway. Arriving at the reception room, the group takes off their slippers and lines them up in pairs along the wall, entering the room one by one.

The room's interior betrays the bland appearance from the hallway: the interior side of the sliding doors is revealed to be an ornate painting of pine branches, masterpieces painted by the famous Kanō family of artists. The long room overlooks a meticulously maintained tea garden with a pond and stone lanterns. In a nook at the head of the room hangs a larger-than-life-size painting of Bodhidharma (Jp. Daruma), the Indian patriarch credited with bringing Zen to China. Bodhidharma, immediately recognizable in his iconic red cloak amid a ferocious storm, is a fitting image for this hall where the Sanzenkai will gather to listen to a *teishō*.

While both are glossed into English as "sermon," a *teishō* is stylistically different from the more general "Dharma talk" (*hōwa*). A hallmark of the *teishō* is the use of a religious text to provide a structural framework for the speech. Since the texts are most often written in classical Japanese, or even Chinese with diacritical marks (which few Japanese have the training to read), the speaker goes line-by-line through the text, providing examples—occasionally drawn from his own life experiences—to illuminate the meaning of the text for the audience. For the Sanzenkai, the speaker often (but not always) provides a photocopy of the text for the audience to follow along.

Another difference between the two "sermons" is the intended audience. Of the two, *hōwa* are generally more accessible to a lay audience, as they are more or less self-contained entities: even if the *hōwa* makes reference to a religious text, the assumption is that the audience is not familiar with the reference, and therefore emphasis is placed on the overall message of the sermon.

In contrast, *teishō* are traditionally delivered to monastic audiences. In theory, the monks hearing the *teishō* would have been familiar with the text, often having been assigned to study it independently. By emphasizing the text as the foundation for the speaker's interpretation, the *teishō* takes on the aura of "revealed wisdom"; part of the function of the *teishō* is to impart to fledgling clergy the knowledge of how a Sōtō Zen priest should publicly interpret religious texts.

The majority of the people I spoke with considered the *teishō* to be an important part of their weekly *zazen* practice. However, this was far from a universal sentiment, and there was no consensus about what was expected or desired from the *teishō*. One man explained to me that his opinion of the *teishō* changes week by week: "It really depends on the content. Right now I think that the *teishō* lacks in content and goes on for too long. It just gets in the way of our *zazen*." A handful of others echoed the sentiment that the topic and delivery of the *teishō* made all the difference and that an uninspired or uninteresting sermon was wasting time that could be better spent sitting *zazen*.

Because the *teishō* is firmly couched in the cultural norms of a hierarchical master/disciple relationship, there is rarely any formal interaction between speaker and audience and almost no opportunity for clarification or questioning during the *teishō* itself. One result of this is that the speaker has the tendency to lose their audience through disengagement. While an attentive few take notes while the teacher speaks, many spend the session only half listening and checking their watches. Others unabashedly nod off to sleep.

Displacement

Why do the laypersons of the Sanzenkai receive a *teishō* if they are not being groomed as religious specialists? The answer lies in the group's historically complicated relationship to Sōjiji's organizational hierarchy.

From its founding, the Sanzenkai had been an extension of the Western Division (*seibu*) of the temple that oversees the seminary education of the *unsui*. In fact, the official bylaws of the Sanzenkai list the actual head of the group as the Godō-rōshi, with the assistant head being the Tantō-rōshi—the two priests largely responsible for the day-to-day education of the novice *unsui*. Moreover, Sōjiji's abbot and the Seidō-rōshi are listed as "advisors" to the group. Together these four officers and their assistants comprised the Sanzen Department (*Sanzen-ryō*). Administratively speaking, therefore, the Sanzenkai was for many years less a lay organization than an offshoot of the monastic training program.

However, the group's favored status among temple organizations was dramatically changed in 2002 when it was decided that the Sanzenkai, as a lay organization, was more appropriately placed under the auspices of the Propagation Department (*Fukyō-ryō*). There was a practical logic involved: for one, the principal priests of the Western Division already had their hands full with the training and teaching of over a hundred *unsui*, and adding supervisory responsibility for the Sanzenkai was an extra burden on offices already stretched too thin. For another, the Propagation Department staff were already tasked with outreach programming and helping to raise lay interest and participation at Sōjiji. Since the Sanzenkai was already one of the most successful means for bringing people though Sōjiji's doors, it seemed like a natural fit to include the Sanzenkai as part of the temple's propagation efforts. The decision was made to remove the Sanzenkai from the seminary side and give responsibility to the administrative side of the temple. Following this reorganization, the Propagation Department was officially renamed the "Propagation and *Sanzen* Department" (*Fukyō Sanzen-ryō*).

For the Sanzenkai, this restructuring was a humiliating demotion in status. Even now, members of the Sanzenkai remember the time before the change as the golden age of the group, when the members could fully imagine themselves as genuinely participating in the same caliber of *shugyō* as the resident monks. These participants fondly recalled the seminary-side priests who would take the time to sit *zazen* with the group every week. For dedicated members, it was a matter of pride to regularly sit side by side with such high-ranking and respected clergy. After the transition to the Propagation Department, many members of the Sanzenkai felt betrayed and abandoned by the Sōjiji administration and by the seminary-side priests in particular.

This administrative restructuring was traumatic for the Sanzenkai. For years the Sanzenkai had grown comfortable in their liminal status in the temple system. Their position inside the Western Division distinguished the group from other temple organizations. Dedicated members might sometimes even be treated to special privileges—for example, being allowed to meditate with the *unsui* in the Monk's Hall—that were unheard of for other groups.

With the change of hands, the Sanzenkai felt it had lost its special position. Whereas before they could imagine themselves as being "monks for a day" (*ichinichi unsui*), their confidence in the quality of their *shugyō* was shaken by the thought that the temple administration viewed the Sanzenkai as just another group of laypersons. Several longtime practitioners left the group in anger and resentment over what they perceived as a grievous insult. While the Godō-rōshi and Tantō-rōshi still occasionally participated in the group through the sermons, their responsibilities overseeing the *unsui* largely kept these priests from giving the Sanzenkai the personal attention to which it had grown accustomed. In general, there were comparably fewer special privileges afforded to the Sanzenkai than they had received in the past.

There may be another factor in play, however. The groups that traditionally fell under the auspices of the Propagation Department—for example, the Fujinkai and the Baikakō—tended to be comprised primarily of women whose involvement at Sōjiji was centered on somewhat passive participation in the religious and ritual life of the temple. Before the transfer to the administrative side, the majority-male Sanzenkai could entertain the fantasy that since their practice was modeled on that of the training monks, they were more "authentic" than those groups whose practices had no scriptural or doctrinal precedent. After the transition, this conceit was no longer possible.

Perhaps the most significant factor might be that the Sanzenkai generally sees itself as both functionally and philosophically distinct from other lay organizations at Sōjiji. Unlike the Fujinkai and the Baikakō, which serve a ritual role to Sōjiji through their participation in temple ceremonies, the Sanzenkai's role in Sōjiji's ritual life is largely tangential. While the group would always officially accept an invitation to participate in a ceremony, there was a tacit sense among many members that such ritual obligations cut into precious *zazen* sitting time. Indeed, group attendance was generally reduced by a third or more when word got out that that week's meditation time would be cut short by an obligation to participate in a temple ceremony.

This is not to say that the members of the Sanzenkai are necessarily averse to the more obviously religious aspects of temple life. Rather, it is that the Sanzenkai, by and large, hold a different conceptualization than either the clergy or other lay groups for what Zen should be: "pure" Zen is *zazen*—and nothing else.

Recalling the earlier discussion of motivation to practice *zazen*, it should be remembered that members of the Sanzenkai are more likely than their counterparts in other lay organizations to be familiar with the foundational literature of Sōtō Zen, particularly the writings of the patriarchs Dōgen and Keizan. A key argument of the *zazen* purists is that the trappings of institutionalized Buddhism, with its emphasis on funeral and memorial rituals, arcane invocations, and ornate paraphernalia, are nowhere found in these foundational texts. The often-repeated battle cry of this group is "the Buddha didn't perform funerals." What the Buddha *did* do, they argue, was meditate.

This emphasis on *zazen* as the essence of Zen practice is retroactively extended to the Sōtō Zen patriarchs. The most commonly cited reference is the *Bendōwa* fascicle from the *Shōbōgenzō*, in which Dōgen writes:

> From the very moment when a disciple comes to meet face-to-face with the one who is to be his spiritual friend and knowing teacher, there is no need to have the disciple offer incense, make prostrations, chant the names of the Buddhas, do ascetic practices and penances or recite Scriptures: the master just has the disciple do pure *zazen* until he lets his body and mind drop off.[20]

Even Keizan, who is often vilified for "contaminating" Dōgen's approach to Zen by promoting funerals and memorial rites, is used to support the purists' pro-*zazen* argument: "Although grand Buddhist ceremonies or the building of large temples are very good things, people who devote themselves to *zazen* should not be involved in such activities."[21] Especially significant at Sōjiji, this line from Keizan's *Zazen Yōjinki* is often cited as something of a smoking gun, damning proof that Keizan and his disciples knowingly sacrificed the purity of Zen in their pursuit of power and status.

Carl Bielefeldt cautions that, "given the varied ways that Buddhists have used their texts, one cannot help but wonder to what extent they also practiced what is preached in them."[22] What is commonly forgotten—or actively ignored—by the purists is that both Dōgen and Keizan left behind far more than manuals for meditation. Both patriarchs wrote large bodies of written materials that included personal correspondence with the aristocracy, sermons, hagiographical texts, and, especially, detailed monastic rules (*shingi*) written specifically to govern and direct the performance of rituals and ceremonies in the monasteries they founded. That certain texts—especially the *Bendōwa* quote above—have been used opportunistically and out of context by purists and originalists is less a reflection of the Zen practiced by Dōgen and Keizan than it is evidence of an effort to reclaim and redefine the identity of Sōtō Zen vis-à-vis internal rivalries and outside competition from a widening religious field in Japan. As Foulk states, "The claims of twentieth-century Sōtō school scholars that Dōgen rejected the 'syncretic' aspects of Song Chan monastic practice and that he taught a form of 'pure' Zen that consisted of an exclusive devotion to seated meditation are entirely groundless."[23]

Indeed, the idea of a pure form of Zen as transmitted through an originalist reading of certain texts at the expense of others demonstrates not only a concern over legitimacy and authenticity within the Sōtō Zen sect itself but also a desire to establish a well-defined sectarian identity distinct from other schools of Buddhism. All sects of Japanese Buddhism have elaborate ritual, but through an emphasis on *zazen*, Sōtō Zen originalists have sought to establish a practice that is unique to them and, consequently, uniquely theirs.

Enlightenment or Bust

As much as the members of the Sanzenkai wish to imagine themselves to have one foot on either side of the gap that separates the lay and clerical communities of Sōjiji, there are substantial differences that distinguish their *shugyō* from those of the monastic communities.

Despite the fact that members of the Sanzenkai share the interest and experience of *zazen* (both in varying degrees of intensity) with their fellow participants, there is remarkably little sense of camaraderie or community among the group in general. Individual practitioners do form friendships and associations with other members within the group. However, it is seldom that a practitioner identifies with the Sanzenkai as a social unit to which they have an obligation to uphold, in the sense of being a player on a team or an employee in a company. This is in stark contrast not only to the monastic community but also to other lay organizations at Sōjiji whose shared *shugyō* instills a sense of "being in it together." The small cadre of volunteer officers are generally the exception to the rule, and it is they who will most often stand to represent the Sanzenkai at official temple functions.

Several factors likely contribute to this lack of a sense of community. The very nature of *zazen* practice guarantees that the Sanzenkai spends most of its time in self-imposed isolation in the guise of communal activity. The limited time window that the Sanzenkai meets each week does not allow for members to freely discuss or share their experiences with one another. Apart from gatherings to celebrate the end of the year (December), the new year (February), and an overnight meditation retreat (July), the Sanzenkai has no regular outings to socialize over food, drink, and conversation. A result is that the members of the Sanzenkai have few social ties to bind them to the group. Indeed, the wearing of name tags is repeatedly stressed by the officers, lest the group fall into complete anonymity.

Another difference in the lasting results of *shugyō* is related to the intended goal of the disciplining practice. Despite the superficial similarities between the Sanzenkai's schedule and the daily regimen of the *unsui*, the Sanzenkai are not being trained to become religious specialists. The constant disciplinary pressure exerted upon the *unsui* is intended to mold his mind and body to conform to the social identity of a Sōtō Zen priest. As much as they imagine themselves to be "*unsui* for a day," the Sanzenkai is comprised of laypeople—businesspersons, teachers, civil servants, retirees, homemakers, and the unemployed—whose social identities are established on the fact that they are *not* religious specialists.

Still, many members of the Sanzenkai hold themselves to the same standard as the *unsui*, believing that *shugyō* can be distilled into four hours of time, once a week. For some, this can lead to unrealistic expectations. At one meeting the priest giving the lecture decided to use his time to open the floor to questions—a rare occurrence. Toward the end of the period, an elderly gentleman raised his hand and stood up. He passionately described his dedication to *zazen* practice, claiming to have rarely missed a meeting of the Sanzenkai in over eleven years of practice. However, he was upset and frustrated that in those eleven years, he still didn't know whether he had accomplished anything. "[Bodhidharma] practiced *zazen* for nine years and attained enlightenment. I've practiced for eleven years, and I have nothing to show for it. What am I doing wrong?"

The practitioner's question hints at a gap in the way enlightenment is portrayed in books and the way it is doctrinally understood by the Sōtō Zen clergy. As noted above, the Sanzenkai is the best-read of all the lay groups at Sōjiji, and its members are more likely than not to be regular consumers of media relating to Zen practice and philosophy. But this knowledge comes at a price. Biographies of legendary Zen masters and even modern accounts from contemporary authors often contain grand depictions of life-transforming revelation and insight, experiences of sudden realization of peace, or bliss, or oneness with all things, and even the acquisition of superhuman powers.[24] It is not uncommon for those who are familiar with and attracted to Zen by the majesty of enlightenment as presented in these media (as this questioning gentleman likely was) to become frustrated and disillusioned when their experiences do not meet their expectations.

The priests are patient in trying to convey to the laity the humbler, but no less beautiful, idea of *satori* taught in Sōtō Zen: that enlightenment is not a single moment in time but rather a diligent lifelong dedication to *shugyō* that disciplines the practitioner to realize moments of non-thinking for longer periods of time. Moreover, they stress that practitioners— particularly the clergy but lay practitioners as well—must come to see *shugyō* as an immersion program, akin to learning a new language: one's body and mind become "fluent" in the performance of enlightenment only through constant repetition. While teachers are quick to promote the benefits of *zazen* as a means of personal cultivation, they are also faced with the unenviable task of having to regularly temper unrealistic, overromanticized, or fantastical expectations of *zazen* practice.

It is clear that *zazen* purists who decry the emphasis on ritual performance in the modern Sōtō Zen school hold to a very different worldview than the clergy they purport to emulate. By focusing in on meditation as the only path towards enlightenment, the purists make the explicit claim that *shugyō* begins and ends on the meditation cushion. Everything else that takes place in a Zen temple is either secondary or unnecessary. It follows from this criticism that priests who spend their careers ministering to the ritual needs of their parishioners are wasting years that could otherwise be spent in *zazen*. Indeed, to this breed of *zazen* practitioner, the clergy and everyone else who prioritizes the traditional ritual and ceremonial aspects of Zen are simply doing it wrong.[25]

Despite the Sanzenkai's success in bringing thousands of curious and interested people through Sōjiji's doors, the purists' insistence on the centrality of *zazen* over the ritual practice has for years tested the patience of many in Sōjiji's administration. Though never quite rejecting the clergy's authority over religious matters, the Sanzenkai's detachment from Sōjiji's ritual life contributed directly to an increasingly strained relationship between the temple and the group that would eventually bring the situation to a head.

FIVE

Performing Compassion through Goeika Music

"Hey, have you ever heard *goeika*?"

Mr. Yabata was a veteran of over thirty years of *zazen* practice, nineteen retreats, and more pilgrimages to temples across Japan than he could count. As such, he was one of the most highly respected participants at the winter *zazen* retreat, and he held court at the large coffee table that took up most of the men's dormitory room. For the entirety of the retreat period, all of the interesting conversation in the room seemed to center on his place at the table.

With my head buried in my field notes, it took me a moment to realize that he had been talking directly to me. "*Goeika*. Have you ever heard of it?" he asked again. I mentally searched for something to connect with the word but came up short.

Mr. Yabata pointed to my satchel and suggested I take out my audio recorder. "*Goeika* is like a hymn you hear in a church," he said as he thumbed through the pages of his sutra book. He found a page near the back of the book and showed it to me. "The songs are very old," he told me. "Probably three, four hundred years. People sing them when they make pilgrimages to temples." In the book there was no musical notation nor any indication that the words printed on the page were music. I asked how he learned the songs. He said that he's known the melodies from his childhood, when his grandmother used to sing to him.

I placed my recorder on the table in front of him and nodded to indicate that we were recording. Mr. Yabata closed his eyes and began to sing in a voice that was tremulous both with age and the vibrato used in traditional Japanese singing. One by one, the others in the room, who moments before were trying to steal as much sleep as they could between the periods of *zazen*, sat up to listen to the song.

For a full fifteen minutes, no one in the room spoke a word. Mr. Yabata sang three songs, one song blending into the next with neither introduction nor explanation. When he finished, he looked up and simply said, "Like that."

In the weeks that followed Mr. Yabata's demonstration, I tried to find out more about *goeika*. An acquaintance from the Sanzenkai told me there was a *goeika* group known as the Baikakō that met regularly at the temple. I was surprised that I had never heard of it until then. When I mentioned that *goeika* was something I would like to try, he laughed. The Baikakō, he said, is "a thing for old ladies" (*obaachan no tame no mono*). Men were permitted, but it just wasn't something that was ordinarily done.

The Sōtō Zen *Goeika* School

The Honzan Baikakō is one of several *kō*—religious associations or confraternities—that are affiliated with Sōjiji. For centuries the organization of *kō* has been a means of collective cooperation and social welfare in Japan. *Kō* brought together individuals for a common purpose, often to raise money to meet a specific financial need (to pay for repairs to a building or for an unexpected funeral, for example), but just as often to enjoy a shared hobby or interest, or simply to socialize.[1] Temple-affiliated *kō* are a later development of this custom, implemented as a way to encourage lay participation in religious activities while serving as a means for the temple to generate income outside of the usual means of funerals and memorial ceremonies. Today the suffix *kō* retains this nuance of "religious," and in common usage *kō* most often refers to a lay religious association affiliated with a temple or shrine.

Like the *kō* of smaller temples throughout Japan, the membership of Sōjiji's various *kō* are drawn largely from the parishioner families of the temple, though membership is usually extended to parishioners of other Sōtō temples. In this regard, Sōjiji is more fortunate than most, with more than five thousand parishioner families from which to draw. While nominally religious associations, many *kō* have the informal character of a club or "circle"—one priest went so far as to describe the temple's various *kō* to me as "teams" (*chiimu*). Consequently, the degree to which a given *kō* participates in temple-sponsored ceremonies and activities depends greatly on the particular set of interests of its members. Some *kō* do meet semi-regularly at Sōjiji to hear sermons, take part in ceremonies, or participate in *zazen* or sutra copying. Other *kō* never meet at Sōjiji at all, choosing instead to schedule outings to "fun" places such as hot springs, ski resorts, and Tokyo Disneyland.

The idea for a sect-wide Sōtō Zen *goeika-kō* is credited to Niwa Butsuan (d. 1955), who would later become abbot of Eiheiji. Niwa first proposed the creation of a Sōtō Zen *goeika* group in 1950 to be included as part of Eiheij's observances of the seven-hundredth anniversary of Dōgen's death. Niwa's interest in *goeika* as an instrument of propagation was inspired by the successes of Shingon Buddhism, which, since 1926, had been using *goeika* as a means to garner interest and participation among lay adherents. With the backing of many influential clergy in the Sōtō Zen hierarchy, Niwa made repeated appeals to the Sōtō sectarian administration calling for the establishment of a school (*ryū*) of Sōtō Zen *goeika*.[2]

By 1951 the *goeika* movement based out of Dōtōin, Niwa's small parish temple in Shizuoka, had begun to generate momentum within the sect. Increasing support among the clergy and Niwa's many petitions to the sectarian administration were eventually met with success, and the as-yet-unnamed *goeika* school was officially established as an auxiliary organization of the Sōtō Zen sect in June 1951. In October representatives from the Sōtō Zen sect met with teachers from the *goeika* schools of three Shingon sects (Koyasan, Tōji, and Chisan) and the Myōshinji Rinzai Zen sect to evaluate which existing style and practice would be "most compatible with the character of the Sōtō sect."[3] In the end, the Sōtō representatives decided that Sōtō *goeika* practice would be modeled after that of the Mitsugen-ryū of the Chisan Shingon sect.

On December 10, 1951, a meeting of the Sōtō Music Research Committee convened to formally establish the new Sōtō Zen *goeika* school. Chief among their concerns was what to name the sect's nascent *goeika-kō*. Many possibilities were considered, but most were dismissed because they were not used in the writings of either of the sect's founders and therefore had no "meaning."[4] Ultimately the committee decided on the word *baika* (plum blossom), which is found in both Dōgen's *Shōbōgenzō* and in Keizan's *Denkōroku*. The Sōtō Zen sect's *goeika* organization, the committee decided, would henceforth be known as the Baika-ryū—the "Plum Blossom School."[5]

The significance of the plum blossom runs deep in the cultures of East Asia, as well as in Buddhist iconography and in Sōtō Zen doctrine. The life cycle of the plum tree serves as an important measure of the passing of the year. The appearance of the plum blossoms in early February mark the coming of spring and correspond with the celebration of the Lunar New Year. From this, the plum tree, including its blossom and its fruit, can often be seen in the literary and visual arts throughout East Asia as symbols of continuity and renewal. Moreover, as the plum tree blooms amid the backdrop of the biting cold and snows of early February, the plum blossom is often used to represent endurance in the face of great hardship. This imagery was taken up in the Buddhist arts, where the blooming plum tree, like the lotus, is a botanical representation of the awakened Buddha, whose presence in the world stands as a beacon of hope for those who live in the midst of hardship and suffering.

For the Buddhist clergy throughout East Asia, the plum blossom carries additional significance. The early-blooming plum blossom thrives in a time of year and in locations where other flowers cannot. They are symbolic reminders that the monastic ideal is to be an exemplar of disciplined grace in spite of the demands and austerities of *shugyō*. As the blooming plum trees were proof that the worst of the winter retreat had passed, the *baika* was the favorite flower of many in the Buddhist clergy, featuring prominently in painting and verse composed by monks and nuns.

For the Japanese Sōtō Zen sect in particular, the image of a single branch of plum blossoms (*baika isshi*) has considerable significance as a symbol of the unbroken lineage of Zen patriarchs and uninterrupted transmission of the True Dharma realized by the Buddha. Dōgen claimed to have had a vision of the long-dead Zen master Damei Fachang while sitting *zazen* at Daibai-zan (Ch. Damei-shan, "Mountain of the Great Plum Trees"). In the vision, Damei handed Dōgen a single branch of plum blossoms, and in that instant, Dōgen claims to have achieved enlightenment. Dōgen believed that his vision of having received the plum blossom spray from Damei was a botanical "passing of the torch" that Dōgen used to legitimate his claim of being heir to the True Dharma, which he brought to Japan from China.[6]

The choice of the plum blossom—a symbol that encapsulates beauty, resilience, and the historical continuity of Sōtō Zen tradition—was an auspicious choice. More than half a century after its establishment, the Baika-ryū is the single largest official propagation body in the Sōtō Zen sect, with more than 6,400 individual *kō* and over 170,000 registered members.[7] A clear measure of the success of *goeika* as a means of encouraging lay participation can be seen in the fact that the number of Baikakō groups sponsored by Sōtō Zen temples in Japan is significantly greater than the number of *zazen* groups. According to results from a 2015 sectarian survey, only about 2,700 Sōtō Zen temples (1 in 5) currently hold regular *zazen* meetings, compared to the more than 4,000 temples (1 in 3) that sponsor Baikakō rehearsals.[8]

"Women's *Shugyō*"

At Sōjiji the Baikakō falls under the auspices of the temple's Propagation Department (Fukyō-ryō). The Propagation Department handles many of the logistical arrangements for the Baikakō—for example, scheduling rehearsal space and arranging for new *goeika* teachers. In addition, the Propagation Department serves as a liaison between the Sōjiji Baikakō and the sect-level offices of the Baika-ryū. New *kō* members are registered with the Propagation Department, who, in turn, submit the appropriate paperwork to the Baika-ryū offices within the Sōtō Zen central sectarian administration. Similarly, when *kō* members take the official advancement tests through the Baika-ryū, they hear the results from the head of the Propagation Department, who recognizes the successful candidate with a certificate of advancement.

Aside from this logistical assistance from the Propagation Department, the Baikakō itself is mostly autonomous. The group receives no financial assistance from Sōjiji for any of its activities. Rather, the group collects monthly dues of 2,500 yen (US$23.75) from each member. Two-thirds of dues collected are given to the temple to cover operational costs associated with rehearsals, including the teacher's salary and a donation in gratitude for the use of temple space. The remaining one-third is kept by the group to pay for incidentals such as tea and sweets for each rehearsal, as well as occasional expenses such as donations and gifts made in the group's name.

The Baikakō has three officers who are elected by the group membership: a group leader (*kōchō*), an assistant group leader, and a secretary. The primary role of these officers is to serve as representatives to the temple on behalf of the Baikakō. The leader during my fieldwork was Mrs. Sakamoto, a soft-spoken octogenarian who had the prestige of being the longest-participating member of Sōjiji's Baikakō. While she rarely addressed the group directly, her opinion was most often solicited when issues of group policy or procedure arose. Because of her seniority, Mrs. Sakamoto was often the only one able to give insight into the origins and rationale of policy decisions that have since become unspoken traditions. The assistant leader was a jovial man named Mr. Kubota, a longtime friend of Mrs. Sakamoto. They had both come to Tokyo in the early 1960s from Miyagi Prefecture, and he was elected to the assistant position precisely because a conflict or disagreement between the two of them was virtually unthinkable.

In terms of actual authority in the group, the leader and the assistant leader are largely figurehead positions. Either by role or by force of personality, the de facto authority in the group lies in the position of secretary. This office was held by Mrs. Terasawa, a fiery woman in her mid-seventies, who was in charge of the membership roster and responsible for collecting the monthly dues and monitoring the group's finances. Mrs. Terasawa was remarkably computer savvy, and within a short time of her taking on the mantle of secretary, she thoroughly modernized the group's record keeping through her use of computer spreadsheets and digital recording.

The force of Mrs. Terasawa's personality was immense. While she often appeared to defer to the higher ranking *kōchō*, she was widely regarded as both policy maker and enforcer. In contrast to Mrs. Sakamoto's soft-spoken demeanor, Mrs. Terasawa's *shitamachi* ("downtown") upbringing, of which she was very proud, gave her a predisposition toward directness and bluntness in her speech and mannerisms. She would bring the full force of her personality to bear when it came to what she thought was best for the group. Even the teacher knew better than to engage her in open disagreement when she had made up her mind.

The membership of the Honzan Baikakō generally fluctuates between thirty and fifty members, though only twenty-five or so attend any given rehearsal. As long as they pay their monthly dues, members are free to attend or not as they please. Most are diligent in coming to rehearsal as often as they can, but illness, family obligations, and travel plans were the reasons most often given for not being able to make it to a specific rehearsal. Members have no need to explain or excuse their absence to the officers or the group—I simply asked after their well-being when I noticed that someone was not at a previous rehearsal.

One of the most notable features of the Sōtō Baika-ryū movement, and of *goeika* groups generally, is the overwhelming predominance of elderly women among the participants. Of the thirty-five members of Sōjiji's Baikakō, female members outnumber the men by nearly a ten-to-one margin, with only four men included on the roster. Prior to 2001 the group was exclusively female; even after, there have never been more than five men in the group at any one time. These numbers are not uncommon in other temples' Baikakō; if anything, Sōjiji may be exceptional in having so *many* men willing to participate.

There is nothing inherently gendered or "feminine" about *goeika* or its performance. The history of *goeika* in Japan dates back to at least the middle Heian period, around the eleventh century CE. *Goeika* has long been associated with the devotional practices of the laity, most notably temple pilgrimages. Unlike other Japanese musical genres, such as *enka*, in which songs are specifically written for male or female performances, *goeika* is technically gender neutral. As pilgrimage songs, *goeika* were taught and sung by men and women alike. It seems to be only after *goeika* was adopted by the various sects of Japanese Buddhism as a means of propagation in the early to mid-twentieth century that *goeika* took on a reputation for being almost exclusively "women's *shugyō*."

The reasons behind this development are not entirely clear. One male informant suggested half jokingly that women are more suited to *goeika* because their voices are "prettier and easier to listen to" than men's voices. Another longtime Baikakō member (a woman) told me that women prefer *goeika* to things like *zazen* because the "environment isn't as strict."

I suggest that one possibility for the gendering of *goeika* may rest in the fact that despite its successes in attracting lay support, modern *goeika* is perceived by traditionalists within the Sōtō Zen sect as an accessory—in the sense of an ornamentation or a support—in temple life and therefore subordinate to "established" practices such as sutra chanting and *zazen*. While *goeika* may be a touching addition to a funeral or memorial service, many feel that it cannot take the place of the necessary liturgy that gives the ritual its doctrinally established efficacy. This power is the sole purview of the ordained—and nearly always male—clergy.

In this regard, it is not coincidental that the model *goeika* practitioner is personified not in a priest but rather in the temple wife (*jizoku*). Temple wives are expected to be exemplars of Japanese traditional "womanly" gender roles, particularly that of wife and mother, whose virtues should include "patience, diligence, endurance, even-temperedness, compliance, and a positive attitude."[9] Within the Sōtō sect, temple wives are an essential but often invisible part of the day-to-day life of a parish temple, usually working as housekeepers, gardeners, cooks, bookkeepers, or receptionists. Perhaps most important for continuity in what is now essentially a generational family business, they are expected to be mothers to the temple's future heirs.[10] Yet, for all their contributions to the daily life of a functioning temple, temple wives remain effectively marginal to institutional Buddhism: they are essential for its survival into future generations, but they lack (or are denied) the formal qualifications to provide care or services to parishioners.[11]

As we saw in the previous chapter, many people hold the view that activities that allow lay practitioners to participate in the "traditional" monastic *shugyō*, however briefly, are superior to those activities that are perceived as "modern" inventions or as "lay-oriented." It is not enough that *goeika*, as a style of music, predates the arrival of Zen in Japan by almost two hundred years, nor does the fact that many male clergy are themselves accomplished *goeika* practitioners sway their opinion. Rather, the Baikakō's origins as a lay propagation movement and reputation as an activity suitable for grandmothers and temple wives, as well as the relatively recent inclusion of *goeika* as part of the Sōtō Zen ritual repertoire, contribute to an atmosphere in which *goeika* is perceived as being ancillary to—and in many way as less authentic than—other temple practices.[12] It is hard to escape the conclusion that in the eyes of many in the Sōtō Zen institution, *goeika* practice is analogous to the role of women in Zen temples—essential for survival but only with limited visibility, recognition, and influence.[13] The members of Sōjiji's Baikakō were very conscious of this attitude of dismissiveness.

There are, of course, men who would otherwise be attracted to *goeika* but are dissuaded from joining by the Baikakō's reputation for being a women's group. It should not be surprising, however, that many women in the Baikakō have a vested interest in keeping that reputation intact. Mr. Takeuchi told me that when he joined the Baikakō, several women were less than welcoming, treating him coldly in his presence and openly complaining about him in his absence. As he tells it, these women resented his invasion into what they considered to be "their" space. He was not the first man to join the Honzan Baikakō (that was Mr. Kubota), but the women clearly felt that one man was more than enough. Mr. Takeuchi later told me that although he persisted in the group, he never felt truly included in it.

The average age of a member of Sōjiji's Baikakō is seventy-two years, with the majority being in their early sixties when they joined. Far from being a mere statistic, the advanced age of the Baikakō members has much to say about the place that *kō* participation holds in members' lives. According to Japanese tradition, sixty is the age of *kanreki*, where a person's life comes full circle, returning them to a "childlike" state in which familial obligations and social responsibilities are formally passed to their children.[14] Rather than celebration, many Japanese enter their sixties with a sense of trepidation and resentment, feeling they are losing—or, perhaps more accurately, being forced out of—the social identities that have defined them for the entirety of their adult lives.[15] Instead of being a period of carefree living, turning sixty is often a difficult time that is characterized by a loss of purpose and a struggle to redefine oneself after a lifetime spent in the workplace or home, occupations that provided clear coordinates by which one could plot their place in the social world.[16] As Japan's "super-aging society" continues to make senior citizens an ever-larger proportion of the population, the country's social, civic, and fiscal infrastructure is proving unable to meet the demand for necessary programs and services, the costs of which are more and more often borne by the elderly themselves. Increasingly, the onset of old age means confronting the realities of isolation, abandonment, vulnerability, and loss of independence that plague the elderly in Japan.[17]

As the time when one's parents pass away and one's children have children of their own, one's sixth decade also marks a major transitional point in a person's life as they assume new roles in their families as elders and custodians of family traditions. Further, the obligations of funerals, memorial ceremonies, and the rites of ancestor veneration bring many to encounter—often for the first time—their family's religious affiliations. These new responsibilities are often accompanied by increased awareness of one's own mortality and concern regarding what lies in store after death, particularly how their spirits will be cared for and remembered.[18]

Though some retirees have long-standing interests that they can now look forward to spending more time with, many who have had precious little free time during their working lives are forced to face the fact that time—empty and undisciplined—is now all they have. For those without previous interests or hobbies, their sixties can be a time for trying out new and different activities on an experimental basis, searching for a new life purpose (*ikigai*) to which they can devote their time, energy, and attention and from which they can forge a new social identity to sustain them through their winter years.[19] The range of possibilities is, of course, endless. For many, the organized structure and discipline of the traditional arts provide a culturally meaningful context for Japanese to reestablish familiar patterns in their daily lives and reinvent themselves in a navigable social landscape. Despite being a recent innovation, *goeika* practice falls into this category.

Employed or preretirement-age women and men are certainly welcome to join the Baikakō. At least at Sōjiji, however, the rehearsal schedule consisting of a five-hour block on weekdays three times a month does not lend itself to the schedules of those with regular employment or with child-care responsibilities. Even if there were interest in singing *goeika*—uncommon, given the prevalence of other musical outlets, such as karaoke—the situation is that people who have jobs and families simply do not have the free time required to be dedicated members. There are exceptions, of course: the Baikakō is considered an excellent way for temple wives, many of whom are between the ages of thirty and sixty, to actively participate in religious activities. The only other exception to the "*goeika* granny (or grandpa)" stereotype I encountered in the Baikakō was an unmarried woman in her late thirties who worked part time. Predictably, she had no choice but to quit the Baikakō when she found full-time employment.

As members age, participation in the Baikakō plays an increasingly significant role in their lives. Over the course of their years of practice, they come to invest hundreds and eventually thousands of hours of face-to-face rehearsal time with the group. In contrast to the relative anonymity of the Sanzenkai, Baikakō members often form close bonds of friendship with other participants. This is especially true for those who join the group around the same time.

Participation in the Baikakō is most dedicated during one's seventies as members who began in their sixties reach veteran status in the group and the prestige of being counted among the higher ranks in the sect-wide Baika-ryū organization. This is also the time when members' interest in Buddhism begins to flourish: travel, especially religious tourism (to temples and pilgrimage sites) is a frequent topic of conversation. In contrast again with the Sanzenkai, it is quite common for Baikakō members to dabble in other aspects of religious life at Sōjiji such as monthly sermons, sutra copying, or *zazen*, though regular participation in these activities is rare.

By the time a member reaches eighty, however, participation tends to fall off dramatically as infirmity and illness make attending rehearsals increasingly difficult. By the end of their time in the group, a Baikakō member often has had, on average, between ten and twenty years of experience with the group.

During the time that I was a member of the group, there were only three regularly participating members over the age of eighty. All of them were women, and all of them were widows. In our conversations, each of these octogenarians told me that their participation in the Baikakō is really all that remained for them: time took spouses, friends, and, in at least one case, children, and these elderly members seldom left their homes for anything except a Baikakō rehearsal. "Younger" members (themselves in their late sixties to early seventies) spoke of these "elders" with respect but used hushed tones to lament what they see as a lonely, sad existence as a "shut-in" (*hikikomori*). Nevertheless, there was a matter-of-fact acceptance of this fate as the natural and inevitable progression of life.

The Fall and Rise of the Honzan Baikakō

Throughout the 1960s and 1970s, the Baikakō thrived at Sōjiji. By 1980, however, the fortunes of the Baikakō had completely reversed. Despite this period corresponding with the height of religious conspicuous consumption in Japan (as measured by the size and cost of funerals and memorial services, as well as household altars), membership in the Baikakō and interest in singing *goeika* declined precipitously. This inverse correlation resulted from the same cause: the elderly generation that was the backbone of the Baika-ryū movement in the 1960s and 1970s was beginning to die off. The increase in money that the baby boom generation was spending on religious trappings did not reflect an increase in personal religiosity but rather that they had the resources to afford more conspicuous memorial expenditures for their parents. As old age and illness increasingly made it difficult for long-time *goeika* practitioners to continue their participation, there were fewer and fewer interested younger people to take their place.

By the time the Japanese bubble economy collapsed in 1992, the Honzan Baikakō was already in critical condition. As membership declined, their membership dues could no longer afford to support the salary of even a part-time *goeika* teacher. By 1999 only three women remained in the group, and they were left to practice by themselves with tape recordings in the place of an instructor. Without a teacher, and without a group to sing with, these women quickly lost the enjoyment of performing *goeika*.

The three remaining members approached both the head of the Fukyō-ryō and the abbot for permission to officially dissolve the ailing Honzan Baikakō. Mrs. Sakamoto, the current *kō* leader, was one of the three women. She explained to me how the two priests sternly refused to acknowledge the possibility that Sōjiji—one of the two flagships of the Sōtō Zen sect—could be without a Baikakō. "They would not allow us to quit," she told me. "They gave us a phone directory of all of the Sōjiji parishioners and let us use the phones in the Fukyō-ryō. Between the three of us, we called every number on that list, saying that the Baikakō was looking for new members." Despite the herculean effort of making over five thousand phone calls, these cold-calling efforts were met with virtually no interest.

Leaving no possibility unexplored, the two priests approached women who were employed as part-time workers at Sōjiji. For the most part, the part-time workers at the temple had no previous religious ties to Sōjiji or even to the Sōtō sect. Nearly all of them had found employment at Sōjiji based on the temple being within walking distance of their homes. Of the roughly two dozen part-time workers at Sōjiji, only three answered the call to join the Baikakō. None of the three had any experience with *goeika* prior to joining the Baikakō, but their agreeing to participate effectively doubled the membership of the group.

As part of the recruitment effort, posters for the Baikakō were printed and hung around the temple in high-traffic areas to ensure maximum visibility. Those who remember them describe the posters as featuring the text of the Heart Sutra as a background along with a caption promising that Baikakō "members would come to understand the teachings of Buddhism." This poster campaign was demonstrably more successful in attracting new members than cold-calling the temple's parishioner base had been. Interestingly, the majority of the new members attracted by the posters were parishioners of other Sōtō temples who had come to Sōjiji for reasons of religious tourism; as with the cold-calling, the posters generated almost no interest from Sōjiji parishioners themselves. While the reasons why both cold-calling and the poster campaign failed to recruit any members from the Sōjiji parishioner base can only be left to speculation, the end result was that the membership of the Honzan Baikakō became comprised almost exclusively of parishioners of other Sōtō Zen temples and members of other Buddhist sects who are personally associated with Sōjiji.

One of the new members attracted by the posters was Mrs. Muraki, a retired schoolteacher. Her natal family was affiliated with the Nichiren sect of Buddhism (at a loss for the name of the sect, she could only describe it to me as "the one that chants *Namu Myōhōrengekyō*"), but Mrs. Muraki had been a devout Christian for nearly all of her life, regularly attending Sunday mass at a Protestant church near her home. When her husband passed away in 1998, funeral preparations revealed that his family were parishioners of a rural Sōtō Zen temple in northwestern Japan.[20] His funeral and subsequent memorial services were officiated by a Sōtō priest in Yokohama hired for the occasion by the funeral company they used.

The loss of her husband was the start of a difficult time for Mrs. Muraki. She described the year that followed as one in which she was "lost and filled with anxiety" (*mayotte nayamimashita*). Feeling that her new role as a Sōtō Buddhist widow was in conflict with her previous identity as a Christian, she stopped going to church and fully gave up her Christianity. At the time, Mrs. Muraki knew very little about Buddhism and even less about Sōtō Zen. As a Christian, much of her religiosity was bound in reading and a personal understanding of the Bible; however, the fact that she couldn't understand the meaning or even words of the Buddhist sutra that were chanted by the Sōtō priest at her husband's funeral deeply distressed her.

Having been religious her entire life and newly responsible for properly observing memorial obligations to her husband, she found herself between two religious worlds: she felt that she could no longer be a good Christian, but she also felt that she did not know enough to be a good Buddhist.

It was during this period that her granddaughter began attending the kindergarten attached to Sōjiji. Mrs. Muraki first heard about the monthly sermons at Sōjiji through a newsletter her granddaughter brought home one day. Sermons were a part of religious life with which, as a Christian, she felt she could identify, and she began attending these monthly meetings regularly. One day, as she was leaving Sōjiji, Mrs. Muraki noticed the recruitment poster for the Baikakō.

Thinking that the Baikakō was a study group like the Bible-reading circles that she was familiar with at her old church, she nervously approached the reception desk and asked one of the monks staffing the desk about the poster. The young monk, unable to define *goeika* himself, explained that it was "'like' a religious text" (*okyō no yō na mono*). Mrs. Muraki immediately signed up, but it took her several months to gather the courage to attend her first Baikakō rehearsal. Not wanting to be embarrassed by her ignorance of Buddhism, she spent those months practicing chanting sutra at home until she felt she was ready to join her peers. "If I had known it was singing, I wouldn't have been so nervous!" she told me with a laugh.

The recruitment campaign of 1999 was a shot of adrenaline to the group, bringing in ten new members, all but one of them women. In the course of the next several years, membership in the Baikakō gradually recovered in strength, though never as quickly as it had during the first stages of the membership drive. By 2008 the group's official roster had reached thirty-five members, and it has held steady in the years since.

While the same forces of natural attrition—infirmity, illness, and death—continue to impact the group's membership at a constant rate, the reinvigorated Baikakō has had more success in attracting new members to fill vacancies. Word of mouth, with members encouraging friends to join, has been an important part of the group's recovery. An equally powerful recruitment tool has been the recent push to include *goeika* as an essential part of the liturgy in Sōtō Zen funerals and memorial services. In fact, several members I spoke with independently reported that their interest in *goeika* stemmed from first hearing it at a funeral or memorial service.

With the exception of three individuals who had been members of Baikakō at other Sōtō Zen temples, none of the new members had any experience performing *goeika* prior to joining Sōjiji's Baikakō. When I asked what precipitated their decision to begin to practice *goeika*, virtually all responses fit into one of five types of answers, with several reporting a combination of motivations. Predictably, the three part-time workers responded that their interest in *goeika* began when the abbot requested volunteers from among the pool of part-time workers. A similar number joined for social reasons: one told me that she simply "wanted to sing with a group," while one of the three male practitioners was encouraged to join "because there were so few men." Five reported being influenced by the practice of family members, with four of the five describing childhood memories of one or both parents performing *goeika* songs. Four responded that they became interested in the practice of *goeika* as a means of personal or spiritual cultivation; one respondent wrote to me that she began her practice of *goeika* "to quiet [her] mind, and also to turn bad thoughts into good ones" (*kokoro ga yasuraka ni nareru, akushin mo yoi kokoro ni*).

Songs of Loss and Remembrance

In interviews, by far the most common reason given for beginning *goeika* practice was as a way of honoring the memory of a deceased family member, spouse, or friend. Roughly a third of respondents reported that their *goeika* practice originated in a desire to perform *kuyō* (offerings for the dead). Most of those who responded in this way specified the person in whose memory they practice *goeika*; two, however, responded with the more general "*senzo kuyō*," as offerings to one's ancestors.

Much of the appeal of contemporary *goeika* performance stems from its perception as "traditional art." The use of old melodies, antiquated musical notation, and lyrics composed in stylistically classical Japanese lends the music an immediate patina of both history and tradition—even if the song itself is brand-new. This "instant tradition" serves both to legitimize *goeika* performance as a respectable hobby and to deepen the elegiac effect of *goeika* performance, immersing the participant in an emotional setting that invokes nostalgia and longing for a bygone past and allowing for the safe and sanctioned expression of sadness and loss.[21]

In this regard, it is telling that when asked about their favorite song, the overwhelming answer is the "*Tsuizen kuyō* (Memorial Service) *gowasan*." At first consideration, this is a very curious preference. The "*Tsuizen kuyō gowasan*" is a sorrowful, mournful song. The melody is composed in the pentatonic (*yonanuki*) minor mode heard most commonly in contemporary Japanese *enka* songs. With *goeika*, as with *enka*, the pentatonic minor mode is used to great effect to evoke emotions of loss, loneliness, nostalgia, heartbreak, and sadness.[22] These emotions are amplified by the poetic solemnity of the lyrics:

Tama to musubite hachisuba ni	The jewel bound to the lotus flower
Okitaru tsuyu no ichi shizuku	is but one drop of dew.
Nagaki wa hito no negai ni te	Long are the prayers of humans
Mijikaki mono wa inochi nari	and such a short thing is life.
Kinō ari shi wa kyō wa yume	What was here yesterday is today but a dream.
Utsutsu ni miyuru misugata wa	In reality, the forms we see
Kokoro no naka no kage ni shite	are merely the shadows within our heart.
Awaseru te koso makoto naru	Truth exists only in our joined palms.
Mina o shizuka ni tonoureba	If I quietly intone your name,
Omoi wa sara ni iyamashinu	my thoughts will further intensify.
Onozuto nijimu namida ni mo	Naturally, [my eyes] will also blur with tears
Eishi no fukaki yue o shiru	and I will know how deep our connection goes.
Sonau hanabana haewatari	The flowers I offer give off their light,
Magokoro akeki miakashi to	and my sincerity is illumined by candlelight.
Mairasu kō ni tsutsumarete	I am enveloped in the incense I have burned,
Mitama yo towa ni yasurawan	and I find peace in the permanence of your soul.

The song has a powerful vocal swell that reoccurs in the third line of each stanza. As the singers move into the higher ranges of their voices, the music becomes hauntingly reminiscent of a wail of grief. In fact, so moving are performances of the *"Tsuizen kuyō gowasan"* that performers are often led to tears well before the song has ended, sometimes during the first verse.

As its name implies, the song is most often heard in the context of memorial services. Yet, despite these somber association, the *"Tsuizen kuyō gowasan"* was the single most requested song at Baikakō rehearsals. Even if they could not remember the lyrics by heart, most members could sing the melody from memory. With all of the positive, life-affirming songs to choose from, why was so much time and attention given to a *goeika* that spoke only of life's brevity and fragility?

I approached these questions with Mrs. Inamura during a tea break on a particularly warm day in May. With over twenty years of *goeika* practice, Mrs. Inamura was the most experienced member of Sōjiji's Baikakō. Like many others I spoke to, the *"Tsuizen kuyō gowasan"* was her favorite *goeika*.

"*Goeika* is something I do for my father," she told me. She explained that her father was a particularly devout Sōtō layman who idealized the monastic lifestyle and had always dreamed of becoming a monk. Some of her fondest memories are from when she was little, when she would sit with him while he chanted sutra in front of the family altar in their house in Shizuoka. When she was five, her father made the decision to realize his lifelong dream. He took the tonsure and left his family to become an *unsui* at a temple whose name she could not remember.

Tragically, he was dead within three years, felled by heart failure in the course of his training, at the young age of forty-five. Seventy-three years later, Mrs. Inamura still blames his death on the severity of his *shugyō*. "If he hadn't become a monk, maybe he would have lived to be a grandfather," she told me.

"When I sing *goeika*, I feel like my father is watching over me. It is like when I used to chant sutra with him. I remember the sound of his voice. This is *kuyō* for my father."

As the popularity of the *"Tsuizen kuyō gowasan"* suggests, Mrs. Inamura's perspective on *goeika* was not uncommon within the Baikakō. For many in the group, the appeal of *goeika* lay in it being a kind of *naki-bushi*, "crying songs" written specifically to invoke deep emotional responses from both performer and listener, particularly drawing out feelings of grief, sadness, and loss.[23]

However, the regular performance of emotionally evocative songs is not intended to be a masochistic trial of psychological endurance. Just as people watch certain films knowing that they will cry at the end, members of the Baikakō perform the *"Tsuizen kuyō gowasan"* precisely because it invokes an emotion-filled, tearful response: performances "reliev[e] the seriousness behind the tears in the fabric of experience . . . and mak[e] these feelings comforting, even beautiful."[24] That others in the group are likely to understand or at least appreciate the sincerity of the emotions that the songs invoke makes the Baikakō a safe space for practitioners to experience and explore these emotions without fear of censure or judgment.[25] As a result, the regular exposure to feelings of pain and grief can lead to positive transformations and a deeper appreciation for the relationships they share. This effect is particularly pronounced among those who are trying to learn to renavigate their world after a profound personal loss.

As a form of *kuyō*, *goeika* is particularly powerful, as it empowers performers to be active participants in the ritual processes of memorialization that would ordinarily be the sole prerogative of the clergy. In a religious context where the laity are usually relegated to the role of passive observers, *goeika* performance grants performers significant agency in the ritual processes that benefit the dead without requiring an intermediary to do the work for them. It is for this reason that the dedication phrase (*ekōmon*) of a *goeika* performance is carefully worded not to specify a recipient; each individual practitioner is encouraged to privately fill in the blanks for themselves and dedicate the merit generated by their own performance as they see fit. As a result, each *goeika* recitation becomes more than just the mere performance of a song; practitioners are encouraged to treat each song as an act of compassion, empowering them to take an active ritual role on behalf of loved ones who are normally beyond their reach. The more powerful the emotion expressed (especially if there are tears), the more sincere the performer's intention is seen to be and, consequently, the more efficacious the performance in producing karmic merit that will be selflessly transferred to the loved one being memorialized. From such a perspective, an emotionally evocative performance of *goeika* is quite literally a performance of compassion.

The Hall of the Smiling Clouds

For years, the Baikakō has used a multipurpose room in the Shōunkaku (Hall of the Smiling Clouds) for rehearsals. The room sits adjacent to the Propagation Department offices in an area that ranks among the least-trafficked of Sōjiji. To reach it from the temple reception desk, one has to navigate a twisting path along the temple corridors through three separate buildings; past a barricade with a posted sign stating, "No visitors beyond this point"; and finally up a steep carpeted incline. For a person unfamiliar with the layout of Sōjiji, the room—tucked away in the deepest part of the temple complex—is virtually impossible to find without assistance.

The building sits on the highest point of the temple grounds and commands an impressive view over the entire temple precincts. The room used for rehearsal is a simple rectangle, narrow on the eastern and western ends and long on the northern and southern sides. Translucent paper panels separate the western and southern walls from the hallway outside, while opaque sliding doors close off the eastern and northern walls from the rooms behind. Although these panels create a space of relative privacy, one is always aware of the activity going on in other rooms of the building, especially the busy Fukyō-ryō office next door, whose phone and fax machines are perpetually ringing.

Being without furniture, the room is an empty visual space that virtually demands to be defined. For lectures the room's spacious tatami flooring can easily accommodate about eighty people. When "study and training" (*kenshū*) retreat groups come to Sōjiji, low tables are brought into the room so that the guests have space to take notes, copy sutra, and eat. On overnight stays, bedding is brought in from a nearby storage closet to convert the room into sleeping quarters. For *zazen* sessions, *zafu* cushions can be placed around the perimeter of the room to create an impromptu meditation hall. The only fixed pieces of furniture in the room are two small bookshelves off to the side that contain an eclectic variety of Buddhism-related reading material.

The room, as it is, can easily be converted for ritual purposes. In an alcove along the northern wall hangs a scroll painting of the bodhisattva Kannon, beneath which sits a basic altar holding candlesticks, an offering of fresh flowers, and an incense burner. A *kyōsaku* stick lies lengthwise across the altar for use during *zazen*. In front of this sits a tray that can be used to hold offerings such as food, tea, or handwritten sutra. To the sides of the altar are a small bell and hollow wooden drum used to keep time while chanting, and to the side of the alcove is a small cabinet built into the wall, which stores various sutra books in both Japanese and English.

Unlike the spaces used by the monks for meditation and ceremony, which are left in a ready state for immediate use, before anything else, the Baikakō must first transform the empty space of the Shōunkaku to be a space for the performance of *goeika*. The rehearsal space of the Baikakō is arranged to facilitate maximum visibility for everyone.

The room is set up in such a way that a person on one side of the room can easily watch the movements of those sitting across from them while using peripheral vision to follow the motions of those sitting next to them. The rehearsal space is set up in a block-U formation, with members seated single file along both the northern and southern walls of the room, and the bulk of the group seated two rows deep along the bottom of the U. The teacher sits by himself on a cushion at the top of the U, closing the circle. Everyone faces the center of the room.

The astute observer will note that the color of the tassels attached to the bells used during *goeika* practice create a continuum as one's eyes move from left to right along the northern wall, around the bottom of the U, and from right to left along the southern wall. Seating is coordinated according to rank as determined through standardized tests administered yearly

Fig. 14. The members of the Baikakō practice *goeika* while waiting for the teacher to arrive.

by the Baika-ryū. The lower-ranked beginners along the northern wall use purple tassels on their bells and rosaries, while the mid-level members who sit in the curve of the U have light blue tassels. Finally, the veterans along the southern wall are distinguished by their white tassels, as is the teacher.

While tassel color provides a visual means of quickly establishing who should sit where in the room, the truth is that these three colors represent eleven individually named ranks through which a layperson can progress.[26] As a consequence, there is quite a bit of variance within the color groupings themselves. To seat themselves properly, members need to know precisely who outranks them and who is below them. Unlike the Sanzenkai, Baikakō members are not concerned about defending "their" space, as where one sits changes depending on who is present and who is absent. Instead it is a game of navigating to one's proper place within an officially recognized hierarchy. With just a glance, the members are able to judge from who is in attendance roughly where they should be seated for the rehearsal and negotiate from there until they find their proper seat.

In marked contrast to activities in the Daisodō, Sōdō, and Shuryō, which facilitate a hierarchical reading of the space by obscuring and privileging lines of sight, the roughly oval formation used in Baikakō rehearsals creates a communal field of vision. From a musical perspective, this formation makes the most sense, as it allows members to use both their ears and eyes to keep time with the rest of the group, which is why the semicircle is the formation of choice for both orchestral and choral ensembles. On another level, however, the Baikakō's block-U formation conveys a more important message: that no one seat in the room—even that of the teacher—is more privileged than any other. In other words, it is the commonalities of *goeika* practice, not the differences, that give meaning to the *shugyō* being performed in the room.

The empty potential space of the Shōunkaku is transformed by the Baikakō to be an occupied active space that facilitates the performance of *dōgyō*—"shared practice." *Dōgyō* implies simultaneity, unison, and, above all, group harmony. In this regard, *dōgyō* stresses the shared, social aspect of *shugyō*; in the rehearsal space, as in the meditation hall or the ceremony hall, it is vital that one be aware and respectful of the people and activity that is taking place around them. While this is good advice to anyone working closely with others, in a musical context, awareness of one's fellow practitioners is the only thing that allows for the performance of unison. Practitioners cannot be permitted to move too fast, such that they finish before everyone else, but neither can they move too slow, such that they make everyone wait for them. *Dōgyō* therefore requires a person to engage all of their senses to fall in with the rhythm established by the group.

While the emphasis on *dōgyō* can be seen in all facets of temple life from ceremonies to mealtimes, the Baikakō embodies this synchronization of practice over any other ritual context. In virtually no other temple context do all participants do the same thing at the same time, and the focus on mechanical unison in the *goeika* performance can be said to be categorically distinct from what might be described as the "organic simultaneity"— different actors performing different roles at the same time—of a ceremony in the Daisodō.

If coordinated "shared practice" is the goal of the Baikakō's *shugyō*, why go through the trouble of establishing a hierarchy of grades and ranks? My observation is that instead of detracting from the shared experience, the hierarchical arrangement of the *goeika* performance space actually reinforces *shugyō* as a communal disciplining practice. This arrangement, or variations thereof, can be found throughout the traditional Japanese fine arts and martial arts. It forces the novices sitting on one side to observe and learn from the veterans sitting across from them while preventing them from seeing (and thus picking up bad habits from) fellow beginners sitting next to them. Conversely, the veterans, whose skill has been proven and refined from years of practice, can keep a watchful eye on the novices in order to correct mistakes, but they also must be vigilant not to let their own technique slip since, as exemplars, they too are being constantly observed. The middle ranks—not yet experts, not quite beginners—can observe and be observed by the instructor. They are not yet practiced enough for their skill to be taken as a given, but neither are they inexperienced enough to require constant reinforcement. Just as in the Monk's Hall, the careful establishment of hierarchy in the Baikakō's rehearsal space is an important means to the end of ensuring group harmony and uniformity.

Offerings of Song

As a religious organization, the Baikakō brings together a variety of people for the common purpose of performing *goeika*. As a group that performs vocal music in a religious setting, it is very tempting to gloss the Baikakō as a "temple chorus" or "choir." While the Baikakō certainly shares some surface similarities with church choirs or choruses (which provide the closest analogue), there are fundamental differences that distinguish the Baikakō from the typical church choir.

For one, despite fifteen hours of rehearsal a month, the Honzan Baikakō is only rarely invited to perform in ceremonies at Sōjiji, though they are almost always invited to attend. My notes show that the Baikakō was asked to perform in public ceremonies on only four occasions during the year I was an active member of the group. Even the group's yearly recital held in March is attended only by the current members of the Baikakō. To my knowledge, families are never invited, and the clergy (a select number of whom do receive invitations) are often too busy to attend. As a consequence, the Baikakō emphasizes the act of rehearsing (*keiko*) itself rather than on public or ceremonial performance.

Sōjiji's Baikakō meets three times a month on days that end in the number seven—that is, the seventh, the seventeenth, and the twenty-seventh of each month.[27] On rehearsal days, members begin to arrive about fifteen minutes before the scheduled start of practice, greeting those who have arrived before them with a cheerful "*Ohayō gozaimasu!*" (Good morning) as they enter the rehearsal room. There is surprisingly little rushing as they drop off their belongings and begin to prepare the room and themselves for rehearsal. Newly arriving members take quick stock of what remains to be done and divide their labor accordingly. One group takes the stools, desks, and cushions out of storage and arranges them throughout the room, and another group prepares tea and distributes a variety of cookies and sweets into small folded-paper pouches. One woman from this group takes a cup of tea and a bag of sweets and, with a slight bow, places them in the alcove where the scroll painting depicting the bodhisattva Kannon hangs.

After the room is prepared, the members gradually make their way to their seats, setting up their personal space and unpacking their things while continuing to talk with their friends. At their seats, the women don ankle-length blue choir robes over their clothes.[28] Over their shoulders, all members put a thin purple stole known as a *warakusu*, a religious stole identical in symbolism to the *rakusu* (see chapter 4), which is itself a functional adaptation of the monastic *kesa*. In addition to this, everyone wears a beaded rosary on their left wrists.[29] From their bags, the members take out a richly embroidered purple and gold bundle and place it on the desk or floor in front of them. With the sound of ripping Velcro, this bundle is opened to reveal a second bundle wrapped in a green cloth. The outer cover is set aside, and the green bundle is left closed for the time being.

A cushion has been placed in the front of the room for the teacher, who himself casually enters the room minutes before rehearsal begins, wearing his monastic robes and carrying a briefcase. Yamazaki-sensei, the group's teacher, is a handsome monk in his early forties with a clear baritone voice and a warm smile. Three times a month, he braves the two-hour drive through the dense morning rush-hour commute from his home temple to Tsurumi to lead the Baikakō rehearsal. As he takes his materials out of his briefcase, one of the women brings him a cup of tea. He exchanges greetings and casual conversation with the group, and the ease with which he relates to the group is one of the reasons for his popularity.

With a last sip from his teacup, Yamazaki-sensei raises his voice to address the group and begins the rehearsal. The casual, relaxed atmosphere of the prerehearsal is instantly transformed. All conversation immediately stops as everyone sits up straighter in their seats and shifts their attention to the front of the room.

Rehearsal starts with a seated bow with palms together. This bow, similar to the one made before *zazen*, is meant as an acknowledgment of the teacher and the others in the room with whom one will be practicing. It is also a show of respect to the *hōgu* ("Dharma objects") that are contained in the bundles that sit before them. Most significantly, this bow marks the entrance into ritual space and time: until the "parentheses" are closed with a similar bow at the end of rehearsal, everything contained within is meant to be separate and distinct from everyday activity.

Fig. 15. *Goeika* bells and songbook. The handbell (*rei*) stands at the lower left and the flat bell (*shō*) sits at the lower right, with the tasseled hammer (*shumoku*) laying between them.

In silence and with synchronized movements, the members begin to carefully unwrap the bundles that sit in front of them. The green cloth (*fukusa*) that wraps the bundle is unfolded with both hands, first smoothing out the right side, and then the left side. The inside of the cloth is a rich purple with intricate gold embroidery of plum flowers along the edges; the temple crests of both Sōjiji and Eiheiji dominate the center. In addition to containing the items inside for safe transport, the *fukusa* serves as a kind of placemat for the items when they are in use, creating a respectful barrier between the items and the floor.

Opening the *fukusa* cloth reveals several items arranged on top of a thick book. First, a flat, hollow silver bell (*shō*) is removed from the pile and placed on the lower right corner of the mat. A thin hammer (*shumoku*) is placed next to the *shō*, its long tassel arranged carefully alongside it. Next, a tall handbell (*rei*) is stood vertically on the lower left corner of the mat. Care is taken while lifting the handbell to keep the bell quiet as it is moved, but still a number of accidental ringings punctuate the silence, to the embarrassment of their owners. For the moment, the songbook—which, as a religious text, is called a *kyōten*—is left closed in the center of the mat.

The moving and placement of each of the items follows a carefully pre-scribed order and rhythm. The simple act of opening the right flap of the cloth is a complex motion that requires the hands to be placed in line, left over right, with the fabric gripped gently between the index and middle fingers. In a single movement, as the fabric is pulled to the side, the palm of the hand is used to smooth out any wrinkles in the cloth. The hands are then repositioned to open the left flap in a similar fashion. It is important that the proper placement of the different items be accompanied by a graceful, deliberate, and, above all, precise bodily movement: the cloth is not so much opened as it is *placed* in an open position; the handbell is not so much stood up as it is *placed* in a standing position. Like so much of Zen ritual, emphasis is placed not on the efficiency or speed of a movement but rather on the smoothness and grace by which the motion is performed.

Despite being described as "Dharma objects," there is nothing intrinsically special about the items contained within the *hōgu* bundle, any more than there is anything special about the store-bought tea and sweets offered to the image of Kannon. While on the surface it may appear absurd to spend an hour practicing wrapping and unwrapping a set of bells until the group gets it right, the very act of handling the bells with attentiveness and care imbues the items—and the music they will be used to make—with the aura of an "offering" (*osonae*). I was amazed to see how much rehearsal time is spent practicing and reinforcing these very basic movements to make them automatic; indeed, proper handling of the *hōgu* is as much a part of the practice of *goeika* as the music itself.

Harmony in Dissonance

Having prepared their tools and space, the teacher uses his *shumoku* hammer to strike a small wooden clapper, producing a sharp crack. On cue, the group opens their books to the first page and places it in front of them. One of the veteran singers then leads the group in the Baikakō pledge:

Watakushi wa Baikaryū eisanka o tooshite,	Through the songs of the Baika-ryū,
tadashii shinkō ni ikimasu.	we will live in correct belief.
Watakushi wa Baikaryū eisanka o tooshite,	Through the songs of the Baika-ryū,
nakayoi kurashi o itashimasu.	we will live a lifestyle of harmony.
Watakushi wa Baikaryū eisanka o tooshite,	Through the songs of the Baika-ryū,

akarui yo no naka o   we will make a brighter world.
tsukurimasu.

The Baikakō rehearsal opens with three bows (*sanpai*) and the recital of the *Kaikyōge*, an acknowledgment by the assembly that they will do their best to understand the teaching that is to follow. The group continues with a recitation of several more religious texts, most notably the Heart Sutra, which most members can recite from memory. With the final bow that follows the Heart Sutra, the opening service is over and rehearsal begins in earnest.

Rehearsals are full-day events that run from ten in the morning to three in the afternoon with regular bathroom and tea breaks and an hour-long lunch break at noon. While the rehearsal format is highly structured in nature, the rehearsals themselves are actually very relaxed occasions. There are only a few times during the year when there is any kind of itinerary or lesson plan, and these usually precede the yearly testing (for those who wish to advance in rank), a national or regional convention, or before the group is scheduled to participate in a temple ceremony. At all other times the rehearsal is generally left open to requests from the members. Should no one offer a suggestion, the teacher might choose a song thematically related to the closest major Buddhist holiday, but more often than not he chooses a song already familiar to a majority of those present.

Once the song has been decided, the members hold the songbook with both hands, raise it to eye-level, and bow their heads. The members then turn the book to the appropriate page by gripping the back of the book with the left hand and opening the front with the right hand to reveal the song. Similar to most ritual texts used in a Sōtō Zen temple, the songbooks are not bound on their spines but are printed in an accordion-fold fashion such that the entire book, if opened to its full length, would be one continuous page. The accordion-fold printing allows both two- and four-page songs to be read without the need to turn pages.

Yamazaki-sensei often prefaced the *goeika* to be rehearsed with a short, usually anecdotal, speech to elucidate the important themes and meanings of the particular song for the group. Despite the ritual formality of the space, the impromptu nature of this "mini-sermon" also worked to make the atmosphere in the rehearsal more relaxed and conversational. Unlike a formal sermon, the Baikakō members were fully engaged in the teacher's story, reacting with nonverbal cues and at times even interjecting their own opinions. While the majority of the teacher's speeches were brief, the more engaging discussions extended well into the time allotted for rehearsal.

When his talk was finished, Yamazaki-sensei performed the song in its entirety by himself, using the *shumoku* hammer and small wood block to mark the rhythm. About a third of the membership brought personal recording devices to record his recitations, turning their recorders on when he started singing and off when he finished. (I was the only one who recorded full rehearsals.) Members would then use these recordings as a reference for when they practiced at home—one woman, for example, said she listens to her recordings on a loop while she does her daily housework.

To a significant degree, Yamazaki-sensei's recitations—and the mini-sermons that preface them—shape the way in which the *goeika* songs are internalized and their meanings are interpreted by the Baikakō participants. This oral transmission from teacher to student is a fundamental part of *goeika*'s identity as a traditional Japanese art. For much of its history, *goeika* was taught within a "family system" (*iemoto seido*) in which songs, melodies, and techniques would be passed down from teacher to student through example and rote repetition.[30] As a primarily oral tradition, this teaching style allowed for proprietary styles of *goeika* to develop. One elderly informant (though not a Baikakō member herself) vividly recalled learning *goeika* as a child in rural Ibaraki Prefecture during the 1930s in this fashion. Once a week, she told me, neighbors gathered at her house to learn from her grandmother, a respected *goeika* teacher: "On days that my grandmother would teach, our house would be full of people—from wall to wall, only people. She would sing one line, and then everyone would repeat it. Back then, no one read music. We learned by listening and memorizing the songs."

As each Buddhist sect's *goeika* school began to publish its own song-books and sheet music (and, later, audio recordings on cassette tapes, CDs, and downloadable MP3s), *goeika* performance became standardized, leaving less room for individual interpretation of the music. This standardization further lent itself to the development of a progressive ranking system, modeled on the system of clerical ranks, where practitioners could be officially certified by a central authority as having demonstrated correct technique and the ability to correctly perform the music as written. This move toward orthopraxy communicated clearly that *goeika* practice was to be viewed as "a *shugyō* curriculum for lay adherents" (*shinja no shugyō katei*), requiring serious, dedicated, and disciplined practice according to the sect's standards and guidelines.[31]

Because of this standardization, the fact that Yamazaki-sensei's interpretation of a given song (for example, his tone, vibrato, and other vocal ornamentations) is emulated and internalized by the Baikakō members to the best of their ability was viewed by some as deeply problematic. One woman, a longtime member who now attends rehearsals only sporadically, was particularly critical of this practice. Rather than place the blame on the members, who in her opinion were doing what diligent students should, she thought that the teacher himself was acting irresponsibly. In her opinion, a *good* teacher (subtly implying that Yamazaki-sensei was not) would keep his talking during rehearsal to a minimum and during his recitations would sing the songs exactly as they are written on the page—that is, flat and unornamented. "Instead of teaching, he gives us a concert," she told me. "This is not a karaoke group, you know."

It's Harder Than It Looks

After his solo recitation, Yamazaki-sensei leads the group in a line-by-line practice of the song while keeping time with the wood block: first he sings the line, and then the group repeats the line back to him. Other than the crack of the wood block (which is sharp enough to be heard through all other sound), the teacher does not conduct the group in any visible way. The group almost never uses their bells during this part of practice, but it is not uncommon to see members pantomiming the bell movements or trying to match the teacher's rhythm by tapping their knee or thighs with sweeping vertical movements. Predictably, the movements of one or two members, slightly ahead or behind the beat, throws off the members sitting next to them, creating a domino effect through which dissonance ripples throughout the room. It is not uncommon for the group to practice the same line several times in succession as Yamazaki-sensei stops to smooth out difficult or complicated sections of the music.

When each line of the verse has been individually rehearsed, the group practices the verse in its entirety, this time using the handbell and flat bell. Most *goeika* songs, particularly the metered *gowasan*,[32] are written in 4/4 time, with each beat of the measure punctuated by a different hand motion. The handbell is held in the left hand and the hammer in the right. During the song, they are used in conjunction in the following pattern:

Beat one: the hammer is swung to strike the flat bell
Beat two: the head of the hammer is audibly placed on the desk/
    floor
Beat three: the handbell is flicked forward to produce a single ring
Beat four: the handbell is flicked again for a single ring

The combined effect is to produce a distinctive *clang-thud-ring-ring* pattern that is repeated throughout the entire song.

For all but the most experienced (or ambidextrous) of practitioners, proper use of the bells is easily the most difficult part of *goeika* practice. Ringing the bells in a manner that combines a pleasing sound with graceful movement requires a level of precision that comes only from years of dedicated practice.

Take, for example, striking the flat bell with the hammer. While sounding simple in theory, proper form is to hold the hammer with only the thumb and forefinger, creating an axis of motion; the remaining three fingers are used only to hold the long tassel that extends from the end of the hammer to prevent it from flying out of one's hand. The hammer is not used to strike as much as it is made to fall against the flat bell in a controlled manner. Too heavy a fall produces a painful, ear-piercing crack; too light a fall will glance off the bell, producing a muddled sound. Similarly, the handbell is held in an awkward hand position meant to simulate the palms-together *gasshō*; this requires that the entirety of the forearm, and not the fingers, be used to produce a sound. Too much of a flick of the arm will cause the clapper to ring against both the front and the back of the bell, producing two sounds instead of one; too light a flick, or holding the bell in a way that tries to use the fingers to control movement, will result in no sound at all.

For most of these movements, the practitioner has only a fraction of a second to move their hands into proper position. When combined with the reading of music and singing, the movements required for proper use of the bells are simply too fast to be left to conscious thought. For one to gracefully perform *goeika*, it is essential that use of the bells be made automatic and habitual, and—like all other aspects of *shugyō*—this can only be done through diligent and repeated practice. Allowing conscious thought to intrude on one's actions by worrying about timing or technique invariably leads to mistakes. And at the group level, the mistakes of even a single person create irreparable dissonance.

It comes as no surprise, then, that adding the bells to the practice of a song almost always counteracts the work that was done while the song was being practiced line by line with only voices. "Non-thinking" is as elusive an ideal for the Baikakō members as it is for *zazen* practitioners. In *goeika* practice there are many factors to concern oneself with, and it is easy for a practitioner to find their attention split in a myriad of directions: the written music, the words on the page, the rhythm of each syllable, the flow of the song, the placement of one's hands, the movement of the bells, the sound and tempo of one's neighbor, the sharp crack of the teacher's wooden block, errant ringings, missed notes, even the sound of the monks' footsteps in the halls outside. While keeping these thoughts in check is difficult for any individual, such difficulties are cumulative and are multiplied exponentially in a group. The resultant effect is that even the most rehearsed song is constantly under threat of collapsing into cacophony as the individual practitioners and the group as a whole struggle to keep their focus.

Learning to discipline one's body and mind amid this struggle between harmony and discord is precisely the point of the Baikakō's *shugyō*. In a sense, the rehearsal space is the world in microcosm: even when care is taken to set everything in its proper place, life is filled with elements that threaten to destroy the harmony in which one wishes to live. By placing emphasis on the rehearsal rather than the public performance, the practitioners are encouraged to focus not on preparing for one perfect performance of a song (which, even if possible, would be only a fleeting thing) but on the act of disciplining itself.

When each verse has been rehearsed to the teacher's satisfaction—though not necessarily to the satisfaction of the individual members—the song is ready to be "offered." The performance of *goeika*, even in the context of a rehearsal, is treated as an offering from the group, though to whom is deliberately never specified. Two individual members are chosen as leaders—usually in order of decreasing seniority, with the two highest-ranking members getting the first song, the next two highest getting the second song, and so on—to start the performance. While the group positions their hands in *gasshō*, the first leader slowly and solemnly chants the title of the song:

Tonae tatematsuru {title} *goeika/gowasan ni.*

We offer this recitation of the {title} *goeika/gowasan*.

The leader draws out their intonation of the syllable "*ei*" in "*goeika*" (or *wa* in "*gowasan*"), adding a vibrato that vacillates by as much as a half step below the pitch: this is a stylistic signal similar to the one used during a ceremony when the cantor calls the title of the liturgy to be chanted. This vibrato serves as a cue to the assembly that the group will be starting in two syllables.[33] As the leader intones this syllable, the group bows their heads, both in recognition of the leader's call and in respect to the presentation of the offering.

The second leader then sings the first phrase of the song alone while the group brings their bells to a ready position. In addition to the pressure of having to perform solo in front of the entire group, the leader who sings the first phrase has the responsibility of setting the key for the entire song. *Goeika*, like many forms of Japanese music, does not use absolute pitch (C, F-sharp, B-flat, etc.) but instead uses relative pitch (do, mi, sol, etc.). This relies on the ability of the leader to accurately intuit the vocal range of the group as a whole: if the key is set either too high or too low, many of the notes will be out of reach for the group. While the teacher usually uses an electronic pitch pipe to give the leader an appropriate starting pitch beforehand, hearing the person before them recite the title (which can be chanted at any pitch that is comfortable to the chanter) often throws off the pitch of the first line. As a result, the person chosen to perform the first phrase is often unsure of the pitch and uncomfortable with both their solo performance and the responsibility to start the song; more often than not, this is the moment when *goeika* performances break down, to the embarrassment of the leader, who usually asks for a do-over until they get it right. Nervous or struggling leaders are often helped by the group to find the right pitch. For some leaders, it is a welcome relief to have the support of the group behind them; for others, it is an embarrassment to have to rely on the assistance of the group.

Very rarely will the teacher interrupt a song once the entire group starts singing, though he will do so if the tempo, rhythm, or pitch are irrevocably lost. In all other instances, the group sings through—or in some cases, stumbles through—to the end of the song, with the teacher using the wood block to keep tempo or raising his voice to be loud enough to keep the song in key if necessary.

At the end of the song, the group finishes in unison, holding their hammers horizontally in front of them and bowing their heads. The group then carefully—and, ideally, silently—replaces their handbell on the mat and deftly arranges the hammer and its tassel in front of them. Placing their hands together again in *gasshō*, the group bows in unison, and the offering is complete. In almost every case, the teacher is the one to break the silence that follows the last bow, replacing the ritual formality of the performance offering with a more relaxed atmosphere.

All told, it takes roughly an hour to practice one song from start to finish. With the hour-long lunch break at noon, a normal Baikakō rehearsal covers only about four songs, with an average of forty minutes per hour spent in actual practicing. Roughly the first ten minutes of every hour are given as a break for members to use the restroom, drink tea, and socialize, while the next ten are spent listening to Yamazaki-sensei's mini-sermon. Although it would be possible for rehearsals to move through each song at a more rigorous pace, my experience has been that most Baikakō members enjoy the more relaxed pace and atmosphere set by Yamazaki-sensei. This pace is not for everyone, however. As one disapproving member emphatically complained to me, "This isn't *shugyō*; it's a coffee circle!"

As the time approaches three in the afternoon, Yamazaki-sensei brings rehearsal to a close. Recalling the solemn attentiveness of the beginning of rehearsal, the rehearsal ends with the chanting of the *ekōmon*, the "Transfer of Merit" verse, which redistributes the good merit generated by the group's *shugyō* for the betterment of all living things. This is followed by a single sitting bow in *gasshō*, the closing of the ritual parentheses, at which point the rehearsal can be said to be officially over.

The presence of the Transfer of Merit verse at the end of the rehearsal as ritual is expected, but the way in which it is performed is a sharp departure from the norm. In nearly all other ritual instances, the *ekōmon* is chanted by the cantor in a single voice on behalf of the assembly. At the Baikakō rehearsal, all of the participants recite the Transfer of Merit verse in unison, a powerful reinforcement of the principle of *dōgyō*.

As before, the teacher is the one to break the silence with a customary "*otsukaresama deshita*" (You must be tired). The rehearsal has now officially ended. The members carefully—but this time without solemn ceremony—rewrap their bundles for transport. The women remove their choir robes, fold them, and put them away. Once one's personal space is taken care of, members move quickly to return the Shōunkaku to its prerehearsal state, again dividing the labor between them. One group collects the teacups for washing and the candy wrappers for disposal, while another group stacks the stools, desks, and cushions for storage. A third group breaks out brooms and sweeps the tatami for any crumbs that may have fallen during rehearsal. Working together, the entire room is reverted to its original state as a potential space in fewer than five minutes.

Members usually leave the room in small groups, walking together on the way to their cars or the Tsurumi train station. They continue their conversations as they walk through the halls of the temple. As they leave through the entrance to the temple reception, some make a detour to pay their respects at the Daisodō or to visit the shrines dotted throughout the temple grounds. Occasionally, they stop for coffee at one of the many cafés near the station, but most say their good-byes and go directly home, not to meet again until the next rehearsal.

As I have shown, even in its most emotionally raw moments, *goeika* encourages practitioners not to dwell on the pain of loss but to use the pain to cultivate in oneself a greater compassion and grace in the face of hardship. This is not to suggest that *goeika* practice necessitates a funereal atmosphere. Much to the contrary, participation in the Baikakō provides an affirming, positive space in which practitioners can create new social identities for themselves and lasting relationships with others through years of shared practice. Perhaps even more important, *goeika* practice enables the practitioner to face fear, anxiety, and death directly and, in so doing, to reorient themselves to new aspirations, new relationships, new accomplishments, and the discovery of new talents.

Goeika, in the context of the Baikakō, is a performance of group harmony, emotional expression, and compassionate practice. Despite its ability to evoke powerful and raw emotions from participants, *goeika* performance is ultimately a declaration of compassion, hope, and trust that promises to safely bring performers through stressful and painful times with grace and dignity.

SIX

Making Ancestors through Memorial Rituals

The Indefatigable Mrs. Terasawa

Mr. Takeuchi had warned me about Mrs. Terasawa before I joined the Baikakō. She could be very hard on new members, especially men. It took six months before she would even acknowledge his presence, he said. She was vocal in her belief that the Baikakō should be a woman's space: let the men have their *zazen*.[1]

Immediately upon entering the rehearsal room, one could tell that Mrs. Terasawa was the dominant force in the group. She spoke quickly, directly, and informally. She dressed like the other Baikakō women, but her hair was always covered with a head scarf, reminding me of pictures of Rosie the Riveter.

Before and after every rehearsal, Mrs. Terasawa held court, receiving a continuous stream of junior members coming to her with questions and requests. She would answer in a voice that dominated all other conversation in the room. Announcements to the group were made with her permission and at her prerogative. In many ways, Mrs. Terasawa *was* the Baikakō. At the very least, the Baikakō was hers.

At my second rehearsal, as the group was preparing to break for lunchtime, Mrs. Terasawa shouted to me across the room: "*Oniisan, kite yo!*" (Hey, young man, come over here). Already aware of the group dynamics, I hurried across the room and kneeled at the foot of her desk.

"Can you eat this?" she asked. She handed me a handmade *onigiri* rice ball. "I can," I replied. "How about this—can you eat it?" she asked, and passed over a piece of fried egg. She placed several pieces of egg on the plastic the rice ball had been wrapped in. "And this?" she asked again. "I can eat it," I replied. This exchange continued with every item she had brought from home until I had a feast laid out on the plastic wrap in front of me. She handed me a set of chopsticks and indicated that I should start eating.

At the end of the meal, Mrs. Terasawa told me that I shouldn't worry about bringing lunch to Baikakō rehearsal anymore. She would bring lunch for me, and I would eat with her. It wasn't a request. It was a command.

From then on, every time the rehearsal broke for lunch, I would prepare my notes until Mrs. Terasawa was done with Baikakō business. When she was ready for me, she would summon me by shouting over the din, "Joshua-saaan, *gohan!*" (Lunchtime). I would sit on the floor in front of her while she unwrapped all manner of delicious home-cooked food.

As a mother and a housewife, she had cooked for a household of four. Now that her daughters had moved out and married, there were two fewer mouths to feed. The problem was, she never changed her recipes to accommodate fewer people in her household. As a consequence, her refrigerator was always filled with leftovers. I provided a happy solution to that problem. Perhaps it was my ability to eat her home-cooked food or simply my willingness to do so, but Mrs. Terasawa and I bonded quickly.

The other Baikakō women occasionally passed me some of the food they brought from home, but it was never questioned that I "belonged" to Mrs. Terasawa and that her food took priority. As time went on, the members of the Baikakō started referring to Mrs. Terasawa as my "Japanese grandmother" (*Nihon no obaachan*).

Mrs. Terasawa had lived her entire life in Higashi Terao, a neighborhood of Tsurumi immediately adjacent to Sōjiji, and was a treasure trove of interesting stories about Yokohama and Tsurumi. Every day she would walk the kilometer from her house to Sōjiji to pay her respects and visit the various images enshrined on the temple grounds. She would then clean her house from top to bottom, go shopping, prepare meals, and still find time for Baikakō business and *goeika* practice. For a seventy-three-year-old woman, it seemed to everyone as if she had an inexhaustible supply of energy.

However, at our first rehearsal back from the monthlong August break, Mrs. Terasawa seemed different. She had always been thin, but it was clear from her face that she had lost weight, making her look tired and old. She was noticeably less vibrant and energetic. She wasn't wearing her head scarf, revealing for the first time her undyed white hair.

She looked *old*, as if she had aged fifteen years in the past month. She moved slowly, taking hesitant steps and often requiring someone's arm for support. Where she once glowed with contagious energy, Mrs. Terasawa was visibly dimming. Where she once dominated the room, she now seemed to recede into it.

October's rehearsal took place on a rainy and unseasonably chilly day. Mrs. Terasawa announced to the group that she would be taking a leave of absence from the Baikakō until January in order to give her legs time to rest and get stronger. Although she was decidedly not resigning her position as the group secretary, she would be delegating responsibility to another senior member of the group for the time being. During lunch, she apologized and told me that I was going to have to fend for myself for food from now on.

After rehearsal ended, I took her arm and, accompanied by Mrs. Oka, her best friend and fellow Baikakō member, the three of us begin a slow, cautious walk down the hill to Tsurumi Station so that Mrs. Terasawa could take the bus home instead of walking.

As we walked, she spoke about how her legs had been hurting her and how she couldn't walk as she used to. But the real problem, she said, was that she just wasn't hungry anymore. She made food for herself and her husband, but she couldn't bring herself to eat. She had lost ten pounds already. I asked if she had been to the doctor. She replied that she hadn't. She didn't want to be a bother.

There was something more, she told me, but I probably wouldn't believe her:

"Everything started in July after I went to a funeral," she said. "One night, I felt a man's hand on my shoulder, pulling me. I looked around; no one was there. I asked myself, 'Was it *hotoke-sama*?' After that, my legs started to hurt, and I wasn't hungry anymore.

"The other night, while lying in bed, I saw a flash of light. I remember it was around 10:50, because I looked at the clock. I thought to myself, 'Is this my time? Are they coming for me?'"

"Were you afraid?," I asked.

"I am *not* afraid!" (*Kowaku nai yo*), Mrs. Terasawa emphatically responded. In a grandmotherly tone, Mrs. Oka echoed, "You really can't be afraid of such things, you know."

Mrs. Terasawa described having first felt the presence of the *hotoke-sama* in her teens, protecting her and providing for her in times of distress, especially when she was hungry. She said that young people no longer feel a connection to these things, but she volunteered that unless a person has had these experiences for themselves, it's hard to believe. "My daughter thinks I'm crazy," Mrs. Terasawa added.

As we walked down the busy street toward the station, Mrs. Oka asked Mrs. Terasawa if maybe she had missed any annual memorial rites and angered her ancestors. Mrs. Terasawa recalled that she had missed her father's twenty-seventh annual memorial rite in July. It was her custom to go to his grave once a month on his death day (*meinichi*), but she had neglected to go recently on account of her legs. Mrs. Oka suggested that when Mrs. Terasawa was feeling better, maybe she should visit her father's grave, burn incense, and apologize. "I don't know if it will work," she said, "but that's something that I heard a priest say."

When we arrived at Tsurumi Station, I flagged the bus driver to hold Mrs. Terasawa's bus. Mrs. Oka and I watched and waved as she boarded. After the bus departed, Mrs. Oka turned to me and said, "You know, Mrs. Terasawa praises you as if you were her own child."

As I walked home alone, the rain started up again. There is no way I could have known that was the last time I would see Mrs. Terasawa. I wish I had thought of a more appropriate good-bye.

"Raising" the Dead

As we have seen, a Sōtō Zen temple like Sōjiji caters to many and diverse religious needs. Still, the performance of funerary and memorial rituals remains—as it has for nearly four centuries—the primary function of Japanese Buddhist practice, regardless of temple or sectarian affiliation. As the Japanese Buddhist clergy struggles to maintain authority over funerary traditions and practices, so too do parishioners and believers struggle to reconcile traditional memorial practices with life in contemporary Japan.

In this chapter I look at how death and grief are disciplined in the context of Zen practice, transformed ritually and practically into a narrative that is less about the ending of life than it is about the birth and development of a new social person and new social relations. The wake and funeral are critical moments in this new "life" cycle, as they not only establish a new social identity for the deceased, but they also work to renegotiate the social relationships in which the deceased was enmeshed in their old lives. This "work" is done through the practice of *kuyō*.

Like *shugyō*, the concept of *kuyō* is difficult to properly convey into a non-Japanese cultural framework. The most common translation found in the Anglophone literature on Japan is "memorial service."[2] Helen Hardacre translates the term simply as "rites,"[3] an idea that Marilyn Ivy expands as "rites aimed at memorializing the dead, rites which aim to pacify the dead by remembering them through offerings, prayers, and recitations of scripture."[4] Ellen Schattschneider, echoing Ivy, translates the term as "ancestral memorialization."[5] Stephen Covell offers two translations: "memorial services" and "rituals for the dead."[6]

Comparing these translations, it might be assumed that the active part of *kuyō* is the act of memorialization—in other words, that there is something about the process of *memory* and *remembering* that has operative power in the gradual transformation of the dead from human through various stages of an "*after*-life cycle" that culminates in their becoming a household ancestor (*senzo*). Without a doubt, the ways in which the living remember and reimagine the dead are a vital aspect of the ritual efficacy of *kuyō*, but I argue that memorialization is only part of the picture.

I suggest that, for all of its various manifestations, *kuyō* lends itself to a simpler translation. The Japanese *kuyō* originates in the Indian Vedic ritual practice of *pūjanā*, where offerings of flowers, incense, and food were made to the gods, local tutelary deities, or religious teachers as an act of reverence. Later, *pūjanā* came to include donations made to sustain the community of Buddhist monks, which, in turn, generated karmic merit for the donor. As Buddhism made deeper inroads into China in the early centuries of the Common Era, *pūjanā* became syncretized with the local customs of ancestor veneration. The three—Buddhism, ancestor veneration, and the practice of *pūjanā*—arrived together in Japan as "imported commodities" and within the span of several centuries had permeated all levels of Japanese culture.[7]

The Japanese word *kuyō* is comprised of two characters, the first meaning "votive offering" and the second meaning "nourishment," with the added implication of "to raise or rear" as one would a child. Looking at it in this way, rather than being an abstract ritual of memorialization, we can see how *kuyō* creates an "economy of care" that, through material and affective labor, provides nourishment for the gradual transformation of the dead from human beings through their early, vulnerable state as a "newly deceased spirit" (*shinmō shōrei*) into full maturity as a household ancestor. To me, it therefore makes the most sense to understand *kuyō* as "feeding": offerings that nourish and develop the spirits of the dead, in the same way that a parent is responsible for raising their child who cannot fend for itself. In this framework, through *kuyō* the living are responsible for "raising" the dead.

Food, feeding, and the sharing of meals are vital practices by which relationships between individuals and groups are established, negotiated, maintained, and cultivated.[8] It should not be surprising, then, that the most common manifestations of *kuyō* are, in fact, food offerings: a portion of a meal, a cup of tea, some cookies or sweets, or a favorite alcoholic beverage.[9] Moreover, the donation of food to the living—particularly making material donations to support a community of monastics—can also be performed as *kuyō*, with the karmic merit accrued for the donor's act being transferred through a Transfer of Merit verse (*ekōmon*) to the deceased, specifying either a named beneficiary indicated by the donor or to one's ancestors generally. By logical extension, all charitable activities can be seen as providing "sustenance," especially those that are performed specifically for the benefit of the dead. Chanting a sutra, or sponsoring Buddhist clergy who do so, is therefore an act of feeding and is considered a powerful act of *kuyō*.

The process of learning to "do *kuyō*" (*kuyō suru*) is as much a cultivation of the living as it is the dead. More so than any meditative practice, the clergy of Sōjiji advocate the practice of *kuyō* as being truly spiritually transformative for all parties involved: activities performed by the living out of gratitude on behalf of the dead renew and reinvigorate the social bonds that death threatened to sever. Both the living and the dead benefit from of these actions: the dead are sped along on their transformation toward ancestorhood, while the living gradually grow toward a state of selfless compassion.

A Time to Mourn

It was Mrs. Otani, a Baikakō member and part-time employee at Sōjiji, who found me to tell me that Mrs. Terasawa had died. It was the first night of the December meditation retreat, and we had just finished the evening period of *zazen*. I was walking back to the dormitory room from the Monk's Hall when I heard her running down the corridor behind me calling my name.

No one had heard anything from Mrs. Terasawa since the last rehearsal she attended in early October. Her friends had tried calling her, but her cell phone had been disconnected. Worse, no one was returning any calls from her house. I knew something was terribly wrong when Mrs. Sakamoto, one of her longtime friends, asked *me* if I had heard any news from Mrs. Terasawa.

During that last rehearsal, Mrs. Terasawa told the Baikakō that she was heading to a hot spring to help her legs. As we all later found out, she had checked herself into a hospital. Even Mrs. Oka—her best friend—had no idea that anything was amiss.

Wishing to pass from this world with a minimum of fuss is not an uncommon phenomenon in Japan. It is an extension of everyday culture in Japan in which people often go to great lengths (and personal trouble) to avoid inconveniencing other people. In fact, the sentiment is common enough to warrant prayer temples called *pokkuri dera* where the elderly or sick can pray for quick deaths in order to minimize the emotional and financial burden placed on family and friends.[10] In many ways, to die quickly and with minimal inconvenience to others is to die with grace and dignity.[11] It is the ultimate non-imposition.

For the living, however, the news of such a death often comes suddenly and without warning. While the dying may have come to accept their approaching mortality, those who were not privy to the last weeks or days in the life of a friend or loved one are left to mourn a sudden and tragic loss, as if the person had died suddenly in an accident. The news is shocking and the pain is acute.

Becoming a Buddha

In Japan, death of the corporeal body is just the beginning of a multi-decade process whereby the dead undergo a course of development and maturation before they can be counted among the generations of tutelary household ancestors. To understand the process that begins upon crossing the threshold of death, it is important to consider the concept of *hotoke*, a multivalent concept with deep cultural significance to the Japanese. The word *hotoke* is often confusingly glossed into English as "buddha," "spirit," or "soul," reflecting both cultural and scholarly disagreement about the etymological derivation of the word itself.[12] In one rendering, *hotoke-sama* refers to the historical Buddha Śākyamuni. After lay funerals began to promise immediate salvation through enlightenment for the deceased during the medieval period, the phrase *hotoke ni naru* (or its alternate, *jōbutsu suru*)—"to become a buddha"—soon became a euphemism for death in the Japanese language. Because of this, a person who has recently died is also referred to as *hotoke-sama*. More confusingly, *hotoke-sama* can also refer to the nameless generations of a family's ancestors, even those who have moved past the initial transition phase discussed below. Since *hotoke* is used somewhat loosely by the Japanese (who are not generally troubled by such minutiae), when a person honorifically refers to *hotoke-sama*, context is often necessary to establish if the referent is the Buddha himself, the spirit of a specific individual, or all of one's ancestors generally.

A *hotoke* does not appear "fully formed" at the moment of death. Rather, the Japanese funerary and memorial process establishes a context for the future interactions that will take place between the living and the dead. Most postmortem ceremonies pertaining to the body itself are private affairs. The events immediately following the death—the washing of the body, the Buddhist last rites said over the newly deceased (*makuragyō*, "pillow sutra"), and the encoffining—are usually attended only by close family members. The funeral itself (*sōgi* or *sōshiki*) is similarly intimate, most often attended only by immediate family and close friends. Finally, the last moments with the body before and after cremation are also small, private events, usually attended, again, only by family and close friends.

In contrast to these private rituals is the *tsuya*, or wake. In most scholarship on Japanese funerals, the *tsuya* is generally mentioned as a minor part of the mortuary process, despite it being the ceremony that will see the greatest attendance from relatives, friends, and guests. Rather than being an anomaly in an otherwise intimate and subdued ritual process, I argue that the *tsuya* plays a crucial role in laying the groundwork for all future social interactions between those on either side of the threshold of death by establishing the *hotoke* in its new social identity.

The *tsuya* is typically held on the evening of the day after death, with the funeral proper taking place the following day. At a symbolic level, a *tsuya* is a sending-off party. The deceased is imagined as a traveler or pilgrim celebrating their last night with family and friends before undertaking a great journey. Grief is expected, but so too are large quantities of food and alcohol. Indeed, feasting alongside the dead is an essential part of the goings-on.

Many of my middle-aged and elderly informants spoke fondly of *tsuya* from when they were younger. Before funeral companies entered the scene, in many regions of Japan wakes were weeklong community-wide events that, while mournful, were accompanied by feasting and the singing of *goeika* and other traditional songs. If the deceased was young, the *tsuya* presented an opportunity for the community to rally together to support the grieving family. If the dead had lived to a healthy old age, the *tsuya* would be a celebration in honor of a life well lived. One informant gleefully recalled one *tsuya* from her youth where the worldly wealth of the deceased was converted into coins and thrown to the assembled crowd, to the joy of the children, who scrambled to gather as much as they could.

While funerary practices have always varied according to local conventions, memorial customs have changed dramatically in Japan in the decades since the end of the Second World War. Most notably, the increased presence and influence of funeral companies have contributed to a standardization of mourning in Japan. No longer is the *tsuya* or funeral a community-organized event; rather, it has become a ceremonial occasion on par with a wedding, with details and arrangements best left to professionals. Consequently, the roles of the mourners and guests have also become standardized, with the funeral companies and their affiliates publishing books and videos on "proper" funeral and mourning etiquette and protocol.

Standardization of mourning, however, has not necessarily made things easier for the bereaved. Several informants told me that they believe death has actually become more painful in recent years. As one woman poignantly commented to me, grief is now expected to be funneled into a period of less than forty-eight hours between the death and the funeral. Moreover, the seven weekly rituals that allow for an extended period to come to terms with grief have become "optional," even for the mourning family. One informant suggested a possible explanation for this: there is little opportunity for the funeral companies to profit from these rites, and therefore they are not stressed to client families as important.

These changes are generally accepted as a convenience, as the community and mourning family no longer has the time (because of jobs, school, and other obligations) to worry about funeral arrangements. One man I spoke with was particularly ambivalent about these changes to traditional funerary practices: on the one hand, he blamed the younger generations, who no longer take the time to learn from their elders what to do at a wake or a funeral, complaining that nowadays they expect other people to take care of "traditional matters" for them. On the other hand, he acknowledged the convenience of having a funeral company take care of the many arrangements for a funeral, since the newly bereaved family usually cannot and the local community no longer will.

As a result, a *tsuya* provides a fascinating opportunity to comment on the tug-of-war between the Buddhist clergy and the funeral companies over the future of Japanese memorial practice.[13] Prior to the 1950s, the Buddhist priest was an instrumental figure in the process of dying: he was called when death was imminent, and it was the Buddhist priest—not the doctor—who would determine when death had occurred. In Sōtō Zen, once the priest had declared the death, a "pillow sutra" was immediately chanted over the deceased, ritually marking their transition from life to afterlife and the start of the family's period of mourning and ritual obligations.

In previous times, even if the *tsuya* and funeral were held in the home (as they commonly were), the clergy and the temple played a pivotal role in the protracted memorial process. With the shift of the location of death from the home to the hospital in the postwar period, the Buddhist clergy quickly became peripheral to the process of dying.[14] Today, rather than being the first to be called when it appears that death is imminent, the priest is often an afterthought. If the family has no ties to a parish temple or priest, one is suggested by the funeral company, which itself may have been recommended by the hospital.

The result has been a double displacement for the clergy: not only are they removed from their role at the bedside of the dying, but they are further relegated to the appearance of being employees of the funeral company—which in many cases they actually are.[15] A corollary effect of this change is that, in the eyes of many Japanese, the Buddhist temple now appears as merely a backdrop for a *tsuya* or funeral rather than a culturally meaningful site for the gradual transformation of the newly dead into their new life as a *hotoke*.

Waking Mrs. Terasawa

On the day of the wake, the Baikakō gathered in Sōjiji's gift shop while they waited for the ceremony to begin. Everyone's eyes were red from crying, and conversation was quiet and superficial. It quickly became clear that no one knew what really happened to Mrs. Terasawa. There were conflicting reports of her final days, and nobody was certain if she died alone in her home or in a hospital with her family. On several occasions, someone's eyes would begin to well up, but before a tear would fall, they excused themselves from the room to regain their composure. I never actually saw anyone cry.

At the appointed time, the Baikakō was met by an usher who led the group to the large ceremony hall in the Sanshōkaku. Outside the hall, a reception desk had been set up for guests to sign their names in a register and to collect and record the envelopes with money inside, intended to help the family offset the costs of the funeral.[16] People who donated money would receive a receipt that could later be redeemed for a thank-you bag as the visitor left. As secretary, it would have been Mrs. Terasawa's job to sign the registration book and leave the money envelope on behalf of the Baikakō. In her absence, the responsibility had been delegated to another member, who argued that it was appropriate that we should individually write our names in the guest register. After we had all signed the book, white-gloved attendants from the funeral company sat us as a group in the back of the ceremony hall.

While the deceased in the coffin is obviously the focal point of the ceremony, the most conspicuous feature of modern outside-of-the-home funeral proceedings is the *saidan*, an elaborate multitiered wooden altar that dominates the room. The *saidan* is newly constructed for each funeral from fresh cypress wood. Like most trappings of the ceremony, the *saidan* is supplied by the funeral company, with the size and intricacy varying by price.

The arrangement of the *saidan* differs somewhat between funeral companies and religious sects, but some commonalities can be observed. On the uppermost tier of the *saidan* is the mortuary photograph (*iei*), with black ribbons adorning the upper left and right corners of the picture frame. On the tier below the picture sits a temporary paper memorial tablet (*ihai*), upon which is written the deceased's posthumous "precepts name" (*kaimyō*). Immediately below this lies the body in its unadorned pine coffin, elevated on wooden supports. In front of the coffin, a small altar dominated by a sand-filled incense burner is set up, from which lit sticks of incense give off a steady plume of smoke. Large bouquets of colorful flowers are arranged on the sides of the *saidan*.

Like all temple ritual spaces, the room is arranged according to the perspective of the object of veneration—in this case, Mrs. Terasawa's spirit, which now hovered close to the body. From the spirit's perspective, the immediate family—those who are observing the mourning rituals—are given the place of honor on the left-hand side, and the extended family is seated on the right. Guests paying their respects are seated in the back of the room. Mrs. Terasawa's wake was so well attended that the ceremony necessitated a second, spillover room, where guests could listen to the ceremony via speaker but could not see what was taking place.

After the Baikakō was seated, the officiating priest turned to the assembled guests and opened the ceremony with a few words of condolence to the family. Addressing the guests, he took several minutes giving a brief explanation as to what would take place during the ceremony.

An important part of this debut is the giving of a new posthumous name to the deceased.[17] The bestowing of a *kaimyō* does not mark the transition of a person from life to death but rather the transition from the life of a layperson to the life of a world-renouncing monastic. Like the *anmyō* (refuge name) given to novice clergy at their tonsure ceremony, the bestowing of a *kaimyō* is intended to mark the transition from one social life into another, identifying the recipient as a disciple of the Buddha.[18] By being given a new "precepts name," the deceased takes on a new identity distinct and separate from their former social lives and responsibilities. The family and guests attending the wake are the first to greet the deceased—transformed but very much socially "alive"—in their new identity as a *hotoke*. By explaining the significance of the name and the reasons that this particular name has been bestowed upon the deceased, the officiating priest "marks the social status of the deceased in his or her new relationship with the living family."[19]

The *kaimyō* can vary from a minimum of six characters—in the Sōtō Zen sect, four characters plus a two-character suffix granting the clerical rank of *jōza*, identical to novice clergy—up to twelve characters. Ostensibly, the more devoted (*nesshin*) the person was to Buddhism in life, the more characters they will have in their *kaimyō*.[20] Mrs. Terasawa was given a ten-character name.

When the priest finished, the emcee—an employee of the funeral company who manifested over the public address system as a disembodied voice—introduced each participant in the ceremony, beginning with Mrs. Terasawa's husband, who in his role of chief mourner (*moshu*) wore a large black and white ribbon on his coat, and the couple's two daughters. As they lit incense in front of the coffin, two handheld incense burners were passed around to the immediate family and the extended family. After the family offered incense, the assembled guests were invited to burn incense at the table in the back. As the incense was offered, the priest's attendant began chanting.

For an ostensibly Buddhist ritual, it comes as a surprise how very nonstandard the *tsuya* liturgy is. Unlike other temple services, *what* is chanted by the clergy during the *tsuya* is less important than *how long* it is chanted. The chanting must continue until all guests have had the opportunity to burn incense in honor of the deceased. It is common practice for Sōtō Zen priests to chant the entirety of the *Shushōgi*, a much-condensed distillation of essential Sōtō Zen teachings. The five chapters of the *Shushōgi* take about thirty minutes to chant in their entirety, and its duration is sufficient in most cases. However, should the number of guests wishing to pay their respects exceed this duration, a priest has to think on his feet to estimate how much longer the incense-offering portion might take. From this guess, he chooses a sutra of appropriate length, with any luck not falling short or extending too far after the last guest offers incense. A priest commented to me that at one memorable *tsuya* he officiated, there were so many guests that he had to start repeating sutra he had already chanted.

Offering incense is done with the highest formality. Guests, standing with their hands pressed together, bow first to their right (to the immediate family), then to their left (the extended family), and finally toward the *saidan* in the center. After the guest offers incense, they bow again, this time first toward the *saidan* and then to the immediate family and the extended family. Even with guests being called up six at a time, the process can be a long one. It took an hour for all of the guests to pay their respects to Mrs. Terasawa. By the time everyone had done so, the air was heavy and thick with smoke.

When every guest had offered incense, the priest turned to the crowd to deliver a speech that was both a touching eulogy and a moving sermon. In describing Mrs. Terasawa's life, the priest talked about how, as a child and then a teenager, she was forced to grow up quickly during the scarcity and hardships of Japan's protracted Pacific War, how she survived the wartime devastation of Yokohama, and how she persevered through the poverty and starvation that followed. Through it all, she was steadfast in her belief that the *hotoke* would provide for her. The priest noted how auspicious it was that, having lived her life with religious conviction, both Mrs. Terasawa's birthday and her death day fell during the period commemorating the Buddha's enlightenment.

The priest bowed with his palms together in *gasshō*, and the assembled relatives and guests bowed in response. The emcee broke the silence to announce that food would be served in an adjoining room. The funeral company employees led the guests to a room where there was a feast of food and drink—platters of fried meats and sashimi, with large bottles of sake and beer at every table.

This meal is arguably the most important part of the *tsuya*, even more so, perhaps, than the previous ritual proceedings. In the pain of loss and haze of tears, it is difficult to remember that the *tsuya* is ostensibly a celebration not only of the deceased's successful transition from life to new life but also of the bonds of affection and relatedness that join all of the assembled participants—family, loved ones, and friends—to one another through the deceased. As with other mortuary celebrations throughout the world, eating and drinking with the dead is a vital aspect of the Japanese *tsuya*, reaffirming social bonds in the face of severe trauma that would otherwise threaten to sever them. The feasting may start somberly, but the quantities of food and alcohol and the mandate not to restrain themselves give the guests the opportunity to freely share stories and memories with one another. The deceased, who is offered a portion of the food and a cup of sake or beer, is a silent participant in all that is taking place. Gazing down from the *saidan*, they are thought by those in attendance to rejoice in the opportunity to share a meal with their family and guests one last time.

Old Faces, New Bodies

While symbolically the *tsuya* is a farewell gathering, a secondary aspect of the event is that it is the first public appearance—a debut—of the new *hotoke*, who, having crossed the threshold of death, has moved into a new category of social person and into a new social identity. The visual frame created through the ritual space of the *tsuya*, and particularly by the architectural arrangement of the *saidan*, is therefore essential for establishing the relationships of signification between the material objects that are necessary for navigating all future interactions between the living and the *hotoke*. The deceased has already been given a new name, the *kaimyō* as discussed above. And as the physical body is prepared for cremation and burial, the deceased is given a new form—perhaps "presence" might be a better word—in the memorial photograph and memorial tablet, both of which are present on the *saidan* as a proxy for the deceased in the coffin.[21]

The memorial photograph can be either a formal portrait or a snapshot of the deceased in life. Like a passport photo, the photograph chosen is usually one in which the person is looking directly into the camera. If part of a larger picture, it is cropped to show only the head and shoulders. A good picture is often preferred over a recent picture—several memorial photographs I saw during my research were clearly taken years before the person passed away. As can be expected, it is sometimes difficult for a grieving family to locate an appropriately flattering picture in the hours immediately following a death. Since the presence of the portrait during the wake is essential, a recent, blurry picture taken on a cell phone is often given to the funeral company as arrangements are being made. As soon as possible, this picture is often replaced by a more flattering picture of the deceased that serves as the permanent portrait. The most important characteristic of the memorial photograph is that the person be depicted alone. Any other contextualizing features that may have been in the photograph— for example, landscape or other people—are removed and replaced with a gray or light blue background.[22]

In the memorial photograph, the deceased is both there and not-there. As Ellen Schattschneider observes, "A photographic print simultaneously evokes presence and absence. It constitutes on the one hand a compact and proximate object, yet it manifestly depicts something separated from the viewer in space and time."[23] During a visit to the home of an informant, my host showed me pictures from his wedding several years earlier. From where I was sitting, I immediately recognized a family portrait mounted on the wall over the household altar as the source from which his father's

memorial photograph had been taken. While it was undoubtedly a distinguished picture of my informant's father, seeing the two pictures simultaneously was an uncanny experience; in the memorial portrait, gone were
the flowers and decorations of the wedding reception hall, and absent were
his smiling wife and his newlywed son and daughter-in-law. The image
in the photograph, carefully decontextualized from its original source,
communicated the father's continued presence and involvement in the life
of the family. However, what struck me as uncanny was that in order to
accomplish a sense of presence here, the image in the photograph had to
first be carefully decontextualized to be forever nowhere, as if he existed in
a perpetual gray void.

Interestingly, this was not always the case. As Yamada Shin'ya has shown,
prior to the end of the nineteenth century, the Japanese—specifically, those
who could afford to do so—typically produced devotional portraits that
contextualized the dead in the "other world" (*ano yo*), surrounded by food,
riches, as well as objects (a favorite pipe or the name plaque of a store) and
even people (children or spouses) that defined them in life. Other portraits
showed the dead as travelers embarking on a journey or of Amida Buddha coming to retrieve them to bring them to the Pure Land. With the
advent of the use of photographic images for memorialization, however,
the emphasis in funerary portraiture in Japan shifted from imagining the
dead living happily in a parallel yet contemporaneous "other world" to a
permanent freezing of the images of the dead into the faces of their former
lives.[24] Yamada concludes his analysis with the commentary that this is not
necessarily a positive development; by fixing the *hotoke* into their appearance in life, he argues, it has become difficult for modern Japanese to con-
ceive of the dead in a physically or spiritually transformed state.

However, Yamada's analysis does not take into account that acts of
negotiation and recontextualization necessarily occur when deciding on a
suitable image for the memorial portrait. The picture that is chosen for the
iei may depict the deceased as they wanted to be remembered, but more
often than not it depicts the deceased in a manner that reflects how the living wish to remember them.[25] It is for this reason that a flattering picture
is often preferred to a recent one: the photograph chosen will become an
idealized depiction of the deceased that will be the image of reference for
years to come.

While the mortuary photograph may fix a person into an idealized
image, the dead are given a new "body" in the memorial tablet (*ihai*). Modern memorial tablets are usually constructed of black lacquered wood,
standing between 13 and 42 centimeters (5 ½ and 16 ½ inches) from base

Fig. 16. A Sōtō parishioner household altar (*butsudan*). A memorial portrait (*iei*) sits prominently on the top of the cabinet, with a memorial tablet (*ihai*) placed on the top interior shelf on the right.

to tip. While styles of *ihai* vary by sect, the feature common to all *ihai* is the vertically standing tablet known as the *fuda*. On *ihai* that are dedicated to an individual, the *kaimyō* is engraved in gilded calligraphy on the front of the tablet, and the age and date of death are engraved on the back.

Unlike the memorial photograph, which points to one (and only one) person, *ihai* are often shared by two or more individuals. One variation is a wider *fuda* tablet with room for two names to be inscribed side by side. These *ihai* are often purchased when one spouse predeceases another, and it is common to see the living spouse's future posthumous name engraved in red lettering (indicating life) alongside the gilded name of the spouse who has passed away. When the living spouse joins their partner in death, the red lettering is replaced with gold characters. Similarly, many households choose to have a communal *ihai* dedicated to the generations of ancestors of the family.

While the memorial photograph may allow a person to feel that they are once again looking at the face of their loved one, the *ihai* is often treated in a way that more closely resembles that of a physical body: not only can it be seen, but it can also be held, spoken to, cared for, cleaned, and—perhaps most significantly—given nourishment through food offerings.[26] The *ihai* is further given legitimacy as a "second body" through the fact that it must first be activated—that is, awakened—through a special Eye-Opening Ceremony (*kaigen kuyō*).[27] The Eye-Opening Ceremony, which is also performed for other Buddhist icons and imagery, transforms an otherwise static object into a living focus that, with social interactions, can take place.[28]

As with a photograph, copies of an *ihai* are often made so that the *ihai* can be simultaneously venerated in multiple places. Before World War II, it was the legal responsibility of the oldest son to take responsibility for the family's memorial rituals and, therefore, possession of the family's altar and memorial tablets. Today, however, it is not uncommon for all siblings of a generation to want to have a copy of an *ihai* that has been made for one or both of their parents. Many families entrust their parish temples with a copy of an *ihai*, especially one dedicated to the family's community of ancestors, to ensure that the spirits receive the proper respects every morning. Enshrining an *ihai* at Sōjiji comes with a substantial price tag: permanent enshrinement in the Hōkōdō runs one million yen (US$9,500), while enshrinement in the Daisodō can range from five hundred thousand to three million yen (approximately US$4,750–$28,500), depending on size of the tablet and desired proximity to the main altar.

Asking an ordinary layperson where the *hotoke* or *senzo* "are" reveals a fascinating number of answers that, while contradictory in theory, fit together without the appearance of contradiction in practice.[29] The newly deceased and the ancestors are thought to reside within the family *butsudan*, where the *ihai* are kept. This answer is complicated by the fact that, as stated above, copies of the same person's *ihai* can simultaneously be kept in multiple places, with the person believed to be "present" in each one. No one I spoke with raised any issues of authenticity or primacy by saying that one *ihai* is more "original" than any other.

Another response is that the dead are said to be present at the family grave, necessitating visitation (*ohakamairi*) at least once, and preferably multiple times, during the year. In addition to visiting, the family is obliged to keep the area of the grave clean and free from debris and to leave offerings for the ancestors who occupy the gravesite.

A third answer is that the ancestors are on the "other shore" (*higan*) and that they return at set periods of the year, most notably the vernal and autumnal equinoxes (at the festival of Higan, when the equal lengths of day and night are said to allow for easier communication and travel between worlds), at the summer Obon festival (where the ancestors are thought to return to their homes), and at the New Year festivities. These periods correspond with spikes in the number of people throughout Japan who go to temples and cemeteries for grave visitations. Again, no one I spoke with mentioned any contradiction between the belief that the ancestors are always present through the family *butsudan* and the fact that they are thought to "return" at set times of the year.

Yet another answer I heard was that the ancestral spirits live in a Pure Land (*jōdo*) or in a heaven (*tengoku*). These beliefs are not doctrinally a part of Sōtō Zen, which advocates for the immediate enlightenment of the dead and continued existence in this world. Rather, the availability and incorporation of the ideas of a heaven or the Pure Land is owed to the syncretic nature of Japanese religion. I never heard a Sōtō Zen priest make reference to these terms; rather, their use among the laity likely stems from constant exposure to the teachings and language of other Buddhist sects and religions without sectarian or doctrinal boundaries being made clear.

A fifth answer, and one that has gained particular momentum in recent years, is that the spirits of the deceased are present and manifest in the natural world around the living. This view has taken on remarkable strength since 2007, when the song "Sen no kaze ni natte" (an adaptation of the anonymous American poem "A Thousand Winds") exploded onto the scene. Following its performance by Akikawa Masafumi at the 2006 NHK New Year's Eve music program, "Sen no kaze ni natte" quickly reached the top of the Japanese charts. Described as "a message from the dead to ease the sadness of loss" (*sōshitsu no kanashimi o iyasu shisha kara no messeji*),[30] the song became a fixture in popular culture, especially as the summer Obon period draws near. In particular, the song became the go-to soundtrack for TV programs dealing with themes of death and loss. Not surprisingly, it also became quickly incorporated into funeral companies' repertoire; when I discussed the song with Kodama-san, he joked that "the only people in Japan who don't like the song are companies that sell graves."

Many of the people I interviewed at Sōjiji made explicit reference to the song during conversation and interviews. One man enthusiastically explained to me that the song came closest to describing the true relationship between the living and the dead. This relationship, he believed, had been obscured by conflicting traditions, competing doctrines, and the forces of "Westernization" (*seiyōka*). However, in one move, this song came along to remove the fog and reveal that the ancestors are still among the living and watching over them.

One woman I met at a public sermon told me that she comes to Sōjiji once a month on behalf of her recently deceased mother. When I asked her if her family were parishioners of Sōjiji, she said that she was not; when her mother passed away, she and her husband did not see a need to purchase a grave for her. Her justification was that the "costs of grave construction are unreasonable" but also unnecessary, as her mother had "become a thousand winds" (*hahaoya wa sen no kaze ni narimashita*). Therefore, she concluded, her monthly visits to Sōjiji provided the same benefits to herself and her mother as if she had visited a physical grave, because her mother's spirit is everywhere.

Sōtō Zen clergy likewise picked up on the potential for capitalizing on the song's popularity. As early as May 2007, I began hearing references to the song in sermons and lectures at Sōjiji. The clergy I spoke with saw the popularity of the song as an opportunity to reconnect with the laity, who were clearly hungering for a more meaningful relationship with those whom they had lost, as indicated by the song's popularity. That the message of the song resonated with Sōtō Zen doctrine about the immanence of the dead in "this world" was fortuitous. The clergy repeatedly invoked the song's title (but not necessarily the lyrics) to encourage listeners to cultivate a sense of reverence (*sange*) and gratitude for their ancestors and departed loved ones in their daily lives. By extension, the clergy stressed, any devotional practice done on their behalf—listening to a sermon, copying sutra, even doing charity—becomes an opportunity for *kuyō* as a kind of grave visitation (*hakamairi*).

It should be mentioned that I heard virtually nothing regarding reincarnation (*umarekaeri*, or *tenshō*). As Buddhism traveled throughout Asia, the Hindu/Buddhist idea of reincarnation influenced and was influenced by local beliefs about the afterlife. Though many of the Buddhist texts found in Japanese Sōtō Zen temples make explicit reference to reincarnation,[31] the concept itself is largely foreign to Japanese tradition.

Ultimately, my clerical informants told me, making the effort to disentangle popular and doctrinal notions of where the *hotoke* and *senzo* are located is missing the point. More important is that the living understand the importance of properly venerating their ancestors through *senzo kuyō*.

Whether this act of veneration is done at a temple, at the grave, at the household altar, or by honoring the dead in one's daily activities, the *senzo* "are" wherever the living choose to address them. All of the ritual mortuary trappings are merely representations, stand-ins to help comfort the living by providing physical, tactile reminders of their presence. "The dead," I was told, "do not have need for such things."

Still, the fear of becoming a *muen botoke*—a "spirit with no attachments"— remains culturally significant.[32] According to Japanese Buddhist cosmology (itself a syncretic mix of Indian, Chinese, and Japanese cultural influences), a soul that does not receive regular care from its descendants in the form of *kuyō* will be doomed to wander the earth for eternity, quickly descending into madness and becoming a destructive force that seeks vengeance on the living. A person or family who falls into sickness, tragedy, or financial misfortune is often asked if perhaps they have an ancestor who has been neglected.

While virtually none of my informants feared retribution from neglected ancestors, for themselves the possibility of having their souls go neglected and unnourished remains a genuine concern, and many go to great lengths to avoid this fate. A significant number of my informants were vocal about their unwillingness to risk their afterlife on the uncertain guarantee that their descendants will properly care for them. Instead, they made financial plans to cover the costs of regular *kuyō* by the clergy of Sōjiji and the administration fees for their grave into the foreseeable future. This was most often done as a provision in their wills, though some wealthy or financially savvy parishioners may establish an endowment fund in trust, the interest from which will cover the necessary costs in perpetuity.

Others whose fortunes are more modest find themselves with limited options. One man told me with regret that his choice not to have children to further his career seemed like a good idea when he was younger. Now that he is in his seventies, he spends much of his time worrying about what will happen to his soul with no one to visit his grave and properly care for him. He has thought about the possibility of buying into Sōjiji's communal "grave for perpetuity" (*eidai gōsō haka*) so at least the clergy will visit and care for him.[33] However, he finds the prospect of not being buried with his ancestors and abandoning them to neglect while he receives care equally as troubling.

Not everyone faces this possibility with trepidation, however. The above informant's friend, who was sitting with us, encouraged him to take a more pragmatic approach: "You're dead. There is nothing you can do. What's the point of being afraid?" The first man shrugged, and his friend continued: "If you don't have children to care for you, well, your spirit has left your body anyway. I don't think there's anything to worry about."

Farewell

The funeral proper is held the day after the *tsuya*. At Sōjiji the funeral service is often held in the same space as the *tsuya*, with the body having been left overnight, attended by two monks. At Sōjiji the bereaved families are offered guest rooms in the Sanshōkaku, especially if they are coming from out of town.

Mrs. Terasawa's funeral had only a fraction of the attendees of the *tsuya*, and the majority present were her immediate and extended family. Attending the *tsuya* satisfies the social responsibilities of friends and acquaintances, many of whom have jobs or other daytime obligations that would prevent them from attending the funeral. I was surprised to find that even the Baikakō was at half strength at the funeral, with attending members giving explanations for the absences of those who could not be there.

As discussed in chapter 4, modern Zen originalists often appeal to an idealized "pure Zen" that is free from popular ritual practices such as funerals and memorial services. These ritual practices are often viewed as "contaminations" to the purity of Zen or, more generally, Buddhist teachings. As one clerical informant asked rhetorically during an interview, "The Buddha never performed a funeral, so why should we?"

However, it is difficult to overemphasize the significance that lay funerals have played in the establishment and development of Sōtō Zen in Japan since the medieval period. As William Bodiford has shown, medieval Sōtō Zen priests—beginning with Dōgen himself, and reaching its full potential with the itinerant and charismatic Sōjiji-affiliated priests from Gasan's Dharma lineage—pioneered the use of Buddhist funerals for the laity.[34] The Sōtō Zen funeral was based on the model used by Chinese monastics for clerical funerals, but its adaptation for use with the laity was a uniquely Japanese innovation.[35] While the actual funerals themselves were influenced by local customs, that these customs were situated within the framework of a distinctively Sōtō Zen funeral ritual was a clear demonstration of a burgeoning sectarian identity. The widespread popularity and appeal of the Sōtō Zen funeral was such that competing Buddhist sects adapted the Sōtō Zen model for their own sectarian funerals. In the intervening centuries, what had begun as a uniquely Sōtō Zen practice became the foundation for modern Japanese funerary practice.[36]

The most characteristic feature of the Sōtō Zen funeral liturgy is that it is less a ceremony of memorialization than it is an abbreviated tonsure ceremony marking the transition from lay to clerical status. The funeral liturgy is relatively short, taking less than twenty minutes in its entirety. Mrs. Terasawa's funeral followed this pattern.

After some preliminary comments, the priest began with the tonsure (*teihatsu*) itself. Unlike a "living" ordination, the priest does not shave the entirety of the head but symbolically shaves only the forelock. The priest chanted the "shaving verse" three times and then reached into the coffin to shave Mrs. Terasawa's forelock using a straight-edge razor. Though we couldn't see what was happening, the familiar sound of a razor blade scraping skin was picked up by the microphone attached to the priest's collar. One of the Baikakō members sitting next to me leaned over to whisper "*atama*" (head).

The tonsure is followed by the Precepts Ceremony (*jukai*), during which the deceased will silently assent to taking refuge in the Three Jewels of the Buddha, the Dharma, and the Sangha, and accept the Three Pure Precepts and the Ten Prohibitions. The priest punctuated each vow by clacking two lacquered pieces of wood together after each vow.

After the precepts are bestowed, the priest chants the *nenju*, an invocation of the ten names of the Buddha. The *nenju* is a common feature of monastic practice and is recited twice daily as part of the mealtime liturgy. From a doctrinal perspective, the *nenju* invocation is thought to operate in the same "disciplining" manner as *goeika*: the body is held in *gasshō*, the position of gratitude and humility; the voice, chanting the Buddha's names, acknowledges the truth of the impermanence of the world. Performing these bodily actions, it is believed, naturally disciplines the mind to deeply comprehend the fleeting nature of the world and to be thankful for one's time on earth. Though it is never made explicit to the audience, this simple invocation is a demonstration of the immanence of *satori*: both the intonations of the priest and the silence of the deceased are proof of the enlightenment that both share.

The final liturgical aspect of the funeral is the *indō hōgō*, or sermon for the deceased. This sermon was not so much a eulogy than a report of the events in Mrs. Terasawa's life. In many ways it was a final reckoning of the social person that was Mrs. Terasawa, who, being newly ordained, now sat as witness to the events and accomplishments of her own former life. The priest bestowed upon her the *kechimyaku* genealogical chart that is given to all who take the Sōtō Zen precepts, which placed her—now known by her new *kaimyō*—into the lineage of the Buddhist patriarchs descending from the Buddha Śākyamuni himself, with a line drawn between her and the Buddha to close the circle. The priest placed the *kechimyaku* into the coffin, to be consumed with her during her cremation.

When the Buddhist liturgy was completed, the funeral company workers invited those sitting in the rear of the room to offer incense to Mrs. Terasawa, now a newly ordained Buddhist nun. One by one, the assembly offered pinches of incense to the burners. I noted that the memorial pictures of Mrs. Terasawa had been replaced by a more flattering portrait—she looked at least ten years younger, full of vibrancy and life. In the picture, she was wearing her Baikakō robes, an essential part of her former identity.

We returned to our seats while the room was rearranged. All of the chairs flanking the coffin were removed, and the coffin was moved from under the *saidan* toward the center of the room. The lid was fully removed.

As the assembly gathered around the coffin, the priest's assistant began to sing a haunting performance of the recently published "Hymn for the Spirit of the Newly Deceased" ("*Shinmō shōrei kuyō gowasan*"). Though the Baikakō had practiced this song in rehearsal, this was the first time that anyone had ever heard it in its proper context at a funeral:

Towa no inochi to negae domo	Even though we ask for everlasting life
Mujō no kaze ni sasowarete	We are compelled by the winds of impermanence.
Oshimite chireru hana nareba	While we reluctantly scatter flowers
Wakare no namida haha tsutau.	The tears of separation roll down our cheeks.

As the priest's assistant sang, the assembled guests were handed bunches of cut flowers. We were told not to worry, as there were plenty. One by one, the guests placed the flowers in the open coffin, covering Mrs. Terasawa's body.

This was the moment when the reality of her death set in for most people. At once, the sounds and sights of grief filled the room. Mrs. Terasawa's husband sat in a chair with tears streaming down his face. One of her two daughters cried at the front of the coffin, holding on to it for stability, wailing loudly. Mrs. Sakamoto stood on the other side, crying and caressing Mrs. Terasawa's face. She was gently led away by an attendant to make room for other mourners to make their final good-byes.

The family was handed origami cranes in a rainbow of colors, which were added to the flowers in the coffin. Finally, the immediate family was given large chrysanthemums to place around Mrs. Terasawa's face.[37] Her husband lovingly touched her face one last time as he placed his flower.

The emcee introduced Mrs. Terasawa's younger brother, who spoke on behalf of the family. He described in detail her deterioration over the past three months, starting with the weakness in her legs, her loss of appetite, and the stroke that finally claimed her. She had been in the hospital since October, but she had been clinging to life in order to see her seventy-fourth birthday and her granddaughter's wedding—both only a week away.

After he finished, the attendants bought the coffin lid to be placed back on the open casket. At this point, Mrs. Terasawa's eldest daughter was overcome with grief, wailing, "*Iya da yo! Iya da yo!*" (Stop it). She tried to physically prevent the attendants from placing the lid on the coffin until her husband could finally hold her firmly. But there was a sense that she was giving voice to the anguish shared by the assembly of guests, nearly all of whom were now openly sobbing.

When the coffin lid was securely placed, the funeral attendants guided everyone to the front entrance of the Sanshōkaku to send off Mrs. Terasawa's body. I noted that "Sen no kaze ne natte" was playing over the public address system as we slowly walked out into the cold December rain.

Three buses were lined up in front of an ornately decorated hearse to take Mrs. Terasawa's close family to the crematorium. While friends are not prohibited from attending the cremation, by custom the cremation is a private, family affair.

When everyone was lined up, Mrs. Terasawa's coffin was carefully carried out of the hall by six pallbearers—a delicate task, as the coffin had no handles. The coffin was placed into the hearse feet first, and the doors were closed and locked. The driver bowed to the coffin in the hearse, bowed to us, and led Mrs. Terasawa's husband to the passenger side of the hearse, where he would travel with the body.

There was another round of heavy crying. Mrs. Terasawa's two daughters thanked the assembled guests profusely with deep bows, for being there and for taking the trouble to come out in such bad weather. The family boarded the waiting buses, and very soon the funeral procession was on its way. One by one, the vehicles circled the roundabout. The Baikakō bowed in *gasshō* as a final salute to Mrs. Terasawa. As the hearse passed Sōjiji's gate and went out of sight, I heard Mrs. Oka quietly whisper, "*Sayonara, Terasawa-san. Tengoku ni mata aimashō.*"

"Goodbye, Mrs. Terasawa. May we meet again in Heaven."

Cultivating Life

It is unreasonable to expect either the intense grief of loss or the disruption of the social fabric caused by death to be resolved at the end of a funeral, no matter how "affirming" the message of the clergy. Despite the claims of the medieval Sōtō Zen priests that they could bestow immediate enlightenment—and thus salvation—upon the dead, this innovation was never able to supplant the traditional Japanese belief that a newly dead spirit must undergo a process of maturation before it could be counted among the generations of tutelary household ancestors. Rather than being an endpoint, we must see the *tsuya* and the funeral as laying the groundwork for all future social interactions between the living and the dead.

Like *shugyō*, the logic of *kuyō* is steeped in Neo-Confucian notions of filial piety that became intertwined with Buddhist cosmology and, later, with Japanese folk practices. In an idealized parent-child relationship, parents make sacrifices to provide food, clothing, shelter, and education to bring a child safely from dependence through adulthood. Moreover, children would not even be alive in the first place were it not for their parents. This gift of life and the years of care that parents give to their offspring result in an impossible debt (*on*) being placed on the shoulders of the children. As parents age and return to a state of dependency, children are obliged to attempt to repay (*hōon*) the infinite debt that they accrued from being the recipients of life and care.[38] While caring for one's parents is relatively straightforward while they are alive, children are obliged to return the care for their parents in perpetuity after death.[39]

The transformation from human to newly dead to ancestor is a long process, requiring attentive care and nourishment over a period of years and decades. More importantly, this process is not *automatic*, in the same way that a child becoming a functioning adult is not automatic. The nurturing relationship has to be active, intentional, and consistent. In this sense, the process of performing *kuyō* mirrors that of providing care for a child from birth through adolescence and ultimately into a productive (and reproductive) adulthood.

The first forty-nine days after death are traditionally considered to be the most critical time for the establishment of this new relationship. Mourners are expected to observe seven weekly memorial rites at their parish temple, each representing a different stage in the transformation of the dead from the newly deceased (*shinmō*) to an enlightened *hotoke*.

After the cremation ceremony, the ashes are taken home in a white brocaded reliquary box to be placed on the household *butsudan*, where, like a newborn child, they are expected to be cared for around the clock with offerings of food, flowers, incense, and sutra recitations.⁴⁰ The *ihai* with the deceased's new name is placed on the *butsudan*, and the mortuary photograph is hung above the cabinet.

By the second week, the temporary *ihai* that was used in the funeral is replaced with a permanent lacquered *ihai* that is then "awoken" in an Eye-Opening Ceremony. After the fifth week, the ashes are placed in their final resting place, either buried in a permanent cemetery plot or disposed of in some other manner.

The forty-ninth day after death is known as the *Nehan no Hi* (Day of Nirvana), or, more formally, the *Dairenki*. At this point, the deceased are thought to be fully stabilized in their new form as *hotoke*, having attained the full enlightenment of the Buddha.⁴¹ In many ways the *Nehan no Hi* echoes the custom of shrine visitation in which Japanese newborns are "presented" at a local Shintō shrine approximately a month after birth, when an infant's soul is thought to be securely attached to its new body.⁴² Though solemn, the *Nehan no Hi* is an occasion for a modicum of celebration. Following the memorial ceremony, the family usually gathers together for a communal meal—often a catered meal in a restaurant or in the home—in recognition of an important transition point for both the dead and the living.

Reflecting back on his time in mourning, one informant told me that the first week was the hardest, but as each of the seven weekly rituals were conducted, the pain of loss gradually eased. Still, the *Nehan no Hi* was not a "celebration," he explained, because no one can be said to be "happy." "The priest explained to us that my grandfather had attained enlightenment like the Buddha and that we should be happy," he told me, "but that didn't make any of us feel better. We were still sad that our grandfather had died."

After the seven-week mourning period ends, the next major event comes at the first anniversary of death. According to custom, families are expected to mourn for an entire year, with the living entering into a public state of mourning (*mochū*) at the moment a family member dies. An announcement to this effect is posted outside the front gate of the mourner's home, and for the next year, the mourning family is supposed to act and dress somberly. One informant elaborated on this to explain that events like parties, vacations, and social gatherings should be cancelled, and even obligations like writing New Year's cards should be avoided.

Traditionally, the end of mourning on the first anniversary of death is considered a celebration, since it is from this point on that the living are again allowed to "enjoy" life. Again the family gathers for a memorial ceremony at a temple and, afterward, for a communal meal in honor of the dead. From this point forward, memorial observation for the dead falls less under the authority of the temple and priest than it does the particularities of household custom and practice.

How meaningful or frequent these offerings are depends, of course, on the person or family in question. Far and away the most common practice is the offering of food on the household altar. Many of my informants reported interacting with their ancestors enshrined on the family *butsudan* in their home at least once a day, usually at mealtimes. The daily ritual, as it was described to me, is simple: a family member (most often a woman) places a bowl of rice or a cup of tea on the *butsudan*, lights a candle, rings a small bell, places their palms together, and bows their head. While I expected this ritual of offering to be short, I was amazed to see how short it could be: visiting the home of one family, I saw the entire thing done in literally twenty seconds.

Individuals or families may observe the deceased's monthly or annual death days (*meinichi*)[43] with practices such as grave visitation, offerings of the deceased's favorite food or drink, donations to a temple or other charitable organization, or with practices such as sutra copying and chanting. One person I spoke with told me that every month on the day his mother died, he forgoes cigarettes and alcohol, drinks only miso soup, and chants the Heart Sutra thirty-three times. Although this particular individual's practice is unique—and even extreme when compared to more common Japanese memorial observations—it provides an example of the range of activities that can comprise the practice of *kuyō*.[44]

While the Sōtō Zen clergy encourage the performance of *kuyō* in one's everyday life according to one's own ability and preferences, there are important ritual moments when believers and parishioners are encouraged to seek the services of the clergy and a temple. The most common periods for employing the clergy are during the four seasonal festival periods: the two equinoctial Higan celebrations (March and September), the summer Obon festival (July and August), and the winter New Year's celebration (January). During these periods, the normally tranquil garden bursts with foot and motor traffic as parishioners swarm to Sōjiji en masse to visit their family graves. Families have the option of participating and paying to have their names read as donors during the *Sejiki* ceremonies that are scheduled daily to correspond with these periods. The *Sejiki* Ceremony aims to feed wandering hungry ghosts through offerings of rice, water, and the sating power of the Dharma. By donating to this cause, living donors accrue karmic merit that the clergy redirects to the benefit of the deceased. The *Sejiki* ceremonies at Sōjiji are well advertised in advance and often draw more than five hundred lay participants on the busiest days.

Less regular are the semiannual memorial rites known as *onki.* These ceremonies take place on the first, third, seventh, thirteenth, seventeenth, twenty-third, twenty-seventh, and thirty-third anniversaries of a person's death.[45] The Sōtō Zen sect considers a *hotoke* to have officially entered the nameless generations of household ancestors after the thirty-third anniversary of death, freeing the descendants from memorial obligations specific to that individual. Be that as it may, in common practice it is rare for a parishioner household to continue to observe—that is, pay for—memorial rites requiring a temple and clergy past the thirteenth anniversary.

Nevertheless, Sōjiji generates a substantial portion of its income through the performance of these ceremonies, more so than the annual dues of its parishioner households. As a result, much of the temple's efforts go toward accommodating parishioner requests for the performance of memorial ceremonies for ancestors and relatives, categorically referred to as *senzo kuyō.*

In a temple of five thousand parishioners, it is instructive to see how the clergy of Sōjiji attempt to maintain mechanical efficiency and speed while working to avoid the appearance of doing precisely that. While families dressed in black mourning clothing are a common sight in Sōjiji's halls any day of the week, it is, of course, the weekend that sees the most activity. In order to accommodate the high demand for the performance of memorial rituals, morning and afternoon sessions of two hours each are held simultaneously in both the Daisodō and the Hōkōdō on Saturday and Sunday, allowing Sōjiji to minister to upward of sixty families each weekend. Simple math shows that in order to keep this pace, the temple clergy must be able to minister to two families every fifteen minutes.

Families are greeted at the reception desk by a monk who will serve as their guide through the temple and through the ritual protocol of the ceremonies, which the laity are not expected to know. Their monk leads the family to the fourth floor of the Sanshōkaku, where rows of long tables are arranged throughout the hall. Here the families are served tea and cookies while they wait for their turn. A higher-ranking priest from the temple comes to each table in turn to speak with the family, adding a human and compassionate face to what might otherwise seem to be an impersonal process.

About a half hour before the family's ceremony is scheduled to begin, their escort monk guides the family through the temple to the appropriate hall. In the back of the hall, a red carpet is set up, split in two by a low wooden barricade. On the left side of this fence sits the family for whom the ceremony is currently being conducted. On the right side sits the family next in line for the ceremony. The family on the right moves to the left when the current ceremony ends, and the next family is brought in to take their place. The family whose ceremony has just ended is led out of the hall.

While this transition is taking place, a stage crew of monks prepares the main altar for the new family. The lights over the altar are turned off while the monks work, speedily replacing one family's offerings of foodstuffs and flowers on the altar with those from the next. If the family has brought a mortuary photograph with them, this is placed on the altar as well. Fresh candles are placed on the altar and lit, and a new stick of lit incense is placed in the burner. The movements of the stage crew are precise and efficient, and the transition from one family to another takes less than three minutes. When the transfer is complete, the lights are turned back on.

As the altar is prepared, the officiant and the assembly of *unsui* sit quietly, facing the center of the hall. The officiant sits on a lacquered throne in the center of the hall; he is flanked on both sides by the assembly of *unsui*, two rows to a side, fifty monks in total.[46]

In contrast to the *unsui*, who are dressed in their uniform black robes, the officiant wears richly embroidered golden-yellow vestments and a pointed miter and carries the tasseled *nioi* scepter of a ranking priest. That the officiant wears fine clothing is considered to be a display of respect to the sponsoring family rather than a conspicuous show of wealth. Ironically, however, this fact is seldom explained to the family. On several occasions, I heard people ask whether the officiant was the abbot of the temple. (He was not.) One person I spoke with actually came away with the opposite message: he perceived the officiant's rich clothing as evidence that his donations were going to the well-being of the clergy rather than to the benefit of his ancestors.

The *senzo kuyō* ceremonies are superficially similar—and surprisingly brief. The ceremony space is opened with a crash from the large bell, and the *unsui* stand. After brief words of benediction from the officiant, the cantor announces a chant, usually something short like the Dharani of Great Compassion (*Daihi Shin Darani*). As the monks chant, they ambulate through the inner hall in an almost figure-eight path. After they have returned to their places, but while the chanting continues, the family's escort leads the family to the altar, where they offer two pinches of incense and then bow in *gasshō*. They are led back to their seats. When the chanting ends, the officiant announces the name of the donor family, declares the purpose of the offering (most often simply "for the purposes of *senzo kuyō*"), and recites the Transfer of Merit verse that transfers to the dead the karmic merit accrued by the family for hiring the clergy to chant scripture. With a final bow, the ceremony ends.

Once again the stage crew whirrs into action, turning the lights off, and resetting the altar for the next family. If all has gone well, the ritual—from set-up to close—has taken fewer than fifteen minutes. On good days the time is closer to twelve minutes, all told.

Given the importance of the *senzo kuyō* rituals to the financial well-being of the temple, as well as the speed and efficiency by which these rituals are performed, it is perhaps all too easy to give in to the perception that Japanese Buddhist temples—even a training temple like Sōjiji—are in the "business" of grief. The ongoing criticism of the Buddhist institution as parasitic and opportunistic is echoed in the comments of the disgruntled parishioner. A more skeptical Japanese critic may comment that a funeral, or a year of mourning observances, or thirty-three years of memorial observances have no soteriological value, that they are merely tools—invented by the Buddhist institution and, increasingly, the provenance of the funeral industry—of keeping customers paying in perpetuity. Ultimately the question must be asked, Who is *kuyō* for? The dead or the living?

Facing Death

On the morning following Mrs. Terasawa's funeral, Yamadera-rōshi gave a sermon to the *unsui*. I had my notebook open and ready to take notes, but as he spoke, I stared past him to the giant wooden statue of the Buddha that dominated the stage behind him. Occasionally, I looked over to the monks sitting on the other side of the hall. I saw only one or two awake. The rest sat with their shoulders slumped over, and their heads bowed in a way that one might mistake for deep concentration on their notes in front of them. I was impressed with their ability to sleep without falling over.

All of a sudden, Yamadera-rōshi's voice broke my trance:

> It is natural for people to try to avoid death. We go to great lengths not to think about it. In hospitals, we avoid the number four because we say it doesn't sound "pleasant" (*yoku nai*). We're not afraid of the number four. We're afraid of death.
>
> How many times have we heard people say that Buddhist tem-

ples are "gloomy" (*kurai*) and "dangerous" (*abunai*) places? When they visit a temple, it seems to them that it is a place where people go only when someone dies. Furthermore, people don't like hearing sutras. Sutras are the words of the Buddha. They are *good* things! But the average person doesn't think about that. All they think when they hear chanting is a funeral.

In previous times, a Buddhist priest was the one to sit with the dying person to comfort them and their family. Only the priest could say when death had occurred, because the priest had to release their spirit from the body. Now priests are only called after the death takes place. Sometimes we're even accused of getting there too late! When people see priests only at funerals, they come to associate Buddhism with death. They don't respect priests, because they think they should avoid you. But ask those same people who they want to perform their funeral, and most will respond that they want "a priest who practices *shugyō*" (*shugyō shite iru sō*). They're not afraid of the priest. They're afraid of death.

Just like the sunlight, humans can't look for too long at death—it hurts too much. But we [priests] have to learn to face death (*shi o mitsumeru*). We have a responsibility to provide comfort in the face of death. You *will* encounter death. This is certain. There is no perfect world where death doesn't exist. This is the meaning of impermanence. The lesson of *shugyō* is that life exists in this moment—now, here.

Ima, koko. Yamadera-rōshi punctuated his words by waving his hand horizontally on "now" (*ima*) and vertically on "here" (*koko*). Out of context, his gesture might have been mistaken for the sign of the Cross. He continued:

Each of us is fortunate to encounter other people in the world, in every moment of our lives. When a person dies, we perform *kuyō* for them to show our gratitude for the blessing of meeting that person and knowing them in life. If you don't understand this, then you can't share it with the people who need to hear it most.

I was not the only one moved by Yamadera-rōshi's words that morning. Later that day, another retreat participant stopped me to ask if I had ever participated in *dokusan*, a private interview with a master in which the student is encouraged to ask questions to deepen their understanding of their *shugyō*.

I told her that I had not. She said that she wanted to ask someone about the compatibility of different religions, but she didn't know if this would be an inappropriate question. Her family belongs to the Rinzai Zen sect, she said, and she thinks it is important to give them the sect-appropriate funeral. At the same time, she couldn't stop thinking about what Yamadera-rōshi had said. "Sōtō-shū really sounds like it cares about people," she told me. "I know my family is Rinzai, but maybe Sōtō is the right answer for me." She decided that the question she wanted to ask is whether she can be both Rinzai and Sōtō at the same time.

At the evening *zazen* session, a bell was rung seven times to announce that the master was ready to receive visitors. I bowed to the wall, slipped on my shoes, and quickly left the hall. I was directed by the hall monitors to the room that I had only seen used as the Tanga-ryō, now repurposed as a waiting room. There was a red carpet on the floor, which served as a queue for those waiting to see the master. I was third in line.

We were each handed a piece of paper giving detailed directions for entering the master's room and asking our questions. I was nervous, but it occurred to me that most of the *unsui* had never done this before either.

After twenty or so minutes, my turn came. Outside the master's room, I heard the ring of a small handbell. I struck the bell that was waiting outside, asking permission to enter. I heard the handbell ring again— permission granted.

From a kneeling position, I opened the sliding door into the room where the master was waiting. The space itself was small, with fluorescent light illuminating only the front half of the room. I was surprised to see Yamadera-rōshi sitting in the darkened half of the room, almost completely enveloped in shadow. A low table with flowers, incense, and the small handbell sat in front of him. In his hands, he was holding a *kyōsaku* stick.

As instructed, I bowed and made a full prostration on the floor. As I stood up, I forgot that I had been wearing the skirt of my *hakama* garments low to keep my feet covered in the frigid meditation hall. I stepped on the back hem and lost my balance, falling squarely on my behind. Yamadera-rōshi laughed kindly at my awkward display and waved me over, telling me not to worry about protocol.

I nervously walked toward him and raised my hands in *gasshō* before I spoke: "Yesterday I was at the funeral of someone who was very important to me. Today I can't think and I can't concentrate. When I try to meditate, all I can see is her face in the coffin. At today's sermon, you said that we have to learn to face death, but I don't know how to do that."

A look of sympathy crossed his face. "You must mean Mrs. Terasawa.

It really was a shame, wasn't it? Ordinarily, I would have gone to pay my respects. Because it is the *sesshin*, I was only able to send a representative. Please sit."

I nodded and thanked him. I knelt in *seiza* in front of him. In a gentle voice, he began answering my question:

> If you're lucky, death is not really something you think about until you're sixty or so. But then people start thinking about their own death, and they begin to worry about how they are going to die.
>
> Compassion for human beings is the kind of feeling that I try to instill in the *unsui*, but they're like you: they're too young to understand. Most of them still have their parents, and grandparents too. They've *heard* of death, but they have no experience of it. But a priest needs to be able to connect with his parishioners—and those who have died—on a human level. When you do your morning rituals, a priest always has to remember that the names he's reading are not just names. Each one of them is a human being.
>
> Nowadays, the *unsui* think that when they are done at Sōjiji, they'll go to work for their fathers. "'One day,'" they think, "I'll inherit a temple with a lot of parishioners," and that they'll never have any problems. That may have been true fifty or a hundred years ago. But it isn't true anymore, and it won't be true in the future. The *unsui* today are going to have to work hard just to maintain what they have.
>
> I didn't inherit my temple. My father was a priest, but I'm the third son. [He pinches his *kesa*.] All he gave me were these robes. Even if there was a second temple in the family, my older brothers were ahead of me in line.
>
> It took twenty years of teaching for me to be offered my own temple. The temple I was given was in the countryside, and it was very poor. When I started, I had sixty parishioner families. Now I have four hundred. There's no secret to what I did. After I perform a wake or a funeral, I don't just up and leave, like many priests do. Instead, I take off my *kesa*. I revert to "human mode" (*ningen mōdo*). I walk around the room, and I talk to the people there. Even people who have never been to a funeral know this is a rare thing. People who, for whatever reason, would ordinarily not talk to a priest are the ones who most appreciate the effort. People who meet me say, "There's a priest who cares about his parishioners! I want to go to *him* for my funeral." And so they join my temple, transferring their family's membership from their old parish to my temple.

Yamadera-rōshi paused to ask me if I was following along. I nodded, and he continued: "To stare at death means to care for people in this moment." He traced a Venn diagram of two interlocking circles on the floor with the tip of his *kyōsaku*:

Mrs. Terasawa was very special to you. You and the people who are important to you are separate, but you share a human connection. [He points to the center, where the circles overlap.] When a person dies, it leaves an emptiness that will be filled with tears. It would be wrong if it didn't.

I sometimes wonder how many people will cry at my funeral. [He smiles.] Actually, I think about it quite a bit. And, you know, I hope there are a lot! If there are, it will mean I've touched the lives of a lot of people. I'm sixty-three years old now. My mother is in her nineties, but I don't know if I'll live ten, twenty, or thirty more years. All I know is that I have that time to make as many connections with people as I can.

We have a saying in Japanese—"without remembering, without forgetting" (*Omoide sezu ni, wasurezu ni*). We must never forget those people we have lost, but we can't hold on to our grief to the point where we can no longer live. We all have responsibilities, and we can't neglect them out of grief.

It is perfectly normal to cry at a funeral. Japanese people don't always show their emotion, thinking that they need to endure (*ganbare*). We also have difficulty expressing anger in appropriate situations. There is a feeling of frustration all around. I think it would be better if people learned to manage their emotions better and not be afraid to express them.

This is why we encourage everyone to practice *kuyō*. When we act on behalf of people who were important to us, without thinking of ourselves, gradually our sadness becomes gratitude (*arigatasa*) for those we were fortunate to meet in this life. At first it is difficult, but the more you do it, the more natural it becomes.

Mrs. Terasawa cared for you, and you cared for her. She became your grandmother, and you became her grandson. When you prepare to sit *zazen*, or sing *goeika*, or even when you make dinner or wash dishes, you should think of her. When you think of her, be grateful that of all the billions of people in the world, you and she had the chance to meet. This is all that is needed for you to do *kuyō*.

With that, he smiled again and apologized for having to cut our meeting short. There were lots of *unsui* who were waiting to ask him their own questions, and he was determined to answer all of them, even if it took him all night.

"Human Mode"

Yamadera-rōshi's words made it clear that *kuyō*, like *shugyō*, is a long, often painful, but ultimately personally transformative process for the living. The close parallels between *kuyō* and *shugyō* suggest that the two operate from an identical logic and are in fact manifestations of the same process.

As gentle as the clergy would like to make it sound, properly performing *kuyō* demands that the living submit to a process of emotional, mental, and physical redisciplining over a period of years. Like *shugyō*, one begins on the path of *kuyō* with reluctance and great sacrifice; it requires a death, both social and literal. From this departure, one is forced to renegotiate previously lived patterns of social relatedness and relearn to interact with social beings not as they were (or as one imagines them to be) but as they *are*.

In this regard, the elements of *kuyō*—the *tsuya*, funeral, and mourning obligations—mimic the initiation processes that an *unsui* faces upon entrance to his training. That *kuyō* disciplines the deceased (who has been tonsured) is expected; however, that it similarly cultivates the living as well is a significant parallel that has not previously been observed. Like *unsui*, the living are taught how to hold their body, how to speak, and how to act, all of which are familiar parts of monastic life: sitting for long periods in *seiza*, holding one's hands in *gasshō*, a sense of hierarchy and respect, and an understanding and ability to navigate ritual space, among other things.

But most significantly, like *shugyō*, the goal of *kuyō* is *kuyō* itself; even a moment in which a person experiences a sense of gratitude for the dead and for the living and acts accordingly is a moment in which one participates in an ideal state of compassion and thus a state of enlightened grace. The real transformation comes when a person is able to extend these moments for longer periods of time and in different social contexts. A cup of tea placed at the family altar may become a surprise gift of cookies brought to friends, eventually leading to a desire to help those in need who cannot help themselves.

As the Buddha taught, the one universal in life is impermanence (*mujō*). No human who has ever lived is spared the pain of loss, and it is only in this pain that the wisdom of *kuyō*—and true gratitude for the living—can be truly appreciated. The mind and body that has been trained to deeply understand the impermanence of life and selflessness (*muga*) is a "living *hotoke*," living in a state of enlightened and compassionate grace no different from one who has been awakened through meditative practice.

Having undergone *shugyō*, the elder clergy hope that the younger clergy will be more understanding of the importance of the disciplining process of *kuyō* and be uniquely qualified to help the laity through it. One day the *unsui* will come to understand the teaching of impermanence, and it is only from this understanding that the wisdom and compassion to effectively minister to their parishioners will spring.

Complicating this, however, has been the encroachment of the funerary industry on what has previously been Buddhist territory. Increasingly, the mourning process has been made to be a commodity to be purchased more or less à la carte. Indeed, the entire process may be abandoned by mourning families out of disinterest or because it costs too much. Rather than being meaningful, the clergy laments that the transforming and necessary process of *kuyō* has been displaced by a veneer of commercialization and the illusion that proper care of the ancestors is something that discerning customers can choose.

In order to stay competitive in the widening field of Japanese religions, the *unsui*—as future Sōtō Zen priests—must learn to embrace change. Learning to face death is, of course, a part of this, but the priests must also learn to navigate a dynamic relationship with the public in which traditional Buddhist practices are subjected to market forces. For the time being, *kuyō* remains the primary means by which the laity and the clergy relate to and interact with one another. Moving forward, one of the challenges for the Sōtō Zen clergy will be how to convey a sense of the lasting importance of *kuyō* as a valuable form of personal cultivation and discipline to a laity whose religious loyalties are increasingly uncertain.

Conclusion

For a Thousand Years

The year 2011 had every indication that it would be a momentous one for Daihonzan Sōjiji. That year marked the centennial of Sōjiji's reopening after the relocation to Tsurumi from its ancestral home on the Noto Peninsula. Preparations for a calendar filled with media promotion, museum exhibits, symposia, and the publication of commemorative volumes had been in the works for at least three years. The culmination would be a grand public celebration to mark the date of the one-hundredth anniversary on November 1–5.

This is not to say that everything had gone smoothly. In November 2009, Sōjiji's deputy abbot, Saitō Shingi, passed away, necessitating the immediate election of a new successor. On March 4, 2010, Egawa Shinzan (1928-2021) was elected to the deputy abbacy, receiving more than two-thirds of the total votes cast.[1] Like many who had come before him, Egawa previously held the office of rector (*kannin*) at Sōjiji, from 1996 to 2000, and had proven himself a highly capable administrator during his tenure. He was formally installed into his new office as deputy abbot at an "entering-into-residence" ceremony (*menkata shiki*) in Sōjiji's Monk's Hall on the morning of March 30, 2010.

This election was doubly important because Ōmichi-zenji's age and declining health had already raised concerns about succession, and it was rumored that his retirement from Sōjiji's abbacy was planned for the end of the year. To insiders, the timing was not surprising—the optics of the ailing and wheelchair-bound ninety-three-year-old Ōmichi-zenji were in stark contrast with the image of a vital and thriving Sōjiji that the commemorative events sought to portray. Moreover, it was increasingly doubtful that Ōmichi-zenji would be able to publicly officiate the many commemorative events the temple had planned. Since these public responsibilities would fall to his deputy anyway, why not hasten the succession and start Sōjiji's second century in Tsurumi on solid footing?

As with every change in abbacal administration, there would be a shift both in Sōjiji's internal and public-facing direction and policy. Throughout 2010, arrangements were made to bring in new department heads and mid-level appointees to staff the temple's many administrative departments. With this, of course, came some housecleaning; rumors were that the incoming administration had become concerned that discipline among the *unsui* had become lax under the present seminary-side leadership. This was in part due to the fact that the current Ino-rōshi had been ill, so discipline had largely fallen to his subordinates in his absence, many of whom were themselves only barely older than the current *unsui*.

But while these shifts in administrative vision were par for the course, I was nevertheless shocked when I received a New Year's card from Mr. Takeuchi in January 2011 informing me that, in the course of the administrative shake-up, the Nichiyō Sanzenkai had officially been dissolved the previous April. It had been replaced by an informal group managed directly by the Propagation Department and now met only one Sunday a month.

When I had the chance to speak to Mr. Takeuchi in person later that year, he was emphatically blunt in telling me that the former head of the Propagation Department "hated the Sanzenkai" and was personally determined to end it before he left Sōjiji. When I asked him why he thought this, Mr. Takeuchi told me that the former department head believed that hosting a lay meditation group was not something that Sōjiji should be wasting space, time, and resources on. He suspected that the department head could not get rid of the group outright, but with the Propagation Department taking direct control and by moving the format from weekly to monthly, the decision was effective in alienating the long-term members who felt compelled by disrespect and indignation to find somewhere else to go. The (now-former) Nichiyō Sanzenkai members saw this administrative shift as further evidence of an internal conspiracy against them.

While I have no evidence (and, from personal conversations with the priest in question, sincere doubts) related to Mr. Takeuchi's claim that the former department head "hated" lay *zazen* practice in general or the Nichiyō Sanzenkai in particular, I did recognize in the move an administrative logic that could very well have been underscored by accumulated frustration toward the group. Despite their devotion to *zazen* practice, it was hard to deny that the Sanzenkai *was* a major drain on the temple's (and specifically, the Propagation Department's) space, time, and resources. For four hours every week, the Sanzenkai effectively colonized one of the most useful publicly accessible spaces in the temple. On top of that, each meeting required the Propagation Department to dedicate between four and six of its staff for that duration to attend to the group and to serve as hall monitors during the meditation periods. Adding to the burden was the expectation that one of the seminary instructors or a manager within the Propagation Department take time each week to prepare and deliver a forty-minute *teishō* lecture to the Sanzenkai, stretching already overextended resources even further.

Despite having four thousand registered members on the books, and despite drawing between five and fifteen interested guests on average per week, that only the same forty or so members showed up each week was evidence that the Sanzenkai's usefulness as an effective tool for public outreach and engagement for the temple and sect was limited at best. As I suggested earlier in this book, the stern atmosphere and aura of exclusivity that some prospective members—particularly women—experienced may have even worked against the temple's outreach efforts.

That said, I suspect that what ultimately doomed the Sanzenkai was the entrenched disregard many of its members held toward the ritual and religious realities of a Japanese Sōtō Zen temple. With due respect to what Dōgen or Keizan may have written about *zazen*, contemporary Sōtō Zen largely remains—as it has for five centuries—defined by its generational relationships with its parishioners, particularly through the performance of memorial rituals. In particular, life at Sōjiji revolves around the careful cultivation of its *unsui* to be ritual specialists who can effectively minister to the needs of their parishioner bases and, with talent and effort, retain or even attract new parishioners to Sōtō Zen. By ideologically distancing themselves from this reality, by rejecting repeated appeals by Sōjiji's administration to participate more fully in the temple's ritual life, and by its members not forming any personal investment in or relationship to Sōjiji other than as a space to sit *zazen*, the Nichiyō Sanzenkai demanded a lot from Sōjiji and offered very little in return.

Despite the successes of *zazen* in raising the international profile of Zen, it is hard to ignore the fact that the lay *zazen* movement in Japan was a temporary detour that failed to be a viable road for keeping Japanese Sōtō Zen temples solvent.[2] As I see it, the dissolution of Sōjiji's Nichiyō

Sanzenkai represented a decisive top-down rejection by the temple administration of their having to cater to the lay *zazen* practitioners' desire for a nonreligious, obligation-free "pure Zen" that was divorced from the reality of contemporary Sōtō Zen religious practice. While there are still plenty of opportunities for the public to sit *zazen* at Sōjiji, these opportunities—and the narratives about Sōtō Zen history and practices that underlie them—are now offered squarely on the temple administration's terms.

A New World

With major changes already under way, very few observers were surprised when, citing age and health concerns, Ōmichi-zenji's retirement from Sōjiji's abbacy was announced in late January 2011. The plan was for him to formally step down at the end of the annual weeklong Precepts Platform festival (*Jukai-e*) on April 16. Egawa's term as abbot would begin with a grand public installation ceremony the following morning on April 17.

Beginning with the rush of New Years' visitors during Hatsumōde, January and February 2011 proceeded without incident. Throughout the month of January, two long columns of *unsui* emerged from the temple each afternoon in straw hats and sandals to walk through the streets of Tsurumi for their annual "alms begging" (*takuhatsu*), offering the townspeople the opportunity to earn good merit in exchange for donations to the temple that the monks received in their eating bowls. The always-festive Lunar New Year (*Setsubun*) celebration packed the Daisodō with families from throughout Yokohama to catch "lucky beans," with the solemn observance of the Buddha's entrance into Nirvana coming two weeks later. Following these celebrations, the temple calendar quieted down for a bit. In this lull the previous year's class of *unsui* began to depart in groups of threes and fours just as the first crop of new arrivals began to show up at the temple gates.

Preparations for the Higan observances in the third week of March were well under way when, at precisely 2:46 p.m. on Friday, March 11, 2011, the world underneath Japan's—and Sōjiji's—feet changed irrevocably. Over the span of six terrifying minutes, Japan's eastern coast was violently shaken by the most powerful earthquake to strike the country in over a century. The earthquake's epicenter was located just 70 kilometers (44 miles) off Japan's Sanriku Coast and could be felt throughout Japan's north and eastern regions, toppling furniture and breaking windows as far south as Tokyo and Yokohama, more than 300 kilometers (186 miles) away.

The worst was yet to come. Given the earthquake's proximity to the coast, the resulting tsunami struck the heavily populated areas along the shorelines of Fukushima, Miyagi, and Iwate Prefectures, including the regional capital, Sendai, with only minutes' warning. In many places, the tsunami easily crested seawalls that had been constructed to protect against that very thing and surged inland with terrifying speed. Cars and trucks and boats were tossed around like toys, and earthquake-resistant buildings and ferroconcrete structures were obliterated by the tsunami's fury. People in low-lying areas who could not get to higher ground, and even some who had fled to upper stories of buildings or designated tsunami evacuation areas, were caught in the wave's merciless surge, which in some places topped twelve meters. When the floodwaters receded, what remained was death and devastation.

As if nature had not done enough, the tsunami surge had breached the seawalls of Tokyo Electric Power Company's (TEPCO) Fukushima No. 1 nuclear power plant. Although emergency protocols had shut the reactors down as soon as the earthquake struck, the backup generators that provided coolant to the nuclear fuel inside the reactors were themselves knocked out by the seawater that flooded the power plant's facility. With nothing to stop the runaway nuclear reaction, the fissile material in the plant's three active reactors went into full meltdown. Not even forty-eight hours after the earthquake and tsunami, all of those living within twenty kilometers of the Fukushima No. 1 plant—roughly sixty thousand people—were forced to evacuate their homes. Three days after the tsunami, explosions from the three crippled reactors ejected vast amounts of radioactive contaminant into the atmosphere, the countryside, and the ocean, adding injury to already calamitous injury.

It is impossible to overstate the lasting effects of the Great East Japan Disaster (*Higashi Nihon Daishinsai*, or "3.11" as the triple disaster has come to be known) on Japan. All told, nearly sixteen thousand people were confirmed to have lost their lives, most of them in the minutes after the tsunami surge hit the coast. More than twenty-five hundred people remain unaccounted for and presumed dead.[3] More than three hundred thousand people were displaced from the Tōhoku region, with homes within the mandatory evacuation zone near the Fukushima nuclear plant likely to be dangerously contaminated for generations.

Survivors of the triple disaster were left without homes, without families and social support networks, without property, without jobs, facing discrimination for being "contaminated," and struggling with anxiety, depression, and symptoms of severe posttraumatic stress.[4] Regionally, the economies of Iwate, Fukushima, and Miyagi prefectures were devastated, with severe consequences for downstream food and manufacturing supply chains throughout the country. The disaster led to the revelation of systematic negligence and corruption throughout the country's energy sector, a crisis of public confidence in the Japanese government, and a rising vocal opposition to Japan's reliance on nuclear energy.[5]

All told, the Japanese government placed the official cost of the earthquake and tsunami at 16.9 trillion yen. This number, however, does not factor in the costs of the Fukushima nuclear disaster, estimated at upward of 10 trillion yen. Together, the triple disaster of March 11, 2011, cost a mind-boggling 26.9 trillion yen (US$256 billion), making it the most expensive natural disaster in human history.

While the tsunami killed indiscriminately across all strata of society, on a sectarian level, Sōtō Zen was disproportionately affected by the disaster. The Tōhoku region has historically been a stronghold of Sōtō Zen's parishioner support, and the sect's twelve hundred parish temples there account for nearly 40 percent of all Buddhist establishments in the three most affected prefectures.[6] Nearly all of these temples suffered varying degrees of damage from the earthquake and tsunami, and forty-five temples were completely destroyed.[7] Internal estimates put the number of Sōtō Zen parishioners who experienced either a death or a catastrophic loss of property at ten thousand households, with an additional five thousand households evacuated as a consequence of the Fukushima nuclear disaster.[8]

Within hours of the disaster, the Sōtō Zen sectarian administration established a "Disaster Relief Headquarters" (*Saigai Taisaku Honbu*) to coordinate information, donation, and relief efforts.[9] At the grassroots level, the sect's Shanti Volunteer Association and its many regional Young Priest Associations (*seinenkai*) were swiftly mobilized to assist with food distribution, debris removal, and charitable fund-raising. In addition, the sect's General Assembly approved an increase to its special disaster relief fund to 2.2 billion yen (US$20.9 million), earmarking 225 million yen (US$2.1 million) for direct relief payments to affected parishioner families.[10]

Despite the unknown short- or long-term dangers posed by chemical, biological, and nuclear contaminants in the disaster area, clergy and volunteers from across the spectrum of the Japanese religious denominations were on the front lines of the national relief effort, throwing themselves into the herculean task of providing aid and ministering to the physical, mental, emotional, and ritual needs of the survivors.[11] Indeed, for Sōtō Zen clergy throughout Japan, the weeks and months after the Great East Japan Disaster were a time when the lessons of their *shugyō* would be put to the ultimate test. This was particularly true for the young, newly minted priests who were on the front lines of the sect's response efforts. As Yamadera-rōshi predicted, the ability to stare into the face of death and human suffering with disciplined composure and selfless compassion would be the mark of a Sōtō priest who could truly minister in "human mode" to the needs of his parishioners and who could become a trusted leader in his community.

As the recovery efforts progressed, reports and images of Buddhist priests of different denominations working together alongside the Japanese Special Defense Forces (SDF) and the International Red Cross, leading clean-up efforts and providing ministerial care in the affected areas became increasingly commonplace in the national and international media. As the survivors faced the further agony of mass burials without proper memorial rites, the united Buddhist clergy performed funerals and memorial services without expectation of payment, in addition to providing material comfort in the form of new or replacement memorial tablets. As the immediacy of the disaster waned and attention turned to the long-term physical and mental welfare of the survivors, a number of innovative Buddhist clergy dedicated themselves to meeting the emotional needs of their communities.[12] These efforts did not go unnoticed. Levi McLaughlin notes that a "leading image of religion that appears to have taken hold in Japan's newspapers is that of highly educated, proactive priests who 'overcome' their archaic denominational boundaries to provide new types of chaplaincy training in forward-looking ecumenical settings."[13] This new narrative in the Japanese media has begun to chip away at the public opinion of religion as "gloomy" and even "dangerous," and specifically of Buddhist clergy as parasites who, as the proverb goes, "always profits" (*bōzu maru mōke*). In their zeal to serve their communities, the 3.11 disaster provided the Japanese Buddhist clergy with a unique opportunity to reset their relationship with the public and, moreover, regain their trust.[14]

Pivot

At a distance from the earthquake's epicenter, Sōjiji suffered only minor structural damage, mainly to the Daisodō and Butsuden. Watching the disaster unfold from my home in the United States, I found myself surprised by Sōjiji's muted response: on March 14, Ōmichi-zenji released a public statement of condolence and support for the victims of the disasters, but in contrast with the head temples of other sects of Japanese Buddhism, there was otherwise little visible activity from Sōjiji itself. What I mistook at first as institutional paralysis, however, I later came to appreciate as the true uniqueness of Sōtō Zen's dual *honzan* model. With the Sōtō Zen sectarian administration having immediately activated its charitable and volunteer auxiliaries, it was neither the time for Sōjiji or Eiheiji to jockey for leadership of the sectarian relief efforts, nor was it either *honzan*'s place to act unilaterally in the wake of the disaster. Rather, as had been done in past national crises, the two *honzan* presented a united front under the combined auspices of the Sōtō Zen administration that allowed the sect leadership to spearhead the effort to collect and distribute financial assistance to affected parish temples and communities and to coordinate the on-the-ground response and relief efforts. By deferring action to the sect administration, Sōjiji's and Eiheiji's silence communicated a powerful message of unity in the face of great adversity, a signal that was amplified by Sōtō Zen's willingness to put aside sectarian differences to cooperate with other Japanese Buddhist sects on behalf of those in desperate need of help.

Understandably, the 3.11 disaster threw Sōjiji's careful planning for its celebratory centennial year into disarray. For the first time since World War II, the difficult choice was made to cancel the Precepts Platform festival (*Jukai-e*) that was to culminate in the auspicious transfer of power from Ōmichi-zenji to his successor. The Jukai-e was the ideal setting for this kind of major transitional event; held annually from April 10 through April 16, it is the festival in which the clergy and laity formally take refuge in the Buddha, the Dharma, the Sangha, and the Ten Bodhisattva vows. It at once serves as a communal rite of passage for the newly arrived *unsui*, a revival-style religious retreat for upward of two hundred members of the Sōtō laity, a full week of back-to-back public ceremonies and lectures, and a festive homecoming and reunion event for Sōjiji clergy, many of whom come to Tsurumi accompanied by tour buses full of parishioners from their home temples. Timing the transition of abbots around the final day of the Jukai-e was a masterstroke of scheduling that would have guaranteed a massive attendance for both Ōmichi-zenji's farewell and Egawa-zenji's installation from across the spectrum of a thriving contemporary Sōtō Zen community.

In the wake of the 3.11 disaster, and with the entire Japanese nation in mourning, it was immediately apparent that the Jukai-e had to be cancelled and the scope of the abbacal transition curtailed to avoid the appearance of impropriety or, worse, that Sōjiji was diverting resources that were in desperate need elsewhere. It was thus in the shadow of the humanitarian and environmental tragedy still unfolding in the Tōhoku region that Egawa-zenji's installation ceremony (*jinsan shiki*) as twenty-fifth abbot of Sōjiji took place on the morning of April 17, 2011.[15] Beginning with a procession from the Sanmon gate, the solemn three-and-a-half-hour ceremony saw Egawa-zenji ascending the altars of the Butsuden and Daisodō to pay his respects as abbot to the enshrined images of Śākyamuni and the Buddhist and Sōtō patriarchs. The installation concluded with his first sermon as abbot and a ritual question-and-answer (*mondō*) demonstration proving his wisdom and possession of the Dharma.[16]

After the installation ceremony, Egawa-zenji's very first official act as newly installed abbot of Sōjiji was to officiate a memorial service on behalf of the victims of the 3.11 disaster. While a cynical reading might see this memorial service as a means of shielding Sōjiji from the problematic optics of holding an otherwise celebratory ceremony during a period of national mourning, I argue that the decision to place this memorial service had significance that went far beyond the considerations of the present moment. Contextually, *this* specific ritual act, performed at *this* specific moment, during *this* specific historical juncture was the opening stanza of a new telling of Sōjiji's historical narrative in which the aftermath and recovery from the March 11 disaster would be forever written into Egawa-zenji's abbacy and thus into the story of Sōjiji itself.

To see the significance of this decision, it is instructive to understand Sōjiji's master narrative in the century since its move to Tsurumi as a triumphant tale of rebirth from catastrophe through the dedicated efforts of its ambitious caretakers. The major beats of this narrative—establishment, destruction, rebirth, prosperity—are well established in the temple's own promotional material as well as mass media coverage about Sōjiji. The history is almost universally told through "rhyming couplets" that create parallels between Sōjiji's founding in Noto in 1321 by a visionary Keizan and its reestablishment in Tsurumi in 1911 by a visionary Ishikawa Sodō, separated by the catastrophic fire of 1898. While all venerable institutions have, by definition, a long history from which to draw, what makes Sōjiji remarkable and perhaps even unique, is that its story is told largely *without* reference to the deep past. In a fascinating turn, the intervening six centuries of Sōjiji's history—the period when the temple's cultural significance was established and solidified—has in the modern period been treated as little more than ellipses between these two foundational events.

Instead of relying on its past successes to explain its relevance in contemporary society, Sōjiji's story is instead told alongside the growth and development of the modern Japanese nation generally and of Tsurumi and Yokohama in particular. Timelines of the temple's twentieth-century history are clear to show Sōjiji's story as paralleling the arc of its community and country.

From another perspective, however, the reverse is also true: in Sōjiji's retelling, the twentieth-century history of Tsurumi and Japan parallel Sōjiji's narrative pattern of tragedy, difficult but determined recovery, and eventual prosperity. This can best be seen in how Sōjiji's narrative structure is extended to other watershed events in modern Japanese history. In particular, the Great Kantō Earthquake of 1923, the firebombing of Yokohama in 1945, and the "Devil's Saturday" train accident in Tsurumi in 1963 all figure prominently in Sōjiji's retelling of its history in the modern period. If you know where and how to look, this history is written into the daily ritual and the very landscape of the temple. The messaging is subtle but clear: Sōjiji's story is the story of modern Japan, and the story of modern Japan is the story of Sōjiji. As goes Japan, so goes Sōjiji. As goes Sōjiji, so goes Japan.

Unlike an institution that takes pride in being distant from the struggles of the world, there is an awareness that Sōjiji cannot be separated from the events taking place outside its gates. Sōjiji's modern history is thus a "reboot" of its medieval history; it reiterates, in concrete and relatable terms, that it is an outward-facing institution that is deeply involved with its community, in the best of times and in the worst of times.

Incorporating the 3.11 disaster into Sōjiji's story enabled Egawa-zenji to make a powerful statement of hope in the face of adversity to the people of Tōhoku: Sōjiji lost everything, but it survived—and so will you. As people from across Japan came together to help Sōjiji recover, so Sōjiji will be there to help you. Writing 3.11 into Sōjiji's history was therefore not an opportunistic appropriation of a national tragedy but rather a conscientious continuation of a story in which Sōjiji's and Japan's destinies are inextricably intertwined.

Sōjiji at One Hundred

This rescripting was visible in the five days of ceremonies and events that took place from November 1 through November 5, 2011, to mark the one-hundredth anniversary of Sōjiji's founding.[17] Because they are expected to be commemorated in specific ways, events like anniversaries are important moments of history making. Etymologically, "commemoration" (from the Latin *com-memoria*) means "to remember, together." Like the words "community" and "communicate," the word's origins remind us that the act of commemoration is an inherently social activity, a collective and continuous process of transforming various (and often conflicting) threads of "pasts" into a coherent and definitive "history." Rituals that imagine the past as history are instrumental in making communal memories for the future.[18]

A commemorative rite, according to Émile Durkheim, involves "remembering the past and making it present, so to speak, by means of a true dramatic performance."[19] The key word here, however, is "true": the truth presented in the commemorative rite is *performatively* true, in the sense that it enables participants to experience, through reenactment or memorialization, a specific account of the past. But performative truth should not be confused with historical fact. While a ritual of commemoration is first and foremost a ritual of social remembering, it may be better described as an act of *selective* remembering. Constraints—usually concerning time and cost but also political sensibilities—often lead to a judicious streamlining of the narrative, allowing "less important" (or less convenient) details to fall to the wayside. Moreover, there are always factors that risk complicating the narrative being constructed that must be left out. Over time, successive commemorations become even more carefully curated, with a tighter narrative structure and fewer and fewer "problematic" threads. Those details that do not make the cut fall out of collective memory.[20]

Through historical coincidence, Sōjiji is blessed with a roughly fifteen-year window every half century to refine its institutional narrative. Prior to 2011, Sōjiji's last period of celebrations began with its 50th anniversary in Tsurumi in 1961 and continued through Gasan's 600th memorial observances (*daionki*) in 1966, Ishikawa-zenji's 50th memorial observances in 1969, Sōjiji's 650th institutional anniversary in 1971, and, finally, Keizan's 650th memorial observances in 1974. During this period, construction was completed on Sōjiji's iconic Daisodō and its Sanmon gate, both the largest of their kind in Japan. These constructions were conspicuous symbols of a thriving and international-facing Sōjiji that mirrored the Japanese miracle economy that was shown off to the world during the 1964 Tokyo Olympic Games. As is typical, a number of official histories and retrospectives were commissioned and published in commemorative editions, giving concrete form to Sōjiji's story.[21] This narrative sustained Sōjiji, proudly framed as an "international Zen garden," for the second half of the twentieth century.

By 2011, after decades of economic stagnation in Japan and especially in the aftermath of the 3.11 disaster, a new narrative was necessary. Planning for a similar "facelift" for Sōjiji, both literal (in the sense of physical renovation) and figurative (in the sense of narrative revisions), had begun in earnest in early 2008. Pulling back from the grand global vision for Sōjiji that characterized the fiftieth anniversary, the centennial vision focused on Sōjiji's relationships: those who made the move to Tsurumi possible and, through them, its connections to its history, its community, and its country.

Beginning at 9:30 a.m. on November 1, Sōjiji's centennial was a five-day marathon of ceremonies that filled the Daisodō with incense smoke; the continuous sound of chanting voices, bells, and drums; and an ever-changing cast of dignitaries and visiting "pilgrimage" groups (*honzan sanpai dan*).

For the visiting groups, in particular, it was a rare and exciting opportunity to witness the memorable pageant of Sōtō Zen ritual in its highest form, with an assembly full of veteran clergy and officiated by high-ranking Sōtō priests in impressive regalia. At the end of each ceremony, the visiting groups were invited to the altar to offer incense, and the merit from the ceremony was transferred by name to the ancestors of each of their families and to the victims of the 3.11 disaster. These groups were then cycled out of the Daisodō between events to tour the temple grounds and experience other aspects of Sōjiji, and while the hall was reset for the next ceremony, a new group was brought into the hall to take their place.

While I am sure that many of the visiting groups, if asked, would have liked to see more of the ceremonies, there was pragmatic as well as logistical sense in having each group participate only once. With the surface features of the ceremonies—the chanting, the prostrations, the ambulations, the offering of incense—being largely the same, they very quickly began to blend together. The specifics of the centennial, in this respect, were not for the laity.

For anyone familiar with Sōjiji's history, however, the little details of the ceremonies—who was being honored, what order they occurred in, and who was selected to officiate them—served as a meaningful honor roll of Sōjiji's legacy: if Sōjiji reaching a century in Tsurumi was the award, the centennial was the acceptance speech thanking "everyone who made this possible."

The morning of November 3 was the pivot point of the entire celebration and featured the largest and most important ceremonies of the centennial—the ritual commemorating the temple's founders (*kaisan*): Keizan, Gasan, and now, Ishikawa-zenji. Echoing the grand procession that Ishikawa-zenji led to mark the official reopening of Sōjiji in 1911, priests, dignitaries, and representatives from the entire temple community—including, adorably, children from Sōjiji's kindergarten, dressed in traditional aristocratic court attire—processed from the temple gate to the

Fig. 17. Sōjiji's cantor (*ino*) reads the names of donors at a ceremony during Sōjiji's 100ᵗʰ Anniversary celebration.

Daisodō, accompanied by *goeika* music sung by the Baikakō. As the hundreds of people took their places in the great hall, I mentally noted that attendance was among the largest I had ever seen at Sōjiji.

The victims of the 3.11 disaster had been kept at the forefront of the entire centennial event. Immediately following the opening ceremonies, the first memorial ritual was for the victims of the 3.11 disaster. In each ceremony that followed, the victims were collectively named as recipients of the merit the religious activity generated. Egawa-zenji's sermon during these ceremonies for the founders did a lot of the narrative "heavy lifting" work for the centennial by specifically linking the recent 3.11 disaster with the catastrophe that set Sōjiji's next hundred years into motion. As with his installation, the message that Sōjiji wanted to convey was one of solidarity and support with the victims of the disaster but also of hope in the face of grave tragedy.

While the centennial commemorated large portions of Sōjiji's past, it is instructive to see who and what was left out of the story as conveyed by the ceremonial rituals. Other than the descendants of the Maeda family, the parishioners that Sōjiji left behind on the Noto Peninsula received no mention. While the descendants of these families are still parishioners of the reconstructed Sōjiji Soin, no mention was given to the uncomfortable fact that moving Sōjiji took away the livelihood of an area that had depended on the income from the regular visitation of priests and their entourages for over five centuries. Instead, Sōjiji's move to Tsurumi was portrayed as the realization of the vision of Keizan and Gasan and imbued the centennial's narrative with a sense of "fulfilled destiny."

Secondly, whatever role Asano Sōichirō played in facilitating Sōjiji's move to Tsurumi was also written out of the ritual narrative. This is an interesting omission, given that overlooking Asano is literally impossible: Asano's grave, located immediately behind the Butsuden, is one of the most prominent monuments in Sōjiji's cemetery. While it is possible that Asano and his partners' complicated legacy as ruthless industrialists could have led the planners to distance themselves from his contributions, it is also possible that he was a sacrifice in service to narrative simplification. Where there were previously two important figures in the relocation story, there is now only one: in the simplified telling, Ishikawa Sodō is given all of the credit for orchestrating the move to Tsurumi. As Asano faded from view, Ishikawa-zenji was ritually elevated alongside Keizan and Gasan as a "founder" of Sōjiji.

What I found telling was that Dōgen (and thus Eiheiji) was narratively absent from the celebration.[22] In fairness, Dōgen never played a personal role in Sōjiji's story, and Eiheiji's relationship with Sōjiji has largely been that of a foil. However, this is not to say that evidence of the historically complicated relationship between the two temples was entirely absent from the weekend. Curiously, Eiheiji scheduled a symposium on the future of nuclear energy in Japan for November 1 and 2, eclipsing Sōjiji's anniversary celebration and giving Eiheiji publicity and media coverage that by rights could have gone to its sister head temple.[23] My informants could only speculate on whether the timing of this symposium was a scheduling oversight on Eiheiji's part, a petty decision to capture some of Sōjiji's spotlight, or an intentional diversion to move media attention away from a celebration during a time of national mourning. Regardless of the motive, Eiheiji's symposium received national media attention; Sōjiji's centennial, in contrast, went virtually unnoticed, getting only local TV and newspaper coverage.

Legacy

The Tsurumi centennial did not bring Sōjiji the media attention it arguably deserved, but it was nevertheless an ideal jumping-off point for Egawa-zenji's administration to renew, reaffirm, and revitalize the social connections that have made Sōjiji such a significant force in Japanese culture and religion for seven centuries. While it still styled itself as an "international Zen garden" as it had during the heyday of Japan's miracle economy, the new direction was to redirect its attention toward meaningfully deepening its existing community relationships: with its parishioners and Sōtō Zen adherents, of course, but also with Tsurumi, with its sister temple, and with a Japan still reeling from a major environmental and humanitarian disaster. Done correctly, this path could be a model for how Sōtō Zen could thrive in Japan through social work and community partnership—"human mode" on an institutional scale.

With sect-based recovery efforts still ongoing in Tōhoku, Sōjiji and Eiheiji entered into a partnership for the creation of the "Dual Head Temples' Cooperative 'Prayer for Recovery' Sakura Project" (*Ryōhonzan Kyōdō Fukkō Kigan Sakura Purojekuto*) in late 2011. The project was nothing less than a Zen temple's botanical metaphor made real: Sōjiji's *unsui* would plant a veritable forest of hundreds of cherry blossom seedlings along the path leading to the Buddha Hall, where they would be given daily care by the monks during their work detail while also being in proximity to the prayers for recovery and good merit that would emanate from *kuyō* ceremonies performed at the Butsuden and Daisodō. It was a metaphor for the Sōtō sect as well: the "propagation" work—the seeding, nurturing, and eventual transplanting of the saplings—was performed at Sōjiji, while the project's offices and bookkeeping were housed at Eiheiji.

With proper cultivation, in the span of a year these seedlings would grow into two-meter-tall saplings that could then be transplanted onto the grounds of Sōtō temples that were damaged by the 3.11 disaster. In 2012, during the month of July, 370 seedlings were planted at Sōjiji, with a delegation from Eiheiji assisting Sōjiji's *unsui* in planting the trees.[24] A year and a half later, the young saplings were strong enough to be transplanted at more than 170 Sōtō temples throughout the Tōhoku region.[25]

Sōjiji's renewed commitment to community engagement through cultural cultivation could likewise be seen in its hosting new musical programs open to the general public. On the eve of the third memorial anniversary of the 3.11 disaster in 2013, Sōjiji hosted the first "Evening of Prayer" (*Inori no Yūbe*), a two-hour multimedia event that blended Buddhist memorial ritual with contemporary musical performance, featuring a high school choir from Fukushima and headlined by the singer/songwriter (and Jōdō Shinshū priest) Yanase Nana.[26] The concert itself was a success, but what was most significant was the number of local organizations that Sōjiji partnered with to make the concert a reality: in addition to a core executive committee formed from members of the Sōjiji administration, the Tsurumi Cultural Association, the Tsurumi Historical Society, and Tsurumi University, the concert received financial backing and material support from ten other community partners, including local business associations and media outlets. Since then, Sōjiji has hosted a number of additional musical events and performances, further blurring the line between ritual space and community space.[27]

These community partnerships would reap dividends when, in late 2013, Sōjiji officially announced the formal commencement of the ten years of celebration that would be framed by Gasan's 650th memorial (which would be held a year early, in 2015) and Keizan's 700th *daionki*, scheduled for 2024.[28] The theme of the celebratory decade was declared to be *Sōjō*, "inheritance." While the "inheritance" in the theme is explicitly a reference to the generational connection between Keizan and Gasan, the broader implication—as read in the subtitle, "Can you hear the sound of the great footsteps?" (*Ooinaru ashioto ga kikoemasuka?*)—is that the legacies of Keizan and Gasan, like the thundering footsteps of the *unsui* whose *shugyō* is training them to be the future of Sōtō Zen, echo through Sōjiji today. The festival's ubiquitous symbol was the *enso*, the calligraphic circle signifying reality and continuity that is one of Zen's most iconic and recognizable symbols.

Among other planned architectural renovations to Sōjiji's *garan*, the most symbolic was the construction of a northern corridor that linked the Hōkōdō, the Butsuden, and the Daisodō. Since its reconstruction, the residual fear of another catastrophic fire was written into the landscape of the temple itself: in addition to its buildings being spaced widely apart, the Buddha Hall was kept disconnected from the other temple buildings with a wide firebreak on either side. Isolating the Butsuden made accessing the temple's ritual spaces more difficult than in other *shichidō garan*, but it also meant that no fire could fully destroy Sōjiji as it had that fateful night in 1898.[29] Whatever else happened to the campus, the Butsuden—the beating heart of the temple—would survive.[30] With the completion of an above-ground corridor linking the three structures, Sōjiji's campus was now connected in a continuous circuit—an architectural *enso*—for the very first time since its move to Tsurumi. This was not evidence of Sōjiji dismissing or forgetting the lessons of its past (the corridor was specifically constructed from fire-resistant materials with a modern fire-prevention system) as much as it was a statement of a confident Sōjiji looking toward the future.

Gasan's memorial anniversary celebration, like the Tsurumi centennial before it, was marked by a full year of commemorative events, symposia, and historical and art exhibits befitting his legacy as a key popularizer of Sōtō Zen. In early May a delegation from Sōjiji visited the flourishing Sōtō Zen missions in France (Temple Zen de la Gendronniere, two hours outside of Paris), Brazil (Busshinji, in São Paolo), and the United States (Zenshuji, in Los Angeles) for a "preliminary celebration" of Gasan's *daionki*.[31] The Sōjiji delegation brought with them precious cargo—a newly consecrated copy of Gasan's memorial tablet. As a proxy presence, the travelling *ihai* presented not only a rare chance for international Sōtō Zen adherents and practitioners to "meet" Gasan but also an opportunity for Gasan to "witness" firsthand his living legacy in the world outside of Japan.

In Japan, Gasan's legacy was being commemorated in music and performance. At the Sixty-third Annual Baika-ryū National Assembly in late May, a new *goeika* piece, the *Daihonzan Sōjiji niso Gasan Zenji sango gowasan* (Hymn in praise of Daihonzan Sōjiji's second ancestor, Gasan-zenji), was debuted to an audience of more than nine thousand Baikakō practitioners from groups throughout Japan, many of whom also took the opportunity to visit Sōjiji, located just three stops from the convention center by train.[32] The following month, more than a thousand people attended the world premiere of the orchestral piece "Gasandō: The Road of Legend," by composer Ikeba Shin'ichirō, in Yokohama's Minato Mirai Hall.[33] The composition was a unique arrangement that wove together orchestral music performed by the Kanagawa Philharmonic Orchestra with chanting by fifty Sōtō clergy selected from among the Sōjiji *unsui* and the Kanagawa Young Priest Association.

As the year progressed, it was clear that an important shift had taken place in the public-facing advertising and messaging about the festival. While both Sōjiji's and the *daionki*'s informational websites were still clearly focused on the figures of Gasan and Keizan, posters placed in heavily trafficked public spaces promoted the festival as the "Town of Tsurumi's Memorial" (*Tsurumi no Machi no Daionki*). Visually, these posters gave very little recognition to Sōjiji; save for an image of Sōjiji's Sanmon gate that towered over silhouetted images representing a modern, urban Tsurumi, the temple was largely treated as just another festival event venue. Further emphasizing this was Sōjiji taking last billing after the municipal and local

Fig. 18. A poster advertising the 2015 *Tsurumi no machi no daionki*.

organizations that were sponsoring the festival. Festival banners that were hung from lampposts throughout Tsurumi likewise shifted focus away from Sōjiji, placing it squarely on the town itself, proclaiming Tsurumi "a town that touches the heart/mind of Zen" (*Zen no kokoro ga fureau machi Tsurumi*).

As the October start of the *daionki* approached, it seemed almost as if two overlapping festivals—one celebrating a historical religious figure; the other showcasing a town aspiring to be a cultural destination—were taking place simultaneously in the same space. By blurring the conceptual boundaries of the *daionki*, the festival likewise blurred the spatial boundaries between town and temple, making it impossible to determine where Sōjiji ended and Tsurumi began. This, of course, was precisely the point: the *daionki* was a recognition by both town and temple that a close relationship between the two entities was the key to future success for both. In a poetic example of chronological continuity, the *daionki* legitimized Tsurumi's place in Sōjiji's seven-century (and counting) historical narrative; together it was Sōjiji's and Tsurumi's role to remake its industrial image as a cultural and artistic destination.

The *daionki* proper began on October 7, with hundreds of Sōtō clergy convening at Sōjiji for two weeks of back-to-back, large-scale memorial ceremonies taking place in the Daisodō in honor of Gasan. While this was taking place, the lobby of the Sanshōkaku had been transformed into a public art gallery, and several illuminated art installations were being set up throughout Sōjiji's precincts.

These two visions came into focus on the evenings of October 17 and 18 for the "Melody of Prayer" (*Inori no Shirabe*) event. By day Sōjiji was filled with the scent of incense and the sounds of drums, bells, and the rhythmic chanting of hundreds of voices, while guests were invited into the garden for a culinary "Festa," where they could sample *shōjin ryori* vegetarian dishes prepared in the temple kitchens. By night the temple was limned with flickering candles and ethereal LED light installations representing the ever-present spirits of the past—the ancestors, victims of war and disaster, and all who have been touched by Gasan's vision of the future. In the Daisodō, the Kanagawa Philharmonic Orchestra performed an encore performance of the "Gasandō" piece to a sold-out audience of over a thousand attendees, with many thousands more making their way through the temple grounds to enjoy the illuminated landscape.

By the end of Gasan's *daionki*, an estimated thirty thousand people—most from Tsurumi but many from across Japan and around the world—had entered Sōjiji's gates to participate in some way in the festivities. With preparations for Keizan's seven-hundredth memorial now beginning in earnest, Sōjiji's star was shining brightly.

"This Tranquil Field"

In 2021, Sōjiji entered its eighth century. As Keizan envisioned on his deathbed, Sōjiji continues to serve as a fertile soil for Buddhist, Sōtō Zen, and Japanese culture, a tranquil field worked and tilled by millions of people over countless generations.

Throughout its first seven hundred years, the temple and its caretakers left an indelible mark on the culture, the history, the people, and the religious landscape of Japan. By fate or by design, Sōjiji has flourished in periods of prosperity and peace and weathered periods of tragedy and conflict, surviving where many other institutions could not. Even after being utterly destroyed by fire and against all odds, Sōjiji has thrived for more than a century in Tsurumi by being able to continuously reinvent itself alongside an ever-changing world. Sōjiji is simultaneously a vision of Sōtō Zen's future even as it is a touchstone for its storied past.

As it has for centuries, Sōjiji's role as a *shugyō dōjō* imprints a uniquely Sōtō Zen perspective of history, identity, culture, and virtue onto the bodies of all those who enter its gates. Inside the temple walls, the many faces of *shugyō* are steeped in memory and tradition, with participants learning to see themselves both as commemorating and contributing to an ongoing narrative set in motion thousands of years ago by the Buddha and kept alive through generations of Sōtō Zen patriarchs. At the same time, *shugyō* is by definition "forward-looking." As a technique of disciplining and self-cultivation, *shugyō* represents above all else transformation, a "becoming."

In the context of popular discourse on religions that is still dominated by tropes of "belief" and "faith," the emphasis placed on *shugyō* at Sōjiji is a reminder of the need to attend to what religion *does*, not merely what religion *says*. Daily life at Sōjiji reinforces the idea that *shugyō* is an *embodied* process of self-cultivation, in which an individual's ethical responsibility is to be transformed through physical, mental, and emotional hardship into living examples of the Sōtō Zen ideals of discipline, compassion, and enlightenment.

As Sōjiji acts upon those within its walls, so is it acted upon. Like dutiful gardeners, Sōjiji's community—novices and priests, meditators and *goeika* singers, visitors, parishioners, ancestors, and countless others—dedicate themselves and their efforts to preserving the temple's past, cultivating its present, and imagining its future. In so doing, they learn to see themselves as participants in an organic cosmology in which diligent and disciplined practice empowers individuals to work toward an idealized version of the world as well as to continuously refine their understanding of their place within it. Not for themselves, but for the benefit of all.

Epilogue

In Perpetuity

It was lunchtime on a humid day in June when Mr. Kubota, the Baikakō assistant group leader, kneeled in the middle of the rehearsal space to address the group. Wearing a blazer and slacks, Mr. Kubota was sweating in the summer heat, occasionally dabbing at his bald forehead with a handkerchief. His quiet voice barely pierced the din of the room, and he had to start his speech several times before he was able to get the group's attention.

Mr. Kubota explained that he was addressing the group on behalf of Yamazaki-sensei, the Baikakō instructor. Yamazaki-sensei's home temple was in need of substantial renovations. In particular, the three-hundred-year-old roof of the main hall was badly in need of repair. Although long lasting, the large gabled roofs of Japanese temple architecture are expensive to repair and maintain, and there was no way that the small parish temple could pay for the repairs on its own. A common practice for temples in these situations is to host a fund-raiser whereby individuals or groups can sponsor the donation of materials, particularly roof tiles.

The Baikakō unanimously agreed to participate in the fund-raiser for Yamazaki-sensei's temple. Further, it was decided that individual donations should be made rather than a single group donation. Each person in the group, it was agreed, would donate 2,000 yen (US$19) to sponsor their own individual roof tile. To ensure equality and fairness within the group, no one was allowed to donate more, but neither was anyone allowed to donate less.

Mrs. Terasawa pulled out a roster of current Baikakō members from her bag. One by one, each member went up to Mrs. Terasawa's desk to give their donation. She checked their name off the list and wrote down their wish. Most of the members chose "safety of the household" (*kanai anzen*), but several opted for "bodily health" (*shintai kenkō*).

After all of the names and donations had been gathered, Mr. Kubota ceremoniously handed Yamazaki-sensei the manila folder on behalf of the Baikakō. In addition to a list of names and wishes, the envelope now contained close to 60,000 yen (US$570). Yamazaki-sensei received the donation graciously, humbly thanking the Baikakō for their contribution. One of the women in the group responded to Yamazaki-sensei's gratitude with the formal expression "Your thanks are enough" (*Okimochi dake desu*). Mrs. Terasawa quickly and bluntly corrected her: "His thanks *aren't* enough. We're asking him for a favor!" (*Okimochi dake ja nai. Onegai suru koto no yo*).

Later that day, I asked Mrs. Terasawa what she meant by "asking for a favor." She explained to me that our names and requests would be painted onto the underside of the individual roof tiles we donated, where they would be protected from the elements. Every time the hall is used thereafter, the good merit (*kudoku*) generated by the activity will rise with the incense smoke and work to make our wishes come true.

"When the roof was originally built, people wrote their names on the tiles just like we're doing. Right now they're removing the old tiles, and finding the names of people who lived three hundred years ago. Those people have been dead for many years, but their names and wishes are still there.

"Three hundred years from now, when the roof is rebuilt again, someone will turn over the tiles and see our names," Mrs. Terasawa said. "We'll be long gone by then, but we'll be remembered because we will have been part of the temple. Maybe someone will pick up a tile and think, 'What kind of a person was this? What stories could they tell?'

"Isn't that amazing?" she asked me emphatically.

I agreed that it was.

Afterword

Writing Sōjiji

This project began with a proposal to investigate the role that domestic and international religious tourism plays in shaping the practice of everyday life at a major Japanese Zen Buddhist temple. Within weeks of arriving in Japan to do my fieldwork, however, it became clear to me that my question was shortsighted, at least as far as Sōjiji was concerned. While Sōjiji does receive a great number of visitors over the course of a given year, as a working parishioner temple, a seminary for novice priests, and an administrative center Sōjiji's relationship with the public is markedly, and perhaps decidedly, different from that of other large temples throughout Japan.

Seeing Sōjiji in this light opened up far more fruitful avenues of inquiry than did limiting my focus to tourism alone. In the short term, however, this shift away from my intended project was terrifying to me, as the enormity and significance of Sōjiji loomed large in both my eyes and my mind. In many ways this is because Sōjiji can only really be described in superlative terms: in terms of land holdings and architectural size, Sōjiji ranks among the largest temples in Japan, boasting the largest Dharma Hall in the country as well as some of the largest examples of Buddhist statuary and icons. Similarly, Sōjiji's parishioner base of five thousand families likewise distinguishes it from the vast majority of other Japanese Buddhist temples, nearly all of which have parishioner memberships that number in the low hundreds.

As I delved into Sōjiji's history in the premodern and modern periods, it was clear to me that Sōjiji stands tall among the Japanese Buddhist institutions in terms of its lasting cultural significance and influence on the historical development of religious practice, particularly with regard to Japanese funerary and memorial ritual. Perhaps most significant for the future is Sōjiji's role in the spread of Zen—both as a religious practice and as a lucrative commodity—to the world outside of Japan.

There are stories, articles, and volumes about Sōjiji that extend infinitely beyond what I could expect to publish. Trying to figure out which stories portrayed "the real" Sōjiji I wanted to represent was admittedly the biggest obstacle for me in conceiving this project, and my field notes reflect the logistical, emotional, and personal struggles of a researcher consumed by capturing everything there is to know about Sōjiji, both historically and as it is lived today.

At the outset, my notebooks were filled with observations about the architecture and other distinctive features of Sōjiji's landscape, as well as maps of the structural layout and directional orientation of the buildings in relation to one another. I spent my first weeks moving between different "posts" from where I could unobtrusively observe the steady flow of people moving through the temple grounds throughout the day. Using a clicking tally counter, I quickly developed an intuitive sense of the "pulse" of daily life at Sōjiji.

My formal entrée into the temple was thanks in large part to Shimazono Susumu, now Professor Emeritus of the Department of Religious Studies at Tokyo University, who arranged an introductory meeting for me with the late Saitō Shingi, Sōjiji's deputy abbot at the time. Without Saitō-rōshi's endorsement to the temple administration, it's likely that I never would have been able to perform the type and quality of ethnography that ultimately resulted from my fieldwork. Once I was introduced, my daily visits to Sōjiji and regular participation in public ceremonies quickly made me a familiar (but nevertheless curious) face to both the temple administration and *unsui*.

At the same time, I made inroads among the laity by throwing myself wholly into the role of participant-observer as a member of Sanzenkai and the Baikakō. My membership in the Sanzenkai did not distinguish me in the temple community, but my membership in the Baikakō most certainly did. Moreover, I took the Bodhisattva precepts twice during *Jukai-e* festivals and received a Dharma name and *kechimyaku* lineage chart from Ōmichi-zenji.

My dedicated attendance and participation in the religious life of the temple encouraged many of my informants—both lay and clerical—to welcome me into their lives and share personal stories about themselves and their experiences at Sōjiji. Both the Sanzenkai and the Baikakō allowed me to conduct a brief, anonymous written survey that provided insights and directions for later interview questions.

As my field research progressed, my presence became part of the backdrop of the temple, and I was permitted to move with increasing freedom across the explicit spatial and conversational boundaries that distinguish public-facing spaces from the "backstage." In addition to being an active member of the Nichiyō Sanzenkai and the Honzan Baikakō, I participated in every public temple activity that I was eligible for; took part in every retreat period open to the public; periodically assisted with the temple work, including time in the kitchens; and sat in as an observer on nearly every public temple ceremony that took place during that period.

Admittedly, this pace was less ambition as it was a manifestation of an ethnographer's earnestness to find that magic "key" (as if such a thing actually exists!) to unlocking and understanding the secrets of one's field site. The pace was also untenable, and my struggles to harness Sōjiji's physical and historical enormity led to my placing unrealistic pressure on myself for being "only" one person, with a limited supply of energy, time, and money.

Ultimately, however, this struggle to describe the inner workings of Sōjiji—a machine-like bureaucratic apparatus that is both complex and perpetually in motion—was mentally productive. A slow process of "false starts" culminated in my foregrounding person-to-person practice and interaction to outline the architectural, ritual, and experiential spaces and contours of the temple. To tell the story presented here, I chose to follow the trajectory of different groups of people as represented by key informants as they moved through their engagement with the temple. While these trajectories would intersect at various important junctures—public ceremonies, sermons, funerals, and the like—the intention was to demonstrate how the logic of *shugyō* informed each group's experience of the temple.

I have returned to Tsurumi and Sōjiji periodically (though never as often as I would like), and during these trips I have reconnected in person with as many of my informants as time and opportunity allow. In between visits, Facebook, Instagram, and Twitter, the annual exchange of New Year's cards, and the sharing of birth, wedding, and graduation announcements have allowed me to stay connected with and informed about events and developments at the temple and remain a part of my informants' lives.

As an author, I have gone to great lengths to portray life at Sōjiji as honestly and as transparently as the process of writing ethnography allows. Still, from an authorial standpoint, these choices and moments of discovery led to concerns over subjectivity: to what degree have I portrayed Sōjiji "as it really is" versus Sōjiji simply as I experienced it? Would my anonymized informants recognize themselves in my retelling of the stories they told me? Would other scholars' experiences support or contradict my treatment of daily life at Sōjiji? There are no easy answers to these questions, and indeed such questions of subjectivity lie at the core of all ethnographies. I acknowledge that other works about Sōjiji or any other Japanese religious institution may—and indeed should—look very different than this one.

Sōjiji's story began long before the ethnographer arrived and will continue long after the ethnographer leaves. This work is only one of many possible stories.

Postscript: Sōjiji in the Time of COVID-19

I had made travel arrangements to visit Tsurumi during the summer of 2020. My goal was to put a capstone on this book by closing the parenthesis around my experience of Sōjiji, twenty years from when I first entered its gates as a curious graduate student. Having not returned to Japan in several years owing to the demands of family and career, I was looking forward to meeting up with the friends I had kept in touch with over the years. In particular, I hoped to see how Sōjiji's emerging reputation as a destination for culture, music, and art might combine with the 2020 Tokyo Olympics to bring a surge of national and international visitors to the temple.

That was, of course, not to be. Japan, and in particular Yokohama, was one of the first places outside of China that the novel coronavirus, SARS-CoV-2, spread, brought to the country by a tourist from Hong Kong who boarded the cruise ship *Diamond Princess* at the Port of Yokohama in January. This person was diagnosed with COVID-19 after disembarking in Hong Kong, but the disease they had brought with them remained on board and spread unabated throughout the ship's passengers and crew on its next voyage. The people on the *Diamond Princess* were quarantined in Yokohama's harbor as the Japanese Ministry of Health dithered on the best course of action to take with the raging outbreak on the ship. The resultant monthlong deadlock was a political fiasco, and although safety measures were put in place, ultimately over seven hundred of the more than thirty-seven hundred international passengers and crew became infected with the disease. When international pressure led to these passengers being released from their weeks-long quarantine and evacuated to their home countries, they too became another vector through which the disease brought the entire world to a standstill.

As soon as I saw "coronavirus" and "Yokohama" mentioned in the same sentence, I knew that I would not be able to finish this book the way I had intended. I refreshed Sōjiji's web page regularly, waiting for the inevitable announcement that the temple activities would be curtailed. The announcement came in mid-February 2020 as the first Japanese deaths from COVID-19 were reported.

Coronavirus had come to Japan on the eve of the tenth memorial anniversary of the 3.11 disaster. Sōjiji and its community partners had been planning another *Inori no Yūbe* concert for March 8 to mark this occasion, but this was cancelled due to the impossibility of practicing social distancing for a thousand people inside the Daisodō. The memorial services on the March 11 anniversary itself and the Spring Higan observances, however, proceeded as scheduled but without any dignitaries, parishioners, or lay attendees.

The announcement also brought with it the news that all of the lay organizations at Sōjiji—the Baikakō, the Sanzenkai, the Fujinkai, and the rest—would be cancelled until further notice. Parishioner funerals and memorial services, on the other hand, would continue amid strict attendance caps and social distancing guidelines.

In order to keep the temple functioning and to meet the ritual needs of their parishioners, the resident *unsui* and the clerical administration would need to remain at Sōjiji to continue their *shugyō*. This was a risky decision and one that required the utmost discipline from all involved. Given the communal life of the monks, a single break in safety protocol leading to exposure could spread the virus through the temple like a raging fire. Considering the advanced age of many in the administration, an accidental exposure could realistically wipe out centuries of the clergy's accumulated experience and wisdom.

But it was a decision couched in the necessity of maintaining and preserving the daily ritual practices that are the bedrock of Sōtō tradition. Even in the face of previous disasters and plagues, Sōjiji has survived for seven centuries on the discipline and sacrifice demanded of the monastics who had entered its gates to walk the difficult path of the Buddha. Even in the face of personal danger, the light of the Buddha's Dharma must not be extinguished but must instead be a beacon to the world.

After a year of strict restrictions, the daily life of the temple is slowly beginning to return to a new normal with modern COVID safety protocols in place. Pictures posted on Sōjiji's website show the daily liturgy performed in the Daisodō by chanting monks in surgical masks, with two meters of distance—roughly the length of a tatami mat—between them. The grueling weeklong December meditation retreat, already an ideal breeding ground for contagion even in normal years, was cut down to three days for the safety of the *unsui*.

As of December 2021, the Sanzenkai, Baikakō, and other lay organizations have yet to resume their meetings. Wakes, funerals, and memorial services for parishioners never stopped, but are attended by a minimum number of mourners, and attendees are asked to keep their distance from the officiant, the deceased, and from each other. The food and drink of the *tsuya* are likewise kept to a minimum or cut out entirely, and priests are expected to take their leave after the ritual portion is over.

For right now, at least, compassion means strict and careful adherence to the separation between the clergy and laity. Tradition survives at Sōjiji, with a careful and hopeful eye toward the future.

Glossary

ango	安居
anmyō	安名
asan	下山
Asano Sōichirō	浅野總一郎
baika	梅花
Baikakō	梅花講
bodaiji	菩提寺
bunri dokuritsu	分離独立
butsudan	仏壇
Butsuden	仏殿
Chōryū-shitsu	跳龍室
Daijōji	大乗寺
Daisodō	大祖堂
danka seido	檀家制度
Den'e	伝依
Denkōroku	伝光録
Denpō	伝法
Dentō Fugin	伝燈諷經
deshi	弟子
dharani	陀羅尼
dōangosha	同安居者

Dōgen Kigen	道元希玄
dōgyō	同行
eidai gōsō haka	永代合葬墓
Eiheiji	永平寺
ekōmon	回向文
fuda	札
Fujinkai	婦人会
Fukan Zazengi	普勧坐禅儀
fuku-kanshu	副貫首
fukusa	袱紗
Fukyō	布教
furyō bōzu	不良坊主
fushi	不思
Fūsu	副寺
gaitan	外端
garan	伽藍
Gasan Jōseki	峨山韶碩
Gasan-ha	峨山派
gasshō	合掌
genze riyaku	現世利益
Godō	後堂
goeika	御詠歌
gowasan	御和讃
hanami	花見
hankafuza	半跏趺坐
Hatsumōde	初詣
hattō	法堂
Higan	彼岸
hishi	非思
hōgu	法具
hōkei	法系
hōkka jōin	法界定印
hōkō bosatsu	放光菩薩
Hōkōdō	放光堂
hōmyō	法名
honkakuteki	本格的

honzan	本山
hōon	報恩
Hossenshiki	法戦式
hotoke	仏 (or 佛)
hotoke ni naru	仏に成る
hotoke no michi	仏の道
hōwa	法話
iei	遺影
ihai	位牌
indō hōgō	引導法号
Ino	維那
inshō	印證
Ishikawa Sodō	石川素童
ichibutsu ryōso	一仏両祖
ichinichi jūshoku	一日住職
isu seikatsu	椅子生活
jikidō	直堂
Jishin	待眞
Jizō	地蔵
jizoku	寺族
jōbutsu	成仏
jōdo	浄土
jōen	牀
Jōganji	成願寺
jōza	上座
jōzan	上山
jukai-e	授戒会
jūshoku	住職
juzu	數珠
kaigen kuyō	開眼供養
kaimyō	戒名
kanai anzen	家内安全
Kandoku-ryō	看讀寮
kannin	監院
Kannon	観音
kanshu	貫首
kayu	粥
kechimyaku	血脈

keiko	稽古
Keizan Jōkin	瑩山紹瑾
Keizan Shingi	瑩山清規
kekkafuza	結跏趺坐
kenshū	研修
kesa	袈裟
kinhin	経行
kitōji	祈祷寺
kō	講
kōchō	講長
kōhai	後輩
kokusai zen'en	国際禅苑
kokyō shōshin	古教照心
koseki	戸籍
kōso	高祖
kōun ryūsui	行雲流水
kuin	庫院
kuyō	供養
kyōsaku	警策
kyōten (as Bible)	教典
kyōten (sutra book)	経典
matsuji	末寺
Meihō Sotetsu	明峰素哲
meinichi	命日
menkata shiki	掛搭式
Mitama Matsuri	御霊祭り
mochū	喪中
mokusō	黙想
mondō	問答
Monju	文殊
moppan	木版
Morooka	諸岡
mōshigo	申し子
moshu	喪主
muen botoke	無縁仏
muga	無我
mujō	無常
mushin	無心

naitan   内端
nakama ishiki   仲間意識
nehankin   涅槃金
nenju   念誦
nesshin   熱心
Nichiyō Sanzenkai   日曜参禅会
nikujiki saitai   肉食妻帯
ningen mōdo   人間モード
nyūdō shiki   入堂式
nyūkaisha   入会者

Obon   お盆
ohakamairi   お墓参り
on   恩
onki   遠忌
oshō   和尚
osonae   お供え

pokkuri dera   ぽっくり寺

rakusu   絡子
rei   鈴
rinjūsei   輪住制
Rokuji   録事
rōshi   老師
ryōzan ittai funi   両山一体不二

saidan   祭壇
samu   作務
samue   作務衣
sandō   参道
sange   散華
sanmoku dōjō   三黙道場
sanmon   山門
sanpai   参拝
Sanshōkaku   三松閣
sanzen   参禅
satori   悟り
seibu   西部
seichū   制中
seishin antei   精神安定

seiyōka	西洋化
seiza	正座
Sejiki-e	施食会
Senbutsujō	選佛場
Sennen no Mori	千年の森
senpai	先輩
senzo daidai	先祖代々
senzo kuyō	先祖供養
sesshin	攝心
Shakai Jigyō	社会事業
shashu	叉手
shichidō garan	七堂伽藍
shikantaza	只管打坐
shinmō	新亡
shinrei	振鈴
shintai kenkō	身体健康
shinto	信徒
shintō	新倒
shippei	竹箆
shisō	師僧
Shissui	直歳
Shiuntai	紫雲台
shō	鉦
Shōbōgenzō	正法眼蔵
Shōgakusan Sōjiji	諸岡山總持寺
shōjin ryori	精進慮利
Shōunkaku	祥雲閣
shugyō dōjō	修行道場
shugyō	修行
shukke tokudo	出家得度
shumidan	須弥壇
shumoku	撞木
Shuryō	衆寮
shūshin	修身
Shushōgi	修証記
shuso	首座
shushō ittō	修証一等
sōan	送安
sōdō	僧堂
sōgi	葬儀
Sōjiji	總持寺

sōrin	僧林
sōryo	僧侶
sōseki	僧籍
sōshiki	葬式
Taihōkan	待鳳官
taiso	太祖
Tanga-ryō	旦過寮
Tantō	単頭
teishatsu	剃髪
teishō	提唱
tengoku	天国
tenshō	転生
Tenzo Kyōkun	典座教訓
Tenzo	典座
Tettsu Gikai	徹通義介
tōbu	東部
Tōkokki	洞谷記
tōsu	東司
tsuizen kuyō	追善供養
Tsuru-ga-oka	鶴ヶ丘
tsuya	通夜
Undō	雲堂
unsui	雲水
warakusu	輪絡子
Yakushi Nyorai	薬師如来
Yōkōji	永光寺
yokusu	浴司
zafu	坐蒲
zagen	坐元
zaike	在家
Zazen Yōjinki	坐禅用心記
zazen	坐禅
zen'en	禅園
zenji	禅師
zuise haitō	瑞世拝堂

Notes

Introduction

1. While the ceremony is common throughout Japanese Buddhism, the term *sejiki* is specific to the Sōtō Zen sect. Other Japanese Buddhist sects call this ceremony the *segaki-e*. *Gaki* (Skt. *preta*), are miserable wandering "hungry ghosts" of those who have been abandoned by their families and descendants. See also Ashikaga 1950, 1951; and Ikegami 2014.

2. Momose 2002, 245.

3. SSSCI 2017, 57.

4. Several informants specifically drew unfavorable comparisons between Sōjiji and its branch temple Daiyūzan Saijōji, also located in Kanagawa Prefecture near Hakone. Saijōji is absolutely picturesque in a way that Sōjiji is not, with antique wooden buildings situated on a tranquil, forested mountainside complete with cascading waterfalls. Architectural comparisons between Sōjiji and Eiheiji were less common.

5. Collcutt (1981, 184) notes that the configuration of the *shichidō garan* buildings varied by period, location, and sect. Earlier temple complexes in Japan could also be described as "seven-hall" monasteries but had a very different take on which buildings were essential. Ichijō Kanera (1402–1481) was among the first to apply the term *shichidō garan* to Japanese Zen monasteries. See also Sōtōshū Shūmūchō 2005, 14–15.

6. Collcutt 1981, 171–172.

7. Paramore 2016, 6.

8. Schlütter 2008. See also Heine 2011, 158–159.

9. Bahloul 1996, 28. See also Bachelard 1964.

10. Collcutt 1981, 182; Faure 1993, 164; Heine 2008a, 144, 152–153.

11. As a side note, Feng (2012) illustrates how the tree/forest metaphor is extended in Song Dynasty architectural manuals to the buildings themselves, with architectural elements like bracketing and protruding arms referred to as "branches," "flowers," and "sprays of blossoms." These elements were commonly

used construction techniques, and while used in the construction of Song period Buddhist temples, the tree metaphor was not limited to temple buildings.

12. The Japanese *garan* is an abbreviation of *sōgya ranma*, a transliteration of the Sanskrit *saṃgha* (Buddhist monastic order) + *rāma* (garden or park). The term *saṃghārāma* originally referred to the forest retreats, often on donated land, where a community of Buddhist monastics would gather for the duration of the monsoon seasons. As Buddhism developed and spread throughout Asia, these temporary forest retreats were replaced by permanent structures that more closely resemble the term "monastery" as it has come to be used today. While *garan* is not a Japanese transliteration of the English "garden," the botanical imagery of a "monk's garden" is implicit in *saṃghārāma* and thus in *garan*.

13. The image of cultivated fields (*denchi*) plays an important and recurrent metaphorical role in Keizan's writings, particularly in the *Denkōroku*. In Keizan's usage, "Field literally refers to the physical land on which one stands and stakes out a position. Figuratively it denotes a state of affairs or frame of mind. Metaphorically it symbolizes the human heart (or subconscious), where one plants karmic seeds and reaps karmic results (fruits), just as farmers plant seeds and harvest crops in fields of land" (Bodiford 2015, 180). Seen in this light, Keizan's use of horticultural imagery in his death verse is not an isolated instance but rather the continuation of a metaphor that he returned to repeatedly throughout his lifetime.

14. Collcutt 1981, 184; Heine 2008b, 31–32; Winfeld 2015, 268, citing Brinker and Kanazawa 1996.

15. Collcutt (1981, 184–185) notes that this layout, specifically the placement of the storehouse opposite the Monk's Hall as the "hands," reflects the influence of Ōbaku Zen on the Sōtō Zen *shichidō garan* model.

16. Faure 1996, 195.

17. Collcutt 1981, 191.

18. Welch 1967, 37. The metaphorical geography used in Zen temples replicates the orientation of the Chinese Imperial Court. The emperor faced the south, while higher-ranked dignitaries were seated at his left hand (in the west) and lower-ranked dignitaries seated at his right (in the east).

19. Bahloul 1996, 51.

20. For a discussion of the application of traditional Chinese "geomantic" principles (Ch. *fengshui*, Jp. *fūsui*) to Zen temple layout and construction, see Irizarry 2011 and Winfeld 2017. Bruun (2008, 100–117) provides an excellent overview of the cosmology and philosophy upon which *fengshui* is based.

21. See Reader and Tanabe 1998.

22. Rowe (2011), Ambros (2012), and Nelson (2013) each offer several examples of how practical concerns, modern sensibilities, and the realities of urban life have recently led to innovations in Buddhist temple architecture in Japan.

23. Certeau 1984, 117.

24. See, for example, Schattschneider 2003.

25. Kondo 1990, 108.

26. Sawada 2004, 58; Paramore 2016, 45, 67.

27. Gluck 1985, 121.

28. Sharf 1993, 10; Snodgrass 2003, 66–71; Victoria 1997, 115. See also Irizarry 2015, 55.

29. Kawano 2005, 40. See also Benjamin's (1997) ethnography of the Japanese education system, which, she argues, socializes Japanese children into this cultural logic from an early age.

30. Kawano 2005, 47.

31. In an important footnote, John McRae (2003, 163n22) illustrates that despite common translations of *dōjō* as "place of the way," the derivation of the Chinese word *daochang* (from which the Japanese *dōjō* is transliterated) is a translation of the Sanskrit *bodhimaṇḍa*, "the Buddha's 'place of enlightenment' under the *bodhi* tree." The word's origin underscores the point I am making here: that what is important to understanding the *dōjō* is not the activity itself but rather the underlying process of personal cultivation and disciplining that is taking place through the activity.

32. Asad 2003, 90.

33. Komazawa Daigakunai Zengaku Daijiten Henshūshitsu (*ZDJ*) 505; Foulk 2015, 25. Foulk translates *shushō ittō* as the "identity of practice and realization."

34. Since "to elevate and save" (*sukuiaguru* 救い上ぐる) is homophonic with "to scoop out [rice]" (*sukuiaguru* 掬い上ぐる), the two terms are phonetically identical, making the rice spoon a convenient allegorical symbol for the salvation of others. *Aguru* is the classical form of the modern *agaru*.

35. See Odin 1996.

Chapter 1

1. The title of the work is derived from Yōkōji's mountain name, Tōkokusan.

2. Faure 1996, 32.

3. Mitsudzi Eigaku et al. (KZZ) 1980, vol. 8, 96.

4. Mitsudzi Eigaku et al. (KZZ) 1980, vol. 8, 96.

5. Bodiford 1993, 90.

6. Sōtōshū Daihonzan Sōjiji 1996, 111.

7. Ozaki 2016, 12. Bodiford (1993, 64) reports that this meeting between Keizan and Gasan took place in 1295.

8. Faure 1996, 51.

9. Azuma 2005, 187.

10. Nodomi 2007, 2.

11. Seckel 1985, 376; Nodomi 2007, 2.

12. Momose 2002, 209.

13. Momose 2002, 211–212; Ozaki 2016, 16.

14. Tsurumi Toshokan 1987, 10; Momose 2002, 243; Sekiguchi 1995, 2. Bodiford (1993, 101) believes that the documents showing a relationship between Keizan and Go-Daigo are likely forgeries as part of an early rivalry between Sōjiji and Yōkōji. Both temples have similar correspondence between Keizan and the emperor, each purportedly claiming that the holding temple was the one Go-Daigo intended to receive imperial honors.

15. Bodiford 1993, 99. Emperor Go-Daigo's so-called restoration was short-lived, however, and was overthrown and replaced three years later by the Ashikaga Shogunate. Nevertheless, Emperor Go-Daigo is commemorated at Sōjiji in the Goreiden hall, which was dedicated in 1936 in recognition of Sōjiji's long historical relationship with the Imperial Household (and was thus, by extension, a statement of allegiance to the Imperial Japanese polity).

16. Ozaki 2016, 13. Prior to 1873, Japan used the Chinese lunar calendar, which was offset from the Gregorian calendar by about a month. A date such as "the 29th day of the fifth month" of 1324 is not an obtuse way of saying "29 May 1324." Rather, this is the date as recorded on the historical documents of the period. In this case the date corresponds on the modern Gregorian calendar to 21 June 1324.

17. Muromine 1967, 239; Ozaki 2015, 215; Ozaki 2016, 14.

18. Stories from the time tell of Gasan commuting on almost daily basis between the two temples via a fifty-two-kilometer path through the hills of the Noto Peninsula that would become known as the *Gasandō*, "Gasan's Road." Gasan's reported ability to traverse fifty kilometers in a matter of minutes was attributed to special powers earned by his dedication to his Zen practice and became part of the folklore of the Noto region. This legend had a unique and lasting effect on the morning services (*chōka fugin*) at both temples: at Yōkōji the Daihi Shin Darani was chanted at double speed in order to allow Gasan to leave quickly; at Sōjiji the same chant was intoned at half speed in order to give Gasan time to arrive. This stylistic adaptation can still be found in the morning services of both temples today. (See also Ozaki 2015, 227)

19. Yōkōji itself faced repeated setbacks, culminating in its being razed in 1468 during the violent conflicts of the Warring States period. Yōkōji never recovered from its destruction politically or financially and by 1500 had ceased to be a major player in the Sōtō Zen sect. Work was done to recover Yōkōji during the peace of the early Edo period, but the temple was destroyed again—this time by a typhoon—in 1674. Yōkōji was rebuilt in the nineteenth century but is today a mere echo of its former self (Faure 1996, 7–8).

20. Williams 2009, 36.

21. Sōjiji's fortunes were strengthened by the .practice of requiring newly installed abbots to replace their inherited Dharma lineages with the lineage of the founder of their temple. This practice, known as *garanbō* (temple Dharma lineage), was instituted by two of Gasan's disciples, Tsūgen Jakurei (1322–1391) and Baisan Monpon (d. 1417), and had the effect of converting even Eiheiji-line Sōtō priests into Dharma descendants of Gasan and transferring their allegiance to Sōjiji (Bodiford 1991, 429). Since the rapid pace at which Gasan-line clerics founded new branch temples virtually guaranteed that almost all available abbacies were at temples affiliated with Sōjiji, any Sōtō priest aspiring to become abbot of a temple during his career faced a difficult choice: keep his Dharma lineage and potentially never get an abbacy, or convert to a Gasan-line lineage and get the position (Bodiford 1991, 430). While Eiheiji-based lines and Yōkōji-based lines also adopted this practice of *garanbō*, by the time of Manzan Dōhaku's reform movement in the late 1600s, Sōjiji's advantage was so overwhelming as to be virtually insurmountable. Interestingly, when the Tokugawa government's Agency of Temples and Shrines was weighing arguments for and against the practice, representatives from Eiheiji fought to limit government involvement of *garanbō*, while those from Sōjiji actively encouraged governmental efforts to abolish it, essentially trying to end the game before their advantage could be overturned (Bodiford 1991, 447). The practice was officially abolished by government edict in 1703. See also Mohr 1994, 358–363.

22. Bodiford 1993, 110. It is worth noting that a large percentage of these "temples" began, like Sōjiji had, as little more than simple wooden structures, often

but not always housing a Buddhist image and usually lacking a resident priest. It would not be until the seventeenth century that many of these small shrines would become full-fledged temples with clergy and a parishioner base (Williams 2005, 18).

23. Bodiford (1993, 110) puts the number at 17,549; Nodomi (2007, 8) shows 18 additional temples, placing the total at 17,567.

24. Nodomi 2007, 8.

25. Williams 2005, 16.

26. Covell 2005, 24.

27. Covell 2005, 24; Nelson 2013, 35. For a detailed history of the development of the parishioner system, see Marcure 1985.

28. Williams 2005, 21–23.

29. Covell 2005, 25; Nelson 2013, 36.

30. Bodiford 1993, 82, 135.

31. See, for example, Diane Riggs's (2015) account of how competing scriptural interpretations over the style of the monk's *kesa* robe became grounds for yet another proxy battle between Sōjiji and Eiheiji.

32. Bodiford 2008, 275.

33. Nodomi 2007, 14.

34. Muromine 1967, 247; Bodiford 1993, 82.

35. Bodiford 2015, 167. The discovery of a never-before-seen text by Keizan led to immediate accusations of its being apocryphal or a forgery at the time of its first publication in 1857. Since that time, additional pre-1650 versions of the text have surfaced. Moreover, a copy of the *Denkōroku* dating from between 1430 and 1459 was discovered in 1958 at Kenkōin in Aichi Prefecture, supporting the case for its authenticity by locating the text within 125 years of Keizan's lifetime (Bodiford 2015, 169–170).

36. Heine 2003, 174.

37. Muromine 1967, 542.

38. Nodomi 2007, 15. Winfeld (2015, 212n1) notes that *ittai* can also signify a shared "substance" or "essence."

39. Sekiguchi 1995, 4; Sōtōshū Shūmuchō 2005, 22. The use of maternal metaphor and imagery in relation to Keizan and Sōjiji has parallels in the medieval Christian monastic tradition, which utilized idealized notions of motherhood and femininity to attribute qualities of fertility, propagation, nurturance, and compassion within the context of male same-sex communities. This was contrasted with "masculine" qualities of authority, strictness, and discipline (see Bynum 1977 and 1982).

40. Muromine 1967, 112.

41. For a detailed understanding of the Meiji Era persecution of Buddhism and its lasting ramifications, see especially Ketelaar 1990 and Jaffe 2001.

42. Muromine 1967, 114.

43. Kawaguchi 1985, 117.

44. Tsurumi Toshokan 1987, 15; Katō 1990, 116; Sōtōshū Danshintō Hikkei Kaitei Iinkai 2007, 42.

45. Tsurumi was previously notorious as the site of the 1862 Namamugi Incident (also known as the Richardson Affair), in which four foreign nationals were

attacked and wounded, one mortally, after failing to quit the road for the passing entourage of a samurai noble (Tsurumi-ku Shi Kankō Iinkai 1982, 310; Tsurumi Toshokan 1987, 4-6). While the residents of Tsurumi were innocent bystanders—the incident could have happened anywhere—the ripples that were sent forth from this tiny village had immense effects on the international political scene: in addition to increased foreign military presence in Japan, the incident led directly to the Anglo-Satsuma War (1863) and, soon after, an alliance between the English and anti-*bakufu* forces that would be instrumental in the rebellion that would ultimately topple the Tokugawa government.

46. Saitō Umie 2011, 172–173.

47. Saitō Shingi 2007, 54.

48. Sōjiji's official temple history describes the meeting between Jōganji's abbot, Katō Umio, and the delegation from Sōjiji: "Standing at the top of the stairs leading to Jōganji, Katō put forth his wishes to donate his land. With both parties smiling, the delegation conveyed, 'We've arrived!' Katō's smile responded, 'I understand. Welcome.' Wordlessly, their intentions were conveyed to each other" (Muromine 1967, 121).

This "wordless" transition of ownership of Jōganji's land is almost certainly apocryphal, but its inclusion is meant to invoke one of Zen's founding myths, in which the Buddha, holding aloft a flower, wordlessly transmitted authority over the community of Buddhist monastics to his disciple Mahākāśyapa (Jp. Mahakashō). Mahākāśyapa's smile signified that he was a worthy successor, fit to be the next leader of the community. By framing Katō's transfer of Jōganji's holdings to the delegation from Sōjiji in these archetypal terms, Sōjiji's chroniclers are invoking the power of the myth to demonstrate that the voluntary transfer of property was done to ensure the continuity of the Sōtō Zen teachings.

49. Muromine 1967, 117.

50. Although I have not seen (nor do I know of) any evidence disputing the official story of the fire at Noto Sōjiji, the circumstances and timing of the Great Fire have always struck me as suspicious. Given the events of the previous twenty-five years—the loss of regional political and financial patronage, the bitter infighting with Eiheiji, the establishment of the national seat of government in Tokyo, and the rise of Yokohama as a city of international commerce—Sōjiji had everything to lose by being permanently rooted on the Noto Peninsula. If Sōjiji remained where it was, it would have been even more remote from the seat of power than it had been previously. Most other sects of Japanese Buddhism had a head temple in the vicinity of Kyoto, still the cultural capital of the country; Sōtō Zen, in contrast, was burdened by having both of its head temples in remote and rural areas. Viewed in the light of its long-standing conflict with Eiheiji, relocating to a position between the new centers of political (Tokyo) and commercial (Yokohama) power would allow Sōjiji to literally outmaneuver its rival.

51. The Hōkōdō was a much older building, donated in its entirety from a Sōtō temple in Yamagata Prefecture. The structure was disassembled, transported across the country, and reassembled in its new home at Sōjiji (Muromine 1967, 124).

52. Muromine 1967, 124.

53. Muromine 1967, 117; Nodomi 2007, 21.

54. Muromine 1967, 124.

55. Another of many potentially confusing homonyms in Japanese, *shinto* 信徒 as "believer" is not to be confused with *shintō* 新倒 as "new arrival" (discussed in chapter 2), or the religion Shinto 神道.

56. Covell 2005, 98–99; Ives 2009, 23–24; Nelson 2013, 39.

57. Readers will note the number of charitable institutions founded specifically to benefit women and children. Keizan, it is claimed, had been an ardent supporter of women's equality in social and religious matters owing to the lifelong influence of his mother, grandmother, and female followers. While the founding of charitable institutions to support women and children was not unique to Sōtō Zen (see Covell 2005, 98–99), Sōjiji's institutional narrative maintains that establishing these social welfare programs to benefit women—particularly single mothers and their children—was done specifically to continue and further Keizan's forward-thinking and progressive work. See, e.g., Yamaguchi 2011b, 14–15.

58. Though not specific to Sōjiji, Victoria 1997 and Hur 1999 shed light on Sōtō Zen's support of Imperial Japan's military and colonial efforts.

59. Kawaguchi 1985, 121.

60. Katō 1990, 160.

61. Tsurumi-ku Shi Kankō Iinkai 1982, 564–566.

62. Remarkably, the only wartime damage to the temple precincts proper occurred when a crippled American B-29 Superfortress crashed into Sōjiji's cemetery on April 6, 1945 (Saitō Umie 2011, 274).

63. Sōjiji's cemetery's most famous "resident" is Ishihara Yūjirō (1935–1987), beloved actor and younger brother of former (and often controversial) Tokyo mayor Ishihara Shintarō. Yūjirō's grave continues to be a popular tourist attraction, and signs are posted throughout the cemetery to direct visitors who come to pay their respects.

64. See Irizarry 2010, 2015.

65. After nearly fifty years of this color scheme (and fifty years of complaints about it), the Daisodō and the Sanmon were repainted in more subdued browns and tans in 2015 as part of the preparation for Gasan's 650th memorial celebration. While still architecturally distinct from the aged wooden structures that dominate the temple grounds, this color change did help to visually incorporate the modern buildings into the rest of the temple landscape.

66. See Nelson 2012.

Chapter 2

1. *Kata* 掛搭 means to "hang up one's belongings," specifically, one's robes, traveling bag, and eating bowls (ZDJ 162). By extension, *menkata* means to receive permission to take up residence among a community of monastics for a retreat season. See also Sōtōshū Shūmuchō 2006a, 124–125.

2. Seckel 1985, 360.

3. In this book I have elected to distinguish the clergy from the laity by the terms of address I use for them. For Sōjiji and Sōtō clergy generally, I use their family name followed by the Japanese honorific *-san*, or their Japanese clerical titles *-rōshi* or *-zenji*. For laypersons, I use the English Mr./Mrs./Ms. followed by their family name.

While I recognize that this breaks somewhat from ethnographic convention that typically chooses either Japanese-style or English-style of terms of address for informants and sticks with that decision throughout, I found that relying solely on either style complicated my ability to communicate the way that the Japanese themselves use terms of address to convey relative status and social distance, particularly the status differential that existed between my clerical and lay informants at Sōjiji.

For example, Sōtō novice monks have the title *-joza* and newly ordained priests the title *-oshō*, but neither are used in everyday communication, with people addressing them defaulting to the generic *-san*. I considered using "brother" for monastic novices and "father" for priests, but this would have overlaid not only Christian but also familial connotations that are not present in a Japanese Buddhist temple context. On the other hand, *-rōshi* is already commonly translated into English as "Reverend," and Japanese speakers use this title to demonstrate respect (and linguistically elevate) established and higher-ranking clergy. To avoid any incongruity, I opted to keep Japanese terms of address for my clerical informants to reflect how they would be addressed both inside and outside the Sōjiji community.

Having made this decision, I chose to use the English Mr./Mrs./Ms. instead of the generic *-san* for my lay informants to linguistically distinguish them from the clerical community. In a religious and cultural context where the two populations are intended to be socially distinct—so important, in fact, that the distinction is visually and materially reinforced by shaved heads and the wearing of monastic robes—I found this to be a useful technique for the reader who is engaging the ethnography through the written word to understand the social divisions in play at Sōjiji.

4. Sōtōshū Shūsei Sōgō Chōsa Iinkai (SSSCI) 2017, 25.

5. More than 40 percent of current clergy graduated from Komazawa University's Buddhist Studies Department or Aichi Gakuin University's Religion and Culture Section (SSSCI 2017, 26).

6. Readers wishing to further explore the experiences, perspectives, and challenges of women priests in Sōtō Zen would be interested in Paula Arai's *Women Living Zen* (1999) and *Bringing Zen Home* (2011), as well as Mark Rowe's article "Charting Known Territory: Female Buddhist Priests" (2017).

7. Covell 2005, 118.

8. Specifically, Buddhism divides the Buddhist community into four parts: male and female "home-leavers" (Skt. *bhikṣu* and *bhikṣuṇī*) and male and female "house-holders" (Skt. *upāsaka* and *upāsikā*). See Reynolds and Carbine 2000, 74.

9. Borup 2012, 127.

10. This name is also known as *kaimyō*, or "precepts name." While the three terms are technically synonymous, *kaimyō* is typically used in Sōtō Zen to refer to the posthumous name given to the deceased as part of the funeral rite (see chapter 6).

11. Sargent 2001, 130; Matsumoto 1992, 50.

12. See Benedict 1984 [1946], 98–113; Bellah 1985 [1957], 70–73.

13. Most Japanese names use the *kun-yomi*, or "Japanese reading," for the characters used to write them. Buddhist names, in contrast, often use the *on-yomi*, or "Chinese reading," for the characters. In this way the characters that make up a

person's name can be preserved even after the pronunciation is changed, an impossibility in alphabetic languages.

14. At Eiheiji the resident monks and priests are known and addressed by their Dharma names. In contrast, at Sōjiji the clergy are known and addressed by their family names as is typical in Japanese social settings, which may contribute to some *unsui* having difficulty personally identifying with their Dharma names, especially if the name was recently bestowed.

15. Nodomi 2007, 5. This requirement was instituted over the Sōtō Zen sect by governmental edict in 1612 as part of a series of policies aimed at organizing, regulating, and restricting the power and influence of the Japanese Buddhist institutions (see Williams 2009, 348–349).

16. Officially, seniority is calculated by simply comparing the length of time since a given monk formally entered the monastery. This means that an *unsui* who arrived even one day before another is technically the "superior" in the relationship.

In actual practice, however, I never witnessed or heard secondhand of a situation where one new arrival tried to pull rank on another based on relative time spent at the temple. For all intents and purposes, the new arrivals are better understood collectively as a "class of" a given year, similar to college alumni. Among themselves, they refer to others of their cohort as *dōangosha* (literally, "those who participated in the same retreat (*ango*)"). This use of *dō* ("same") parallels that of *dōhai* ("social equal"; "peer") or *dōkyūsei* ("classmate") and indicates that all of the *unsui* who entered around a given time are considered to hold the same position in the hierarchy. They are *kōhai* ("subordinate") to previous classes of monks and *senpai* ("superior") to the entrants of the following retreat period and later.

17. *Senbutsujō* and *Undō* ("Cloud Hall," referring to the *unsui* training inside) are common synonyms for the Monk's Hall in Japanese Zen monasteries. See Collcutt 1981, 207.

18. Previously there were very few photographs that show the actual inside of the Monk's Hall at Sōjiji. Most photographs of monastic practice at Sōjiji—for example, those used in magazine features about Zen, or the cover of Heine and Wright's edited volume *Zen Ritual* (2008)—show the *unsui* sitting in the outer hall or in the Community Hall (*shuryō*), which superficially resembles the Monk's Hall. This has changed somewhat since the advent of social media—the Sōtō Zen official Instagram account now routinely posts pictures of temple scenes previously hidden from the public eye, including the interior of Sōjiji's Monk's Hall.

19. The number 108 appears regularly in Buddhist contexts, usually signifying "all" or "completion," often of a circuit. It can refer to the 108 levels of concentration (Skt. *samadhi*; Jp. *sanmai*) to be attained through meditation or the 108 forms of desire that plague humans. Temple bells are rung 108 times every morning and also to bring in the New Year, and some styles of Buddhist rosaries (*juzu*) have 108 beads (ZDJ 1052).

20. The Monk's Hall, toilet, and bath are collectively referred to as the "Three Silent Halls" (*sanmoku dōjō*) where speaking is forbidden (Sōtōshū Shūmuchō 1991, 137; Sōtōshū Danshintō Hikkei Kaitei Iinkai 2007, 50).

21. Foucault 1977, 146.

22. When I experienced this ritual in the Monk's Hall for the first time, I found

it curious that in Japanese the *kesa* 袈裟 (a transliteration of the Sanskrit *kasaya*) is homophonic with *kesa* 今朝, or "this morning." Without any additional information, *kesa o itadakimasu* could also be understood as "we receive this morning." This was reinforced by the fact that the *kesa* (as Dharma robe) is "received" in such a manner only during the morning hours. My informants, however, insisted that this is merely a linguistic coincidence.

23. Sōtō-shū Nikka Kyō Daizen, 157; Sōtō School Scriptures for Daily Services and Practice, 72.

24. Faure 1995, 347.

25. Diane Riggs (2017, 200–201) discusses how the resemblance of the patchwork pattern of the *kesa* to a landscape of rice paddies has come to also metaphorically symbolize a monastic's role as a "field of merit" (*fuku denchi*) whereby the laity can "sow" seeds of karmic merit through material donations to the sangha.

26. During the Tang Dynasty (618–907) in China, Buddhist monastics of the emerging Ch'an school used this story to advocate the legitimacy of Ch'an over competing lineages as the vehicle of the "True Dharma" taught by the historical Buddha. The *kesa*, not surprisingly, became a key symbol of this claim to legitimacy: citing this story, the Ch'an patriarchs claimed to have in their possession the original *kesa* worn by the Buddha. This *kesa* supposedly survived time and the elements by being passed by hand from a master to a student. Naturally, competing lineages within the Ch'an school were ingenious in producing stories of how they had come to possess the "true" Dharma robe of the Buddha. Reports of theft, clandestine transmission ceremonies, and even magical acquisition of the true *kesa* fill the Ch'an literature of the time. Keizan's *Denkōroku* is characteristic of this genre, with the transmission of the *kesa* featuring prominently in his reckoning of the Sōtō Zen lineage. See Diane E. Riggs 2015.

27. Nishijima and Cross 1994, 21, 138.

28. Nearman 2001, 155.

29. See Nonomura's (2008, 169–170) description of his and his cohorts' painful experiences with beriberi at Eiheiji.

30. Japanese schoolchildren are commonly tasked with cleaning their schoolrooms and, in particular, cleaning the floors. In addition to promoting group responsibility, cleaning "encourages students to think of the school as theirs, as a place they each have a stake in" (Benjamin 1997, 34).

31. Reader (1995, 170–173) expands on the apparent "non-productivity" of *samu* in Sōtō Zen temples.

32. As Goffman (1959, 112–134) discusses, the figurative "backstage"—which includes break rooms—is almost universally an area where the "performers" can relax and step out of their character. As a consequence, the activities of the back room must be kept hidden from the "audience" in order to preserve the illusion of what takes place in public. This is particularly true in religious settings, in which breaches of decorum risk undermining the authority and faith of the clergy or the sacredness of the site itself.

33. Throughout *Eat Sleep Sit* (2008), Nonomura Kaoru viscerally describes the severe physical and psychological abuse that he claims Sōtō Zen *unsui* routinely experience during their *shugyō*. In reflecting on his first days at Eiheiji, Nonomura recalls that he would sometimes be awoken by "a great noise. It was the sound

of someone slamming into a glass-paned wooden sliding door, and it was always followed by what sounded, through the intervening walls, like a muffled scream" (148). Throughout his year in *shugyō*, slaps, punches, kicks, and other abuses were routine.

Nonomura rationalizes the violence he experienced as a pedagogical tool: "A little thought will show that in the context of Zen discipline, the fundamental purpose of a beating or thrashing is not to inflict injury or pain. Such acts are rather a means of conveying living truth from body to body and mind to mind, a form of spiritual training and cultivation" (149). This abuse, Nonomura argues, serves the important purpose of "self-annihilation," and he even expresses "relief" whenever he was personally the recipient of such abuse, because he felt "like an artificial pearl whose false exterior was being scraped away. . . . I knew that whatever remained, exposed for all to see, was nothing less than my true self. The discovery of my own insignificance brought instant, indescribable relief" (149).

Nonomura's rationalization for the abuse he and his peers suffered at Eiheiji demonstrates the degree to which coercive pressure and corporal punishment are culturally entrenched as necessary aspects of *shugyō*, impersonal and inflicted for the "benefit" of the recipient (see also Hori 1994, 21–22). I accept that the incidents Nonomura describes took place, especially given my older informants' recounting of having experienced similar events at Sōjiji.

The question for the present study, however, is to ask how relevant Nonomura's account of these abuses are in understanding an *unsui*'s training at Sōjiji today. To answer this, we need to recognize that Nonomura entered Eiheiji in 1990 and that as of this writing, a generation and a half have passed between his training and the monks being trained today. In the intervening years, a conversation about the "bullying problem" (*ijime mondai*) endemic throughout Japanese society has taken shape. This conversation has brought efforts at systemic reform—for example, the institutional changes that Sōjiji's administration took to encourage the reporting and monitoring of bullying incidents already mentioned. Still, even with education and attentive monitoring, bullying incidents persist at all levels and in all contexts within Japanese society. As my informants at Sōjiji indicate, such efforts can only have so much effect, especially if incidents go unreported, which they often do.

A second consideration is that Eiheiji has traditionally had a reputation for stricter discipline than Sōjiji. While the physical abuses that Nonomura describes may still take place at Eiheiji, my interviews, conversations, and observations at Sōjiji do not indicate a similar routinization of physical violence against current *unsui* there. I recognize, however, that a victim would likely have been reluctant to confide the abuse they were suffering to me, a researcher who could potentially get them in worse trouble by making public their private ordeal. I also concede that many abusers know exactly how to hide evidence of physical abuse by targeting parts of their victim's body that can be concealed. In the case of abuse, an absence of evidence is not evidence of absence.

Lastly, while Nonomura describes superiors inflicting traumatic injuries on their subordinates, it is important to recognize that violence and abuse are not always physical. I did not observe any black eyes or swollen cheeks among the *unsui* during my research, but I did occasionally witness situations in which certain *unsui* were mocked, shamed, and alienated by their peers, and to a lesser degree, by their superiors. These incidents were immediately reminiscent of reports of bullying in Japanese schools and workplaces and, I argue, are better understood in the larger social context of bullying in Japan (see Benjamin 1997, 219–20; Allison 2013, 94).

34. *Obon* is observed from the thirteenth through the fifteenth of July in the Kantō region, which includes metropolitan Tokyo and Yokohama. Elsewhere in Japan, it is observed on the thirteenth through the fifteenth of August.

Chapter 3

1. The characters for "descending the mountain" 下山 can be read either as *gezan* (more common) or *asan* (less common). Within a training temple like Sōjiji, however, the two words have very different meanings. *Asan* can best be thought of as an "honorable discharge" from one's training. *Gezan*, however, has the opposite meaning, implying that the person in question was dishonorably dismissed from the monastery for violating the rules.

2. Sōjiji is not alone among Japanese Zen temples as having free-standing gates that do not connect to walls, allowing anyone to just as easily walk around them as through them. The gates are more symbolic than practical, and passing through the gate is therefore a symbolic act of passing between "the secular and the religious worlds, between the realms of attachment and liberation" (Collcutt 1981, 189).

3. Nara 1995, 21.

4. Sōtō-shū, like other sects of Japanese Buddhism, has separate systems for clerical titles and clerical ranks (*sōkai*), which are based on a priest's meeting certain educational and experiential requirements and are used internally to determine eligibility for different positions within the sect, such as the abbacy of a temple. The requirements for each of the Sōtō clerical ranks can be found in the bylaws printed in the *Sōtōshū Shūsei* (Sōtōshū Shūmuchō 2007).

5. Momose 2002, 144.

6. See Sōtōshū Shūgaku Kenkyūsho 2006.

7. The *shuso* is the representative of the community of *unsui* and is distinguished visually by his black and white *kesa*, which contrasts with the *unsui*'s standard black *kesa*. At Sōjiji and Eiheiji, the *shuso* is elected by his peers and is usually a monk who has been at the temple for an extended period of time. In previous eras the role of *shuso* was given many more responsibilities than the position holds now. Today the position is similar to a valedictorian, with only nominal administrative duties. He is elected for the duration of the *angō* retreat period, so of the 150 or so resident *unsui* at Sōjiji, only two can hold the title per year.

8. There is a long tradition in Zen of using light or flame—an active, vital force capable of burning away ignorance and illusion—as a metaphor for the Buddha's Dharma. This imagery can be found in the genre of Buddhist biographic genealogies known as "transmission of the lamp" (Ch. *ch'uan-teng*; Jp. *dentō*) records, which trace successive generations of Dharma transmission from master to disciple. Keizan's *Denkōroku* ("Record of the Transmission of the Light/Illumination") shares many characteristics with this literature. See also Faure (1996, 152) and Bodiford (2000, 303; 2015, 172).

9. See especially Foulk 1993 and Bodiford 1991, 1999, and 2008.

10. These colors are meant to symbolically reference the discoloration (through

dirt, mud, and other contaminants) of the robes sewn from white funeral shrouds that ancient Indian mendicants would wear to show that they had transcended material concerns of purity or pollution.

11. Nearman 2001, 7. Foulk (2017, 12n1) notes that, by this line, Keizan is likely arguing that even though the tale of Mahākāśyapa and the flower is well known throughout the Ch'an/Zen traditions, there is a true version of the story that has "been passed down only by word of mouth . . . *individually transmitted* from master to disciple" through the lineage that Keizan himself has inherited. See also Bodiford 2000.

12. McRae 2003, 2–9; Borup 2008, 9–15.

13. Johnson (2002, 3) defines "secretism" as "the active milling, polishing, and promotion of the reputation of secrets."

14. To this we can also add the Orientalist image of the "enlightened Zen master" as imagined in the West, whose "express mission it is to transmit his ancient spiritual heritage" to a worthy Western pupil (Iwamura 2011, 51).

15. McRae 2003, 6; Bodiford 2008, 268.

16. Foulk 1993, 154.

17. Bodiford 2008, 269.

18. Sargent 2001, 15.

19. Borup (2008, 111) reports a similar reticence to discuss the topic of *satori* at Myōshinji-branch Rinzai Zen temples in Japan.

20. Leighton 2008, 169.

21. Goffman 1959, 216; Asad 1993, 62; Sharf 2005, 266.

22. Bodiford 1993, 105; Yamaguchi 2011a, 145.

23. Nodomi 2007, 6.

24. Williams 2009, 36.

25. Bodiford 2003, 253.

26. The *zuise* ceremony (historically distinct from the rotating abbot system) actually began at Eiheiji, where the title of "former abbot" was exchanged for monetary and material donations (Bodiford 1993, 74). However, unlike Sōjiji, the "former abbot" title was decidedly honorary; while priests could use the title of "former abbot of Eiheiji" among their credentials, they were not included in the official record of the abbacy.

27. Sōtōshū Shūmuchō (2005, 66); Nodomi (2007, 7). The exhaustive list of each of these former abbots was published in 2011 in the commemorative volume *Jūzanki* ["Record of Temple Abbots"] (Nodomi and Ozaki 2011).

28. Ozaki 2015, 234–235.

29. In the Rinzai Zen sects, the usage of *rōshi* and *zenji* is effectively reversed from the way the titles are used in Sōtō Zen. Rinzai priests are referred to as *zenji*, while the term *rōshi* is used only for abbots of training temples.

30. *Oshō* is often glossed into English as "preceptor." I prefer not to use this translation, as preceptor usually carries the meaning of "teacher" or "instructor" rather than the intended meaning of "one who observes the precepts."

31. See Bodiford 1996.

32. The tenure of Egawa Shinzan-zenji, who held Sōjiji's abbacy from 2011 until his death in 2021, is discussed in the concluding chapter.

33. Recall that East/West are determined by the orientation of the central

image of the temple and do not necessarily correspond with actual geographical direction.

34. The Tenzo-ryō has a similarly outfitted satellite kitchen in the basement of the Sanshōkaku, which feeds visiting dignitaries, guests, and tour groups.

35. Foulk 2001, 9.

36. Sōtōshū Shūmuchō 1991, 208–209.

37. I admit that it is only when revising this section for publication that I realized Kodama-san's movie trivia mistake—namely, that Marlon Brando wasn't in *Rebel without a Cause*. Kodama-san was likely thinking of Brando in *The Wild One* or was thinking of James Dean. Either way, I understood his point and opted to keep his quote verbatim here.

38. David E. Riggs 2015, 191. See also Bodiford 2005a.

39. Bodiford 2005b, 185.

40. Okumura 2004, 1.

41. According to David E. Riggs (2015, 189–190), the story of Dōgen importing this list of sixteen Bodhisattva precepts to Japan is apocryphal, with the modern form of the Sōtō Zen Bodhisattva precepts crystallizing during the Tokugawa period (1600–1868).

42. This translation is slightly modified from the list found in the English-language *Sōtō-Shū Sutras* (Sōtōshū Shūmuchō 1982, 32).

43. Sōtō Shūmuchō 2006b, 189.

44. Jaffe 2001, 21–22.

45. Jaffe 2001, 95. See also Jaffe 2005.

46. A sermon reported by Rowe (2011, 143) echoes this more permissive take on the Buddhist precepts within contemporary Sōtō Zen.

47. Further complicating the situation is the fact that modern Japanese translations of the precepts (and from Japanese into other languages like English) are mediated interpretations that must account for cultural, political, and religious differences across time and place, not just in Japan but throughout the Buddhist world generally.

A case in point is the third precept: it is easy to imagine how its meaning shifted through centuries of translation, localization, and interpretation, morphing from a series of *vinaya* regulations prohibiting specific sexual actions and behaviors into a singular injunction against "licentiousness" or "sexual lust" and finally into a loose proscription against "improper sexual relations" that permits clerical sex and marriage but warns against extramarital affairs (see Faure 1998a).

Similarly, as several of my monastic informants were quick to mention, the precept "do not kill" technically says nothing that would prevent Buddhist clergy from eating meat. Early Buddhist mendicants, they told me, were beholden to eat anything that was put into their begging bowls, be it meat, vegetable, or grain. Indeed, the Buddha himself is said to have died from eating spoiled or poisoned pork. Nearly all of the clergy I spoke with had no compunction about the regular consumption of meat, provided, of course, that they did not kill it themselves (see Jaffe 2005).

The fifth precept, prohibiting consumption of "intoxicants," is seemingly even more flexible. The precept as used today in Sōtō Zen specifies "no alcohol" (*fuko-shu*), but in their explanations, my informants took the emphasis off of the medium (the alcohol) in order to stress instead the dangers of excessiveness. Their logic was that any activity done to an extreme is "intoxicating" by virtue of its interfering with a person's ability act responsibly and to be aware of their surroundings. Therefore, a priest can drink alcohol, even to the point of drunkenness, as long as they do not do it to "to excess." Conveniently, what "to excess" means is left to the interpretation of the individual (see Nelson 2020).

48. As Covell (2005, 76) shows, the pressure on contemporary clergy to renegotiate one's identity in relation to past interpretations of the precepts continues to take place throughout all Japanese Buddhist denominations.

49. According to the 2015 Sōtō-shū General Survey, a combined 59.4 percent of Sōtō priests strongly or somewhat disagree with the statement, "A priest should not eat meat or drink alcohol"; a further 32.8 percent report that they "can't say either way" (SSSCI 2017, 175).

50. During this same conversation, Yanagi-san ventured a joke: "Do you know why Japanese women wear headwraps during the wedding ceremony? To hide their horns."

The "jealous demon woman/wife" is a very old trope in Japanese Buddhism. Barbara Ambros (2015, 91) describes how, during Japan's medieval period, Buddhist texts and Noh plays demonized femaleness by attributing qualities like jealousy, anger, and pollution to women: "Such depictions render the jealous woman as a powerful being, victimizing men in a reversal of expected power relations." Through their dedication to *shugyō*, celibate Buddhist clergy had the power to exorcize these demons and were the demons' natural dramatic foils in religious texts, theater, and literature.

Knowingly or not, Yanagi-san was channeling this dramatic trope of "virtuous monk" versus "demon woman" through his description of his marriage. While he did not explicitly define his situation in such terms, he may have felt that his inability to "exorcize" this demon from his life was a consequence of his "delinquent" actions and what he perceived to be his shortcomings as a clergyman unable to maintain his vows and his *shugyō*.

51. Nevertheless, Borup (2008, 73–74) notes that the pressures placed on temple families result in "remarkably high" divorce rates in clerical marriages in Japan.

52. On the stigma of literally being X'ed out of the family register (*kōseki*), see Alexy 2020, 137–140.

53. Faure (1998a, 16); Meeks (2016, 139). Later derivative narratives describe Śākyamuni's son, Rāhula (Jp. Ragora; alternatively, Raun), as joining his father's monastic community at the age of nine. His young age and subordinate position in the *sangha* allowed for an easy identification between Rāhula and newly ordained novice monks and nuns. While Meeks (2016, 132, 149) notes that "there is little evidence that widespread cults to . . . Rāhula ever existed in Japan," certain medieval texts such as the *Raun kōshiki* encouraged novice monks to "venerate [Rāhula] as a means of cultivating and protecting their own practice."

54. To the question "As a priest, I want to live my life proudly" (*sōryo to shite hokori wo moteru ikikata wo shitai*), 88.2 percent of respondents reported "agreement" (59.4%) or "strong agreement" (28.8%). To the question "As a priest, I want to be a model for my parishioners/adherents" (*sōryo to shite danshintō no tehon ni naritai*), 78.4 percent of respondents reported "agreement" (59.1%) or "strong agreement" (19.3%). SSSCI (2017, 175).

55. See also Borup 2008, 66.

56. Agency for Cultural Affairs 2019, 74–75. Of this number, 97 percent identify as male, and 3 percent identify as female.

57. SSSCI 2017, 19.

58. SSSCI 2017, 25.

59. SSSCI 2017, 22.

60. SSSCI 2017, 37.

61. SSSCI 2017, 172.

Chapter 4

1. Sharf 1995a, 260; Faure 2009, 77; Mohr 2012, 115.

2. SZBIC 2002, 69.

3. SZBIC 2002, 91.

4. Reader 1991, 103; SSSCI 2017, 93.

5. See especially Bodiford 1993.

6. Victoria 1997, 99, 144.

7. Victoria 1997, 101. Sharf (1995b, 437) further identifies the "democratization of enlightenment" as a feature of Japanese New Religions.

8. Davis 1989, 331; Covell 2005, 98–99.

9. Sōtōshū Shūmuchō 2004.

10. From what I observed in the reception room, there was never pressure placed on visitors to join the group. However, there did seem to be a momentum that built after one person in the reception line decided to become a member; the very act of seeing the person ahead in line receive the membership packet for just five hundred yen more seemed to motivate the people waiting behind them to do the same, even if they came to Sōjiji for only the one-day experience.

The timing of this decision presents an interesting problem: a visitor is asked if they want to pay for a one-day participation or for full membership at the registration desk *before* they actually sit their first session of *zazen*. At the time of decision, the visitor will likely have no idea whether *zazen* practice is something that they even like, much less want to continue.

Since no personal information other than a name was collected at the time of membership, there was no way of contacting those who registered for the group and showed up only one or two more times, or those who simply never returned. It was, of course, impossible to tell at a glance who would return to the Sanzenkai and who would not.

11. See Rohlen 1979 and Victoria 1997.

12. Bielefeldt 1988, 178–79.

13. SZBIC 2002, 89.

14. I came to take this leniency for granted and was personally censured for my attire on two occasions. Once, during my first weeks in Japan, I was asked to leave an evening *zazen* group at a small temple in Tokyo because I was wearing a very comfortable but apparently "distasteful" (*iya na*) red and yellow soccer jersey that I had worn to Sōjiji's Sanzenkai that same day without issue. The second occasion occurred many months later when one of the women of the Sōjiji Sanzenkai pulled me aside and told me that wearing shorts in the meditation hall was "disrespectful" (*shitsurei*). I explained to her that I was wearing shorts because there was a typhoon

raging outside and, having walked over a kilometer from my apartment to Sōjiji, they were the only thing I could reasonably expect to keep dry in such weather.

15. In theory, the attention to detail begins even before this, as practitioners are instructed to eat a light meal so as not to be so full that they fall asleep but not hungry enough to cause a person to focus on their desire to eat. Similarly, sect-published *zazen* manuals provide instructions for washing the feet, but this practice is not observed by the Sanzenkai or at any other *zazen* group that I have observed.

16. The practice has its roots in the daily customs of India that were later imported to China and Japan as part of Buddhist practice. In these customs the right hand is favored over the "unclean" left hand. Thus, if one is circumambulating a religious image, it is proper to always keep the right hand facing it.

17. While the cross-legged positions are the most common, it is also acceptable to do *zazen* while kneeling in *seiza* with cushions between the legs to reduce pressure on the joints, as well as sitting flat-footed in chairs. These methods are by far the exception and not the rule.

18. Bielefeldt 1988, 178.
19. Bielefeldt 1988, 146, 189.
20. Nearman 2007, 4.
21. SZBIC 2002, 90.
22. Bielefeldt 2005, 241.
23. Foulk 2008, 42.
24. McMahan (2008, 121-128) traces modern Zen practitioners' fascination with these powerful experiences to the ideal of the *epiphany* as imagined by nineteenth century European Romantic and American Transcendentalist authors. The through line of this connection is the work of D. T. Suzuki who, responding to Orientalist critiques of Buddhism and Asian religions generally, used his familiarity with Western philosophy (particularly that of William James) to reframe Zen as a means of accessing "true reality," "pure experience," and one's "creative spirit," which he later associated with Japanese culture generally (see Faure 1993, Sharf 1993, 1998 and Yamada Shoji 2009).

25. As Sharf (1995b) demonstrates, this type of critique was characteristic of the teachings of the Sanbōkyōdan (recently rebranded as Sanbō-Zen International), an independent and anti-establishment Zen movement that has been disproportionately influential in shaping the narrative about Zen since the 1960s.

Chapter 5

1. See Embree 1939, 138–153; Robertson 1991, 141–143; Kawano 2005, 107.
2. Sōtōshū Shūmuchō 2008, 401.
3. Sōtōshū Shūmuchō 2008, 404.
4. Sōtōshū Shūmuchō 2008, 404.
5. The *ka* (花, "blossom") of *baika* is unrelated to the *ka* (歌, "song") of *goeika*. *Baika* and *goeika* therefore cannot be used interchangeably.
6. This was not Dōgen's first encounter with plum blossom imagery. According to hagiographical accounts in the *Kenzeiki* (a fifteenth century biography of Dōgen) and Keizan's *Denkōroku*, Dōgen was once offered a cloth "transmission document" embroidered with a pattern of plum blossoms by a Chinese priest who believed that his chance meeting with Dōgen was foretold in a dream (Faure 1996,

119). The Chinese priest explained to Dōgen that the woven document contained the "lessons of the Buddhas and Patriarchs for teaching the Dharma" (*busso no kyōhō ni tsuite no kyōkun*) (KZZ, vol. 4, 270). Dōgen politely refused the document, making the plum blossom's second appearance in his dream even more meaningful.

7. Sōtō Shūmuchō 2008, 3. Virtually all Baika-ryū members are Japanese living in Japan. However, there are four international *goeika kō* affiliated with Sōtō international communities in Maui, Los Angeles, San Francisco, and São Paulo.

8. SSSCI 2017, 92–93.

9. Lock 1988, 46. These virtues originate in Neo-Confucian ideals of womanhood that laid the foundation for the state-regulated role of "good wife, wise mother" (*ryōsai kenbo*) in the first decades of the twentieth century (Robertson 1998a, 62; Starling 2019, 15). In the postwar period, these virtues have been reinforced by conservative policies and rules within Japanese governmental, business, and religious organizations that reasserted, "The ideal femininity consist[s] of wifehood and motherhood" (Ambros 2015, 136).

10. Underscoring this point, section 2 of the "Regulations for Sōtō Temples" (*Sōtōshū Jiin Kitei*) is explicit in stating that "a *jizoku* must believe in the doctrine of the sect and work together with the abbot to ensure the prosperity of the temple, raising the abbot's successor, and providing instruction to parishioners" (*jizoku wa, honshū no shūshi o shinpō shi, jūshoku ni kyōka shi, tomo ni jimon no kōryū, jūshoku no kōkeisha no ikusei oyobi danshintō no kyōka ni tsutomenakereba naranai*) (SSSCI 2017, 46).

11. As Kumamoto (2004, 468) comments, this invisibility of monastic spouses extends to the highest institutional levels: the Sōtō Sect Constitution (*shūken*) all but denies the existence of priests' spouses and families along doctrinal grounds, wherein ordained Sōtō clergy are still officially identified (and many still identify) as celibate world renunciants that, by definition, cannot have spouses or families. This, according to Jaffe (2001, 239), "has helped ensure the survival of an ideal that stands in stark relief to the lived practice of [Sōtō] clerics."

Previous to 2015, section 32 of the Sōtō Sect Constitution read, "*Jizoku* are those outside of the clergy who reside at the temple" (*jiin ni zaijū suru sōryō igai no sha*). This section was amended to define *jizoku* as "a person who believes in the doctrine of this sect, and who has been recorded on the register of temple wives" (*honshū no shūshi o shinpō shi, jiin ni zaijū suru jizokubo ni tōroku sareta sha*) (SSSCI 2017, 46n7). As Kawahashi (2017) describes, to those advocating for a more equitable recognition of the wife's status and role in Sōtō Zen temples, this was arguably not much of an improvement. See also Kawahashi 1995, 2012, 2017; Schrimpf 2015; and Rowe 2017.

12. As the members of the Baika-ryū Eisanka Research Project discuss in their report, it is important to situate the Sōtō Zen *goeika* movement within the larger context of the postwar religious boom in Japan (Sōtōshū Sōgō Kenkyū Sentaa [SSKS] 2019, 14–24). Religious movements that creatively blend traditional Buddhist or Shinto teachings with populist practices are well documented throughout modern Japanese history, but the enshrinement of religious freedom in the postwar Japanese Constitution led to an explosion of new religious movements from 1947 onward and peaking during the 1970s. The popular appeal of the Japanese New Religions is in their offering "comprehensive religious teachings embedded

in religious practice," particularly in an approachable group setting (Prohl 2012, 248–249). With established religious institutions being dominated by men and male-facing practices, many New Religions represented an attractive alternative for women. (For a concise overview of the scholarship pertaining to Japanese New Religions, see Prohl 2012.)

The dismissiveness by some Sōtō clergy toward *goeika* practice likely stems in part from the fact that the Sōtō Zen *goeika* movement straddles the divide between institutional and "new" religious practice. Despite *goeika* practice being firmly situated in the traditional male-dominated hierarchical and ritual authority of the Sōtō institution, *goeika*'s populist appeal (particularly how it attracts women practitioners) and emphasis on shared practice and intergroup relationships represent the same criticisms of institutional religion that made the Japanese New Religions such compelling alternatives (see Shimazono 2004).

13. It is instructive here to compare the status of temple wives in Sōtō Zen with that of temple wives in the Jōdō Shin (True Pure Land) sect, where clerical marriage has been permitted since the thirteenth century. As Starling (2013, 2019) shows, Jōdō Shinshū temple wives play a more recognized and direct role in the religious life of their temples and denomination, but even as their position gives them the status of "de facto religious professionals," Jōdō Shinshū temple wives are not exempt from having to navigate the gender biases and stratification that permeate Japanese and Buddhist culture.

14. Danely 2014, 2.

15. Current employment law gives Japanese companies the right to set a mandatory retirement age for their employees. Companies can set their mandatory retirement age as early as sixty years, but since Japanese senior citizens become eligible for their governmental social security pensions at sixty-five, employers must guarantee employment until the age of sixty-five for all employees who wish to work. This makes sixty-five the de facto retirement age in Japan. However, the law does not require that employees keep their same jobs, so from the age of sixty to sixty-five, employees may find themselves transferred to subsidiary companies, given reduced job portfolios, or offered employment only on the basis of short-term contracts. Predictably, this increases senior citizens' sense of role loss, financial precarity, and feelings of anxiety.

16. See White 2002, 154–164.

17. See Allison 2013 and Danely 2014, 2019.

18. See Rowe 2011.

19. Traphagan (2004, 62, 73–77) describes how the Japanese government has mobilized the concept of *ikigai* to encourage continued self-cultivation among the elderly, not so subtly implying that it is a person's moral and civic responsibility to keep themselves physically and mentally healthy in old age so as not to become a burden on the family, community, or state. See also Danely 2014, 26.

20. Reader (1991, 89), Covell (2005, 33), and others have shown that it is not uncommon for Japanese to be unfamiliar with the teachings or even the name of the sect to which their families are registered. For many Japanese families, this information becomes relevant only when a family member dies, and a common service provided by funeral companies is to locate this information for the bereaved family.

21. Yano (2002) discusses how the popular musical genre of *enka* is a similarly "invented tradition" that utilizes themes of loss and nostalgia, emotionally evocative language, and a "sense of temporal and spatial otherness" in its musical composition that gives *enka* a feeling of timelessness and tradition, even as the industry continues to produce new songs regularly.

22. Yano 2002, 105.

23. *Naki-bushi* are songs intended to invoke tears and are so popular in Japan as to be its own subgenre. See Yano 2002, 3.

24. Danely 2014, 21.

25. See also Arai 2011, 191–193.

26. The entire course requires a minimum of fourteen years to achieve the highest rank. However, few of the members of the Sōjiji Baikakō feel the need to progress quickly through the official ranks. As a result, only very seldom do rank and length of membership correspond.

27. The Baikakō's rehearsal schedule is based on the ten-day monastic "week," in which regularly occurring ceremonies, activities (like head shaving), and days of relaxation are matched with days ending in a specific number. Days ending in the number seven were chosen for the Baikakō rehearsal because they do not conflict with anything else on the monastic schedule.

28. Men are exempt from wearing these robes. Most men instead wear blazers and slacks, though this is only an unofficial dress code.

29. Each sect of Japanese Buddhism has a different approved style of *juzu*. Although all are similar in outward appearance, the length, number of beads on the strand, and ornamentation is standardized according to sect. The Sōtō-shū *juzu* has fifty-four beads, one of which is larger than the rest. This bead, known as the *oyadama* ("parent bead"), has two tassels hanging from it. As used in the Baika-ryū, the color of the *juzu* corresponds to the color of the tassels on one's *hōgu*.

30. Shimbori 2006, 2–3.

31. Shimbori 2008, 68.

32. *Gowasan* is a style of metered *goeika* written in four verses of seven and five syllable phrases.

33. The purpose of this vacillation was made clear to me after I participated in a ceremony during which the officiant failed to perform the drop in tone that serves as the audible cue to the assembly to begin. I watched in amused disbelief as the assembled *unsui*, though clearly aware that they should be chanting, did not get the necessary cue and thought better of joining in. As a result, the officiant—a high ranking and respected priest—recited the entire fifteen-minute sutra by himself. I witnessed similar miscues a handful of other times over the course of my fieldwork.

Chapter 6

1. Portions of this chapter have been previously published in Irizarry 2014a.
2. See, for example, Embree 1939, 218; Reader 1991, 91; and Rocha 2006, 156.
3. Hardacre 1999, 2.
4. Ivy 1995, 145–146.
5. Schattschneider 2003, 49.
6. Covell 2005, 43, 208n1.
7. Glassman 2009, 391.

8. Feeley-Harnik 1994, 2, 11.

9. See Smith 1974, 133–139.

10. See Reader 1995; Traphagan 2004, 25.

11. See Wöss 1993.

12. Walter (2008) cautions against "soul" as a gloss, since it is laden with Christian connotations that are not necessarily found in the Japanese concept of *hotoke*. See especially Smith 1974 and Sasaki 1993.

13. See Murakami 2000, Rowe 2000 and 2009, and Kawano 2012 for discussions of the changes to Japanese funerary customs from the Meiji period to the present.

14. Lock 2002, 216; Tomatsu 2012, 38.

15. Covell 2008, 316; Rowe 2011, 144–145.

16. Donations can be made toward specific funeral costs, such as flower money (*hana dai*), oil money (*abura dai*), and salt money (*shio dai*).

17. Despite (or because of) the granting of *kaimyō* being a common feature of Buddhist funerals in Japan, only 12.3 percent of Sōtō priests report that they explain the meaning or significance of an individual's *kaimyō* to attendees during the funeral (SSSCI 2017, 172).

18. From a theological standpoint, *kaimyō* and *anmyō* are synonymous and functionally interchangeable (Matsumoto 1992, 41). The cultural distinction between the two terms lies in traditional usage: similar to the avoidance of the number 4 (homophonic with "death"), the practice of bestowing *kaimyō* primarily in funerary contexts has led to the word becoming associated with death and mourning. Japanese priests began using "*anmyō*" to refer to their own naming practices seeking to avoid unlucky associations.

19. Covell 2008, 300.

20. It is difficult to objectively measure a person's religiosity; it is comparably easier to measure monetary donations. Media attention to the practices of bestowing *kaimyō* throughout all sects of Japanese Buddhism have "revealed" a correlation between private donations and the length of a persons' *kaimyō*. These pay-per-character practices were met with public indignation over the perceived exploitation at the hands of unscrupulous clergy who used guilt tactics to make vulnerable families pay for longer names for the sake of their loved ones.

However, it is important to note that the practice of bestowing posthumous names to the laity has nearly always contained an element of privilege and conspicuous consumption. In longer *kaimyō*, the additional characters often highlight a person who has made substantial material donations to the Buddhist institution——for example, as a benefactor who provided the monetary backing to establish or rebuild a temple.

That certain members of the clergy have capitalized on a family's vulnerability to guilt them into "purchasing" a longer *kaimyō* for their loved one is an unfortunate outgrowth of this practice. Nevertheless, it should not be forgotten that the practice of granting more prestigious *kaimyō* to wealthy patrons of Buddhism—thus perpetuating social hierarchies, even in death—is not a recent development (see Williams 2005, 29 and Heine 2008b, 149).

21. For a semiotic analysis of how the relationships of signification are established between the body, the memorial portrait, and the memorial tablet, see Irizarry 2014a, S172-S177.

22. All of my inquiries regarding the memorial picture indicate that the choice of the background color is a matter of preference and does not constitute any belief as to the qualities of the place where the dead currently resides.

23. Schattschneider 2003, 204.

24. Yamada Shin'ya 2002, 45.

25. See Danely 2014.

26. Edwards 2012, 224.

27. See Sōtōshū Shūmuchō 2006a, 362.

28. Levine 2006; Faure 1995, 1996.

29. Japanese has two closely related verbs for "to be." As a rule of thumb, *aru* (有る) is used for nonliving, inanimate objects, while *iru* (居る) is used for living, animate things such as people and animals. *Hotoke* and *senzo* are spoken of using the *iru* form and are thus linguistically demonstrated to be "alive." See also Plath 1964, Williams 2008, and Rowe 2011.

30. As promoted on the cover of the CD book "Sen no kaze ni natte" (Arai Man 2003).

31. In particular, public and textual references to "outcastes" (Jp. *burakumin*)—a discriminated underclass traditionally blamed for their own discrimination by virtue of having committed sins in previous lives—have led to embarrassing public incidents for the Sōtō Zen sect, famously the 1984 Machida Incident (Bodiford 1996).

32. See especially Rowe 2004 and 2011.

33. See Rowe 2011.

34. Bodiford 1992 and 1993.

35. Bodiford 1993, 195.

36. Williams 2005 and 2008; Walter 2008.

37. Being homophones the noun *kiku* (菊, "chrysanthemum") and the verb *kiku* (聞く, "to hear") have an associative relationship: chrysanthemums are said to be able to facilitate communication between the newly deceased and the living by permitting both sides to "hear" the other. After a funeral, chrysanthemums are placed on the household *butsudan*, from where they serve as communicative devices that connect with the flowers that were placed in the coffin. In so doing, the dead can still hear what is going on in the home, and the family—ostensibly—can hear the voice of their departed loved one.

38. Lancaster 1984, 141.

39. Davis 1989, 307.

40. I was told that if the family cannot, or is unwilling, to keep the ashes, the reliquary can be left with a temple priest who will give them the appropriate care.

41. Stone (2005, 62–63) notes that while a forty-nine-day "interim period" between physical death and the next stage of existence (however conceived) is a common feature of Buddhist death customs throughout Asia, ideas of what actually takes place during this period vary widely, influenced both by doctrinal and philosophical interpretations as well as local cultural traditions and practices.

42. Hendry 1995, 134.

43. *Meinichi* literally translates as "day of life," reinforcing the cultural idea that an individual is reborn into a new existence after corporeal death.

44. See Smith 1974 and Nelson 2008.

45. Fiftieth and hundredth anniversaries (and multiples thereof, i.e., 150, 200, etc.) are also celebrated, though they are usually reserved for famous or historic figures.

46. This is assuming that the ceremony is held in the Daisodō. The Hōkōdō can accommodate between only twelve and twenty monks.

Conclusion

1. "*Sōtō-shū Fuku Kanshu Sen Egawa-shi no Tōsen Kettei.*" *Bukkyō Times*, March 18, 2010.

2. See Nelson 2013, 199.

3. National Police Agency of Japan 2020.

4. Samuels 2013, 6.

5. Starrs 2014, 16-19.

6. Agency for Cultural Affairs 2019.

7. Initial estimates placed the number of destroyed temples at thirty-seven (thirty-one temples in Miyagi Prefecture and six in Iwate Prefecture), but this was later revised upward to forty-five lost, with nine abandoned in the contamination zone in Fukushima Prefecture ("*Sōtō-shū Tsunami Shōshitsu 37 ka ji; Shisha, Fumei 13 nin.*" *Bukkyō Times*, April 28, 2011; McLaughlin 2013a, 299).

8. Like most other Japanese Buddhist sects, Sōtō Zen tabulates its total membership by counting registered parishioner households and, from there, roughly estimating the number of individual adherents. See Roemer 2009.

9. "*Higashi Nihon Daishinsai Tohoku Jiin wo Chokugeki.*" *Bukkyō Times*, March 18, 2011.

10. Specifically, funds for onetime payments of 20,000 yen (US$190) were earmarked for parishioner households that suffered a death or total loss of property. Parishioner households forced to evacuate from the nuclear contamination zone would be offered 5,000 yen (US$47.50) ("*Sōtōshū Shūgikai Hisai Danshinto ni Tokubetsu Mimaikin.*" *Bukkyō Times*, June 30, 2011).

11. Levi McLaughlin (2013a, 2013b, 2013c, 2016) has performed an invaluable service in his overviews and analyses of the Japanese religious responses to the 3.11 disaster.

12. See Shimazono 2012, 214-218 and Takahashi 2016, 191–194.

13. McLaughlin 2016, 127.

14. Nevertheless, Horie (2016, 210) questions whether the reported increase in religious sentiment following the 3.11 disaster (particularly regarding the belief in the continuation of life after death) is evidence of a revitalized relationship between the clergy and laity or, rather, a reflection of survivors' continuing emotional and affective bonds with the deceased which are traditionally performed in the ritual space of a Buddhist temple.

15. Having stepped down from the abbacy, Ōmichi-zenji returned to his home temple in Hokkaidō, where he died on June 25, 2011.

16. Daihonzan Sōjiji Fukyōshi-kai 2003, 31.

17. Portions of this section were previously presented in Irizarry 2014b.

18. See Robertson 1991, 1998b; Vlastos 1998; Schnell 1999.

19. Durkheim 1995 [1912], 376.

20. Nelson 2000, 89.

21. See, e.g., Matsuyama 1967; Muromine 1967.

22. It should be noted that Eiheiji's abbot did attend the centennial and even officiated a service on behalf of Keizan and Gasan on the second-to-last day of the celebration. Eiheiji also sent flowers.

23. This Eiheiji-sponsored symposium (titled "To Love Life: Choosing to Live without Nuclear Energy" [*Inochi wo Itsukushimu: Genpatsu wo Erabanai to iu Ikikata*]) was newsworthy because Eiheiji was the first major Buddhist temple in Japan to take a public position against the country's reliance on nuclear energy following the 3.11 disaster.

24. "'*Fukkō Kigen Sakura Purojekuto' Sakura no Engi ga Daihonzan Sōjiji ni Todokeraremashita*," sotozen-net.or.jp/newstopics/j20120709.html

25. "'*Ryōhonzan Fukkō Kigen Sakura Purojekuto' Sakura no Itoki ga Hisai Jiin ni Okuraremshita*," sotozen-net.or.jp/syumucyo/j20131219.html

26. Memorial anniversaries are determined using the traditional *kazoedoshi* counting system, which marks year transitions at the time of the Lunar New Year. In this system the date of birth or death begins "Year One," with the *second* memorial anniversary taking place one year after that. As a consequence, the two-year anniversary of 3.11 in 2013 was calculated as the *third* memorial anniversary.

27. Nelson (2013, 165–177) discusses how an increasing number of Buddhist temples—especially those with the space to do so—have been electing to utilize their landscapes and ritual space for music and theater performance. There are a variety of reasons for doing so: to deepen community engagement, as a means of cultural/religious innovation, and as a means of bringing in people who might not otherwise have cause or desire to visit a Buddhist temple. Also facilitating this innovation are a number of contemporary Buddhist priests who are well-known musicians and performers in their own right.

28. The 750th anniversary of Keizan's birth also fell into this time period and was observed with a classical music concert on September 27, 2014.

29. Previously, the Butsuden was only connected to the Hōkōdō and Daisodō by a subterranean tunnel that could only be accessed via steep staircases. While the tunnel and its modern fire prevention system protected the temple from disaster, it also made the three ritual halls inaccessible for people with mobility issues.

30. As Margaret Lock (2002) observes in her study of organ donation in Japan, traditional Japanese ideas about death use "heart death" (the cessation of a heartbeat) as the end of life, not "brain death" (the cessation of brain activity). Recalling the biologic metaphor that treats a Zen temple as being analogous to a human body, isolating the Butsuden meant that even if the rest of the "body" of the temple was destroyed, the "heart" of the temple—and thus the temple itself—would survive.

31. "Memorial Ceremony for the 650th Anniversary of Daihonzan Sojiji's Second Abbot, Gasan Joseki Zenji,"sotozen.com/eng/activity/report/special_events/650th_anniversary2.html

32. "*Sōtō-shū Baika-ryū Zenkoku Hōei Taikai Yokohama ni 9000 nin, Gasan Zenji Hōsan mo.*" *Bukkyō Times*, June 4, 2015.

33. The piece's subtitle, "The Road of Legend," was written using transliterated English loan words ("*Za Rōdo obu Regendo*").

Bibliography

Agency for Cultural Affairs, Government of Japan. 2019. *Shūkyō Nenkan* [Religious Yearbook]. https://www.bunka.go.jp/tokei_hakusho_shuppan/hakusho_nenji-hokokusho/shukyo_nenkan/index.html. Accessed July 23, 2020.

Alexy, Allison. 2020. *Intimate Disconnection: Divorce and the Romance of Independence in Contemporary Japan*. Chicago: University of Chicago Press.

Allison, Anne. 2013. *Precarious Japan*. Durham, NC: Duke University Press.

Ambros, Barbara B. 2012. *Bones of Contention: Animals and Religion in Contemporary Japan*. Honolulu: University of Hawaii Press.

Ambros, Barbara B. 2015. *Women in Japanese Religions*. New York: New York University Press.

Arai, Paula Kane Robinson. 1999. *Women Living Zen: Japanese Sōtō Buddhist Nuns*. London: Oxford University Press.

Arai, Paula Kane Robinson. 2011. *Bringing Zen Home: The Healing Heart of Japanese Women's Rituals*. Honolulu: University of Hawaii Press.

Arai Man. 2003. *Sen no Kaze ni Natte* [A Thousand Winds]. Tokyo: Kōdansha.

Asad, Talal. 1993. *Genealogies of Religion: Discipline and Reasons of Power in Christianity and Islam*. Baltimore: Johns Hopkins University Press.

Asad, Talal. 2003. *Formations of the Secular: Christianity, Islam, Modernity*. Stanford: Stanford University Press.

Ashikaga Ensho. 1950. "The Festival for the Spirits of the Dead in Japan." *Western Folklore* 9(3): 217–228.

Ashikaga Ensho. 1951. "Notes on Urabon ('Yü Lan P'ên, Ullambana')." *Journal of the American Oriental Society* 71(1): 71–75.

Azuma Ryūshin. 2005. *Sōtōshū Shingyō Kyōten*. Tokyo: Kamakura Shinsho.

Bachelard, Gaston. 1958. *The Poetics of Space*. Boston: Beacon Press.

Bahloul, Joëlle. 1996. *The Architecture of Memory: A Jewish-Muslim Household in Colonial Algeria 1937–1962*. Cambridge: Cambridge University Press.

Bellah, Robert. 1985 [1957]. *Tokugawa Religion: The Cultural Roots of Modern Japan*. New York: Free Press.

Benedict, Ruth. 1984 [1946]. *The Chrysanthemum and the Sword: Patterns of Japanese Culture*. Boston: Houghton Mifflin.

Benjamin, Gail R. 1997. *Japanese Lessons: A Year in a Japanese School through the Eyes of an American Anthropologist and Her Children*. New York: New York University Press.

Bielefeldt, Carl. 1988. *Dōgen's Manuals of Zen Meditation*. Berkeley: University of California Press.

Bielefeldt, Carl. 2005. "Practice." In *Critical Terms for the Study of Buddhism*, edited by Donald S. Lopez, 229–244. Chicago: University of Chicago Press.

Bodiford, William M. 1991. "Dharma Transmission in Sōtō Zen: Manzan Dōhaku's Reform Movement." *Monumenta Nipponica* 46(4): 423–51.

Bodiford, William M. 1992. "Zen in the Art of Funerals: Ritual Salvation in Japanese Buddhism." *History of Religions* 32(2): 146–64.

Bodiford, William M. 1993. *Sōtō Zen in Medieval Japan*. Honolulu: University of Hawaii Press.

Bodiford, William M. 1996. "Zen and the Art of Religious Prejudice: Efforts to Reform a Tradition of Social Discrimination." *Japanese Journal of Religious Studies* 23(1–2): 1–27.

Bodiford, William M. 2000. "Emptiness and Dust: Zen Dharma Transmission Rituals." In *Tantra in Practice*, edited by David Gordon White, 299–307. Princeton: Princeton University Press.

Bodiford, William M. 2003. "The Enlightenment of Kami and Ghosts: Spirit Ordinations in Japanese Sōtō Zen." In *Chan Buddhism in Ritual Context*, edited by Bernard Faure, 250–265. London: RoutledgeCurzon.

Bodiford, William M. 2005a. "Introduction." In *Going Forth: Visions of Buddhist Vinaya*, edited by William M. Bodiford, 1–16. Honolulu: University of Hawaii Press.

Bodiford, William M. 2005b. "Bodhidharma's Precepts in Japan." In *Going Forth: Visions of Buddhist Vinaya*, edited by William M. Bodiford, 210–235. Honolulu: University of Hawaii Press.

Bodiford, William M. 2008. "Dharma Transmission in Theory and Practice." In *Zen Ritual: Studies of Zen Buddhist Theory in Practice*, edited by Steven Heine and Dale S. Wright, 261–282. Oxford: Oxford University Press.

Bodiford, William M. 2015. "Keizan's *Denkōroku*: A Textual and Contextual Overview." In *Dōgen and Sōtō Zen*, edited by Steven Heine, 167–187. New York: Oxford University Press.

Borup, Jørn. 2008. *Japanese Rinzai Zen Buddhism*. Leiden: Brill.

Borup, Jørn. 2012. "Contemporary Buddhist Priests and Clergy." In *Handbook of Japanese Religions*, edited by Inken Prohl and John K. Nelson, 107–132. Leiden: Brill.

Brinker, Helmut, and Hiroshi Kanazawa. 1996. *Zen: Masters of Meditation in Images and Writing*. Translated by Andreas Leisinger. Zurich: Artibus Asiae.

Bruun, Ole. 2008. *An Introduction to Feng Shui*. Cambridge: Cambridge University Press.

Bynum, Caroline Walker. 1977. "Jesus as Mother and Abbot as Mother: Some Themes in Twelfth-Century Cistercian Writing." *Harvard Theological Review* 70(3/4): 257–284.

Bynum, Caroline Walker. 1982. *Jesus as Mother: Studies in the Spirituality of the High Middle Ages*. Berkeley: University of California Press.

Certeau, Michel de. 1984. *The Practice of Everyday Life*. Translated by Steven Randall. Berkeley: University of California Press.

Collcutt, Martin. 1981. *Five Mountains: The Rinzai Zen Monastic Institution in Medieval Japan*. Cambridge, MA: Harvard University Press.

Covell, Stephen G. 2005. *Japanese Temple Buddhism: Worldliness in a Religion of Renunciation*. Honolulu: University of Hawaii Press.

Covell, Stephen G. 2008. "The Price of Naming the Dead: Posthumous Precept Names and Critiques of Contemporary Japanese Buddhism." In *Death and the Afterlife in Japanese Buddhism*, edited by Jacqueline I. Stone and Mariko Namba Walter, 293–324. Honolulu: University of Hawaii Press.

Daihonzan Sōjiji Fukyōshi-kai. 2003. *Sōtōshū Hōyō Kaisetsu Hikkei* [Handbook for Explaining Sōtō-shū Ceremonies]. Tsurumi: Daihonzan Sōjiji Shuppanbu.

Danely, Jason. 2014. *Aging and Loss: Mourning and Maturity in Contemporary Japan*. New Brunswick, NJ: Rutgers University Press.

Davis, Winston. 1989. "Buddhism and the Modernization of Japan." *History of Religions* 28(4): 304–339.

Durkheim, Émile. 1995 [1912]. *The Elementary Forms of Religious Life*. Translated by Karen E. Fields. New York: Free Press.

Edwards, Elizabeth. 2012. "Objects of Affect: Photography beyond the Image." *Annual Review of Anthropology* 41: 221–234.

Embree, John F. 1939. *Suye Mura: A Japanese Village*. Michigan Classics in Japanese Studies, 14. Ann Arbor: University of Michigan Press.

Faure, Bernard. 1993. *Chan Insights and Oversights: An Epistemological Critique of the Chan Tradition*. Princeton: Princeton University Press.

Faure, Bernard. 1995. "*Quand l'habit fait le moine*: The Symbolism of the Kāṣāya in Sōtō Zen." *Cahiers d'Extrême-Asie* 8: 335–369.

Faure, Bernard. 1996. *Visions of Power: Imagining Medieval Japanese Buddhism*. Translated by Phyllis Brooks. Princeton: Princeton University Press.

Faure, Bernard. 1998a. *The Red Thread: Buddhist Approaches to Sexuality*. Princeton: Princeton University Press.

Faure, Bernard. 2009. *Unmasking Buddhism*. Malden, MA: Wiley-Blackwell.

Feeley-Harnik, Gillian. 1994. *The Lord's Table: The Meaning of Food in Early Judaism and Christianity*. Washington, DC: Smithsonian.

Feng Jiren. 2012. *Chinese Architecture and Metaphor: Song Culture in the* Yingzao Fashi *Building Manual*. Honolulu: University of Hawaii Press.

Foucault, Michel. 1977. *Discipline and Punish: The Birth of the Prison*. New York: Vintage.

Foulk, T. Griffith. 1993. "Myth, Ritual, and Monastic Practice in Sung Ch'an Buddhism." In *Religion and Society in T'ang and Sung China*, edited by Patricia Buckley Ebrey and Peter N. Gregory, 147–208. Honolulu: University of Hawaii Press.

Foulk, T. Griffith. 2001. *Tenzo Kyōkun* [Instructions for the Cook]. http://hcbss. stanford.edu/research/projects/sztp/translations/eihei_shingi/translations/ tenzo_kyokun/translation.html. Accessed August 15, 2011.

Foulk, T. Griffith. 2008. "Ritual in Japanese Zen Buddhism." In *Zen Ritual: Studies of Zen Buddhist Theory in Practice*, edited by Steven Heine and Dale S. Wright, 21–82. Oxford: Oxford University Press.

Foulk, T. Griffith. 2015. "Dōgen's Use of Rujing's 'Just Sit' (*shikan taza*) and Other Kōans." In *Dōgen and Sōtō Zen*, edited by Steven Heine, 23–45. New York: Oxford University Press.

Foulk, T. Griffith, ed. 2017. *Record of the Transmission of Illumination by the Great Ancestor, Zen Master Keizan*. https://global.sotozen-net.or.jp/eng/library/den-koroku/index.html. Accessed October 29, 2019.

Glassman, Hank. 2009. "Chinese Buddhist Death Ritual and the Transformation of Japanese Kinship." In *The Buddhist Dead: Practices, Discourses, Representations*, edited by Bryan J. Cuevas and Jacqueline I. Stone, 378–404. Honolulu: University of Hawaii Press.

Gluck, Carol. 1985. *Japan's Modern Myths: Ideology in the Late Meiji Period*. Princeton: Princeton University Press.

Goffman, Erving. 1959. *The Presentation of Self in Everyday Life*. New York: Anchor Books.

Hardacre, Helen. 1999. *Marketing the Menacing Fetus in Japan*. Berkeley: University of California Press.

Heine, Steven. 2003. "Abbreviation or Aberration: The Role of the *Shushōgi* in Modern Sōtō Zen Buddhism." In *Buddhism in the Modern World: Adaptations of an Ancient Tradition*, edited by Steven Heine and Charles S. Prebish, 169–192. Oxford: Oxford University Press.

Heine, Steven. 2008a. "Is Dōgen's Eiheiji Temple 'Mt. T'ien-t'ung East'?: Geo-Ritual Perspectives on the Transition from Chinese Ch'an to Japanese Zen." In *Zen Ritual: Studies of Zen Buddhist Theory in Practice*, edited by Steven Heine and Dale S. Wright, 139–165. Oxford: Oxford University Press.

Heine, Steven. 2008b. *Zen Skin, Zen Marrow: Will the Real Zen Buddhism Please Stand Up?* New York: Oxford University Press.

Heine, Steven. 2011. "Not So Quiet on the Eastern Front: On Deconstructing and Reconstructing Traditional Zen Narratives." *Religious Studies Review* 37(3): 157–164.

Heine, Steven, and Dale S. Wright, eds. 2008. *Zen Ritual: Studies of Zen Buddhist Theory in Practice*. Oxford: Oxford University Press.

Hendry, Joy. 1995. *Understanding Japanese Society*, 2nd ed. London: Routledge.

Hori, G. Victor Sōgen. 1994. "Teaching and Learning in the Rinzai Zen Monastery." *Journal of Japanese Studies* 20(1): 5–35.

Horie Norichika. 2016. "Continuing Bonds in the Tōhoku Disaster Area: Locating the Destinations of Spirits." *Journal of Religion in Japan* 5(2–3): 199–226.

Hur, Nam-lin. 1999. "The Sōtō Sect and Japanese Military Imperialism in Korea." *Japanese Journal of Religious Studies* 26(1–2): 107–134.

Ikegami Yoshimasa. 2014. "Shūkyōgaku no kenkyū kadai toshite no 'segaki.'" [The Subject of 'Segaki' in Religious Studies Research.] *Komazawa Daigaku Bunka* 32: 69-94.

Irizarry, Joshua A. 2010. "Cultivating an 'International Zen Garden': Daihonzan Sōjiji in the 21st Century." Paper presented at the Twentieth Congress of the International Association for the History of Religions, Toronto, Canada, August 15.

Irizarry, Joshua A. 2011. *A Forest for a Thousand Years: Cultivating Life and Disciplining Death at Daihonzon Sōjiji, a Japanese Zen Temple*. PhD diss. University of Michigan.

Irizarry, Joshua A. 2014a. "Signs of Life: Grounding the Transcendent in Japanese Memorial Objects." *Signs and Society* 2 (S1): S160-S187.

Irizarry, Joshua A. 2014b. "Building on History: Commemorating Sōtō-shū Daihonzan Sōjiji at 100." Paper presented at the Annual Meeting of the Association for Asian Studies, Philadelphia, March 28.

Irizarry, Joshua A. 2015. "Putting a Price on Zen: The Business of Redefining Religion for Global Consumption." *Journal of Global Buddhism* 16: 51–69.

Ives, Christopher. 2009. *Imperial-Way Zen: Ichikawa Hakugen's Critique and Lingering Questions for Buddhist Ethics*. Honolulu: University of Hawaii Press.

Ivy, Marilyn. 1995. *Discourses of the Vanishing: Modernity, Phantasm, Japan*. Chicago: University of Chicago Press.

Iwamura, Jane Naomi. 2011. *Virtual Orientalism: Asian Religions and American Popular Culture*. New York: Oxford University Press.

Jaffe, Richard M. 2001. *Neither Monk nor Layman: Clerical Marriage in Modern Japanese Buddhism*. Princeton: Princeton University Press.

Jaffe, Richard M. 2005. "The Debate over Meat Eating in Japanese Buddhism." In *Going Forth: Visions of Buddhist Vinaya*, edited by William M. Bodiford, 255–275. Honolulu: University of Hawaii Press.

Johnson, Paul Christopher. 2002. *Secrets, Gossip, and Gods: The Transformation of Brazilian Candomblé*. Oxford: Oxford University Press.

Katō Yūzō, ed. 1990. *Yokohama: Past and Present*. Yokohama: Yokohama City University.

Kawaguchi Masahide. 1985. *Meiji no "Yokohama no Hito"* [People of Yokohama of the Meiji Era]. Tokyo: Seiunsha.

Kawahashi Noriko. 1995. "*Jizoku* (Priests' Wives) in Sōtō Zen Buddhism: An Ambiguous Category." *Japanese Journal of Religious Studies* 22(1–2): 161–183.

Kawahashi Noriko. 2012. "Re-imagining Buddhist Women in Contemporary Japan." In *Handbook of Contemporary Japanese Religions*, edited by Inken Prohl and John K. Nelson, 197–214. Leiden: Brill.

Kawahashi Noriko. 2017. "Women Challenging the 'Celibate' Buddhist Order: Recent Cases of Progress and Regress in the Sōtō School." *Japanese Journal of Religious Studies* 44(1): 55–74.

Kawano Satsuki. 2005. *Ritual Practice in Modern Japan*. Honolulu: University of Hawaii Press.

Kawano Satsuki. 2012. "From the 'Tradition' to a Choice: Recent Developments in Japanese Mortuary Practices." In *Handbook of Contemporary Japanese Religions*, edited by Inken Prohl and John K. Nelson, 413–430. Leiden: Brill.

Ketelaar, James Edward. 1990. *Of Heretics and Martyrs in Meiji Japan: Buddhism and Its Persecution*. Princeton: Princeton University Press.

Komazawa Daigakunai Zengaku Daijiten Henshūshitsu (ZDJ). 1985. *Shinban Zengaku Daijiten* [Dictionary of Zen Studies, New Edition]. Tokyo: Daishukan Shoten.

Kondo, Dorinne K. 1990. *Crafting Selves: Power, Gender, and Discourses of Identity in a Japanese Workplace*. Chicago: University of Chicago Press.

Kumamoto Einin. 2004. "Shut Up, Zen Priest: A Review of Minami Jikisai's *The Zen Priest Speaks* and Other Works." *Japanese Journal of Religious Studies* 31(2): 465–487.

Lancaster, Lewis R. 1984. "Buddhism and Family in East Asia." In *Religion and the Family in East Asia*, edited by George A. DeVos and Takao Sofue, 139–151. Berkeley: University of California Press.

Leighton, Taigen Dan. 2008. "Zazen as an Enactment Ritual." In *Zen Ritual: Studies of Zen Buddhist Theory in Practice*, edited by Steven Heine and Dale S. Wright, 167–184. Oxford: Oxford University Press.

Levine, Gregory P. A. 2006. *Daitokuji: The Visual Cultures of a Zen Monastery*. Seattle: University of Washington Press.

Lock, Margaret. 1988. "New Japanese Mythologies: Faltering Discipline and the Ailing Housewife." *American Ethnologist* 15(1): 43–61.

Lock, Margaret. 2002. *Twice Dead: Organ Transplants and the Reinvention of Death*. Berkeley: University of California Press.

Marcure, Kenneth. 1985. "The Danka System." *Monumenta Nipponica* 40(1): 39–67.

Matsumoto Jikei. 1992. *Kaimyō no Hanashi* [A Discussion of *Kaimyō*]. Tokyo: Kunisha Inkōkai.

Matsuyama Sogen, ed. 1967. *Tsuru-ga-oka: Rokujūgo nen no Ayumi* [Tsuru-ga-oka: The Progress of 65 Years]. Tokyo: Sankyō Bijutsu Insatsu.

McLaughlin, Levi. 2013a. "What Have Religions Done after 3.11?" (Part 1). *Religion Compass* 7(8): 294–308.

McLaughlin, Levi. 2013b. "What Have Religions Done after 3.11?" (Part 2). *Religion Compass* 7(8): 309–325.

McLaughlin, Levi. 2013c. "Reconnecting with Everyday Life: Buddhism through Simple Gestures in the Café de Monk." *Dharma World* 40 (July–September): 22–25.

McLaughlin, Levi. 2016. "Hard Lessons Learned: Tracking Changes in Media Presentations of Religion and Religious Aid Mobilization after the 1995 and 2011 Disasters in Japan." *Asian Ethnology* 75(1): 105–138.

McMahan, David L. 2008. *The Making of Buddhist Modernism*. Oxford: Oxford University Press.

McRae, John R. 2003. *Seeing through Zen: Encounter, Transformation, and Genealogy in Chinese Chan Buddhism*. Berkeley: University of California Press.

Meeks, Lori. 2016. "Imagining Rāhula in Medieval Japan: The *Raun kōshiki*." *Japanese Journal of Religious Studies* 43(1): 131–151.

Mitsudzi Eigaku, Matsuda Fumio and Arai Kōhei, eds. (KZZ). 1980. *Keizan Zen* [The Zen of Keizan]. 12 volumes. Tokyo: Sankibō Butsushorin.

Mohr, Michel. 1994. "Zen Buddhism during the Tokugawa Period: The Challenge to Go beyond Sectarian Consciousness." *Japanese Journal of Religious Studies* 21(4): 341–372.

Mohr, Michel. 2012. "Plowing the Zen Field: Trends since 1989 and Emerging Perspectives." *Religion Compass* 6(2): 113–124.

Momose Meiji. 2002. *Keizan Jōkin no Shōgai* [The Life of Keizan Jōkin]. Tokyo: Mainichi Shinbunsha.

Murakami Kōkyō. 2000. "Changes in Japanese Urban Funeral Customs during the Twentieth Century." *Japanese Journal of Religious Studies* 27(3–4): 335–352.

Muromine Bai'itsu, ed. 1967. *Sōjiji shi* [History of Sōjiji]. Tokyo: Jitsugetsu Insatsu.

Nara Yasuaki. 1995. "May the Deceased Get Enlightenment!: An Aspect of the Enculturation of Buddhism in Japan." *Buddhist-Christian Studies* 15: 19–42.

National Police Agency of Japan. 2020. "Police Countermeasures and Damage Situation Associated with the 2011 Tōhoku District—Off the Pacific Coast Earthquake." Rev. June 10, 2020. https://www.npa.go.jp/news/other/earthquake2011/pdf/higaijokyo-e.pdf. Accessed July 24, 2020.

Nearman, Hubert, trans. 2001. *The Denkōroku*, 2nd ed. Mount Shasta, CA: Shasta Abbey Press.

Nearman, Hubert, trans. 2007. *Shōbōgenzō: A Trainee's Translation of Great Master Dōgen's Spiritual Masterpiece*. Mount Shasta, CA: Shasta Abbey Press.

Nelson, John K. 2000. *Enduring Identities: The Guise of Shinto in Contemporary Japan*. Honolulu: University of Hawaii Press.

Nelson, John K. 2008. "Household Altars in Contemporary Japan: Rectifying Buddhist 'Ancestor Worship' with Home Décor and Consumer Choice." *Japanese Journal of Religious Studies* 27(3–4): 335–352.

Nelson, John K. 2012. "Japanese Secularities and the Decline of Temple Buddhism." *Journal of Religion in Japan* 1(1): 37–60.

Nelson, John K. 2013. *Experimental Buddhism: Innovation and Activism in Contemporary Japan*. Honolulu: University of Hawaii Press.

Nelson, John K. 2020. "Japan's 'Priest's Bars': 'Bad Buddhism' or Hope for the Future?" *Journal of Global Buddhism* 21: 241–260.

Nishijima Gudo and Chodo Cross, trans. 1994. *Shōbōgenzō*, v. 1. Charleston, SC: BookSurge.

Nodomi Jōten. 2007. "*Sōjiji no Konjaku: Tsurumi Goiten Zengo wo Chūshin ni*" [Sōjiij's Past and Present: Focusing on the Move to Tsurumi]. *Kyōdo Tsurumi* 62: 1–22.

Nodomi Jōten and Ozaki Shōzen, eds. 2011. *Jūzanki: Sōji Zendera Kaisan Irai Jūji no Shidai* [Record of Temple Abbots: From the Founder of Zen Temple Sōjiji to Future Generations of Abbots]. Kure City: Unix Corp.

Nonomura Kaoru. 2008. *Eat Sleep Sit: My Year at Japan's Most Rigorous Zen Temple*. Translated by Juliet Winters Carpenter. Tokyo: Kodansha.

Odin, Steve. 1996. *The Social Self in American and Zen Pragmatism*. Albany: SUNY Press.

Okumura Shohaku. 2004. "The Bodhisattva Precepts in Sōtō Zen Buddhism." *Dharma Eye* 13: 1–3.

Ozaki Shōzen. 2015. "Gasan Jōseki Zenji no Goitoku: 650dai Daionki ni mukete" [The Virtue of Zen Master Gasan Jōseki: Towards the 650th Memorial Anniversary]. *Tsurumi Daigaku Bukkyō Bunkagaku Kenkyūshitsu Kiyō* 20: 213–250.

Ozaki Shōzen. 2016. "Gasan Jōseki Zenji no Gyōseki: Danshintō to no Kankei ni tsuite" [The Contributions of Zen Master Gasan Jōseki: Focusing on His Relationships with His Lay Followers]. *Tsurumi Daigaku Bukkyō Bunkagaku Kenkyūshitsu Kiyō* 21: 11–30.

Paramore, Kiri. 2016. *Japanese Confucianism: A Cultural History*. Cambridge: Cambridge University Press.

Plath, David W. 1964. "Where the Family of God Is the Family: The Role of the Dead in Japanese Households." *American Anthropologist* 66(2): 300–317.

Prohl, Inken. 2012. "New Religions in Japan: Adaptations and Transformations in Contemporary Society." In *Handbook of Contemporary Japanese Religions*, edited by Inken Prohl and John K. Nelson, 241–268. Leiden: Brill.

Reader, Ian. 1991. *Religion in Contemporary Japan*. Honolulu: University of Hawaii Press.

Reader, Ian. 1995. "Cleaning Floors and Sweeping the Mind: Cleaning as a Ritual Process." In *Ceremony and Ritual in Japan: Religious Practices in an Industrialized Society*, edited by Jan van Bremen and D. P. Martinez, 169–181. London: Routledge.

Reader, Ian, and George J. Tanabe Jr. 1998. *Practically Religious: Worldly Benefits and the Common Religion of Japan*. Honolulu: University of Hawaii Press.

Reynolds, Frank E., and Jason A. Carbine, eds. 2000. *The Life of Buddhism*. Berkeley: University of California Press.

Riggs, David E. 2015. "Are Sōtō Zen Precepts for Ethical Guidance or Ceremonial Transformation? Menzan's Attempted Reforms and Contemporary Practices."

In *Dōgen and Sōtō Zen*, edited by Steven Heine, 188–209. New York: Oxford University Press.

Riggs, Diane E. 2015. "Interpreting the Material Heritage of the 'Elephant Trunk Robe' in Sōtō Zen." In *Dōgen and Sōtō Zen*, edited by Steven Heine, 235–259. New York: Oxford University Press.

Riggs, Diane E. 2017. "Golden Robe or Rubbish Robe? Interpretations of the Transmitted Robe in Tokugawa Period Zen Buddhist Thought." In *Zen and Material Culture*, edited by Steven Heine and Pamela D. Winfeld, 197–228. Oxford: Oxford University Press.

Robertson, Jennifer. 1991. *Native and Newcomer: Making and Remaking a Japanese City*. Berkeley: University of California Press.

Robertson, Jennifer. 1998a. *Takarazuka: Sexual Politics and Popular Culture in Modern Japan*. Berkeley: University of California Press.

Robertson, Jennifer. 1998b. "It Takes a Village: Internationalization and Nostalgia in Postwar Japan." In *Mirror of Modernity: Invented Traditions of Modern Japan*, edited by Stephen Vlastos, 110–129. Berkeley: University of California Press.

Rocha, Cristina. 2006. *Zen in Brazil: The Quest of Cosmopolitan Modernity*. Honolulu: University of Hawaii Press.

Roemer, Michael. 2009. "Religious Affiliation in Japan: Untangling the Enigma." *Review of Religious Research* 50(3): 298–320.

Rohlen, Thomas P. 1979. *For Harmony and Strength: Japanese White-Collar Organization in Anthropological Perspective*. Berkeley: University of California Press.

Rowe, Mark. 2000. "Stickers for Nails: The Ongoing Transformation of Roles, Rites, and Symbols in Japanese Funerals." *Japanese Journal of Religious Studies* 27(3–4): 353–378.

Rowe, Mark. 2004. "Where the Action Is: Sites of Contemporary Sōtō Buddhism." *Japanese Journal of Religious Studies* 31(2): 357–388.

Rowe, Mark. 2009. "Death, Burial, and the Study of Contemporary Japanese Buddhism." *Religion Compass* 3(1): 18–30.

Rowe, Mark. 2011. *Bonds of the Dead: Temples, Burial, and the Transformation of Contemporary Japanese Buddhism*. Chicago: University of Chicago Press.

Rowe, Mark. 2017. "Charting Known Territory: Female Buddhist Priests." *Japanese Journal of Religious Studies* 44(1): 75–101.

Saitō Shingi. 2007. *"Jihi no Zazen" wo Ikiru* [Living "Compassionate Zen"]. Tokyo: Shunjūsha.

Saitō Umie. 2011. *Tsurumi Sōjiji Monogatari.* [The Story of Tsurumi Sōjiji]. Yokohama: Kanagawa Shinbunsha Eigyōkyoku Shuppanbu.

Samuels, Richard J. 2013. *3.11: Disaster and Change in Japan*. Ithaca, NY: Cornell University Press.

Sargent, Jihō. 2001. *Asking about Zen: 108 Answers*. New York: Weatherhill.

Sasaki Kōkan. 1993. *Hotoke to Tama no Jinruigaku: Bukkyō Bunka no Shinsō Kōzō* [The Anthropology of *Hotoke* and *Tama*: The Deep Structure of Buddhist Culture]. Tokyo: Shunjūsha.

Sawada, Janine Tasca. 2004. *Practical Pursuits: Religion, Politics, and Personal Cultivation in Nineteenth-Century Japan*. Honolulu: University of Hawaii Press.

Schattshneider, Ellen. 2003. *Immortal Wishes: Labor and Transcendence on a Japanese Mountain*. Durham, NC: Duke University Press.

Schlütter, Morten. 2008. *How Zen Became Zen: The Dispute over Enlightenment and the Formation of Chan*. Honolulu: University of Hawaii Press.

Schnell, Scott. 1999. *The Rousing Drum: Ritual Practice in a Japanese Community*. Honolulu: University of Hawaii Press.

Schrimpf, Monika. 2015. "Children of Buddha, or Caretakers of Women?: Self-Understandings of Ordained Buddhist Women in Contemporary Japan." *Journal of Religion in Japan* 4(2–3): 184–211.

Seckel, Dietrich. 1985. "Buddhist Temple Names in Japan." *Monumenta Nipponica* 40(4): 359–386.

Sekiguchi Dōjun. 1995. *Sōtōshū Daihonzan Sōjiji Soin*. Kanezawa: Yoshida Insatsu.

Sharf, Robert H. 1993. "The Zen of Japanese Nationalism." *History of Religions* 33(1): 1–43.

Sharf, Robert H. 1995a. "Buddhist Modernism and the Rhetoric of Meditative Experience." *Numen* 42: 228–281.

Sharf, Robert H. 1995b. "Sanbōkyōdan: Zen and the Way of the New Religions." *Japanese Journal of Religious Studies* 22(3–4): 417–458.

Sharf, Robert H. 1998. "Experience." In *Critical Terms for Religious Studies*, edited by Mark C. Taylor, 94–116. Chicago: University of Chicago Press.

Sharf, Robert H. 2005. "Ritual." In *Critical Terms for the Study of Buddhism*, edited by Donald S. Lopez, 245–270. Chicago: University of Chicago Press.

Shimazono Susumu. 2004. *From Salvation to Spirituality: Popular Religious Movements in Modern Japan*. Melbourne: Trans Pacific Press.

Shimazono Susumu. 2012. "Japanese Buddhism and the Public Sphere: From the End of World War II to the Post–Great East Japan Earthquake and Nuclear Power Plant Accident." *Journal of Religion in Japan* 1(3): 203–225.

Shimbori Kanno. 2006. "Mitsugon-ryū Goeika no Gakufu to Kutō Denshō ga Hen'yō Suru Shukumi: Kihan to Kosei no Kankei wo Megutte" [The Mechanism of the Changes in the Notation and the Oral Tradition of the Mitsugon-school Go-eika: The Relationship between the Norm and Creativity]. *Tōyō Ongaku Kenkyū* 71: 1–20.

Shimbori Kanno. 2008. "1920–1930 Nendai ni Okeru Yamato-ryū Goeika no Seiritsu Katei" [The Formation Process of the Yamato School *Go-eika* in the 1920s–30s]. *Tōyō Ongaku Kenkyū* 73: 63–75.

Smith, Robert J. 1974. *Ancestor Worship in Contemporary Japan*. Stanford: Stanford University Press.

Snodgrass, Judith. 2003. *Presenting Japanese Buddhism to the West: Orientalism, Occidentalism, and the Columbian Exposition*. Chapel Hill: University of North Carolina Press.

Sōtōshū Daihonzan Sōjiji. 1996. *Sōtōshū Daihonzan Sōjiji.* Yokohama: Sōtōshū Daihonzan Sōjiji Shuppanbu.

Sōtōshū Danshintō Hikkei Kaitei Iinkai. 2007. *Sōtōshū Danshintō Hikkei* [Handbook for Sōtō-shū Parishioners and Believers]. Tokyo: Sōtō Shūmuchō.

Sōtōshū Shūgaku Kenkyūsho. 2006. *Hossenshiki Yōgo Kaisetsu* [Explanation of the Language of the Dharma Combat Ceremony]. Tokyo: Sōtō Shūmuchō.

Sōtōshū Shūmuchō. 1982. *Sōtō-shū Sutras.* Tokyo: Kinko Iinsatsu.

Sōtōshū Shūmuchō. 1991. *Sōtōshū wo Shiru: Sōdō Dokuhon* [Learning about Sōtō-shū: A Guidebook for the Monk's Hall]. Tokyo: Sōtō Shūmuchō.

Sōtōshū Shūmuchō. 2004. *Sanzen Yōten* [Essentials of Sanzen]. Tokyo: Sōtō Shūmuchō.

Sōtōshū Shūmuchō. 2005. *Shūryo Hikkei* [Handbook for Sect Clergy]. Tokyo: Sōtō Shūmuchō.

Sōtōshū Shūmuchō. 2006a. *Sōtōshū Gyōji Kihan* [Sōtō-shū Ritual Handbook]. Tokyo: Sōtō Shūmuchō.

Sōtōshū Shūmuchō. 2006b. *Sōtōshū Nikka Gongyō Seiten* [Sōtō-shū Scriptures for Daily Religious Service], 12th ed. Sankyō Bijutsu Insatsu.

Sōtōshū Shūmuchō. 2007. *Sōtōshū Shūsei* [Sōtō-shū Organization]. Tokyo: Sōtō Shūmuchō

Sōtōshū Shūmuchō. 2008. *Baikaryū Shidō Hikkei* [Handbook for Baika-ryū Instruction]. Tokyo: Sōtō Shūmuchō.

Sōtōshū Shūsei Sōgō Chōsa Iinkai (SSSCI). 2017. *Sōtōshū Shūsei Sōgō Chōsa Hōgoku shō*, 2015 (Heisei 27) *nenhan*. [Report on the Sōtō Sect General Survey, 2015 ed.]. Tokyo: Sōtō Shūmuchō.

Sōtōshū Sōgō Kenkyū Sentaa (SSKS). 2019. *Sōtōshū Kyōdanshi ni okeru Baikaryū* [The Baika School within the Sōtō Sect Religious Organization]. Tokyo: Sankyō Bijutsu Insatsu.

Sōtō Zen Buddhism International Center (SZBIC). 2002. *Sōtō Zen: An Introduction to Zazen.* Tokyo: Sōtōshū Shūmuchō.

Starling, Jessica. 2013. "Neither Nun nor Laywoman: The Good Wives and Wise Mothers of Jōdo Shinshū Temples." *Japanese Journal of Religious Studies* 40(2): 277–301.

Starling, Jessica. 2019. *Guardians of the Buddha's Home: Domestic Religion in Contemporary Jōdo Shinshū.* Honolulu: University of Hawaii Press.

Starrs, Roy.2014. "Introduction: Cultural Responses to Disaster in Japan." In *When the Tsunami Came to Shore: Culture and Disaster in Japan*, edited by Roy Starrs, 1-20. Boston: Global Oriental.

Stone, Jacqueline I. 2005. "Death." In *Critical Terms for the Study of Buddhism*, edited by Donald S. Lopez, 56–76. Chicago: University of Chicago Press.

Takahashi Hara. 2016. "The Ghosts of the Tsunami Dead and *Kokoro no kea* in Japan's Religious Landscape." *Journal of Religions in Japan* 5(2–3): 176–198.

Tomatsu Yoshiharu. 2012. "Tear Down the Wall: Bridging the Premortem and

Postmortem Worlds in Medical and Spiritual Care." In *Buddhist Care for the Dying and Bereaved: Global Perspectives*, edited by Jonathan S. Watts and Yoshiharu Tomatsu, 37–56. Boston: Wisdom Publications.

Traphagan, John W. 2004. *The Practice of Concern: Ritual, Well-Being, and Aging in Rural Japan*. Durham, NC: Carolina Academic Press.

Tsurumi-ku Shi Kankō Iinkai. 1982. *Tsurumi-ku shi* [History of Tsurumi Ward]. Tokyo: Gyōsei.

Tsurumi Toshokan. 1987. *Tsurumi no Hyakunen* [Tsurumi's Hundred Years]. Yokohama: Zentomo Insatsu.

Victoria, Brian A. 1997. *Zen at War*. New York: Weatherhill.

Vlastos, Stephen. 1998. "Tradition: Past/Present Culture and Modern Japanese History." In *Mirror of Modernity: Invented Traditions of Modern Japan*, edited by Stephen Vlastos, 1–16. Berkeley: University of California Press.

Walter, Mariko Namba. 2008. "The Structure of Japanese Buddhist Funerals." In *Death and the Afterlife in Japanese Buddhism*, edited by Jacqueline I. Stone and Mariko Namba Walter, 247–292. Honolulu: University of Hawaii Press.

Welch, Holmes. 1967. *The Practice of Chinese Buddhism 1900–1950*. Cambridge, MA: Harvard University Press.

White, Merry Isaacs. 2002. *Perfectly Japanese: Making Families in an Era of Upheaval*. Berkeley: University of California Press.

Williams, Duncan Ryūken. 2005. *The Other Side of Zen: A Social History of Sōtō Zen Buddhism in Tokugawa Japan*. Princeton: Princeton University Press.

Williams, Duncan Ryūken. 2008. "Funerary Zen: Sōtō Zen Death Management in Tokugawa Japan." In *Death and the Afterlife in Japanese Buddhism*, edited by Jacqueline I. Stone and Mariko Namba Walter, 207–246. Honolulu: University of Hawaii Press.

Williams, Duncan Ryūken. 2009. "The Purple Robe Incident and the Formation of the Early Modern Sōtō Zen Institution." *Japanese Journal of Religious Studies* 36(1): 27–43.

Winfeld, Pamela D. 2015. "Embodying Sōtō Zen: Institutional Identity and Ideal Body Image at Daihonzan Eiheiji." In *Dōgen and Sōtō Zen*, edited by Steven Heine, 260–286. Oxford: Oxford University Press.

Winfeld, Pamela D. 2017. "Materializing the Zen Monastery." In *Zen and Material Culture*, edited by Steven Heine and Pamela D. Winfeld, 37–69. Oxford: Oxford University Press.

Wöss, Fleur. 1993. "*Pokkuri*-Temples and Aging: Rituals for Approaching Death." In *Religion and Society in Modern Japan*, edited by Mark R. Mullins, Shimazono Susumu, and Paul L. Swanson, 191–202. Berkeley: Asian Humanities Press.

Wright, Dale S. 2008. "Introduction: Rethinking Ritual Practice in Zen Buddhism." In *Zen Ritual: Studies of Zen Buddhist Theory in Practice*, edited by Steven Heine and Dale S. Wright, 3–19. Oxford: Oxford University Press.

Yamada Shin'ya. 2002. "Nakihito wo Omou: Iei no Tanjō" [Remembering the Dead: The Emergence of the Memorial Photograph]. In *Ikai Dangi*, edited by Ikegami Yoshimasa, et al. Tokyo: Uokawa Shoten.

Yamada Shoji. 2009. *Shots in the Dark: Japan, Zen, and the West*. Chicago: University of Chicago Press.

Yamaguchi Seishō. 2011a. "Tsūgen Jakurei Zenji to Sono Monryū" [Zen Master Tsūgen Jakurei and His Branch]. In *Sōtōshū Daihonzan Sōjiji Goin Monogatari*, 121–253. Yokohama: Kanagawa Shinbunsha Eigyōkyoku Shuppanbu.

Yamaguchi Seishō. 2011b. *Gakkyō no Toki—moment musical*. Yokohama: Kanagawa Shinbunsha Eigyōkyoku Shuppanbu.

Yano, Christine R. 2002. *Tears of Longing: Nostalgia and the Nation in Japanese Popular Song*. Cambridge, MA: Harvard University Press.

Index